M
ANNOTATED ST

General Editors

MARK ROBERTS
*Professor of English
The Queen's University of Belfast*

and

DEREK ROPER
University of Sheffield

Editorial Board

BRIAN W. DOWNS
*Professor Emeritus and sometime Master of
Christ's College, Cambridge*

KENNETH MUIR
Professor of English Literature, University of Liverpool

F. W. BATESON
*Fellow and University Lecturer in English
Corpus Christi College, Oxford*

M. L. BURCHNALL
Senior English Master, Winchester College

M & E ANNOTATED STUDENT TEXTS

M & E ANNOTATED STUDENT TEXTS

WILLIAM WORDSWORTH

and

SAMUEL TAYLOR COLERIDGE

Lyrical Ballads 1805

Edited by

DEREK ROPER, B.A., B.Litt.

*Senior Lecturer in English Literature,
Sheffield University*

SECOND EDITION

MACDONALD AND EVANS

MACDONALD & EVANS LTD
Estover, Plymouth PL6 7PZ

First published 1968
Reprinted 1973
Second edition January 1976
Reprinted 1979
Reprinted 1982

ISBN: 0 7121 0140 3

Printed in Great Britain by Fletcher & Son Ltd, Norwich

Contents

Acknowledgments

The Editors and Publishers desire to make grateful acknowledgment to the following for permission to include copyright material as stated:

The Clarendon Press, Oxford, for the extract on page 415 from the Introduction to *Wordsworth: Poetry and Prose* by David Nichol Smith;

Oxford University Press for the extract on page 418 from *The Romantic Imagination* by C. M. Bowra.

Note on the Text

THERE IS NO STANDARD text of *Lyrical Ballads*; earlier reprints have been based on the editions of 1798, 1800, or 1805, or on combinations of these. The present text follows the fourth and final edition of 1805, which gives a complete text of Wordsworth's Preface and seems to me critically preferable to any of the earlier editions. (For an account of the original editions and modern reprints see pp. 261-8 and 420.) As in other volumes of this series the spelling, capitals and punctuation have been modernised, though the deliberate archaisms of *The Ancient Mariner* have of course been retained. Quotations in the notes have likewise been modernised. Wordsworth's Preface has been thoroughly repunctuated (he confessed himself to be 'no adept' at punctuation), and it is hoped that as a result many passages have become easier to follow at a first reading. The poems have been more conservatively treated.

A large selection of textual variants has been included in the notes, so that in most cases the reader should be able to follow all revisions of real critical importance made either before or after 1805. In the case of *The Ancient Mariner* and *Tintern Abbey* I have tried to record all substantive printed variants. For these readings and for much other information I am indebted to Ernest de Selincourt and Helen Darbishire's edition of Wordsworth's *Poetical Works* (O.U.P., 1940-9), and to E. H. Coleridge's edition of Coleridge's *Poetical Works* (O.U.P., 1912).

The notes of this second edition have been revised in the light of recent scholarship. The bibliography has likewise been revised and expanded, and a bibliographical section added.

D.S.R.

Editor's Preface

Lyrical Ballads is worth studying, in the first place, because it contains some of the best poems ever written in English. *The Ancient Mariner*, *Tintern Abbey* and *Michael* are great achievements by any standard. They are achievements, too, of quite different kinds: the reader who understands and appreciates all three has come some distance in his critical development. The many good shorter poems are likewise very different one from another—*Goody Blake*, *It is the first mild day of March*, *A slumber did my spirit seal*, *The Nightingale*, *The Old Cumberland Beggar*. Few original publications can have shown such variety. Naturally there are dull poems and failures among the fifty-nine, but these should be seen as 'so many light or inferior coins in a rouleau of gold, not as so much alloy in a weight of bullion' (Coleridge, *Biographia Literaria*, ch. iv.).

It is worth studying, secondly, as a literary landmark. The beginning of the Romantic movement in English poetry is usually dated from the first publication of *Lyrical Ballads* in 1798. Like many physical landmarks, the work is in some ways more striking at a distance than when seen in its immediate setting. Poems like *Simon Lee* seem wholly revolutionary if placed against a supposedly orthodox background of ornate and elevated poetry such as Gray and Johnson wrote, and Wordsworth himself had written. But in fact the late eighteenth century had been a period of development and experiment. Humble and rustic themes, ballad techniques, simple language—these features would not in themselves have been surprising to a poetry-reader of 1798. What is really new is the seriousness, the daring and the poetic power that Wordsworth brings to his experiments, and the enlarged conceptions of poetry that he develops while pursuing them. Coleridge's *Ancient Mariner* was indeed puzzling to contemporaries, more so than anything by Wordsworth. Coleridge himself could not give any satisfying explanation of its strange power; nor, probably, was any available until our own century. But its power was increasingly acknowledged, and nineteenth-century writers inherited both from Coleridge and from Wordsworth new ideas of what was possible in poetry. *Lyrical Ballads* is, at least, as true a landmark as most.

Lastly, Wordsworth's Preface is as rewarding of study as any of the poems, and in a few passages almost as impressively written. Between 1798 and 1802 Wordsworth formed new conceptions of the nature, scope, language and function of poetry, derived for the most part from a searching examination of his own experience as a reader and as a creative artist. These conceptions make up part of our modern attitude to poetry. Helen Darbishire writes:

> Thanks to Wordsworth, Browning could take as subject Mr. Sludge the medium no less than Fra Lippo Lippi. Tennyson could develop a rustic theme with even a banal simplicity. . . . And our twentieth-century poets can sweep, as we know, from Byzantine glories to damp housemaids on area steps, and can freely explore the possibilities of a poetic language which may range from the charged words of inscrutable nursery rhymes through every compelling idiosyncrasy of elliptical speech to the allusive lingo of learned scholarship.
>
> (*The Poet Wordsworth*, pp. 56-7.)

Despite occasional distortions, inconsistencies and obscurities the Preface is probably the most important single document in English criticism, and to master it is an enlarging experience. But the poems themselves are more immediately rewarding, and are best approached without too many preconceptions derived from Wordsworth's theories. Many of them present no real difficulty; in other cases it is hoped that the notes will be of use. New readers might do well to get to know the poems first, and explore the Preface afterwards.

Wordsworth: Principal Dates

1770 Born, April 7th, at Cockermouth in Cumberland.

1778 His mother dies.

1779–87 At Hawkshead Grammar School. His father dies, 1783; W. spends summers with relations at Penrith.

1787–90 At St. John's College, Cambridge. Walking-tour of fourteen weeks in France and Switzerland, with Robert Jones (July-October 1790).

1791 To France again; Paris (November), then Orleans.

1792 Moves to Blois (spring). Friendship with Michel Beaupuy, love-affair with Annette Vallon; she gives birth to W.'s daughter Caroline, December 15th; W. returns to England.

1793 Restless unhappy period begins. *Letter to Bishop of Llandaff, by a Republican* written, though not pubd. *An Evening Walk* and *Descriptive Sketches* pubd. Walking-tour by Salisbury, Stonehenge, Bristol, Tintern Abbey to N. Wales.

1794 With Dorothy Wordsworth at Windy Brow, Keswick (spring). Wanders through Lake country. Seeks employment. Nurses Raisley Calvert.

1795 Legacy of £900 from Calvert. Meets Coleridge at Bristol (autumn). Settles at Racedown, in Dorset, with Dorothy.

1797 Close friendship with Coleridge begins (June). W. and Dorothy move to Alfoxden, in Somerset, to be near Coleridge at Stowey.

1798 Intense poetic activity (spring and summer): writes most of his contributions to first edn. of *Lyrical Ballads*, also *Peter Bell* and other work. *L.B.* pubd. (September). W., Dorothy, Coleridge and John Chester sail for Germany; W. and Dorothy take lodgings at Goslar, near the Harz Forest (October). W. begins work on *The Prelude* (winter of 1798-9).

1799 Leaves Goslar (April). Settles with Dorothy at Town End, Grasmere, his home until 1808.

1800 In close touch with Coleridge; preparing new edn. of *L.B.* (dated 1800, pubd. January 1801).

1802 W. and Dorothy visit Annette and Caroline at Calais (August). W. marries Mary Hutchinson (October 4th). Writes patriotic sonnets.

1803 First tour in Scotland; meets Walter Scott.

1805 W.'s favourite brother John drowned at sea.

1806–7 Spends winter at Coleorton in Leicestershire; long visit by Coleridge.

1807 *Poems in Two Volumes* pubd.

1808 Moves from Town End to Allan Bank, Grasmere.

1809 *Convention of Cintra* pubd.

1810 Serious quarrel with Coleridge (reconciled 1812). *Guide to the Lakes* pubd. as intro. to Joseph Wilkinson's *Select Views in Cumberland*, etc.

1811 Moves from Allan Bank to the Rectory, Grasmere.

1813 Appointed Stamp-Distributor for Westmorland (a government sinecure). Settles at Rydal Mount, his home for the rest of his life.

1814 Second tour in Scotland. *The Excursion* pubd.

1815 *Poems* (first collected edn.) and *The White Doe of Rylstone* pubd.

1819 *The Waggoner* (written 1805) and *Peter Bell* pubd.

1820 *The River Duddon: a Series of Sonnets* pubd. Visits Switzerland, Italy and France.

1822 *Memorials of a Tour on the Continent* and *Ecclesiastical Sketches* pubd.

1828 Tour up the Rhine with his daughter Dora and Coleridge.

1835 *Yarrow Revisited* pubd.

1842 Resigns post of Stamp-Distributor; receives pension of £300 p.a. from Civil List.

1843 Appointed Poet Laureate at Southey's death. Dictates series of notes on poems to Isabella Fenwick.

1844 *Kendal and Windermere Railway* pubd.

1849–50 Sixth edn. of *Poetical Works* (6 vols.), the last to be revised by W.

1850 Dies, April 23rd. *The Prelude* (completed 1805, subsequently much revised), pubd. after his death.

Coleridge: Principal Dates

1772 Born, October 21st, at Ottery St. Mary, Devon.

1781 C.'s father dies.

1782–91 At school at Christ's Hospital, London. Meets Mary Evans.

1791–3 At Jesus College, Cambridge; becomes a Unitarian and a democrat; in love with Mary Evans; in debt; enlists in 15th Dragoons (December 1793).

1794 Bought out of army, returns to Cambridge (April). Visits Southey at Oxford and forms scheme of settlement in America (Pantisocracy). With Southey writes *The Fall of Robespierre* (pubd. October). Becomes engaged to Sarah Fricker; breaks with Mary Evans. Leaves Cambridge without degree.

1795 At Bristol, living with Southey. Gives lectures, pubd. as *Conciones ad Populum*. Meets Wordsworth. Marries Sarah Fricker, October 4th. Disintegration of Pantisocracy and quarrel with Southey (November).

1796 Takes laudanum (March), an opiate to which he eventually becomes addicted. Produces short-lived periodical, *The Watchman*. First child (David Hartley) born September 19th. Tries to find work. *Poems on Various Subjects* and *Ode to the Departing Year* pubd.

1797 At Nether Stowey in Somerset. Writes *Osorio*. Visits Wordsworths (June) and 'settles' them at Alfoxden. Writes *Kubla Khan*, begins *The Ancient Mariner*.

1798 On point of becoming Unitarian minister, accepts annuity of £150 from the Wedgwoods. Completes *The Ancient Mariner*, writes Part I of *Christabel*. Satirised by Charles Lloyd in *Edmund Oliver* (pubd. April). *Lyrical Ballads* pubd., also C.'s *Fears in Solitude, France* and *Frost at Midnight*. To Germany with the Wordsworths and John Chester; with Chester to Ratzeburg and Göttingen.

1799 Returns from Germany (July). Walking-tour in the Lakes with William and John Wordsworth. Visits Sockburn and falls in love with Sara Hutchinson. To London, works on *Morning Post*. Writes *Love*, begins translating Schiller's *Wallenstein*.

1800 *Wallenstein* pubd. Settles at Greta Hall, Keswick, 13 miles from the Wordsworths. Active in preparing 2nd edn. of *Lyrical Ballads*; writes Part II of *Christabel*.

1802 Health declining. *Dejection* written as verse letter to Sara Hutchinson (April); a version pubd. in *Morning Post* (October).

1804–5 To Malta as Temporary Public Secretary; visits Sicily, Rome and Naples.

1806–7 Returns to England (August 1806). With the Wordsworths and Sara Hutchinson at Coleorton.

1807 Separates from his wife. Lectures on literature at the Royal Institution.

1808–10 With the Wordsworths and Sara Hutchinson at Grasmere. Pubs. new periodical, *The Friend* (June 1809–March 1810).

1810 To London. Quarrel with Wordsworth (reconciled 1812).

1811 Josiah Wedgwood withdraws his share of annuity.

1811–12 Lectures on Shakespeare.

1813 *Remorse* (a recast of *Osorio*) successfully produced at Drury Lane.

1816 Takes up residence with Dr. James Gillman at Highgate, his home for the rest of his life. *Christabel, Kubla Khan, Pains of Sleep* pubd.

1817 *Sibylline Leaves* and *Biographia Literaria* pubd.

1818 More lectures; C. attracts circle of young disciples.

1824 The 'Highgate Thursday evenings.'

1825 *Aids to Reflection* pubd. C. becomes Associate of the Royal Society of Literature, with annuity of £125.

1828 Tour up Rhine with Wordsworth and Dora Wordsworth.

1829 *Poetical Works* pubd. (dated 1828).

1830 *Constitution of Church and State* pubd.

1834 New edn. of *Poetical Works*. C. dies, July 25th.

Lyrical Ballads 1805

VOLUME I[1]

[1] With four exceptions, marked thus *, Volume I contains poems
published in the original one-volume edition of 1798 and Volume
II contains poems added in 1800. For the starred poems, see
notes.

LYRICAL BALLADS 1805

VOLUME II

LYRICAL BALLADS,

WITH

PASTORAL

AND OTHER

POEMS.

IN TWO VOLUMES.

BY W. WORDSWORTH.

Quam nihil ad genium, Papiniane, tuum!

VOL. I.

FOURTH EDITION.

LONDON:

PRINTED FOR LONGMAN, HURST, REES, AND ORME,

By R. Taylor and Co. 38, Shoe-Lane.

1805.

Wordsworth's Preface

THE FIRST VOLUME of these poems has already been submitted to general perusal. It was published as an experiment, which I hoped might be of some use to ascertain how far, by fitting to metrical arrangement a
5 selection of the real language of men in a state of vivid sensation, that sort of pleasure and that quantity of pleasure may be imparted which a poet may rationally endeavour to impart.

I had formed no very inaccurate estimate of the
10 probable effect of those poems: I flattered myself that they who should be pleased with them would read them with more than common pleasure; and on the other hand I was well aware that by those who should dislike them they would be read with more than com-
15 mon dislike. The result has differed from my expectation in this only, that I have pleased a greater number than I ventured to hope I should please.

For the sake of variety, and from a consciousness of my own weakness, I was induced to request the assist-
20 ance of a friend, who furnished me with the poems of *The Ancient Mariner*, *The Foster-Mother's Tale*, *The Nightingale*, and the poem entitled *Love*. I should not, however, have requested this assistance had I not believed that the poems of my friend would in a great
25 measure have the same tendency as my own, and that though there would be found a difference, there would be found no discordance in the colours of our style; as our opinions on the subject of poetry do almost entirely coincide.

Several of my friends are anxious for the success of these poems from a belief that if the views with which they were composed were indeed realised, a class of poetry would be produced well adapted to interest mankind permanently, and not unimportant in the 5 multiplicity and in the quality of its moral relations; and on this account they have advised me to prefix a systematic defence of the theory upon which the poems were written. But I was unwilling to undertake the task, because I knew that on this occasion the reader 10 would look coldly upon my arguments, since I might be suspected of having been principally influenced by the selfish and foolish hope of *reasoning* him into an approbation of these particular poems; and I was still more unwilling to undertake the task, because ade- 15 quately to display my opinions and fully to enforce my arguments would require a space wholly dispro- portionate to the nature of a preface. For to treat the subject with the clearness and coherence of which I believe it susceptible, it would be necessary to give a 20 full account of the present state of the public taste in this country, and to determine how far this taste is healthy or depraved; which, again, could not be deter- mined without pointing out in what manner language and the human mind act and react on each other, and 25 without retracing the revolutions, not of literature alone, but likewise of society itself. I have therefore altogether declined to enter regularly upon this defence; yet I am sensible that there would be some impro- priety in abruptly obtruding upon the public, without 30 a few words of introduction, poems so materially different from those upon which general approbation is at present bestowed.

It is supposed that by the act of writing in verse an author makes a formal engagement that he will 35 gratify certain known habits of association; that he not

only thus apprises the reader that certain classes of ideas and expressions will be found in his book, but that others will be carefully excluded. This exponent or symbol held forth by metrical language must in
5 different eras of literature have excited very different expectations: for example, in the age of Catullus, Terence and Lucretius, and that of Statius or Claudian; and in our own country, in the age of Shakespeare and Beaumont and Fletcher, and that of Donne and Cow-
10 ley, or Dryden, or Pope. I will not take upon me to determine the exact import of the promise which, by the act of writing in verse, an author in the present day makes to his reader; but I am certain it will appear to many persons that I have not fulfilled the terms of an
15 engagement thus voluntarily contracted. They who have been accustomed to the gaudiness and inane phraseology of many modern writers, if they persist in reading this book to its conclusion, will no doubt frequently have to struggle with feelings of strangeness
20 and awkwardness; they will look round for poetry, and will be induced to enquire by what species of courtesy these attempts can be permitted to assume that title. I hope therefore the reader will not censure me if I attempt to state what I have proposed to myself to
25 perform, and also (as far as the limits of a preface will permit) to explain some of the chief reasons which have determined me in the choice of my purpose; that at least he may be spared any unpleasant feeling of disappointment, and that I myself may be protected
30 from the most dishonourable accusation which can be brought against an author—namely, that of an indolence which prevents him from endeavouring to ascertain what is his duty, or, when his duty is ascertained, prevents him from performing it.
35 The principal object, then, which I proposed to myself in these poems was to choose incidents and

situations from common life, and to relate or describe
them throughout, as far as was possible, in a selection
of language really used by men; and at the same time
to throw over them a certain colouring of imagination,
whereby ordinary things should be presented to the 5
mind in an unusual way; and further, and above all, to
make these incidents and situations interesting by
tracing in them, truly though not ostentatiously, the
primary laws of our nature: chiefly as far as regards the
manner in which we associate ideas in a state of excite- 10
ment. Low and rustic life was generally chosen, because in that condition the essential passions of the
heart find a better soil in which they can attain their
maturity, are less under restraint, and speak a plainer
and more emphatic language; because in that condition 15
of life our elementary feelings co-exist in a state of
greater simplicity, and consequently may be more
accurately contemplated and more forcibly communicated; because the manners of rural life germinate from
those elementary feelings, and from the necessary char- 20
acter of rural occupations are more easily compre-
hended, and are more durable; and lastly, because in
that condition the passions of men are incorporated
with the beautiful and permanent forms of nature. The
language, too, of these men is adopted (purified indeed 25
from what appear to be its real defects, from all lasting
and rational causes of dislike or disgust) because such
men hourly communicate with the best objects from
which the best part of language is originally derived;
and because, from their rank in society and the same- 30
ness and narrow circle of their intercourse being less
under the influence of social vanity, they convey their
feelings and notions in simple and unelaborated expressions. Accordingly such a language, arising out of
repeated experience and regular feelings, is a more 35
permanent and a far more philosophical language than

that which is frequently substituted for it by poets, who think that they are conferring honour upon themselves and their art in proportion as they separate themselves from the sympathies of men, and indulge
5 in arbitrary and capricious habits of expression in order to furnish food for fickle tastes and fickle appetites of their own creation.*

I cannot, however, be insensible of the present outcry against the triviality and meanness both of thought
10 and language which some of my contemporaries have occasionally introduced into their metrical compositions; and I acknowledge that this defect, where it exists, is more dishonourable to the writer's own character than false refinement or arbitrary innovation,
15 though I should contend at the same time that it is far less pernicious in the sum of its consequences. From such verses the poems in these volumes will be found distinguished at least by one mark of difference, that each of them has a worthy *purpose*. Not that I mean to
20 say that I always began to write with a distinct purpose formally conceived; but I believe that my habits of meditation have so formed my feelings, as that my descriptions of such objects as strongly excite those feelings will be found to carry along with them a *purpose*. If in this opinion I am mistaken, I can have little
25 *pose*. If in this opinion I am mistaken, I can have little right to the name of a poet. For all good poetry is the spontaneous overflow of powerful feelings; but though this be true, poems to which any value can be attached were never produced on any variety of subjects but by
30 a man who, being possessed of more than usual organic sensibility, had also thought long and deeply. For our continued influxes of feeling are modified and directed by our thoughts, which are indeed the representatives

*It is worth while here to observe that the affecting parts of Chaucer are almost always expressed in language pure and universally intelligible to this day. [In the MS. this note is in Coleridge's handwriting.]

of all our past feelings; and as by contemplating the relation of these general representatives to each other we discover what is really important to men, so by the repetition and continuance of this act our feelings will be connected with important subjects, till at length, if 5 we be originally possessed of much sensibility, such habits of mind will be produced that, by obeying blindly and mechanically the impulses of those habits, we shall describe objects and utter sentiments of such a nature and in such connection with each other that 10 the understanding of the being to whom we address ourselves, if he be in a healthful state of association, must necessarily be in some degree enlightened and his affections ameliorated.

I have said that each of these poems has a purpose. I 15 have also informed my reader what this purpose will be found principally to be: namely, to illustrate the manner in which our feelings and ideas are associated in a state of excitement. But speaking in language somewhat more appropriate, it is to follow the fluxes and 20 refluxes of the mind when agitated by the great and simple affections of our nature. This object I have endeavoured in these short essays to attain by various means: by tracing the maternal passion through many of its more subtle windings, as in the poems of *The* 25 *Idiot Boy* and *The Mad Mother*; by accompanying the last struggles of a human being at the approach of death, cleaving in solitude to life and society, as in the poem of *The Forsaken Indian*; by showing, as in the stanzas entitled *We are Seven*, the perplexity and ob- 30 scurity which in childhood attend our notion of death, or rather our utter inability to admit that notion; or by displaying the strength of fraternal or, to speak more philosophically, of moral attachment when early associated with the great and beautiful objects of nature, as 35 in *The Brothers*; or, as in the incident of *Simon Lee*, by

placing my reader in the way of receiving from ordinary moral sensations another and more salutary impression than we are accustomed to receive from them. It has also been part of my general purpose to attempt to
5 sketch characters under the influence of less impassioned feelings, as in *The Two April Mornings*, *The Fountain*, *The Old Man Travelling*, *The Two Thieves*, etc., characters of which the elements are simple, belonging rather to nature than to manners, such as exist
10 now and will probably always exist, and which from their constitution may be distinctly and profitably contemplated. I will not abuse the indulgence of my reader by dwelling longer upon this subject, but it is proper that I should mention one other circumstance
15 which distinguishes these poems from the popular poetry of the day: it is this, that the feeling therein developed gives importance to the action and situation, and not the action and situation to the feeling. My meaning will be rendered perfectly intelligible by re-
20 ferring my reader to the poems entitled *Poor Susan* and *The Childless Father*, particularly to the last stanza of the latter poem.

I will not suffer a sense of false modesty to prevent me from asserting that I point my reader's attention
25 to this mark of distinction far less for the sake of these particular poems than from the general importance of the subject. The subject is indeed important! For the human mind is capable of being excited without the application of gross and violent stimulants; and he
30 must have a very faint perception of its beauty and dignity who does not know this, and who does not further know that one being is elevated above another in proportion as he possesses this capability. It has therefore appeared to me that to endeavour to produce
35 or enlarge this capability is one of the best services in which, at any period, a writer can be engaged; but this

service, excellent at all times, is especially so at the present day. For a multitude of causes unknown to former times are now acting with a combined force to blunt the discriminating powers of the mind and, unfitting it for all voluntary exertion, to reduce it to a 5 state of almost savage torpor. The most effective of these causes are the great national events which are daily taking place and the increasing accumulation of men in cities, where the uniformity of their occupations produces a craving for extraordinary incident, 10 which the rapid communication of intelligence hourly gratifies. To this tendency of life and manners the literature and theatrical exhibitions of the country have conformed themselves. The invaluable works of our elder writers, I had almost said the works of 15 Shakespeare and Milton, are driven into neglect by frantic novels, sickly and stupid German tragedies, and deluges of idle and extravagant stories in verse. When I think upon this degrading thirst after outrageous stimulation, I am almost ashamed to have spoken of 20 the feeble effort with which I have endeavoured to counteract it; and, reflecting upon the magnitude of the general evil, I should be oppressed with no dishonourable melancholy, had I not a deep impression of certain inherent and indestructible qualities of the human 25 mind, and likewise of certain powers in the great and permanent objects that act upon it which are equally inherent and indestructible; and did I not further add to this impression a belief that the time is approaching when the evil will be systematically opposed by men of 30 greater powers, and with far more distinguished success.

Having dwelt thus long on the subjects and aim of these poems, I shall request the reader's permission to apprise him of a few circumstances relating to their 35 *style*, in order, among other reasons, that I may not be

censured for not having performed what I never attempted. The reader will find that personifications of abstract ideas rarely occur in these volumes, and, I hope, are utterly rejected as an ordinary device to
5 elevate the style and raise it above prose. I have proposed to myself to imitate, and as far as is possible to adopt, the very language of men; and assuredly such personifications do not make any natural or regular part of that language. They are, indeed, a figure of
10 speech occasionally prompted by passion, and I have made use of them as such; but I have endeavoured utterly to reject them as a mechanical device of style, or as a family language which writers in metre seem to lay claim to by prescription. I have wished to keep my
15 reader in the company of flesh and blood, persuaded that by so doing I shall interest him. I am, however, well aware that others who pursue a different track may interest him likewise; I do not interfere with their claim, I only wish to prefer a different claim of my own.
20 There will also be found in these volumes little of what is usually called poetic diction; I have taken as much pains to avoid it as others ordinarily take to produce it; this I have done for the reason already alleged, to bring my language near to the language of men, and further,
25 because the pleasure which I have proposed to myself to impart is of a kind very different from that which is supposed by many persons to be the proper object of poetry. I do not know how, without being culpably particular, I can give my reader a more exact notion of
30 the style in which I wished these poems to be written, than by informing him that I have at all times endeavoured to look steadily at my subject: consequently I hope that there is in these poems little falsehood of description, and that my ideas are expressed in
35 language fitted to their respective importance. Something I must have gained by this practice, as it is

26

friendly to one property of all good poetry, namely good sense; but it has necessarily cut me off from a large portion of phrases and figures of speech which from father to son have long been regarded as the common inheritance of poets. I have also thought it 5 expedient to restrict myself still further, having abstained from the use of many expressions in themselves proper and beautiful, but which have been foolishly repeated by bad poets till such feelings of disgust are connected with them as it is scarcely possible by any 10 art of association to overpower.

If in a poem there should be found a series of lines or even a single line in which the language, though naturally arranged and according to the strict laws of metre, does not differ from that of prose, there is a 15 numerous class of critics who when they stumble upon these prosaisms, as they call them, imagine that they have made a notable discovery, and exult over the poet as over a man ignorant of his own profession. Now these men would establish a canon of criticism which 20 the reader will conclude he must utterly reject, if he wishes to be pleased with these volumes. And it would be a most easy task to prove to him that not only the language of a large portion of every good poem, even of the most elevated character, must necessarily (ex- 25 cept with reference to the metre) in no respect differ from that of good prose, but likewise that some of the most interesting parts of the best poems will be found to be strictly the language of prose, when prose is well written. The truth of this assertion might be demon- 30 strated by innumerable passages from almost all the poetical writings, even of Milton himself. I have not space for much quotation; but to illustrate the subject in a general manner I will here adduce a short composition of Gray, who was at the head of those who by 35 their reasonings have attempted to widen the space of

27

separation betwixt prose and metrical composition, and was more than any other man curiously elaborate in the structure of his own poetic diction.

> In vain to me the smiling mornings shine,
> 5 And reddening Phoebus lifts his golden fire:
> The birds in vain their amorous descant join,
> Or cheerful fields resume their green attire.
> These ears, alas! for other notes repine;
> *A different object do these eyes require;*
> 10 *My lonely anguish melts no heart but mine;*
> *And in my breast the imperfect joys expire;*
> Yet morning smiles the busy race to cheer,
> And new-born pleasure brings to happier men;
> The fields to all their wonted tribute bear;
> 15 To warm their little loves the birds complain.
> *I fruitless mourn to him that cannot hear,*
> *And weep the more because I weep in vain.*

It will easily be perceived that the only part of this sonnet which is of any value is the lines printed in 20 italics: it is equally obvious that except in the rhyme, and in the use of the single word 'fruitless' for fruitlessly, which is so far a defect, the language of these lines does in no respect differ from that of prose.

By the foregoing quotation I have shown that the 25 language of prose may yet be well adapted to poetry; and I have previously asserted that a large portion of the language of every good poem can in no respect differ from that of good prose. I will go further. I do not doubt that it may be safely affirmed, that there 30 neither is, nor can be, any essential difference between the language of prose and metrical composition. We are fond of tracing the resemblance between poetry and painting, and accordingly we call them sisters: but where shall we find bonds of connection sufficiently 35 strict to typify the affinity betwixt metrical and prose composition? They both speak by and to the same

organs; the bodies in which both of them are clothed
may be said to be of the same substance, their affections are kindred and almost identical, not necessarily
differing even in degree. Poetry* sheds no tears 'such
as angels weep,' but natural and human tears; she can 5
boast of no celestial ichor that distinguishes her vital
juices from those of prose; the same human blood cir-
culates through the veins of them both.

If it be affirmed that rhyme and metrical arrangement of themselves constitute a distinction which over- 10
turns what I have been saying on the strict affinity of
metrical language with that of prose, and paves the
way for other artificial distinctions which the mind
voluntarily admits, I answer that the language of such
poetry as I am recommending is, as far as is possible, a 15
selection of the language really spoken by men; that
this selection, wherever it is made with true taste and
feeling, will of itself form a distinction far greater than
would at first be imagined, and will entirely separate
the composition from the vulgarity and meanness of 20
ordinary life; and if metre be superadded thereto I believe a dissimilitude will be produced altogether sufficient for the gratification of a rational mind. What
other distinction would we have? Whence is it to come?
And where is it to exist? Not, surely, where the poet 25
speaks through the mouths of his characters: it cannot
be necessary here, either for elevation of style or any
of its supposed ornaments; for if the poet's subject be
judiciously chosen it will naturally, and upon fit occa-

*I here use the word *poetry* (though against my own judgment) as
opposed to the word *prose*, and synonymous with metrical composition. But much confusion has been introduced into criticism
by this contradistinction of poetry and prose, instead of the more
philosophical one of poetry and matter of fact, or science. The
only strict antithesis to prose is metre; nor is this in truth a *strict*
antithesis, because lines and passages of metre so naturally occur
in writing prose that it would be scarcely possible to avoid them,
even were it desirable.

sion, lead him to passions the language of which, if
selected truly and judiciously, must necessarily be dignified and variegated, and alive with metaphors and
figures. I forbear to speak of an incongruity which
5 would shock the intelligent reader, should the poet
interweave any foreign splendour of his own with that
which the passion naturally suggests; it is sufficient to
say that such addition is unnecessary. And surely it is
more probable that those passages which with pro-
10 priety abound with metaphors and figures will have
their due effect if upon other occasions, where the
passions are of a milder character, the style also be
subdued and temperate.

But as the pleasure which I hope to give by the
15 poems I now present to the reader must depend entirely on just notions upon this subject, and as it is in
itself of the highest importance to our taste and moral
feelings, I cannot content myself with these detached
remarks. And if in what I am about to say it shall
20 appear to some that my labour is unnecessary, and that
I am like a man fighting a battle without enemies, I
would remind such persons that whatever may be the
language outwardly holden by men, a practical faith in
the opinions which I am wishing to establish is almost
25 unknown. If my conclusions are admitted, and carried
as far as they must be carried if admitted at all, our
judgments concerning the works of the greatest poets
both ancient and modern will be far different from
what they are at present, both when we praise and
30 when we censure; and our moral feelings influencing
and influenced by these judgments will, I believe, be
corrected and purified.

Taking up the subject, then, upon general grounds,
I ask what is meant by the word *poet*? What is a poet?
35 To whom does he address himself? And what language
is to be expected from him? He is a man speaking to

men: a man, it is true, endued with more lively sensibility, more enthusiasm and tenderness, who has a greater knowledge of human nature, and a more comprehensive soul, than are supposed to be common among mankind; a man pleased with his own passions 5 and volitions, and who rejoices more than other men in the spirit of life that is in him; delighting to contemplate similar volitions and passions as manifested in the goings-on of the universe, and habitually impelled to create them where he does not find them. To these 10 qualities he has added a disposition to be affected more than other men by absent things as if they were present: an ability of conjuring up in himself passions which are indeed far from being the same as those produced by real events, yet (especially in those parts of the 15 general sympathy which are pleasing and delightful) do more nearly resemble the passions produced by real events than anything which, from the motions of their own minds merely, other men are accustomed to feel in themselves; whence, and from practice, he has ac- 20 quired a greater readiness and power in expressing what he thinks and feels, and especially those thoughts and feelings which by his own choice, or from the structure of his own mind, arise in him without immediate external excitement. 25

But whatever portion of this faculty we may suppose even the greatest poet to possess, there cannot be a doubt but that the language which it will suggest to him must in liveliness and truth fall far short of that which is uttered by men in real life under the actual pressure 30 of those passions, certain shadows of which the poet thus produces or feels to be produced in himself. However exalted a notion we would wish to cherish of the character of a poet, it is obvious that while he describes and imitates passions his situation is altogether 35 slavish and mechanical compared with the freedom

and power of real and substantial action and suffering.
So that it will be the wish of the poet to bring his feelings near to those of the persons whose feelings he
describes—nay, for short spaces of time perhaps to let
himself slip into an entire delusion, and even confound
and identify his own feelings with theirs; modifying
only the language which is thus suggested to him by
a consideration that he describes for a particular purpose, that of giving pleasure. Here, then, he will apply
the principle on which I have so much insisted,
namely that of selection: on this he will depend for
removing what would otherwise be painful or disgusting in the passion; he will feel that there is no
necessity to trick out or to elevate nature; and the more
industriously he applies this principle, the deeper will
be his faith that no words which his fancy or imagination can suggest will be to be compared with those
which are the emanations of reality and truth.

But it may be said by those who do not object to
the general spirit of these remarks that, as it is impossible for the poet to produce upon all occasions
language as exquisitely fitted for the passion as that
which the real passion itself suggests, it is proper that
he should consider himself as in the situation of a
translator, who deems himself justified when he sub-
stitutes excellences of another kind for those which are
unattainable by him; and endeavours occasionally to
surpass his original in order to make some amends for
the general inferiority to which he feels that he must
submit. But this would be to encourage idleness and
unmanly despair. Further, it is the language of men
who speak of what they do not understand; who talk of
poetry as of a matter of amusement and idle pleasure;
who will converse with us as gravely about a *taste* for
poetry, as they express it, as if it were a thing as indifferent as a taste for rope-dancing, or Frontiniac, or

sherry. Aristotle, I have been told, hath said that poetry is the most philosophic of all writing: it is so: its object is truth, not individual and local, but general and operative; not standing upon external testimony, but carried alive into the heart by passion; truth which 5 is its own testimony, which gives strength and divinity to the tribunal to which it appeals, and receives them from the same tribunal. Poetry is the image of man and nature. The obstacles which stand in the way of the fidelity of the biographer and historian, and of their 10 consequent utility, are incalculably greater than those which are to be encountered by the poet who has an adequate notion of the dignity of his art. The poet writes under one restriction only, namely, that of the necessity of giving immediate pleasure to a human 15 being possessed of that information which may be expected from him, not as a lawyer, a physician, a mariner, an astronomer or a natural philosopher, but as a man. Except this one restriction, there is no object standing between the poet and the image of things: 20 between this and the biographer and historian there are a thousand.

Nor let this necessity of producing immediate pleasure be considered as a degradation of the poet's art. It is far otherwise. It is an acknowledgment of the 25 beauty of the universe, an acknowledgment the more sincere because it is not formal, but indirect; it is a task light and easy to him who looks at the world in the spirit of love; further, it is a homage paid to the native and naked dignity of man, to the grand elementary 30 principle of pleasure, by which he knows, and feels, and lives, and moves. We have no sympathy but what is propagated by pleasure: I would not be misunderstood; but wherever we sympathise with pain it will be found that the sympathy is produced and carried 35 on by subtle combinations with pleasure. We have no

knowledge, that is no general principles drawn from the contemplation of particular facts, but what has been built up by pleasure, and exists in us by pleasure alone. The man of science, the chemist and mathe-
5 matician, whatever difficulties and disgusts they may have had to struggle with, know and feel this. However painful may be the objects with which the anatomist's knowledge is connected, he feels that his knowledge is pleasure; and where he has no pleasure he has no
10 knowledge. What then does the poet? He considers man and the objects that surround him as acting and re-acting upon each other so as to produce an infinite complexity of pain and pleasure; he considers man in his own nature and in his ordinary life as contemplating
15 this with a certain quantity of immediate knowledge, with certain convictions, intuitions, and deductions which by habit become of the nature of intuitions; he considers him as looking upon this complex scene of ideas and sensations, and finding everywhere objects
20 that immediately excite in him sympathies which, from the necessities of his nature, are accompanied by an overbalance of enjoyment.

To this knowledge which all men carry about with them, and to these sympathies in which without any
25 other discipline than that of our daily life we are fitted to take delight, the poet principally directs his atten-tion. He considers man and nature as essentially adapted to each other, and the mind of man as naturally the mirror of the fairest and most interesting qualities
30 of nature. And thus the poet, prompted by this feeling of pleasure which accompanies him through the whole course of his studies, converses with general nature with affections akin to those which, through labour and length of time, the man of science has raised up in
35 himself by conversing with those particular parts of nature which are the objects of his studies. The know-

ledge both of the poet and the man of science is pleasure: but the knowledge of the one cleaves to us as a necessary part of our existence, our natural and unalienable inheritance; the other is a personal and individual acquisition, slow to come to us, and by no habitual and direct sympathy connecting us with our fellow-beings. The man of science seeks truth as a remote and unknown benefactor; he cherishes and loves it in his solitude: the poet, singing a song in which all human beings join with him, rejoices in the presence of truth as our visible friend and hourly companion. Poetry is the breath and finer spirit of all knowledge; it is the impassioned expression which is in the countenance of all science. Emphatically may it be said of the poet, as Shakespeare hath said of man, 'that he looks before and after.' He is the rock of defence of human nature, an upholder and preserver, carrying everywhere with him relationship and love. In spite of difference of soil and climate, of language and manners, of laws and customs, in spite of things silently gone out of mind and things violently destroyed, the poet binds together by passion and knowledge the vast empire of human society, as it is spread over the whole earth, and over all time. The objects of the poet's thoughts are everywhere: though the eyes and senses of men are, it is true, his favourite guides, yet he will follow wheresoever he can find an atmosphere of sensation in which to move his wings. Poetry is the first and last of all knowledge: it is as immortal as the heart of man. If the labours of men of science should ever create any material revolution, direct or indirect, in our condition and in the impressions which we habitually receive, the poet will sleep then no more than at present, but he will be ready to follow the steps of the man of science, not only in those general indirect effects, but he will be at his side, carrying sensation into the midst of the

objects of the science itself. The remotest discoveries
of the chemist, the botanist or mineralogist will be as
proper objects of the poet's art as any upon which it
can be employed, if the time should ever come when
5 these things shall be familiar to us, and the relations
under which they are contemplated by the followers of
these respective sciences shall be manifestly and palpably material to us as enjoying and suffering beings.
If the time should ever come when what is now called
10 science, thus familiarised to men, shall be ready to put
on, as it were, a form of flesh and blood, the poet will
lend his divine spirit to aid the transfiguration, and
will welcome the being thus produced as a dear and
genuine inmate of the household of man. It is not,
15 then, to be supposed that any one who holds that sublime notion of poetry which I have attempted to convey will break in upon the sanctity and truth of his
pictures by transitory and accidental ornaments, and
endeavour to excite admiration of himself by arts the
20 necessity of which must manifestly depend upon the
assumed meanness of his subject.

What I have thus far said applies to poetry in
general, but especially to those parts of composition
where the poet speaks through the mouths of his
25 characters; and upon this point it appears to have such
weight that I will conclude: there are few persons of
good sense who would not allow that the dramatic
parts of composition are defective in proportion as they
deviate from the real language of nature and are
30 coloured by a diction of the poet's own, either peculiar
to him as an individual poet or belonging simply to
poets in general—to a body of men who, from the circumstance of their compositions being in metre, it is
expected will employ a particular language.

35 It is not, then, in the dramatic parts of composition
that we look for this distinction of language; but still

it may be proper and necessary where the poet speaks
to us in his own person and character. To this I answer
by referring my reader to the description which I have
before given of a poet. Among the qualities which I
have enumerated as principally conducing to form a 5
poet is implied nothing differing in kind from other
men, but only in degree. The sum of what I have there
said is that the poet is chiefly distinguished from other
men by a greater promptness to think and feel without
immediate external excitement, and a greater power in 10
expressing such thoughts and feelings as are produced
in him in that manner. But these passions and thoughts
and feelings are the general passions and thoughts and
feelings of men. And with what are they connected?
Undoubtedly with our moral sentiments and animal 15
sensations, and with the causes which excite these:
with the operations of the elements and the appearances of the visible universe; with storm and sunshine,
with the revolutions of the seasons, with cold and heat,
with loss of friends and kindred, with injuries and re- 20
sentments, gratitude and hope, with fear and sorrow.
These and the like are the sensations and objects which
the poet describes, as they are the sensations of other
men and the objects which interest them. The poet
thinks and feels in the spirit of the passions of men. 25
How then can his language differ in any material degree
from that of all other men who feel vividly and see
clearly? It might be *proved* that it is impossible. But
supposing that this were not the case, the poet might
then be allowed to use a peculiar language when ex- 30
pressing his feelings for his own gratification, or that
of men like himself. But poets do not write for poets
alone, but for men. Unless therefore we are advocates
for that admiration which depends upon ignorance,
and that pleasure which arises from hearing what we 35
do not understand, the poet must descend from this

supposed height, and in order to excite rational sympathy he must express himself as other men express themselves. To this it may be added that while he is only selecting from the real language of men (or,
5 which amounts to the same thing, composing accurately in the spirit of such selection), he is treading upon safe ground, and we know what we are to expect from him. Our feelings are the same with respect to metre: for as it may be proper to remind the
10 reader, the distinction of metre is regular and uniform and not, like that which is produced by what is usually called poetic diction,[1] arbitrary and subject to infinite caprices upon which no calculation whatever can be made. In the one case the reader is utterly at the mercy
15 of the poet respecting what imagery or diction he may choose to connect with the passion, whereas in the other the metre obeys certain laws to which the poet and reader both willingly submit because they are certain, and because no interference is made by them
20 with the passion but such as the concurring testimony of ages has shown to heighten and improve the pleasure which co-exists with it.

It will now be proper to answer an obvious question, namely 'Why, professing these opinions, have I
25 written in verse?' To this, in addition to such answer as is included in what I have already said, I reply in the first place: because however I may have restricted myself, there is still left open to me what confessedly constitutes the most valuable object of all writing, whether
30 in prose or verse—the great and universal passions of men, the most general and interesting of their occupations, and the entire world of nature, from which I am at liberty to supply myself with endless combinations of forms and imagery. Now, supposing for a moment
35 that whatever is interesting in these objects may be as

[1]See Wordsworth's Appendix, p. 252.

vividly described in prose, why am I to be condemned
if to such description I have endeavoured to superadd
the charm which by the consent of all nations is acknowledged to exist in metrical language? To this, by
such as are unconvinced by what I have already said, 5
it may be answered that a very small part of the
pleasure given by poetry depends upon the metre, and
that it is injudicious to write in metre unless it be
accompanied with the other artificial distinctions of
style with which metre is usually accompanied; and 10
that by such deviation more will be lost from the
shock which will be thereby given to the reader's
associations than will be counterbalanced by any
pleasure which he can derive from the general power
of numbers. In answer to those who still contend for 15
the necessity of accompanying metre with certain
appropriate colours of style in order to the accom-
plishment of its appropriate end, and who also, in my
opinion, greatly under-rate the power of metre in itself, it might perhaps, as far as relates to these poems, 20
have been almost sufficient to observe that poems are
extant written upon more humble subjects, and in a
more naked and simple style than I have aimed at,
which poems have continued to give pleasure from
generation to generation. Now, if nakedness and sim- 25
plicity be a defect, the fact here mentioned affords a
strong presumption that poems somewhat less naked
and simple are capable of affording pleasure at the
present day; and what I wished *chiefly* to attempt, at
present, was to justify myself for having written under 30
the impression of this belief.

But I might point out various causes why, when the
style is manly and the subject of some importance,
words metrically arranged will long continue to impart
such a pleasure to mankind as he who is sensible of the 35
extent of that pleasure will be desirous to impart. The

end of poetry is to produce excitement in co-existence
with an over-balance of pleasure. Now, by the sup-
position, excitement is an unusual and irregular state
of the mind: ideas and feelings do not in that state suc-
5 ceed each other in accustomed order. But if the words
by which this excitement is produced are in themselves powerful, or the images and feelings have an
undue proportion of pain connected with them, there
is some danger that the excitement may be carried
10 beyond its proper bounds. Now the co-presence of
something regular, something to which the mind has
been accustomed in various moods and in a less excited
state, cannot but have great efficacy in tempering and
restraining the passion by an inter-texture of ordinary
15 feeling, and of feeling not strictly and necessarily connected with the passion. This is unquestionably true;
and hence, though the opinion will at first appear para-
doxical, from the tendency of metre to divest language
in a certain degree of its reality, and thus to throw a
20 sort of half-consciousness of unsubstantial existence
over the whole composition, there can be little doubt
but that more pathetic situations and sentiments (that
is, those which have a greater proportion of pain connected with them) may be endured in metrical com-
25 position, especially in rhyme, than in prose. The metre
of the old ballads is very artless, yet they contain many
passages which would illustrate this opinion; and I
hope if the following poems be attentively perused
similar instances will be found in them. This opinion
30 may be further illustrated by appealing to the reader's
own experience of the reluctance with which he comes
to the re-perusal of the distressful parts of *Clarissa
Harlowe*, or *The Gamester*; while Shakespeare's writings, in the most pathetic scenes, never act upon us as
35 pathetic beyond the bounds of pleasure—an effect
which, in a much greater degree than might at first be

imagined, is to be ascribed to small but continual and
regular impulses of pleasurable surprise from the metrical arrangement. On the other hand (what it must be
allowed will much more frequently happen), if the
poet's words should be incommensurate with the 5
passion and inadequate to raise the reader to a height
of desirable excitement, then (unless the poet's choice
of his metre has been grossly injudicious) in the feelings of pleasure which the reader has been accustomed
to connect with metre in general, and in the feeling, 10
whether cheerful or melancholy, which he has been
accustomed to connect with that particular movement
of metre, there will be found something which will
greatly contribute to impart passion to the words, and
to effect the complex end which the poet proposes to 15
himself.

If I had undertaken a systematic defence of the
theory upon which these poems are written, it would
have been my duty to develop the various causes upon
which the pleasure received from metrical language 20
depends. Among the chief of these causes is to be
reckoned a principle which must be well known to
those who have made any of the arts the object of
accurate reflection: I mean the pleasure which the
mind derives from the perception of similitude in dis- 25
similitude. This principle is the great spring of the
activity of our minds, and their chief feeder. From this
principle the direction of the sexual appetite, and all
the passions connected with it, take their origin; it is
the life of our ordinary conversation; and upon the 30
accuracy with which similitude in dissimilitude, and
dissimilitude in similitude, are perceived depend our
taste and our moral feelings. It would not have been
a useless employment to have applied this principle
to the consideration of metre, and to have shown that 35
metre is hence enabled to afford much pleasure, and

to have pointed out in what manner that pleasure is produced. But my limits will not permit me to enter upon this subject, and I must content myself with a general summary.

5   I have said that poetry is the spontaneous overflow of powerful feelings; it takes its origin from emotion recollected in tranquillity; the emotion is contemplated till by a species of reaction the tranquillity gradually disappears, and an emotion, kindred to that which was 10 before the subject of contemplation, is gradually produced and does itself actually exist in the mind. In this mood successful composition generally begins, and in a mood similar to this it is carried on; but the emotion, of whatever kind and in whatever degree, from various 15 causes is qualified by various pleasures, so that in describing any passions whatsoever which are voluntarily described the mind will upon the whole be in a state of enjoyment. Now, if Nature be thus cautious in preserving in a state of enjoyment a being thus employed, 20 the poet ought to profit by the lesson thus held forth to him, and ought especially to take care that whatever passions he communicates to his reader, those passions, if his reader's mind be sound and vigorous, should always be accompanied with an overbalance of 25 pleasure. Now the music of harmonious metrical language, the sense of difficulty overcome, and the blind association of pleasure which has been previously received from works of rhyme or metre of the same or similar construction, an indistinct perception per- 30 petually renewed of language closely resembling that of real life, and yet in the circumstance of metre differing from it so widely—all these imperceptibly make up a complex feeling of delight, which is of the most important use in tempering the painful feeling which 35 will always be found intermingled with powerful descriptions of the deeper passions. This effect is

always produced in pathetic and impassioned poetry;
while in lighter compositions the ease and gracefulness
with which the poet manages his numbers are themselves confessedly a principal source of the gratification of the reader. I might perhaps include all which it 5
is *necessary* to say upon this subject by affirming, what
few persons will deny, that of two descriptions either
of passions, manners or characters, each of them
equally well executed, the one in prose and the other in
verse, the verse will be read a hundred times where the 10
prose is read once. We see that Pope, by the power of
verse alone, has contrived to render the plainest common sense interesting, and even frequently to invest it
with the appearance of passion. In consequence of
these convictions I related in metre the tale of *Goody* 15
Blake and Harry Gill, which is one of the rudest of this
collection. I wished to draw attention to the truth, that
the power of the human imagination is sufficient to
produce such changes even in our physical nature as
might almost appear miraculous. The truth is an im- 20
portant one: the fact (for it is a *fact*) is a valuable illustration of it. And I have the satisfaction of knowing
that it has been communicated to many hundreds of
people who would never have heard of it had it not
been narrated as a ballad, and in a more impressive 25
metre than is usual in ballads.

Having thus explained a few of the reasons why I
have written in verse, and why I have chosen subjects
from common life and endeavoured to bring my
language near to the real language of men, if I have 30
been too minute in pleading my own cause, I have at
the same time been treating a subject of general
interest; and it is for this reason that I request the
reader's permission to add a few words with reference
solely to these particular poems, and to some defects 35
which will probably be found in them. I am sensible

that my associations must have sometimes been particular instead of general, and that consequently, giving to things a false importance, sometimes from diseased impulses I may have written upon unworthy subjects;
5 but I am less apprehensive on this account, than that my language may frequently have suffered from those arbitrary connections of feelings and ideas with particular words and phrases, from which no man can altogether protect himself. Hence I have no doubt that
10 in some instances feelings even of the ludicrous may be given to my readers by expressions which appeared to me tender and pathetic. Such faulty expressions, were I convinced they were faulty at present and that they must necessarily continue to be so, I would will-
15 ingly take all reasonable pains to correct. But it is dangerous to make these alterations on the simple authority of a few individuals, or even of certain classes of men; for where the understanding of an author is not convinced or his feelings altered, this cannot be
20 done without great injury to himself: for his own feelings are his stay and support, and if he sets them aside in one instance he may be induced to repeat this act till his mind loses all confidence in itself and becomes utterly debilitated. To this it may be added that the
25 reader ought never to forget that he is himself exposed to the same errors as the poet, and perhaps in a much greater degree: for there can be no presumption in saying that it is not probable he will be so well acquainted with the various stages of meaning through
30 which words have passed, or with the fickleness or stability of the relations of particular ideas to each other; and above all, since he is so much less interested in the subject, he may decide lightly and carelessly.

Long as I have detained my reader, I hope he will
35 permit me to caution him against a mode of false criticism which has been applied to poetry in which

the language closely resembles that of life and nature.
Such verses have been triumphed over in parodies of
which Dr. Johnson's stanza is a fair specimen:

> I put my hat upon my head,
> And walked into the Strand, 5
> And there I met another man
> Whose hat was in his hand.

Immediately under these lines I will place one of the
most justly admired stanzas of *The Babes in the Wood*:

> These pretty babes with hand in hand 10
> Went wandering up and down;
> But never more they saw the man
> Approaching from the town.

In both these stanzas the words, and the order of the
words, in no respect differ from the most unimpas- 15
sioned conversation. There are words in both, for
example 'the Strand' and 'the town,' connected with
none but the most familiar ideas; yet the one stanza
we admit as admirable, and the other as a fair example
of the superlatively contemptible. Whence arises this 20
difference? Not from the metre, not from the language,
not from the order of the words: but the *matter* expressed in Dr. Johnson's stanza is contemptible. The
proper method of treating trivial and simple verses to
which Dr. Johnson's stanza would be a fair parallelism 25
is not to say 'This is a bad kind of poetry,' or 'This is
not poetry,' but 'This wants sense; it is neither interesting in itself, nor can *lead* to anything interesting; the
images neither originate in that sane state of feeling
which arises out of thought, nor can excite thought or 30
feeling in the reader.' This is the only sensible manner
of dealing with such verses. Why trouble yourself
about the species till you have previously decided upon
the genus? Why take pains to prove that an ape is not a
Newton, when it is self-evident that he is not a man? 35

I have one request to make of my reader, which is

45

that in judging these poems he would decide by his own feelings genuinely, and not by reflection upon what will probably be the judgment of others. How common it is to hear a person say, 'I myself do not object to this style of composition, or this or that expression, but to such and such classes of people it will appear mean or ludicrous.' This mode of criticism, so destructive of all sound unadulterated judgment, is almost universal: I have therefore to request that the reader would abide independently by his own feelings, and that if he finds himself affected he would not suffer such conjectures to interfere with his pleasure.

If an author by any single composition has impressed us with respect for his talents, it is useful to consider this as affording a presumption that on other occasions where we have been displeased he nevertheless may not have written ill or absurdly; and further, to give him so much credit for this one composition as may induce us to review what has displeased us with more care than we should otherwise have bestowed upon it. This is not only an act of justice but, in our decisions upon poetry especially, may conduce in a high degree to the improvement of our own taste: for an *accurate* taste in poetry and in all the other arts, as Sir Joshua Reynolds has observed, is an *acquired* talent, which can only be produced by thought and a long-continued intercourse with the best models of composition. This is mentioned, not with so ridiculous a purpose as to prevent the most inexperienced reader from judging for himself (I have already said that I wish him to judge for himself), but merely to temper the rashness of decision; and to suggest that if poetry be a subject on which much time has not been bestowed the judgment may be erroneous, and that in many cases it necessarily will be so.

I know that nothing would have so effectually con-

tributed to further the end which I have in view as to
have shown of what kind the pleasure is, and how that
pleasure is produced, which is confessedly produced
by metrical composition essentially different from that
which I have here endeavoured to recommend: for the 5
reader will say that he has been pleased by such composition, and what can I do more for him? The power
of any art is limited; and he will suspect that if I propose to furnish him with new friends, it is only upon
condition of his abandoning his old friends. Besides, 10
as I have said, the reader is himself conscious of the
pleasure which he has received from such composition,
composition to which he has peculiarly attached the
endearing name of *poetry*; and all men feel an habitual
gratitude, and something of an honourable bigotry, for 15
the objects which have long continued to please them;
we not only wish to be pleased, but to be pleased in
that particular way in which we have been accustomed
to be pleased. There is a host of arguments in these
feelings; and I should be the less able to combat them 20
successfully, as I am willing to allow that in order entirely to enjoy the poetry which I am recommending it
would be necessary to give up much of what is ordinarily enjoyed. But would my limits have permitted
me to point out how this pleasure is produced I might 25
have removed many obstacles, and assisted my reader
in perceiving that the powers of language are not so
limited as he may suppose; and that it is possible that
poetry may give other enjoyments of a purer, more
lasting, and more exquisite nature. This part of my 30
subject I have not altogether neglected; but it has been
less my present aim to prove that the interest excited
by some other kinds of poetry is less vivid and less
worthy of the nobler powers of the mind, than to offer
reasons for presuming that if the object which I have 35
proposed to myself were adequately attained, a species

LYRICAL BALLADS,

WITH

PASTORAL

AND

OTHER POEMS.

Pectus enim id est quod disertos facit,
et vis mentis; ideoque imperitis quoque,
si modo sint aliquo affectu concitati,
verba non desunt.

EXPOSTULATION AND REPLY

'Why, William, on that old grey stone,
Thus for the length of half a day,
Why, William, sit you thus alone,
And dream your time away?

'Where are your books?—that light   5
        bequeathed
To beings else forlorn and blind!
Up! up! and drink the spirit breathed
From dead men to their kind.

'You look round on your mother earth,
As if she for no purpose bore you;   10
As if you were her first-born birth,
And none had lived before you!'

One morning thus, by Esthwaite lake,
When life was sweet, I knew not why,
To me my good friend Matthew spake,   15
And thus I made reply:

'The eye it cannot choose but see;
We cannot bid the ear be still;
Our bodies feel, where'er they be,
Against, or with our will.   20

'Nor less I deem that there are powers
Which of themselves our minds impress;
That we can feed this mind of ours
In a wise passiveness.

'Think you, 'mid all this mighty sum   25
Of things for ever speaking,
That nothing of itself will come,
But we must still be seeking?

'—Then ask not wherefore, here, alone,
Conversing as I may,   30
I sit upon this old grey stone,
And dream my time away.'

THE TABLES TURNED

AN EVENING SCENE, ON THE SAME SUBJECT

Up! up! my friend, and clear your looks;
Why all this toil and trouble?
Up! up! my friend, and quit your books,
Or surely you'll grow double.

The sun, above the mountain's head,   5
A freshening lustre mellow
Through all the long green fields has spread,
His first sweet evening yellow.

Books! 'tis a dull and endless strife:
Come, hear the woodland linnet,   10
How sweet his music! on my life
There's more of wisdom in it.

And hark! how blithe the throstle sings!
And he is no mean preacher:
Come forth into the light of things,   15
Let Nature be your teacher.

She has a world of ready wealth,
Our minds and hearts to bless—
Spontaneous wisdom breathed by health,
Truth breathed by cheerfulness.   20

One impulse from a vernal wood
May teach you more of man,
Of moral evil and of good,
Than all the sages can.

Sweet is the lore which Nature brings;   25
Our meddling intellect
Misshapes the beauteous forms of things—
We murder to dissect.

Enough of science and of art;
Close up these barren leaves;   30
Come forth, and bring with you a heart
That watches and receives.

ANIMAL TRANQUILLITY AND DECAY

A SKETCH

        The little hedge-row birds
That peck along the road, regard him not.
He travels on, and in his face, his step,
His gait, is one expression; every limb,
His look and bending figure, all bespeak   5
A man who does not move with pain, but moves
With thought. He is insensibly subdued
To settled quiet: he is one by whom
All effort seems forgotten; one to whom
Long patience hath such mild composure given,   10
That patience now doth seem a thing of which
He hath no need. He is by nature led
To peace so perfect, that the young behold
With envy, what the old man hardly feels.
I asked him whither he was bound, and what   15
The object of his journey: he replied
That he was going many miles to take
A last leave of his son, a mariner,
Who from a sea-fight had been brought to
        Falmouth,
And there was dying in an hospital.   20

GOODY BLAKE AND HARRY GILL

A TRUE STORY

Oh! what's the matter? what's the matter?
What is't that ails young Harry Gill?
That evermore his teeth they chatter,
Chatter, chatter, chatter still.
Of waistcoats Harry has no lack,   5
Good duffle grey, and flannel fine;
He has a blanket on his back,
And coats enough to smother nine.

In March, December, and in July,
'Tis all the same with Harry Gill;   10
The neighbours tell, and tell you truly,
His teeth they chatter, chatter still.
At night, at morning, and at noon,
'Tis all the same with Harry Gill;
Beneath the sun, beneath the moon,   15
His teeth they chatter, chatter still.

Young Harry was a lusty drover,
And who so stout of limb as he?
His cheeks were red as ruddy clover;
His voice was like the voice of three.   20
Old Goody Blake was old and poor;
Ill fed she was, and thinly clad;
And any man who passed her door
Might see how poor a hut she had.

All day she spun in her poor dwelling;   25
And then her three hours' work at night!
Alas! 'twas hardly worth the telling,
It would not pay for candle-light.
This woman dwelt in Dorsetshire,
Her hut was on a cold hill-side,   30
And in that country coals are dear,
For they come far by wind and tide.

By the same fire to boil their pottage,
Two poor old dames, as I have known,
Will often live in one small cottage;   35
But she, poor woman! dwelt alone.
'Twas well enough when summer came,
The long, warm, lightsome summer-day,
Then at her door the canty dame
Would sit, as any linnet gay.   40

But when the ice our streams did fetter,
Oh! then how her old bones would shake!
You would have said if you had met her
'Twas a hard time for Goody Blake.
Her evenings then were dull and dead;   45
Sad case it was, as you may think,
For very cold to go to bed;
And then for cold not sleep a wink.

Oh joy for her! whene'er in winter
The winds at night had made a rout,   50
And scattered many a lusty splinter
And many a rotten bough about.
Yet never had she, well or sick,
As every man who knew her says,
A pile beforehand, wood or stick,   55
Enough to warm her for three days.

Now, when the frost was past enduring,
And made her poor old bones to ache,
Could any thing be more alluring
Than an old hedge to Goody Blake?   60
And now and then, it must be said,
When her old bones were cold and chill,
She left her fire, or left her bed,
To seek the hedge of Harry Gill.

39. *canty:* cheerful

Now Harry he had long suspected   65
This trespass of old Goody Blake;
And vowed that she should be detected,
And he on her would vengeance take.
And oft from his warm fire he'd go,
And to the fields his road would take;   70
And there, at night, in frost and snow,
He watched to seize old Goody Blake.

And once, behind a rick of barley,
Thus looking out did Harry stand:
The moon was full and shining clearly,   75
And crisp with frost the stubble land.
He hears a noise—he's all awake—
Again?—on tip-toe down the hill
He softly creeps—'tis Goody Blake,
She's at the hedge of Harry Gill.   80

Right glad was he when he beheld her:
Stick after stick did Goody pull:
He stood behind a bush of elder,
Till she had filled her apron full.
When with her load she turned about,   85
The bye-road back again to take,
He started forward with a shout,
And sprang upon poor Goody Blake.

And fiercely by the arm he took her,
And by the arm he held her fast,   90
And fiercely by the arm he shook her,
And cried, 'I've caught you then at last!'
Then Goody, who had nothing said,
Her bundle from her lap let fall;
And, kneeling on the sticks, she prayed   95
To God that is the judge of all.

She prayed, her withered hand uprearing,
While Harry held her by the arm—
'God! who art never out of hearing,
O may he never more be warm!'   100
The cold, cold moon above her head,
Thus on her knees did Goody pray.
Young Harry heard what she had said,
And icy cold he turned away.

He went complaining all the morrow   105
That he was cold and very chill:
His face was gloom, his heart was sorrow,
Alas! that day for Harry Gill!
That day he wore a riding-coat,
But not a whit the warmer he: 110
Another was on Thursday brought,
And ere the Sabbath he had three.

'Twas all in vain, a useless matter,
And blankets were about him pinned;
Yet still his jaws and teeth they clatter,   115
Like a loose casement in the wind.
And Harry's flesh it fell away;
And all who see him say, 'tis plain
That live as long as live he may,
He never will be warm again.   120

No word to any man he utters,
Abed or up, to young or old;
But ever to himself he mutters,
'Poor Harry Gill is very cold.'
Abed or up, by night or day;   125
His teeth they chatter, chatter still.
Now think, ye farmers all, I pray,
Of Goody Blake and Harry Gill.

THE LAST OF THE FLOCK

In distant countries I have been,
And yet I have not often seen
A healthy man, a man full-grown,
Weep in the public roads alone.
But such a one, on English ground,   5
And in the broad high-way, I met;
Along the broad high-way he came,
His cheeks with tears were wet.
Sturdy he seemed, though he was sad;
And in his arms a lamb he had.   10

He saw me, and he turned aside,
As if he wished himself to hide;
Then with his coat he made essay
To wipe those briny tears away.
I followed him, and said, 'My friend,   15
What ails you? wherefore weep you so?'
'Shame on me, sir! this lusty lamb,
He makes my tears to flow.
Today I fetched him from the rock;
He is the last of all my flock.   20

'When I was young, a single man,
And after youthful follies ran,
Though little given to care and thought,
Yet so it was, a ewe I bought;
And other sheep from her I raised,   25
As healthy sheep as you might see;
And then I married, and was rich
As I could wish to be;
Of sheep I numbered a full score,
And every year increased my store.   30

'Year after year my stock it grew,
And from this one, this single ewe,

57

Full fifty comely sheep I raised,
As sweet a flock as ever grazed!
Upon the mountain did they feed,   35
They throve, and we at home did thrive.
—This lusty lamb of all my store
Is all that is alive;
And now I care not if we die,
And perish all of poverty.   40

'Six children, sir! had I to feed,
Hard labour in a time of need!
My pride was tamed, and in our grief
I of the parish asked relief.
They said I was a wealthy man;   45
My sheep upon the mountain fed,
And it was fit that thence I took
Whereof to buy us bread.
"Do this: how can we give to you,"
They cried, "what to the poor is due?"   50

'I sold a sheep, as they had said,
And bought my little children bread,
And they were healthy with their food;
For me—it never did me good.
A woeful time it was for me,   55
To see the end of all my gains,
The pretty flock which I had reared
With all my care and pains,
To see it melt like snow away!
For me it was a woeful day.   60

'Another still; and still another;
A little lamb, and then its mother.
It was a vein that never stopped:
Like blood-drops from my heart they dropped.
Till thirty were not left alive   65
They dwindled, dwindled, one by one,

And I may say that many a time
I wished they all were gone:
They dwindled one by one away;
For me it was a woeful day.   70

'To wicked deeds I was inclined,
And wicked fancies crossed my mind;
And every man I chanced to see
I thought he knew some ill of me.
No peace, no comfort could I find,   75
No ease, within doors or without,
And crazily, and wearily,
I went my work about.
Oft-times I thought to run away;
For me it was a woeful day.   80

'Sir! 'twas a precious flock to me,
As dear as my own children be;
For daily with my growing store
I loved my children more and more.
Alas! it was an evil time;   85
God cursed me in my sore distress;
I prayed, yet every day I thought
I loved my children less;
And every week, and every day,
My flock, it seemed to melt away.   90

'They dwindled, sir, sad sight to see!
From ten to five, from five to three,
A lamb, a wether, and a ewe;
And then, at last, from three to two;
And of my fifty, yesterday   95
I had but only one:
And here it lies upon my arm,
Alas! and I have none;
Today I fetched it from the rock;
It is the last of all my flock.'   100

LINES

LEFT UPON A SEAT IN A YEW-TREE, WHICH STANDS NEAR THE LAKE OF ESTHWAITE, ON A DESOLATE PART OF THE SHORE, YET COMMANDING A BEAUTIFUL PROSPECT.

Nay, traveller! rest. This lonely yew-tree stands
Far from all human dwelling: what if here
No sparkling rivulet spread the verdant herb?
What if these barren boughs the bee not loves?
Yet, if the wind breathe soft, the curling waves,   5
That break against the shore, shall lull thy mind
By one soft impulse saved from vacancy.

                      Who he was
That piled these stones, and with the mossy sod
First covered o'er, and taught this aged tree   10
With its dark arms to form a circling bower,
I well remember. He was one who owned
No common soul. In youth by science nursed,
And led by nature into a wild scene
Of lofty hopes, he to the world went forth   15
A favoured being, knowing no desire
Which genius did not hallow, 'gainst the taint
Of dissolute tongues, and jealousy, and hate,
And scorn, against all enemies prepared,
All but neglect. The world, for so it thought,   20
Owed him no service: wherefore he at once
With indignation turned himself away,
And with the food of pride sustained his soul
In solitude. — Stranger! these gloomy boughs
Had charms for him; and here he loved to sit,   25
His only visitants a straggling sheep,
The stone-chat, or the glancing sand-piper;
And on these barren rocks, with juniper
And heath and thistle thinly sprinkled o'er,

60

Fixing his down-cast eye, he many an hour   30
A morbid pleasure nourished, tracing here
An emblem of his own unfruitful life;
And lifting up his head, he then would gaze
On the more distant scene—how lovely 'tis
Thou seest—and he would gaze till it became   35
Far lovelier, and his heart could not sustain
The beauty still more beauteous. Nor, that time,
When Nature had subdued him to herself,
Would he forget those beings to whose minds,
Warm from the labours of benevolence,   40
The world, and man himself, appeared a scene
Of kindred loveliness: then he would sigh
With mournful joy, to think that others felt
What he must never feel: and so, lost man!
On visionary views would fancy feed,   45
Till his eye streamed with tears. In this deep vale
He died,—this seat his only monument.

If thou be one whose heart the holy forms
Of young imagination have kept pure,
Stranger! henceforth be warned; and know that pride, 50
Howe'er disguised in its own majesty,
Is littleness; that he who feels contempt
For any living thing, hath faculties
Which he has never used; that thought with him
Is in its infancy. The man whose eye   55
Is ever on himself doth look on one,
The least of nature's works, one who might move
The wise man to that scorn which wisdom holds
Unlawful, ever. O be wiser, thou!
Instructed that true knowledge leads to love,   60
True dignity abides with him alone
Who, in the silent hour of inward thought,
Can still suspect, and still revere himself,
In lowliness of heart.

THE FOSTER-MOTHER'S TALE[1]

A NARRATION IN DRAMATIC BLANK VERSE

MARIA

But that entrance, mother!

FOSTER-MOTHER

Can no one hear? It is a perilous tale!

MARIA

No one.

FOSTER-MOTHER

    My husband's father told it me,
Poor old Leoni! Angels rest his soul!
He was a woodman, and could fell and saw   5
With lusty arm. You know that huge round beam
Which props the hanging wall of the old chapel;
Beneath that tree, while yet it was a tree,
He found a baby wrapped in mosses lined
With thistle-beards, and such small locks of wool   10
As hang on brambles. Well, he brought him home,
And reared him at the then Lord Velez's cost.
And so the babe grew up a pretty boy,
A pretty boy, but most unteachable;
And never learnt a prayer, nor told a bead,   15
But knew the names of birds, and mocked their notes,
And whistled, as he were a bird himself:
And all the autumn 'twas his only play
To gather seeds of wild flowers, and to plant them
With earth and water on the stumps of trees.   20
A friar, who sought for simples in the wood,
A grey-haired man, he loved this little boy,
The boy loved him; and when the friar taught him
He soon could write with the pen; and from that time
Lived chiefly at the convent or the castle.   25
So he became a very learned youth.

[1]By Coleridge.

But, oh! poor wretch, he read, and read, and read,
Till his brain turned; and ere his twentieth year
He had unlawful thoughts of many things:
And though he prayed, he never loved to pray   30
With holy men, nor in a holy place;
But yet his speech, it was so soft and sweet,
The late Lord Velez ne'er was wearied with him.
And once, as by the north side of the chapel
They stood together, chained in deep discourse,   35
The earth heaved under them with such a groan
That the wall tottered, and had well-nigh fallen
Right on their heads. My lord was sorely frightened;
A fever seized him, and he made confession
Of all the heretical and lawless talk   40
Which brought this judgment: so the youth was
          seized
And cast into that cell. My husband's father
Sobbed like a child—it almost broke his heart;
And once as he was working near the cell
He heard a voice distinctly: 'twas the youth's,   45
Who sang a doleful song about green fields,
How sweet it were on lake or wild savannah
To hunt for food, and be a naked man,
And wander up and down at liberty.
Leoni doted on the youth, and now   50
His love grew desperate; and defying death,
He made that cunning entrance I described:
And the young man escaped.

MARIA
                    'Tis a sweet tale.
And what became of him?

FOSTER-MOTHER
                    He went on ship-board,
With those bold voyagers who made discovery   55
Of golden lands. Leoni's younger brother

Went likewise; and when he returned to Spain,
He told Leoni that the poor mad youth,
Soon after they arrived in that new world,
In spite of his dissuasion, seized a boat,   60
And, all alone, set sail by silent moonlight
Up a great river, great as any sea,
And ne'er was heard of more: but 'tis supposed
He lived and died among the savage men.

THE THORN

I

There is a thorn—it looks so old,
In truth you'd find it hard to say
How it could ever have been young,
It looks so old and grey.
Not higher than a two years' child   5
It stands erect, this aged thorn;
No leaves it has, no thorny points;
It is a mass of knotted joints,
A wretched thing forlorn.
It stands erect, and like a stone   10
With lichens it is overgrown.

II

Like rock or stone, it is o'ergrown
With lichens to the very top,
And hung with heavy tufts of moss,
A melancholy crop: 15
Up from the earth these mosses creep,
And this poor thorn they clasp it round
So close, you'd say that they were bent
With plain and manifest intent
To drag it to the ground: 20
And all had joined in one endeavour
To bury this poor thorn for ever.

III

High on a mountain's highest ridge,
Where oft the stormy winter gale
Cuts like a scythe, while through the clouds 25
It sweeps from vale to vale;
Not five yards from the mountain path,
This thorn you on your left espy;
And to the left, three yards beyond,
You see a little muddy pond 30
Of water never dry;
I've measured it from side to side:
'Tis three feet long, and two feet wide.

IV

And close beside this aged thorn
There is a fresh and lovely sight, 35
A beauteous heap, a hill of moss,
Just half a foot in height.
All lovely colours there you see,
All colours that were ever seen;
And mossy net-work too is there, 40
As if by hand of lady fair
The work had woven been;
And cups, the darlings of the eye,
So deep is their vermilion dye.

V

Ah me! what lovely tints are there! 45
Of olive green and scarlet bright,
In spikes, in branches, and in stars,
Green, red, and pearly white.
This heap of earth o'ergrown with moss,
Which close beside the thorn you see, 50
So fresh in all its beauteous dyes,
Is like an infant's grave in size,
As like as like can be:
But never, never anywhere
An infant's grave was half so fair. 55

VI

Now would you see this aged thorn,
This pond, and beauteous hill of moss,
You must take care and choose your time
The mountain when to cross.
For oft there sits, between the heap   60
That's like an infant's grave in size,
And that same pond of which I spoke,
A woman in a scarlet cloak,
And to herself she cries,
'Oh misery! oh misery!   65
Oh woe is me! oh misery!'

VII

At all times of the day and night
This wretched woman thither goes;
And she is known to every star,
And every wind that blows;   70
And there beside the thorn she sits
When the blue daylight's in the skies,
And when the whirlwind's on the hill,
Or frosty air is keen and still,
And to herself she cries,   75
'Oh misery! oh misery!
Oh woe is me! oh misery!'

VIII

'Now wherefore thus, by day and night,
In rain, in tempest and in snow,
Thus to the dreary mountain-top   80
Does this poor woman go?
And why sits she beside the thorn
When the blue daylight's in the sky,
Or when the whirlwind's on the hill,
Or frosty air is keen and still,   85
And wherefore does she cry?
Oh wherefore? wherefore? tell me why
Does she repeat that doleful cry?'

IX

I cannot tell; I wish I could;
For the true reason no one knows: 90
But if you'd gladly view the spot,
The spot to which she goes;
The heap that's like an infant's grave,
The pond—and thorn, so old and grey;
Pass by her door—'tis seldom shut—   95
And, if you see her in her hut,
Then to the spot away!
I never heard of such as dare
Approach the spot when she is there.

X

'But wherefore to the mountain-top   100
Can this unhappy woman go,
Whatever star is in the skies,
Whatever wind may blow?'
Nay, rack your brain—'tis all in vain,
I'll tell you everything I know;   105
But to the thorn, and to the pond
Which is a little step beyond,
I wish that you would go:
Perhaps, when you are at the place,
You something of her tale may trace.   110

XI

I'll give you the best help I can:
Before you up the mountain go,
Up to the dreary mountain-top,
I'll tell you all I know.
'Tis now some two-and-twenty years   115
Since she (her name is Martha Ray)
Gave with a maiden's true good will
Her company to Stephen Hill;
And she was blithe and gay,
And she was happy, happy still   120
Whene'er she thought of Stephen Hill.

XII

And they had fixed the wedding-day,
The morning that must wed them both;
But Stephen to another maid
Had sworn another oath;   125
And with this other maid to church
Unthinking Stephen went—
Poor Martha! on that woeful day
A cruel, cruel fire, they say,
Into her bones was sent: 130
It dried her body like a cinder,
And almost turned her brain to tinder.

XIII

They say, full six months after this,
While yet the summer leaves were green,
She to the mountain-top would go,   135
And there was often seen.
'Tis said, a child was in her womb,
As now to any eye was plain;
She was with child, and she was mad;
Yet often she was sober sad   140
From her exceeding pain.
Oh me! ten thousand times I'd rather
That he had died, that cruel father!

XIV

Sad case for such a brain to hold
Communion with a stirring child!   145
Sad case, as you may think, for one
Who had a brain so wild!
Last Christmas when we talked of this,
Old farmer Simpson did maintain
That in her womb the infant wrought   150
About its mother's heart, and brought
Her senses back again:
And when at last her time drew near,
Her looks were calm, her senses clear.

XV

No more I know, I wish I did,   155
And I would tell it all to you;
For what became of this poor child
There's none that ever knew:
And if a child was born or no,
There's no one that could ever tell;   160
And if 'twas born alive or dead,
There's no one knows, as I have said;
But some remember well
That Martha Ray about this time
Would up the mountain often climb.   165

XVI

And all that winter, when at night
The wind blew from the mountain-peak,
'Twas worth your while, though in the dark,
The churchyard path to seek:
For many a time and oft were heard   170
Cries coming from the mountain-head:
Some plainly living voices were;
And others, I've heard many swear,
Were voices of the dead:
I cannot think, whate'er they say,   175
They had to do with Martha Ray.

XVII

But that she goes to this old thorn,
The thorn which I've described to you,
And there sits in a scarlet cloak,
I will be sworn is true.   180
For one day with my telescope,
To view the ocean wide and bright,
When to this country first I came,
Ere I had heard of Martha's name,
I climbed the mountain's height: 185
A storm came on, and I could see
No object higher than my knee.

XVIII

'Twas mist and rain, and storm and rain,
No screen, no fence could I discover,
And then the wind! in faith, it was   190
A wind full ten times over.
I looked around, I thought I saw
A jutting crag, and off I ran,
Head-foremost, through the driving rain,
The shelter of the crag to gain,   195
And, as I am a man,
Instead of jutting crag, I found
A woman seated on the ground.

XIX

I did not speak—I saw her face,
In truth it was enough for me;   200
I turned about and heard her cry,
'Oh misery! Oh misery!'
And there she sits, until the moon
Through half the clear blue sky will go;
And when the little breezes make   205
The waters of the pond to shake,
As all the country know,
She shudders, and you hear her cry,
'Oh misery! Oh misery!'

XX

'But what's the thorn? and what's the pond? 210
And what's the hill of moss to her?
And what's the creeping breeze that comes
The little pond to stir?'
I cannot tell; but some will say
She hanged her baby on the tree;   215
Some say she drowned it in the pond
Which is a little step beyond:
But all and each agree
The little babe was buried there,
Beneath that hill of moss so fair.   220

XXI

I've heard, the moss is spotted red
With drops of that poor infant's blood:
But kill a new-born infant thus,
I do not think she could.
Some say, if to the pond you go, 225
And fix on it a steady view,
The shadow of a babe you trace,
A baby and a baby's face,
And that it looks at you;
Whene'er you look on it, 'tis plain 230
The baby looks at you again.

XXII

And some had sworn an oath that she
Should be to public justice brought;
And for the little infant's bones
With spades they would have sought. 235
But then the beauteous hill of moss
Before their eyes began to stir;
And for full fifty yards around
The grass it shook upon the ground;
But all do still aver 240
The little babe is buried there,
Beneath that hill of moss so fair.

XXIII

I cannot tell how this may be:
But plain it is, the thorn is bound
With heavy tufts of moss, that strive 245
To drag it to the ground;
And this I know, full many a time,
When she was on the mountain high,
By day, and in the silent night,
When all the stars shone clear and bright, 250
That I have heard her cry,
'Oh misery! Oh misery!
Oh woe is me! Oh misery!'

WE ARE SEVEN

A simple child, dear brother Jim,
That lightly draws its breath,
And feels its life in every limb,
What should it know of death?

I met a little cottage girl: 5
She was eight years old, she said;
Her hair was thick with many a curl
That clustered round her head.

She had a rustic, woodland air,
And she was wildly clad;   10
Her eyes were fair, and very fair;
Her beauty made me glad.

'Sisters and brothers, little maid,
How many may you be?'
'How many? Seven in all,' she said,   15
And wondering looked at me.

'And where are they? I pray you tell.'
She answered, 'Seven are we;
And two of us at Conway dwell,
And two are gone to sea.   20

'Two of us in the churchyard lie,
My sister and my brother;
And in the churchyard cottage I
Dwell near them with my mother.'

'You say that two at Conway dwell,   25
And two are gone to sea,
Yet you are seven; I pray you tell,
Sweet maid, how this may be?'

Then did the little maid reply,
'Seven boys and girls are we;   30
Two of us in the churchyard lie,
Beneath the churchyard tree.'

'You run about, my little maid,
Your limbs they are alive;
If two are in the churchyard laid,   35
Then ye are only five.'

'Their graves are green, they may be seen,'
The little maid replied,
'Twelve steps or more from mother's door,
And they are side by side.   40

'My stockings there I often knit,
My kerchief there I hem;
And there upon the ground I sit—
I sit and sing to them.

'And often after sunset, sir,   45
When it is light and fair,
I take my little porringer,
And eat my supper there.

'The first that died was little Jane;
In bed she moaning lay,   50
Till God released her of her pain;
And then she went away.

'So in the churchyard she was laid;
And all the summer dry
Together round her grave we played,   55
My brother John and I.

'And when the ground was white with snow,
And I could run and slide,
My brother John was forced to go,
And he lies by her side.'   60

'How many are you then,' said I,
'If they two are in Heaven?'
The little maiden did reply,
'O master! we are seven.'

'But they are dead: those two are dead!   65
Their spirits are in Heaven!'
'Twas throwing words away; for still
The little maid would have her will,
And said, 'Nay, we are seven!'

ANECDOTE FOR FATHERS

SHOWING HOW THE PRACTICE OF LYING MAY BE TAUGHT.

I have a boy of five years old;
His face is fair and fresh to see;
His limbs are cast in beauty's mould,
And dearly he loves me.

One morn we strolled on our dry walk,   5
Our quiet home all full in view,
And held such intermitted talk
As we are wont to do.

My thoughts on former pleasures ran:
I thought of Kilve's delightful shore,   10
Our pleasant home, when spring began,
A long, long year before.

A day it was when I could bear
To think, and think, and think again;
With so much happiness to spare,   15
I could not feel a pain.

My boy was by my side, so slim
And graceful in his rustic dress!
And oftentimes I talked to him,
In very idleness.   20

The young lambs ran a pretty race;
The morning sun shone bright and warm;
'Kilve,' said I, 'was a pleasant place;
And so is Liswyn farm.

'My little boy, which like you more,'   25
I said, and took him by the arm—
'Our home by Kilve's delightful shore,
Or here at Liswyn farm?

'And tell me, had you rather be,'
I said, and held him by the arm,   30
'At Kilve's smooth shore by the green sea,
Or here at Liswyn farm?'

In careless mood he looked at me,
While still I held him by the arm,
And said, 'At Kilve I'd rather be   35
Than here at Liswyn farm.'

'Now, little Edward, say why so;
My little Edward, tell me why.'
'I cannot tell, I do not know.'
'Why, this is strange,' said I.   40

'For here are woods, and green-hills warm:
There surely must some reason be
Why you would change sweet Liswyn farm
For Kilve by the green sea.'

At this, my boy hung down his head,   45
He blushed with shame, nor made reply;
And five times to the child I said,
'Why, Edward, tell me why?'

75

His head he raised: there was in sight—
It caught his eye, he saw it plain—   50
Upon the house-top, glittering bright,
A broad and gilded vane.

Then did the boy his tongue unlock;
And thus to me he made reply:
'At Kilve there was no weather-cock,   55
And that's the reason why.'

O dearest, dearest boy! My heart
For better lore would seldom yearn,
Could I but teach the hundredth part
Of what from thee I learn.   60

LINES

WRITTEN AT A SMALL DISTANCE FROM MY HOUSE,
AND SENT BY MY LITTLE BOY TO THE PERSON TO
WHOM THEY ARE ADDRESSED.

It is the first mild day of March:
Each minute sweeter than before,
The redbreast sings from the tall larch
That stands beside our door.

There is a blessing in the air,   5
Which seems a sense of joy to yield
To the bare trees, and mountains bare,
And grass in the green field.

My sister! ('tis a wish of mine)
Now that our morning meal is done,   10
Make haste, your morning task resign;
Come forth and feel the sun.

Edward will come with you; and pray,
Put on with speed your woodland dress,
And bring no book: for this one day   15
We'll give to idleness.

No joyless forms shall regulate
Our living calendar:
We from today, my friend, will date
The opening of the year.   20

Love, now an universal birth,
From heart to heart is stealing,
From earth to man, from man to earth:
It is the hour of feeling.

One moment now may give us more   25
Than fifty years of reason:
Our minds shall drink at every pore
The spirit of the season.

Some silent laws our hearts may make,
Which they shall long obey: 30
We for the year to come may take
Our temper from today.

And from the blessed power that rolls
About, below, above,
We'll frame the measure of our souls: 35
They shall be tuned to love.

Then come, my sister! come, I pray,
With speed put on your woodland dress;
And bring no book: for this one day
We'll give to idleness.   40

THE FEMALE VAGRANT

My father was a good and pious man,
An honest man by honest parents bred;
And I believe that soon as I began
To lisp, he made me kneel beside my bed,
And in his hearing there my prayers I said: 5
And afterwards, by my good father taught,
I read, and loved the books in which I read;
For books in every neighbouring house I sought,
And nothing to my mind a sweeter pleasure brought.

The suns of twenty summers danced along,—   10
Ah! little marked how fast they rolled away:
Then rose a stately hall our woods among,
And cottage after cottage owned its sway.
No joy to see a neighbouring house, or stray
Through pastures not his own, the master took;   15
My father dared his greedy wish gainsay:
He loved his old hereditary nook,
And ill could I the thought of such sad parting brook.

But when he had refused the proffered gold,
To cruel injuries he became a prey,   20
Sore traversed in whate'er he bought and sold:
His troubles grew upon him day by day,
And all his substance fell into decay.
They dealt most hardly with him, and he tried
To move their hearts—but it was vain—for they   25
Seized all he had; and, weeping side by side,
We sought a home where we uninjured might abide.

It was in truth a lamentable hour,
When from the last hill-top my sire surveyed,
Peering above the trees, the steeple tower   30
That on his marriage-day sweet music made.

Till then he hoped his bones might there be laid,
Close by my mother, in their native bowers;
Bidding me trust in God, he stood and prayed,—
I could not pray: through tears that fell in showers   35
I saw our own dear home, that was no longer ours.

There was a youth, whom I had loved so long
That when I loved him not I cannot say.
'Mid the green mountains many and many a song
We two had sung, like gladsome birds in May.   40
When we began to tire of childish play
We seemed still more and more to prize each other;
We talked of marriage and our marriage-day;
And I in truth did love him like a brother;
For never could I hope to meet with such another.   45

Two years were passed, since to a distant town
He had repaired to ply the artist's trade.
What tears of bitter grief till then unknown!
What tender vows our last sad kiss delayed!
To him we turned: we had no other aid.   50
Like one revived, upon his neck I wept;
And her whom he had loved in joy, he said
He well could love in grief: his faith he kept;
And in a quiet home once more my father slept.

We lived in peace and comfort; and were blest   55
With daily bread, by constant toil supplied.
Three lovely infants lay upon my breast;
And often, viewing their sweet smiles, I sighed,
And knew not why. My happy father died
When sad distress reduced the children's meal: 60
Thrice happy! that from him the grave did hide
The empty loom, cold hearth, and silent wheel,
And tears that flowed for ills which patience could
       not heal.

'Twas a hard change, an evil time was come;
We had no hope, and no relief could gain.   65
But soon, day after day, the noisy drum
Beat round, to sweep the streets of want and pain.
My husband's arms now only served to strain
Me and his children hungering in his view;
In such dismay my prayers and tears were vain: 70
To join those miserable men he flew;
And now to the sea-coast, with numbers more, we drew.

There, long were we neglected, and we bore
Much sorrow ere the fleet its anchor weighed;
Green fields before us and our native shore,   75
We breathed a pestilential air that made
Ravage for which no knell was heard. We prayed
For our departure; wished and wished—nor knew
'Mid that long sickness, and those hopes delayed,
That happier days we never more must view;   80
The parting signal streamed, at last the land withdrew.

But the calm summer season now was past.
On as we drove, the equinoctial deep
Ran mountains-high before the howling blast;
And many perished in the whirlwind's sweep.   85
We gazed with terror on their gloomy sleep,
Untaught that soon such anguish must ensue,
Our hopes such harvest of affliction reap,
That we the mercy of the waves should rue.
We reached the western world, a poor, devoted crew. 90

The pains and plagues that on our heads came down,
Disease and famine, agony and fear,
In wood or wilderness, in camp or town,
It would thy brain unsettle, even to hear.
All perished: all, in one remorseless year,   95

Husband and children! one by one, by sword
And ravenous plague, all perished: every tear
Dried up, despairing, desolate, on board
A British ship I waked, as from a trance restored.

Peaceful as some immeasurable plain   100
By the first beams of dawning light impressed,
In the calm sunshine slept the glittering main.
The very ocean has its hour of rest.
I too was calm, though heavily distressed;
Oh me, how quiet sky and ocean were!   105
My heart was healed within me, I was blest
And looked, and looked along the silent air,
Until it seemed to bring a joy to my despair.

Ah! how unlike those late terrific sleeps!
And groans, that rage of racking famine spoke;   110
The unburied dead that lay in festering heaps;
The breathing pestilence that rose like smoke;
The shriek that from the distant battle broke;
The mine's dire earthquake, and the pallid host
Driven by the bomb's incessant thunder-stroke   115
To loathsome vaults, where heart-sick anguish tossed,
Hope died, and fear itself in agony was lost!

At midnight once the storming army came;
Yet do I see the miserable sight,
The bayonet, the soldier, and the flame   120
That followed us and faced us in our flight;
When Rape and Murder by the ghastly light
Seized their joint prey, the mother and the child!
But I must leave these thoughts. From night to night,
From day to day, the air breathed soft and mild;   125
And on the gliding vessel Heaven and Ocean smiled.

Some mighty gulf of separation past,
I seemed transported to another world:—
A thought resigned with pain, when from the mast
The impatient mariner the sail unfurled,   130
And, whistling, called the wind that hardly curled
The silent sea. From the sweet thoughts of home
And from all hope I was for ever hurled.
For me—farthest from earthly port to roam
Was best, could I but shun the spot where man might
      come.   135

And oft I thought (my fancy was so strong)
That I at last a resting-place had found;
'Here will I dwell,' said I, 'my whole life long,
Roaming the illimitable waters round;
Here will I live—of every friend disowned,   140
Here will I roam about the ocean flood.'
To break my dream the vessel reached its bound:
And homeless near a thousand homes I stood,
And near a thousand tables pined, and wanted food.

By grief enfeebled was I turned adrift,   145
Helpless as sailor cast on desert rock;
Nor morsel to my mouth that day did lift,
Nor dared my hand at any door to knock.
I lay where, with his drowsy mates, the cock
From the cross-timber of an out-house hung;   150
Dismally tolled, that night, the city clock!
At morn my sick heart hunger scarcely stung,
Nor to the beggar's language could I frame my tongue.

So passed another day, and so the third;
Then did I try in vain the crowd's resort.   155
—In deep despair by frightful wishes stirred,
Near the sea-side I reached a ruined fort:
There, pains which nature could no more support,

With blindness linked, did on my vitals fall,
And I had many interruptions short   160
Of hideous sense; I sank, nor step could crawl,
And thence was carried to a neighbouring hospital.

Recovery came with food; but still my brain
Was weak, nor of the past had memory.
I heard my neighbours in their beds complain   165
Of many things which never troubled me:
Of feet still bustling round with busy glee;
Of looks where common kindness had no part;
Of service done with careless cruelty,
Fretting the fever round the languid heart;   170
And groans which, as they said, would make a dead man
          start.

These things just served to stir the torpid sense,
Nor pain nor pity in my bosom raised.
My memory and my strength returned; and thence
Dismissed, again on open day I gazed,   175
At houses, men, and common light amazed.
The lanes I sought, and, as the sun retired,
Came where beneath the trees a faggot blazed;
The travellers saw me weep, my fate enquired,
And gave me food—and rest, more welcome, more
          desired.   180

My heart is touched to think that men like these,
Wild houseless wanderers, were my first relief:
How kindly did they paint their vagrant ease,
And their long holiday that feared not grief!
For all belonged to all, and each was chief.   185
No plough their sinews strained; on grating road
No wain they drove; and yet the yellow sheaf
In every vale for their delight was stowed;
In every field with milk their dairy overflowed.

They with their panniered asses semblance made 190
Of potters wandering on from door to door:
But life of happier sort to me portrayed,
And other joys my fancy to allure;
The bagpipe dinning on the midnight moor
In barn uplighted, and companions boon 195
Well met from far with revelry secure
Among the forest glades, when jocund June
Rolled fast along the sky his warm and genial moon.

But ill they suited me: those journeys dark
O'er moor and mountain, midnight theft to hatch! 200
To charm the surly house-dog's faithful bark,
Or hang on tip-toe at the lifted latch;
The gloomy lantern and the dim blue match,
The black disguise, the warning whistle shrill,
And ear still busy on its nightly watch 205
Were not for me, brought up in nothing ill:
Besides, on griefs so fresh my thoughts were brooding
      still.

What could I do, unaided and unblest?
My father! gone was every friend of thine;
And kindred of dead husband are at best 210
Small help; and after marriage such as mine
With little kindness would to me incline.
Ill was I then for toil or service fit:
With tears whose course no effort could confine,
By the road-side forgetful would I sit 215
Whole hours, my idle arms in moping sorrow knit.

I led a wandering life among the fields;
Contentedly, yet sometimes self-accused,
I lived upon what casual bounty yields,
Now coldly given, now utterly refused. 220
The ground I for my bed have often used:

But what afflicts my peace with keenest ruth
Is that I have my inner self abused,
Forgone the home delight of constant truth,
And clear and open soul, so prized in fearless youth. 225

Three years thus wandering, often have I viewed,
In tears, the sun towards that country tend
Where my poor heart lost all its fortitude:
And now across this moor my steps I bend—
Oh! tell me whither; for no earthly friend   230
Have I.—She ceased, and weeping turned away;
As if because her tale was at an end
She wept; because she had no more to say
Of that perpetual weight which on her spirit lay.

LINES WRITTEN IN EARLY SPRING

I heard a thousand blended notes,
While in a grove I sate reclined,
In that sweet mood when pleasant thoughts
Bring sad thoughts to the mind.

To her fair works did Nature link   5
The human soul that through me ran;
And much it grieved my heart to think
What man has made of man.

Through primrose tufts, in that sweet bower,
The periwinkle trailed its wreaths;   10
And 'tis my faith that every flower
Enjoys the air it breathes.

The birds around me hopped and played;
Their thoughts I cannot measure:
But the least motion which they made,   15
It seemed a thrill of pleasure.

The budding twigs spread out their fan,
To catch the breezy air;
And I must think, do all I can,
That there was pleasure there. 20

If I these thoughts may not prevent,
If such be of my creed the plan,
Have I not reason to lament
What man has made of man?

SIMON LEE, THE OLD HUNTSMAN,
WITH AN INCIDENT IN WHICH
HE WAS CONCERNED.

In the sweet shire of Cardigan,
Not far from pleasant Ivor Hall,
An old man dwells, a little man,
I've heard he once was tall.
Of years he has upon his back, 5
No doubt, a burthen weighty;
He says he is threescore and ten,
But others say he's eighty.

A long blue livery-coat has he,
That's fair behind, and fair before; 10
Yet meet him where you will, you see
At once that he is poor.
Full five-and-twenty years he lived
A running huntsman merry;
And though he has but one eye left, 15
His cheek is like a cherry.

No man like him the horn could sound,
And no man was so full of glee;
To say the least, four counties round
Had heard of Simon Lee: 20
His master's dead, and no one now
Dwells in the Hall of Ivor;
Men, dogs, and horses, all are dead;
He is the sole survivor.

And he is lean and he is sick,   25
His dwindled body's half awry;
His ankles they are swollen and thick;
His legs are thin and dry.
When he was young he little knew
Of husbandry or tillage;   30
And now he's forced to work, though weak,
—The weakest in the village.

He all the country could outrun,
Could leave both man and horse behind;
And often, ere the race was done,   35
He reeled and was stone-blind.
And still there's something in the world
At which his heart rejoices;
For when the chiming hounds are out,
He dearly loves their voices!   40

His hunting feats have him bereft
Of his right eye, as you may see:
And then, what limbs those feats have left
To poor old Simon Lee!
He has no son, he has no child,   45
His wife, an aged woman,
Lives with him near the waterfall,
Upon the village common.

36. *stone-blind:* utterly blind

Old Ruth works out of doors with him,
And does what Simon cannot do; 50
For she, not over-stout of limb,
Is stouter of the two.
And though you with your utmost skill
From labour could not wean them,
Alas! 'tis very little, all 55
Which they can do between them.

Beside their moss-grown hut of clay,
Not twenty paces from the door,
A scrap of land they have, but they
Are poorest of the poor. 60
This scrap of land he from the heath
Enclosed when he was stronger;
But what avails the land to them,
Which they can till no longer?

Few months of life has he in store, 65
As he to you will tell,
For still, the more he works, the more
His poor old ankles swell.
My gentle reader, I perceive
How patiently you've waited, 70
And I'm afraid that you expect
Some tale will be related.

O reader! had you in your mind
Such stores as silent thought can bring,
O gentle reader! you would find 75
A tale in everything.
What more I have to say is short,
I hope you'll kindly take it:
It is no tale; but, should you think,
Perhaps a tale you'll make it. 80

One summer day I chanced to see
This old man doing all he could
About the root of an old tree,
A stump of rotten wood.
The mattock tottered in his hand;   85
So vain was his endeavour
That at the root of the old tree
He might have worked for ever.

'You're overtasked, good Simon Lee,
Give me your tool,' to him I said;   90
And at the word right gladly he
Received my proffered aid.
I struck, and with a single blow
The tangled root I severed,
At which the poor old man so long   95
And vainly had endeavoured.

The tears into his eyes were brought,
And thanks and praises seemed to run
So fast out of his heart, I thought
They never would have done.   100
—I've heard of hearts unkind, kind deeds
With coldness still returning.
Alas! the gratitude of men
Has oftener left me mourning.

THE NIGHTINGALE[1]

No cloud, no relic of the sunken day
Distinguishes the west, no long thin slip
Of sullen light, no obscure trembling hues.
Come, we will rest on this old mossy bridge!
You see the glimmer of the stream beneath,   5
But hear no murmuring: it flows silently
O'er its soft bed of verdure. All is still,
A balmy night! and though the stars be dim,
Yet let us think upon the vernal showers
That gladden the green earth, and we shall find   10
A pleasure in the dimness of the stars.
And hark! the nightingale begins its song,
'Most musical, most melancholy' bird!
A melancholy bird? O idle thought!
In nature there is nothing melancholy.   15
But some night-wandering man, whose heart was
        pierced
With the remembrance of a grievous wrong,
Or slow distemper, or neglected love,
(And so, poor wretch! filled all things with himself,
And made all gentle sounds tell back the tale   20
Of his own sorrows) he and such as he
First named these notes a melancholy strain;
And many a poet echoes the conceit:
Poet, who hath been building up the rhyme
When he had better far have stretched his limbs   25
Beside a brook in mossy forest-dell
By sun- or moon-light, to the influxes
Of shapes and sounds and shifting elements
Surrendering his whole spirit, of his song
And of his fame forgetful! so his fame   30

[1] By Coleridge.

Should share in nature's immortality,
A venerable thing! and so his song
Should make all nature lovelier, and itself
Be loved, like nature!—But 'twill not be so;
And youths and maidens most poetical   35
Who lose the deep'ning twilights of the spring
In ballrooms and hot theatres, they still
Full of meek sympathy must heave their sighs
O'er Philomela's pity-pleading strains.

My friend, and my friend's sister! we have learnt   40
A different lore: we may not thus profane
Nature's sweet voices always full of love
And joyance! 'Tis the merry nightingale
That crowds, and hurries, and precipitates
With fast thick warble his delicious notes,   45
As he were fearful that an April night
Would be too short for him to utter forth
His love-chant, and disburthen his full soul
Of all its music! And I know a grove
Of large extent, hard by a castle huge   50
Which the great lord inhabits not: and so
This grove is wild with tangling underwood,
And the trim walks are broken up, and grass,
Thin grass and king-cups grow within the paths.
But never elsewhere in one place I knew   55
So many nightingales: and far and near
In wood and thicket over the wide grove
They answer and provoke each other's songs—
With skirmish and capricious passagings,
And murmurs musical and swift jug jug   60
And one low piping sound more sweet than all—
Stirring the air with such an harmony,
That should you close your eyes, you might almost
Forget it was not day.

                    A most gentle maid
Who dwelleth in her hospitable home   65
Hard by the castle, and at latest eve
(Even like a lady vowed and dedicate
To something more than nature in the grove)
Glides through the pathways; she knows all their
            notes,
That gentle maid! and oft, a moment's space,   70
What time the moon was lost behind a cloud,
Hath heard a pause of silence: till the moon
Emerging, hath awakened earth and sky
With one sensation, and those wakeful birds
Have all burst forth with choral minstrelsy,   75
As if one quick and sudden gale had swept
An hundred airy harps! And she hath watched
Many a nightingale perch giddily
On blosmy twig still swinging from the breeze,
And to that motion tune his wanton song,   80
Like tipsy Joy that reels with tossing head.

Farewell, O warbler! till tomorrow eve,
And you, my friends! farewell, a short farewell!
We have been loitering long and pleasantly,
And now for our dear homes.—That strain again!   85
Full fain it would delay me! My dear babe,
Who, capable of no articulate sound,
Mars all things with his imitative lisp,
How he would place his hand beside his ear,
His little hand, the small forefinger up,   90
And bid us listen! And I deem it wise
To make him Nature's playmate. He knows well
The evening star; and once when he awoke
In most distressful mood (some inward pain
Had made up that strange thing, an infant's dream)   95
I hurried with him to our orchard plot,
And he beholds the moon, and hushed at once

Suspends his sobs, and laughs most silently,
While his fair eyes that swam with undropped tears
Did glitter in the yellow moonbeam! Well—   100
It is a father's tale. But if that Heaven
Should give me life, his childhood shall grow up
Familiar with these songs, that with the night
He may associate joy! Once more farewell,
Sweet nightingale! once more, my friends! farewell.   105

THE IDIOT BOY

'Tis eight o'clock—a clear March night,
The moon is up—the sky is blue,
The owlet in the moonlight air,
He shouts from nobody knows where;
He lengthens out his lonely shout,   5
Halloo! halloo! a long halloo!

Why bustle thus about your door,
What means this bustle, Betty Foy?
Why are you in this mighty fret?
And why on horseback have you set   10
Him whom you love, your idiot boy?

Beneath the moon that shines so bright,
Till she is tired, let Betty Foy
With girth and stirrup fiddle-faddle;
But wherefore set upon a saddle   15
Him whom she loves, her idiot boy?

There's scarce a soul that's out of bed:
Good Betty, put him down again;
His lips with joy they burr at you;
But, Betty! what has he to do   20
With stirrup, saddle, or with rein?

The world will say 'tis very idle,
Bethink you of the time of night;
There's not a mother, no not one,
But when she hears what you have done,   25
O Betty, she'll be in a fright.

But Betty's bent on her intent;
For her good neighbour, Susan Gale,
Old Susan, she who dwells alone,
Is sick, and makes a piteous moan,   30
As if her very life would fail.

There's not a house within a mile,
No hand to help them in distress:
Old Susan lies abed in pain,
And sorely puzzled are the twain,   35
For what she ails they cannot guess.

And Betty's husband's at the wood,
Where by the week he doth abide,
A woodman in the distant vale;
There's none to help poor Susan Gale: 40
What must be done? what will betide?

And Betty from the lane has fetched
Her pony, that is mild and good,
Whether he be in joy or pain,
Feeding at will along the lane,   45
Or bringing faggots from the wood.

And he is all in travelling trim,
And by the moonlight Betty Foy
Has up upon the saddle set—
The like was never heard of yet—   50
Him whom she loves, her idiot boy.

And he must post without delay
Across the bridge that's in the dale,
And by the church, and o'er the down,
To bring a doctor from the town, 55
Or she will die, old Susan Gale.

There is no need of boot or spur,
There is no need of whip or wand,
For Johnny has his holly-bough,
And with a hurly-burly now 60
He shakes the green bough in his hand.

And Betty o'er and o'er has told
The boy who is her best delight
Both what to follow, what to shun,
What do, and what to leave undone, 65
How turn to left, and how to right.

And Betty's most especial charge
Was, 'Johnny! Johnny! mind that you
Come home again, nor stop at all,
Come home again, whate'er befall, 70
My Johnny, do, I pray you do.'

To this did Johnny answer make,
Both with his head, and with his hand,
And proudly shook the bridle too,
And then! his words were not a few, 75
Which Betty well could understand.

And now that Johnny is just going,
Though Betty's in a mighty flurry,
She gently pats the pony's side
On which her idiot boy must ride, 80
And seems no longer in a hurry.

But when the pony moved his legs,
Oh! then for the poor idiot boy!
For joy he cannot hold the bridle,
For joy his head and heels are idle,   85
He's idle all for very joy.

And while the pony moves his legs,
In Johnny's left hand you may see
The green bough's motionless and dead:
The moon that shines above his head   90
Is not more still and mute than he.

His heart it was so full of glee,
That till full fifty yards were gone,
He quite forgot his holly whip
And all his skill in horsemanship;   95
Oh, happy, happy, happy John!

And Betty's standing at the door,
And Betty's face with joy o'erflows,
Proud of herself, and proud of him,
She sees him in his travelling trim;   100
How quietly her Johnny goes.

The silence of her idiot boy,
What hopes it sends to Betty's heart!
He's at the guide-post—he turns right,
She watches till he's out of sight,   105
And Betty will not then depart.

Burr, burr—now Johnny's lips they burr,
As loud as any mill, or near it;
Meek as a lamb the pony moves,
And Johnny makes the noise he loves,   110
And Betty listens, glad to hear it.

Away she hies to Susan Gale:
And Johnny's in a merry tune,
The owlets hoot, the owlets curr,
And Johnny's lips they burr, burr, burr,   115
And on he goes beneath the moon.

His steed and he right well agree,
For of this pony there's a rumour,
That should he lose his eyes and ears,
And should he live a thousand years,   120
He never will be out of humour.

But then, he is a horse that thinks!
And when he thinks his pace is slack;
Now, though he knows poor Johnny well,
Yet for his life he cannot tell   125
What he has got upon his back.

So through the moonlight lanes they go,
And far into the moonlight dale,
And by the church, and o'er the down,
To bring a doctor from the town,   130
To comfort poor old Susan Gale.

And Betty, now at Susan's side,
Is in the middle of her story,
What comfort Johnny soon will bring,
With many a most diverting thing   135
Of Johnny's wit and Johnny's glory.

And Betty's still at Susan's side;
By this time she's not quite so flurried:
Demure with porringer and plate
She sits, as if in Susan's fate   140
Her life and soul were buried.

But Betty, poor good woman! she,
You plainly in her face may read it,
Could lend out of that moment's store
Five years of happiness or more   145
To any that might need it.

But yet I guess that now and then
With Betty all was not so well,
And to the road she turns her ears,
And thence full many a sound she hears,   150
Which she to Susan will not tell.

Poor Susan moans, poor Susan groans;
'As sure as there's a moon in heaven,'
Cries Betty, 'he'll be back again;
They'll both be here—'tis almost ten—   155
They'll both be here before eleven.'

Poor Susan moans, poor Susan groans;
The clock gives warning for eleven;
'Tis on the stroke—'If Johnny's near,'
Quoth Betty, 'he will soon be here,   160
As sure as there's a moon in heaven.'

The clock is on the stroke of twelve,
And Johnny is not yet in sight:
The moon's in heaven, as Betty sees,
But Betty is not quite at ease;   165
And Susan has a dreadful night.

And Betty, half an hour ago,
On Johnny vile reflections cast:
'A little idle sauntering thing!'
With other names, an endless string,   170
But now that time is gone and past.

And Betty's drooping at the heart,
That happy time all past and gone;
'How can it be he is so late?
The doctor he has made him wait,   175
Susan! they'll both be here anon.'

And Susan's growing worse and worse,
And Betty's in a sad quandary;
And then there's nobody to say
If she must go or she must stay!   180
She's in a sad quandary.

The clock is on the stroke of one;
But neither doctor nor his guide
Appear along the moonlight road;
There's neither horse nor man abroad,   185
And Betty's still at Susan's side.

And Susan she begins to fear
Of sad mischances not a few:
That Johnny may perhaps be drowned,
Or lost, perhaps, and never found,   190
Which they must both for ever rue.

She prefaced half a hint of this
With 'God forbid it should be true!'
At the first word that Susan said
Cried Betty, rising from the bed,   195
'Susan, I'd gladly stay with you.

'I must be gone, I must away,
Consider, Johnny's but half-wise;
Susan, we must take care of him,
If he is hurt in life or limb—'   200
'Oh God forbid!' poor Susan cries.

'What can I do?' says Betty, going,
'What can I do to ease your pain?
Good Susan tell me, and I'll stay;
I fear you're in a dreadful way,   205
But I shall soon be back again.'

'Nay, Betty, go! good Betty, go!
There's nothing that can ease my pain.'
Then off she hies, but with a prayer
That God poor Susan's life would spare,   210
Till she comes back again.

So, through the moonlight lane she goes,
And far into the moonlight dale;
And how she ran, and how she walked,
And all that to herself she talked,   215
Would surely be a tedious tale.

In high and low, above, below,
In great and small, in round and square,
In tree and tower was Johnny seen,
In bush and brake, in black and green,   220
'Twas Johnny, Johnny, everywhere.

She's past the bridge that's in the dale,
And now the thought torments her sore,
Johnny perhaps his horse forsook
To hunt the moon that's in the brook,   225
And never will be heard of more.

And now she's high upon the down,
Alone amid a prospect wide;
There's neither Johnny nor his horse
Among the fern or in the gorse;   230
There's neither doctor nor his guide.

'Oh saints! what is become of him?
Perhaps he's climbed into an oak,
Where he will stay till he is dead;
Or sadly he has been misled,   235
And joined the wandering gipsy-folk.

'Or him that wicked pony's carried
To the dark cave, the goblin's hall;
Or in the castle he's pursuing
Among the ghosts his own undoing; 240
Or playing with the waterfall.'

At poor old Susan then she railed,
While to the town she posts away:
'If Susan had not been so ill,
Alas! I should have had him still, 245
My Johnny, till my dying day.'

Poor Betty, in this sad distemper,
The doctor's self would hardly spare;
Unworthy things she talked and wild,
Even he of cattle the most mild, 250
The pony, had his share.

And now she's got into the town,
And to the doctor's door she hies;
'Tis silence all on every side;
The town so long, the town so wide, 255
Is silent as the skies.

And now she's at the doctor's door,
She lifts the knocker, rap, rap, rap;
The doctor at the casement shows
His glimmering eyes that peep and doze; 260
And one hand rubs his old night-cap.

'Oh doctor! doctor! where's my Johnny?'
'I'm here, what is't you want with me?'
'Oh sir! you know I'm Betty Foy,
And I have lost my poor dear boy,   265
You know him—him you often see;

'He's not so wise as some folks be.'
'The devil take his wisdom!' said
The doctor, looking somewhat grim,
'What, woman, should I know of him?'   270
And grumbling he went back to bed.

'Oh woe is me! Oh woe is me!
Here will I die; here will I die;
I thought to find my Johnny here,
But he is neither far nor near,   275
Oh! what a wretched mother I!'

She stops, she stands, she looks about,
Which way to turn she cannot tell.
Poor Betty! it would ease her pain
If she had heart to knock again;   280
The clock strikes three—a dismal knell!

Then up along the town she hies,
No wonder if her senses fail;
This piteous news so much it shocked her,
She quite forgot to send the doctor   285
To comfort poor old Susan Gale.

And now she's high upon the down,
And she can see a mile of road;
'Oh cruel! I'm almost threescore;
Such night as this was ne'er before,   290
There's not a single soul abroad.'

She listens, but she cannot hear
The foot of horse, the voice of man;
The streams with softest sounds are flowing,
The grass you almost hear it growing, 295
You hear it now if e'er you can.

The owlets through the long blue night
Are shouting to each other still:
Fond lovers! yet not quite hob nob,
They lengthen out the tremulous sob, 300
That echoes far from hill to hill.

Poor Betty now has lost all hope,
Her thoughts are bent on deadly sin:
A green-grown pond she just has passed,
And from the brink she hurries fast, 305
Lest she should drown herself therein.

And now she sits her down and weeps;
Such tears she never shed before;
'Oh dear, dear pony! my sweet joy!
Oh carry back my idiot boy! 310
And we will ne'er o'erload thee more.'

A thought is come into her head:
'The pony he is mild and good,
And we have always used him well;
Perhaps he's gone along the dell, 315
And carried Johnny to the wood.'

Then up she springs, as if on wings;
She thinks no more of deadly sin;
If Betty fifty ponds should see,
The last of all her thoughts would be 320
To drown herself therein.

Oh, reader! now that I might tell
What Johnny and his horse are doing!
What they've been doing all this time,
Oh could I put it into rhyme,   325
A most delightful tale pursuing!

Perhaps, and no unlikely thought,
He with his pony now doth roam
The cliffs and peaks so high that are,
To lay his hands upon a star,   330
And in his pocket bring it home.

Perhaps he's turned himself about,
His face unto his horse's tail,
And still and mute, in wonder lost,
All like a silent horseman-ghost,   335
He travels on along the vale.

And now, perhaps, he's hunting sheep,
A fierce and dreadful hunter he;
Yon valley that's so trim and green,
In five months' time, should he be seen,   340
A desert wilderness will be.

Perhaps, with head and heels on fire,
And like the very soul of evil,
He's galloping away, away,
And so he'll gallop on for aye,   345
The bane of all that dread the devil.

I to the Muses have been bound
These fourteen years, by strong indentures:
O gentle Muses! let me tell
But half of what to him befell,   350
He surely met with strange adventures.

O gentle Muses! is this kind?
Why will ye thus my suit repel?
Why of your further aid bereave me?
And can ye thus unfriendly leave me,   355
Ye Muses, whom I love so well?

Who's yon, that near the waterfall
Which thunders down with headlong force,
Beneath the moon, yet shining fair,
As careless as if nothing were,   360
Sits upright on a feeding horse?

Unto his horse, that's feeding free,
He seems, I think, the rein to give;
Of moon or stars he takes no heed;
Of such we in romances read—   365
'Tis Johnny! Johnny! as I live.

And that's the very pony too.
Where is she, where is Betty Foy?
She hardly can sustain her fears:
The roaring waterfall she hears,   370
And cannot find her idiot boy.

Your pony's worth his weight in gold,
Then calm your terrors, Betty Foy!
She's coming from among the trees,
And now all full in view she sees   375
Him whom she loves, her idiot boy.

And Betty sees the pony too:
Why stand you thus, good Betty Foy?
It is no goblin, 'tis no ghost,
'Tis he whom you so long have lost,   380
He whom you love, your idiot boy.

She looks again—her arms are up—
She screams—she cannot move for joy;
She darts, as with a torrent's force,
She almost has o'erturned the horse, 385
And fast she holds her idiot boy.

And Johnny burrs, and laughs aloud,
Whether in cunning or in joy
I cannot tell; but while he laughs,
Betty a drunken pleasure quaffs, 390
To hear again her idiot boy.

And now she's at the pony's tail,
And now she's at the pony's head,
On that side now, and now on this,
And almost stifled with her bliss, 395
A few sad tears does Betty shed.

She kisses o'er and o'er again
Him whom she loves, her idiot boy,
She's happy here, she's happy there,
She is uneasy everywhere; 400
Her limbs are all alive with joy.

She pats the pony, where or when
She knows not, happy Betty Foy!
The little pony glad may be,
But he is milder far than she, 405
You hardly can perceive his joy.

'Oh, Johnny! never mind the doctor;
You've done your best, and that is all.'
She took the reins, when this was said,
And gently turned the pony's head 410
From the loud waterfall.

By this the stars were almost gone,
The moon was setting on the hill,
So pale you scarcely looked at her;
The little birds began to stir,   415
Though yet their tongues were still.

The pony, Betty, and her boy
Wind slowly through the woody dale;
And who is she, betimes abroad,
That hobbles up the steep rough road?   420
Who is it, but old Susan Gale?

Long Susan lay deep lost in thought,
And many dreadful fears beset her,
Both for her messenger and nurse;
And as her mind grew worse and worse,   425
Her body it grew better.

She turned, she tossed herself in bed,
On all sides doubts and terrors met her;
Point after point did she discuss;
And while her mind was fighting thus,   430
Her body still grew better.

'Alas! what is become of them?
These fears can never be endured,
I'll to the wood.'—The word scarce said,
Did Susan rise up from her bed,   435
As if by magic cured.

Away she posts up hill and down,
And to the wood at length is come,
She spies her friends, she shouts a greeting;
Oh me! it is a merry meeting,   440
As ever was in Christendom.

The owls have hardly sung their last,
While our four travellers homeward wend;
The owls have hooted all night long,
And with the owls began my song, 445
And with the owls must end.

For while they all were travelling home,
Cried Betty, 'Tell us, Johnny, do,
Where all this long night you have been,
What you have heard, what you have seen, 450
And Johnny, mind you tell us true.'

Now Johnny all night long had heard
The owls in tuneful concert strive;
No doubt too he the moon had seen;
For in the moonlight he had been 455
From eight o'clock till five.

And thus, to Betty's question, he
Made answer like a traveller bold—
His very words I give to you:
'The cocks did crow to-whoo, to-whoo, 460
And the sun did shine so cold.'
Thus answered Johnny in his glory,
And that was all his travel's story.

LOVE[1]

All thoughts, all passions, all delights,
Whatever stirs this mortal frame,
All are but ministers of Love,
    And feed his sacred flame.

Oft in my waking dreams do I 5
Live o'er again that happy hour,
When midway on the mount I lay
    Beside the ruined tower.

[1]By Coleridge.

The moonshine stealing o'er the scene
Had blended with the lights of eve;   10
And she was there, my hope, my joy,
    My own dear Genevieve!

She leaned against the arméd man,
The statue of the arméd knight;
She stood and listened to my harp   15
    Amid the lingering light.

Few sorrows hath she of her own,
My hope, my joy, my Genevieve!
She loves me best whene'er I sing
    The songs that make her grieve.   20

I played a soft and doleful air,
I sang an old and moving story—
An old rude song that fitted well
    The ruin wild and hoary.

She listened with a flitting blush,   25
With downcast eyes and modest grace;
For well she knew, I could not choose
    But gaze upon her face.

I told her of the knight that wore
Upon his shield a burning brand;   30
And that for ten long years he wooed
    The lady of the land.

I told her how he pined: and ah!
The low, the deep, the pleading tone
With which I sang another's love   35
    Interpreted my own.

She listened with a flitting blush,
With downcast eyes and modest grace;
And she forgave me, that I gazed
    Too fondly on her face!   40

But when I told the cruel scorn
Which crazed this bold and lovely knight,
And that he crossed the mountain woods
    Nor rested day nor night;

That sometimes from the savage den,   45
And sometimes from the darksome shade,
And sometimes starting up at once
    In green and sunny glade,

There came, and looked him in the face,
An angel beautiful and bright;   50
And that he knew it was a fiend,
    This miserable knight!

And how, unknowing what he did,
He leapt amid a murderous band,
And saved from outrage worse than death   55
    The lady of the land;

And how she wept and clasped his knees,
And how she tended him in vain;
And ever strove to expiate
    The scorn that crazed his brain;   60

And that she nursed him in a cave;
And how his madness went away
When on the yellow forest leaves
    A dying man he lay;

His dying words—but when I reached   65
That tenderest strain of all the ditty,

My faltering voice and pausing harp
    Disturbed her soul with pity!

All impulses of soul and sense
Had thrilled my guileless Genevieve,   70
The music, and the doleful tale,
    The rich and balmy eve;

And hopes, and fears that kindle hope,
An undistinguishable throng!
And gentle wishes long subdued,   75
    Subdued and cherished long!

She wept with pity and delight,
She blushed with love and maiden shame;
And, like the murmur of a dream,
    I heard her breathe my name.   80

Her bosom heaved—she stepped aside;
As conscious of my look, she stepped—
Then suddenly with timorous eye
    She fled to me and wept.

She half enclosed me with her arms,   85
She pressed me with a meek embrace;
And bending back her head looked up,
    And gazed upon my face.

'Twas partly love, and partly fear,
And partly 'twas a bashful art   90
That I might rather feel than see
    The swelling of her heart.

I calmed her fears; and she was calm,
And told her love with virgin pride.
And so I won my Genevieve,   95
    My bright and beauteous bride!

III

THE MAD MOTHER

Her eyes are wild, her head is bare,
The sun has burnt her coal-black hair,
Her eyebrows have a rusty stain,
And she came far from over the main.
She has a baby on her arm,   5
Or else she were alone;
And underneath the haystack warm,
And on the greenwood stone,
She talked and sung the woods among;
And it was in the English tongue.   10

'Sweet babe! they say that I am mad,
But nay, my heart is far too glad;
And I am happy when I sing
Full many a sad and doleful thing:
Then, lovely baby, do not fear!   15
I pray thee have no fear of me,
But safe as in a cradle here,
My lovely baby! thou shalt be,
To thee I know too much I owe;
I cannot work thee any woe.   20

'A fire was once within my brain;
And in my head a dull, dull pain;
And fiendish faces one, two, three,
Hung at my breasts, and pulled at me.
But then there came a sight of joy;   25
It came at once to do me good:
I waked, and saw my little boy,
My little boy of flesh and blood;
Oh joy for me that sight to see!
For he was here, and only he.   30

'Suck, little babe, oh suck again!
It cools my blood; it cools my brain;

Thy lips I feel them, baby! they
Draw from my heart the pain away.
Oh! press me with thy little hand;   35
It loosens something at my chest;
About that tight and deadly band
I feel thy little fingers pressed.
The breeze I see is in the tree;
It comes to cool my babe and me.   40

'Oh! love me, love me, little boy!
Thou art thy mother's only joy;
And do not dread the waves below,
When o'er the sea-rock's edge we go;
The high crag cannot work me harm,   45
Nor leaping torrents when they howl;
The babe I carry on my arm,
He saves for me my precious soul:
Then happy lie, for blest am I;
Without me my sweet babe would die.   50

'Then do not fear, my boy! for thee
Bold as a lion I will be;
And I will always be thy guide,
Through hollow snows and rivers wide.
I'll build an Indian bower; I know   55
The leaves that make the softest bed:
And if from me thou wilt not go,
But still be true till I am dead,
My pretty thing! then thou shalt sing
As merry as the birds in spring.   60

'Thy father cares not for my breast,
'Tis thine, sweet baby, there to rest:
'Tis all thine own! and if its hue
Be changed, that was so fair to view,
'Tis fair enough for thee, my dove!   65
My beauty, little child, is flown;

But thou wilt live with me in love,
And what if my poor cheek be brown?
'Tis well for me, thou canst not see
How pale and wan it else would be.   70

'Dread not their taunts, my little life!
I am thy father's wedded wife;
And underneath the spreading tree
We two will live in honesty.
If his sweet boy he could forsake,   75
With me he never would have stayed;
From him no harm my babe can take,
But he, poor man! is wretched made,
And every day we two will pray
For him that's gone and far away.   80

'I'll teach my boy the sweetest things;
I'll teach him how the owlet sings.
My little babe! thy lips are still,
And thou hast almost sucked thy fill.
—Where art thou gone, my own dear child? 85
What wicked looks are those I see?
Alas! alas! that look so wild,
It never, never came from me:
If thou art mad, my pretty lad,
Then I must be for ever sad.   90

'Oh! smile on me, my little lamb!
For I thy own dear mother am.
My love for thee has been well tried:
I've sought thy father far and wide.
I know the poisons of the shade,   95
I know the earth-nuts fit for food;
Then pretty dear, be not afraid;
We'll find thy father in the wood.
Now laugh and be gay, to the woods away!
And there, my babe, we'll live for aye.'   100

THE ANCIENT MARINER[1]

I

[An ancient Mariner meeteth three Gallants bidden to a wedding feast, and detaineth one.]

It is an ancient Mariner,
    And he stoppeth one of three:
'By thy long gray beard and thy glittering eye,
    Now wherefore stoppest me?

'The Bridegroom's doors are opened wide,   5
    And I am next of kin;
The Guests are met, the Feast is set—
    May'st hear the merry din.'

But still he holds the wedding-guest—
    'There was a Ship,' quoth he—   10
'Nay, if thou'st got a laughsome tale,
    Mariner! come with me.'

He holds him with his skinny hand,
    Quoth he, 'There was a Ship—'
'Now get thee hence, thou gray-beard   15
    Loon!
Or my Staff shall make thee skip.'

[The Wedding-Guest is spell-bound by the eye of the old sea-faring man, and constrained to hear his tale.]

He holds him with his glittering eye—
    The wedding-guest stood still
And listens like a three years' child;
    The Mariner hath his will.   20

The wedding-guest sate on a stone,
    He cannot choose but hear;
And thus spake on that ancient man,
    The bright-eyed Mariner.

[1]By Coleridge. The 'gloss' or marginal commentary here printed within square brackets was not published until 1817 (see notes).

'The Ship was cheered, the Harbour 25
    cleared—
  Merrily did we drop
Below the Kirk, below the Hill,
  Below the Light-house top.

[The Mariner tells how the ship sailed southward with a good wind and fair weather, till it reached the line.]

The Sun came up upon the left,
  Out of the Sea came he: 30
And he shone bright, and on the right
  Went down into the sea.

Higher and higher every day,
  Till over the mast at noon—'
The wedding-guest here beat his breast, 35
  For he heard the loud bassoon.

[The Wedding-Guest heareth the bridal music; but the Mariner continueth his tale.]

The Bride hath paced into the Hall,
  Red as a rose is she;
Nodding their heads before her go
  The merry Minstrelsy. 40

The wedding-guest he beat his breast,
  Yet he cannot choose but hear:
And thus spake on that ancient Man,
  The bright-eyed Mariner:

[The ship driven by a storm towards the south pole.]

'But now the North wind came more 45
    fierce,
  There came a Tempest strong!
And southward still for days and weeks
  Like Chaff we drove along.

And now there came both Mist and Snow,
  And it grew wondrous cold; 50
And Ice mast-high came floating by
  As green as Emerald.

[The land
of ice, and
of fearful
sounds
where no
living thing
was to be
seen.]

And through the drifts the snowy clifts
    Did send a dismal sheen;
Nor shapes of men nor beasts we ken—   55
    The Ice was all between.

The Ice was here, the Ice was there,
    The Ice was all around:
It cracked and growled, and roared and
      howled,
    A wild and ceaseless sound.   60

[Till a great
sea-bird,
called the
Albatross,
came
through
the snow-
fog, and
was re-
ceived with
great joy
and
hospitality.]

At length did cross an Albatross,
    Thorough the Fog it came;
As if it had been a Christian Soul,
    We hailed it in God's name.

The Mariners gave it biscuit-worms,   65
    And round and round it flew.
The Ice did split with a Thunder-fit;
    The Helmsman steered us through.

[And lo!
the Alba-
tross
proveth a
bird of
good omen,
and fol-
loweth the
ship as it
returned
northward
through fog
and float-
ing ice.]

And a good South wind sprung up behind,
    The Albatross did follow;   70
And every day for food or play
    Came to the Mariner's hollo!

In mist or cloud on mast or shroud
    It perched for vespers nine,
Whiles all the night through fog-smoke   75
      white
    Glimmered the white moon-shine.'

[The
ancient
Mariner in-
hospitably
killeth the
pious bird
of good
omen.]

'God save thee, antient Mariner,
    From the fiends that plague thee thus!
Why look'st thou so?'—'With my crossbow
    I shot the Albatross.'   80

II

'The Sun now rose upon the right,
　　Out of the Sea came he;
Still hid in mist; and on the left
　　Went down into the Sea.

And the good South wind still blew　　　　85
　　　　behind,
　　But no sweet Bird did follow,
Nor any day for food or play
　　Came to the Mariner's hollo!

[His ship-
mates cry
out against
the
ancient
Mariner,
for killing
the bird of
good luck.]

And I had done an hellish thing,
　　And it would work 'em woe:　　　　　90
For all averred, I had killed the Bird
　　That made the Breeze to blow.

[But when
the fog
cleared off,
they justify
the same,
and thus
make
themselves
accomplices
in the
crime.]

Nor dim nor red, like an Angel's head,
　　The glorious Sun uprist:
Then all averred, I had killed the Bird　　95
　　That brought the fog and mist.
'Twas right, said they, such birds to slay
　　That bring the fog and mist.

[The fair
breeze con-
tinues; the
ship enters
the Pacific
Ocean, and
sails north-
ward, even
till it
reaches
the Line.]

The breezes blew, the white foam flew,
　　The furrow followed free:　　　　　100
We were the first that ever burst
　　Into that silent Sea.

[The ship
hath been
suddenly
becalmed.]

Down dropt the breeze, the Sails dropt down,
　　'Twas sad as sad could be;
And we did speak only to break　　　　105
　　The silence of the Sea.

All in a hot and copper sky
　　The bloody Sun, at noon,
Right up above the mast did stand,
　　No bigger than the moon.　　　　　110

Day after day, day after day,
　　We stuck, nor breath nor motion,
As idle as a painted Ship
　　Upon a painted Ocean.

[And the
Albatross
begins to be
avenged.]

Water, water, every where,　　　　　115
　　And all the boards did shrink;
Water, water, every where,
　　Nor any drop to drink.

The very deeps did rot: O Christ!
　　That ever this should be!　　　　120
Yea, slimy things did crawl with legs
　　Upon the slimy Sea.

About, about, in reel and rout
　　The Death-fires danced at night;
The water, like a witch's oils,　　　125
　　Burnt green and blue and white.

[A Spirit
had fol-
lowed
them; one
of the in-
visible in-
habitants
of this
planet,

And some in dreams assuréd were
　　Of the Spirit that plagued us so:
Nine fathom deep he had followed us
　　From the Land of Mist and Snow.　130

neither departed souls nor angels; concerning whom the learned Jew Josephus, and
the Platonic Constantinopolitan, Michael Psellus, may be consulted. They are very
numerous, and there is no climate or element without one or more.]

And every tongue through utter drouth
　　Was withered at the root;
We could not speak, no more than if
　　We had been choked with soot.

[The ship-
mates, in
their sore
distress,
would fain
throw the
whole guilt
on the
ancient

Ah well-a-day! what evil looks　　　135
　　Had I from old and young!
Instead of the Cross the Albatross
　　About my neck was hung.'

Mariner: in sign whereof they hang the dead sea-bird round his neck.]

III

'So passed a weary time; each throat
    Was parched, and glazed each eye.   140
When, looking westward, I beheld
    A something in the sky.

[The
ancient
Mariner
beholdeth
a sign in
the element
afar off.]

At first it seemed a little speck,
    And then it seemed a mist;
It moved and moved, and took at last   145
    A certain shape, I wist.

A speck, a mist, a shape, I wist!
    And still it ner'd and ner'd;
And as if it dodged a water-sprite
    It plunged and tacked and veered.   150

[At its
nearer
approach,
it seemeth
him to be
a ship; and
at a dear
ransom he
freeth his
speech
from the
bonds of
thirst.]

With throat unslaked, with black lips
        baked,
    We could nor laugh nor wail;
Through utter drouth all dumb we stood
Till I bit my arm and sucked the blood,
    And cried, A sail! a sail!   155

With throat unslaked, with black lips
        baked,
    Agape they heard me call:
[A flash of
joy;
Gramercy! they for joy did grin,
And all at once their breath drew in
    As they were drinking all.   160

And horror
follows.
For can it
be a ship
that comes
onward
without
wind or
tide?]
See! See! (I cried) she tacks no more!
    Hither to work us weal
Without a breeze, without a tide,
    She steddies with upright keel!

The western wave was all a flame.   165
  The day was well-nigh done!
Almost upon the western wave
  Rested the broad bright Sun;
When that strange shape drove suddenly
  Betwixt us and the Sun.   170

[It seemeth him but the skeleton of a ship.]

And straight the Sun was flecked with
    bars
  (Heaven's Mother send us grace!)
As if through a dungeon grate he peered
  With broad and burning face.

Alas! (thought I, and my heart beat   175
    loud)
  How fast she neres and neres!
Are those *her* Sails that glance in the
    Sun
  Like restless gossameres?

[And its ribs are seen as bars on the face of the setting Sun. The Spectre-Woman and her Death-mate, and no other on board the skeleton ship.]

Are those *her* Ribs, through which the Sun
  Did peer, as through a grate?   180
And are those two all, all her crew,
  That Woman, and her Mate?

His bones were black with many a crack,
  All black and bare, I ween;
Jet-black and bare, save where with rust   185
Of mouldy damps and charnel crust
  They were patched with purple and green.

[Like vessel, like crew!]

Her lips were red, *her* looks were free,
  Her locks were yellow as gold:
Her skin was as white as leprosy,   190
And she was far liker Death than he;
  Her flesh made the still air cold.

121

[Death and Life-in-Death have diced for the ship's crew, and she (the latter) winneth the ancient Mariner.]

The naked Hulk alongside came
   And the Twain were playing dice;
'The Game is done! I've won, I've   195
    won!'
   Quoth she, and whistled thrice.

A gust of wind sterte up behind
   And whistled through his bones;
Thro' the holes of his eyes and the hole
    of his mouth
   Half-whistles and half-groans.   200

With never a whisper in the Sea
   Off darts the Spectre-ship;
[At the rising of the Moon,While clombe above the Eastern bar
The hornéd Moon, with one bright Star
   Almost between the tips.   205

One after another.One after one by the hornéd Moon
   (Listen, O Stranger, to me!)
Each turned his face with a ghastly pang
   And cursed me with his ee.

His ship-mates drop down dead.]Four times fifty living men,   210
   With never a sigh or groan,
With heavy thump, a lifeless lump,
   They dropped down one by one.

[But Life-in-Death begins her work on the ancient Mariner.]Their souls did from their bodies fly—
   They fled to bliss or woe!   215
And every soul it passed me by,
   Like the whiz of my cross-bow.'

IV

[The Wedding-Guest feareth that a Spirit is talking to him;

'I fear thee, ancient Mariner!
  I fear thy skinny hand;
And thou art long and lank and brown   220
  As is the ribbed Sea-sand.

'I fear thee and thy glittering eye
  And thy skinny hand so brown.'

But the ancient Mariner assureth him of his bodily life, and proceedeth to relate his horrible penance.]

'Fear not, fear not, thou wedding-guest!
  This body dropt not down.   225

Alone, alone, all all alone,
  Alone on the wide wide Sea;
And Christ would take no pity on
  My soul in agony.

[He despiseth the creatures of the calm.]

The many men so beautiful,   230
  And they all dead did lie!
And a million million slimy things
  Lived on—and so did I.

[And envieth that they should live, and so many lie dead.]

I looked upon the rotting Sea,
  And drew my eyes away;   235
I looked upon the ghastly deck,
  And there the dead men lay.

I looked to Heaven, and tried to pray;
  But or ever a prayer had gusht,
A wicked whisper came and made   240
  My heart as dry as dust.

I closed my lids and kept them close,
  Till the balls like pulses beat;
For the sky and the sea, and the sea
    and the sky
Lay like a load on my weary eye,   245
  And the dead were at my feet.

[But the
curse liveth
for him in
the eye of
the dead
men.]

The cold sweat melted from their limbs,
   Nor rot nor reek did they;
The look with which they looked on me
   Had never passed away.   250

An orphan's curse would drag to Hell
   A spirit from on high:
But oh! more horrible than that
   Is the curse in a dead man's eye!
Seven days, seven nights I saw that   255
    curse,
   And yet I could not die.

[In his
loneliness
and fixed-
ness he
yearneth
towards the
journeying
Moon, and
the stars

The moving Moon went up the sky
   And no where did abide;
Softly she was going up
   And a star or two beside—   260

that still sojourn, yet still move onward; and everywhere the blue sky belongs to
them, and is their appointed rest, and their native country and their own natural
homes, which they enter unannounced, as lords that are certainly expected and yet
there is a silent joy at their arrival.]

Her beams bemocked the sultry main
   Like April hoar-frost spread;
But where the Ship's huge shadow lay,
The charmèd water burnt alway
   A still and awful red.   265

[By the
light of the
Moon he
beholdeth
God's crea-
tures of the
great calm.]

Beyond the shadow of the ship
   I watched the water-snakes:
They moved in tracks of shining white;
And when they reared, the elfish light
   Fell off in hoary flakes.   270

Within the shadow of the ship
   I watched their rich attire:
Blue, glossy green, and velvet black
They coiled and swam; and every track
   Was a flash of golden fire.   275

[Their
beauty and
their
happiness.]

O happy living things! no tongue
   Their beauty might declare:
A spring of love gusht from my heart,
   And I blessed them unaware!

[He blesseth
them in his
heart.]

Sure my kind saint took pity on me,   280
   And I blessed them unaware.

[The spell
begins to
break.]

The self-same moment I could pray;
   And from my neck so free
The Albatross fell off, and sank
   Like lead into the sea.'   285

V

'Oh sleep, it is a gentle thing
   Beloved from pole to pole!
To Mary-queen the praise be given,
She sent the gentle sleep from heaven
   That slid into my soul.   290

[By grace
of the holy
Mother,
the ancient
Mariner is
refreshed
with rain.]

The silly buckets on the deck
   That had so long remained,
I dreamt that they were filled with dew,
   And when I awoke it rained.

My lips were wet, my throat was cold,   295
   My garments all were dank;
Sure I had drunken in my dreams,
   And still my body drank.

I moved and could not feel my limbs,
   I was so light, almost   300
I thought that I had died in sleep,
   And was a blessed Ghost.

[He heareth
sounds and
seeth
strange
sights and
commotions
in the sky
and the
element.]

And soon I heard a roaring wind,
  It did not come anear;
But with its sound it shook the sails   305
  That were so thin and sere.

The upper air burst into life,
  And a hundred fire-flags sheen
To and fro they were hurried about;
And to and fro, and in and out,   310
  The wan stars danced between.

And the coming wind did roar more loud;
  And the sails did sigh like sedge;
And the rain poured down from one
    black cloud;
  The moon was at its edge.   315

The thick black cloud was cleft, and still
  The Moon was at its side;
Like waters shot from some high crag,
The lightning fell with never a jag
  A river steep and wide.   320

[The bodies
of the ship's
crew are
inspired
and the
ship moves
on;]

The loud wind never reached the Ship,
  Yet now the Ship moved on!
Beneath the lightning and the moon
  The dead men gave a groan.

They groaned, they stirred, they all   325
    uprose,
  Nor spake, nor moved their eyes:
It had been strange even in a dream
  To have seen those dead men rise.

The helmsman steered, the ship moved
    on;
  Yet never a breeze up-blew;   330
The Mariners all 'gan work the ropes,
  Where they were wont to do:
They raised their limbs like lifeless
    tools—
  We were a ghastly crew.

The body of my brother's son   335
  Stood by me knee to knee:
The body and I pulled at one rope,
  But he said nought to me.'

'I fear thee, ancient Mariner!'
  'Be calm, thou wedding-guest!   340

[But not by
the souls of
the men,
nor by
dæmons of
earth or
middle air,
but by a
blessed
troop of
angelic
spirits, sent
down by
the invoca-
tion of the
guardian
saint.]

'Twas not those souls, that fled in pain,
Which to their corses came again,
  But a troop of Spirits blest:

For when it dawned—they dropped their
    arms,
  And clustered round the mast: 345
Sweet sounds rose slowly through their
    mouths,
  And from their bodies passed.

Around, around, flew each sweet sound,
  Then darted to the sun;
Slowly the sounds came back again,   350
  Now mixed, now one by one.

Sometimes a-dropping from the sky
  I heard the Sky-lark sing;
Sometimes all little birds that are,
How they seemed to fill the sea and air   355
  With their sweet jargoning!

And now 'twas like all instruments,
   Now like a lonely flute;
And now it is an angel's song
   That makes the heavens be mute.   360

It ceased: yet still the sails made on
   A pleasant noise till noon,
A noise like of a hidden brook
   In the leafy month of June,
That to the sleeping woods all night   365
   Singeth a quiet tune.

Till noon we silently sailed on,
   Yet never a breeze did breathe:
Slowly and smoothly went the Ship
   Moved onward from beneath.   370

[The lonesome spirit from the south-pole carries on the ship as far as the Line, in obedience to the angelic troop, but still requireth vengeance.]

Under the keel nine fathom deep
   From the land of mist and snow
The Spirit slid: and it was He
   That made the ship to go.
The sails at noon left off their tune,   375
   And the Ship stood still also.

The Sun right up above the mast
   Had fixed her to the ocean:
But in a minute she 'gan stir
   With a short uneasy motion—   380
Backwards and forwards half her length,
   With a short uneasy motion.

Then, like a pawing horse let go,
   She made a sudden bound:
It flung the blood into my head,   385
   And I fell into a swound.

[The Polar
Spirit's
fellow-
dæmons,
the
invisible
inhabitants
of the
element,
take part
in his
wrong;
and two of
them relate,
one to the
other, that
penance
long and
heavy for
the ancient
Mariner
hath been
accorded to
the Polar
Spirit, who
returneth
southward.]

How long in that same fit I lay,
  I have not to declare;
But ere my living life returned,
I heard and in my soul discerned   390
  Two voices in the air.

"Is it he?" quoth one, "Is this the man?
  By him who died on cross,
With his cruel bow he laid full low
  The harmless Albatross.   395

"The Spirit who bideth by himself
  In the land of mist and snow,
He loved the bird that loved the man
  Who shot him with his bow."

The other was a softer voice,   400
  As soft as honey-dew;
Quoth he, "The man hath penance done,
  And penance more will do." '

VI

FIRST VOICE

' "But tell me, tell me! speak again,
  Thy soft response renewing—   405
What makes that ship drive on so fast?
  What is the Ocean doing?" '

SECOND VOICE

"Still as a Slave before his Lord,
  The Ocean hath no blast:
His great bright eye most silently   410
  Up to the moon is cast—

"If he may know which way to go,
   For she guides him smooth or grim.
See, brother, see! how graciously
   She looketh down on him."   415

FIRST VOICE

[The
Mariner
hath been
cast into a
trance; for
the angelic
power
causeth
the vessel
to drive
northward
faster than
human life
could
endure.]

"But why drives on that ship so fast
   Without or wave or wind?"

SECOND VOICE

"The air is cut away before,
   And closes from behind.

"Fly, brother, fly! more high, more high,   420
   Or we shall be belated:
For slow and slow that ship will go,
   When the Mariner's trance is abated."

[The super-
natural
motion is
retarded;
the Mariner
awakes,
and his
penance
begins
anew.]

I woke, and we were sailing on
   As in a gentle weather;   425
'Twas night, calm night, the moon was
      high;
   The dead men stood together.

All stood together on the deck,
   For a charnel-dungeon fitter;
All fixed on me their stony eyes   430
   That in the moon did glitter.

The pang, the curse, with which they died
   Had never passed away;
I could not draw my eyes from theirs,
   Nor turn them up to pray.   435

[The curse is finally expiated.]

And now this spell was snapt: once more
   I viewed the ocean green,
And looked far forth, yet little saw
   Of what had else been seen—

Like one, that on a lonesome road   440
   Doth walk in fear and dread,
And having once turned round, walks on
   And turns no more his head;
Because he knows a frightful fiend
   Doth close behind him tread.   445

But soon there breathed a wind on me,
   Nor sound nor motion made:
Its path was not upon the sea
   In ripple or in shade.

It raised my hair, it fanned my cheek,   450
   Like a meadow-gale of spring—
It mingled strangely with my fears,
   Yet it felt like a welcoming.

Swiftly, swiftly flew the ship,
   Yet she sailed softly too;   455
Sweetly, sweetly blew the breeze—
   On me alone it blew.

[And the ancient Mariner beholdeth his native country.]

O dream of joy! is this indeed
   The light-house top I see?
Is this the Hill? Is this the Kirk?   460
   Is this mine own countrée?

We drifted o'er the Harbour-bar,
   And I with sobs did pray—
'O let me be awake, my God!
   Or let me sleep alway.'   465

The harbour-bay was clear as glass,
　So smoothly it was strewn!
And on the bay the moonlight lay,
　And the shadow of the moon.

The rock shone bright, the kirk no less　　470
　That stands above the rock:
The moonlight steeped in silentness
　The steady weathercock.

And the bay was white with silent light,
　Till rising from the same　　475
Full many shapes, that shadows were,
　In crimson colours came.

A little distance from the prow
　Those crimson shadows were:
I turned my eyes upon the deck—　　480
　O Christ! what saw I there?

Each corse lay flat, lifeless and flat,
　And, by the Holy rood,
A man all light, a seraph-man,
　On every corse there stood.　　485

This seraph-band, each waved his hand,
　It was a heavenly sight!
They stood as signals to the land,
　Each one a lovely light:

This seraph-band, each waved his hand,　　490
　No voice did they impart—
No voice; but oh! the silence sank
　Like music on my heart.

But soon I heard the dash of oars,
    I heard the pilot's cheer: 495
My head was turned perforce away,
    And I saw a boat appear.

The pilot and the pilot's boy,
    I heard them coming fast:
Dear Lord in Heaven! it was a joy   500
    The dead men could not blast.

I saw a third—I heard his voice:
    It is the Hermit good!
He singeth loud his godly hymns
    That he makes in the wood.   505
He'll shrieve my soul, he'll wash away
    The Albatross's blood.'

VII

[The Hermit of the wood.

'This Hermit good lives in that wood
    Which slopes down to the Sea.
How loudly his sweet voice he rears!   510
He loves to talk with Mariners
    That come from a far countrée.

He kneels at morn and noon and eve—
    He hath a cushion plump:
It is the moss that wholly hides   515
    The rotted old Oak-stump.

The Skiff-boat ner'd: I heard them talk,
    "Why, this is strange, I trow!
Where are those lights so many and fair
    That signal made but now?"   520

"Strange, by my faith!" the Hermit said,
  "And they answered not our cheer.
The planks look warped, and see those
      sails
  How thin they are and sere!
I never saw aught like to them   525
  Unless perchance it were

"The skeletons of leaves that lag
  My forest brook along;
When the Ivy-tod is heavy with snow,
And the Owlet whoops to the wolf below   530
  That eats the she-wolf's young."

"Dear Lord! it has a fiendish look,"
  The pilot made reply,
"I am a-feared."—"Push on, push on!"
  Said the Hermit cheerily.   535

The Boat came closer to the Ship,
  But I nor spake nor stirred;
The Boat came close beneath the Ship,
  And straight a sound was heard.

Under the water it rumbled on,   540
  Still louder and more dread;
It reached the ship, it split the bay:
  The ship went down like lead.

Stunned by that loud and dreadful sound,
  Which sky and ocean smote,
Like one that hath been seven days   545
      drowned
  My body lay afloat;
But, swift as dreams, myself I found
  Within the Pilot's boat.

134

Upon the whirl, where sank the Ship,   550
  The boat spun round and round,
And all was still, save that the hill
  Was telling of the sound.

I moved my lips: the Pilot shrieked
  And fell down in a fit.   555
The Holy Hermit raised his eyes
  And prayed where he did sit.

I took the oars: the Pilot's boy,
  Who now doth crazy go,
Laughed loud and long, and all the while 560
  His eyes went to and fro,
"Ha! ha!" quoth he, "full plain I see
  The devil knows how to row."

And now all in mine own countrée
  I stood on the firm land!   565
The Hermit stepped forth from the boat,
  And scarcely he could stand.

[The ancient Mariner earnestly entreateth the Hermit to shrieve him; and the penance of life falls on him.]

"O shrieve me, shrieve me, holy Man!"
  The Hermit crossed his brow.
"Say quick," quoth he, "I bid thee say 570
  What manner of man art thou?"

Forthwith this frame of mine was wrenched
  With a woeful agony,
Which forced me to begin my tale,
  And then it left me free.   575

[And ever and anon throughout his future life an agony constraineth him to travel from land to land;]

Since then, at an uncertain hour,
  That agony returns;
And till my ghastly tale is told
  This heart within me burns.

I pass, like night, from land to land;   580
  I have strange power of speech;
The moment that his face I see
I know the man that must hear me;
  To him my tale I teach.

What loud uproar bursts from that door!   585
  The wedding-guests are there;
But in the garden-bower the bride
  And bride-maids singing are;
And hark the little vesper-bell,
  Which biddeth me to prayer.   590

O wedding-guest! this soul hath been
  Alone on a wide wide sea:
So lonely 'twas, that God himself
  Scarce seeméd there to be.

O sweeter than the marriage-feast,   595
  'Tis sweeter far to me
To walk together to the Kirk
  With a goodly company:

To walk together to the Kirk
  And all together pray,   600
While each to his great Father bends,
Old men, and babes, and loving friends,
  And youths, and maidens gay.

[And to
teach by
his own
example,
love and
reverence
to all
things that
God made
and
loveth.]

Farewell, farewell! But this I tell
  To thee, thou wedding-guest!   605
He prayeth well who loveth well
  Both man and bird and beast.

He prayeth best who loveth best
   All things both great and small:
For the dear God, who loveth us,   610
   He made and loveth all.'

The Mariner, whose eye is bright,
   Whose beard with age is hoar,
Is gone; and now the wedding-guest
   Turned from the bride-groom's door.   615

He went, like one that hath been stunned
   And is of sense forlorn:
A sadder and a wiser man
   He rose the morrow morn.

LINES

WRITTEN A FEW MILES ABOVE TINTERN ABBEY, ON
REVISITING THE BANKS OF THE WYE DURING A TOUR.
JULY 13, 1798.

Five years have passed; five summers, with the length
Of five long winters! and again I hear
These waters, rolling from their mountain-springs
With a sweet inland murmur. Once again
Do I behold these steep and lofty cliffs,   5
Which on a wild secluded scene impress
Thoughts of more deep seclusion ; and connect
The landscape with the quiet of the sky.
The day is come when I again repose
Here, under this dark sycamore, and view   10
These plots of cottage-ground, these orchard-tufts,
Which, at this season, with their unripe fruits,
Are clad in one green hue, and lose themselves
Among the woods and copses, nor disturb
The wild green landscape. Once again I see   15
These hedge-rows—hardly hedge-rows, little lines
Of sportive wood run wild; these pastoral farms
Green to the very door; and wreaths of smoke
Sent up, in silence, from among the trees,
With some uncertain notice, as might seem,   20
Of vagrant dwellers in the houseless woods,
Or of some hermit's cave, where by his fire
The hermit sits alone.

                   Though absent long,
These forms of beauty have not been to me
As is a landscape to a blind man's eye;   25
But oft, in lonely rooms, and 'mid the din
Of towns and cities, I have owed to them,
In hours of weariness, sensations sweet,

Felt in the blood, and felt along the heart,
And passing even into my purer mind   30
With tranquil restoration:—feelings too
Of unremembered pleasure: such, perhaps,
As may have had no trivial influence
On that best portion of a good man's life,
His little, nameless, unremembered acts   35
Of kindness and of love. Nor less, I trust,
To them I may have owed another gift,
Of aspect more sublime: that blessed mood
In which the burthen of the mystery,
In which the heavy and the weary weight   40
Of all this unintelligible world
Is lightened; that serene and blessed mood
In which the affections gently lead us on
Until, the breath of this corporeal frame
And even the motion of our human blood   45
Almost suspended, we are laid asleep
In body, and become a living soul;
While with an eye made quiet by the power
Of harmony, and the deep power of joy,
We see into the life of things.

                      If this   50
Be but a vain belief, yet, oh! how oft,
In darkness, and amid the many shapes
Of joyless daylight; when the fretful stir
Unprofitable, and the fever of the world,
Have hung upon the beatings of my heart,   55
How oft, in spirit, have I turned to thee,
O sylvan Wye! Thou wanderer through the woods,
How often has my spirit turned to thee!

And now, with gleams of half-extinguished thought,
With many recognitions dim and faint,   60
And somewhat of a sad perplexity,

The picture of the mind revives again:
While here I stand, not only with the sense
Of present pleasure, but with pleasing thoughts
That in this moment there is life and food   65
For future years. And so I dare to hope,
Though changed, no doubt, from what I was when first
I came among these hills: when like a roe
I bounded o'er the mountains, by the sides
Of the deep rivers, and the lonely streams,   70
Wherever nature led; more like a man
Flying from something that he dreads, than one
Who sought the thing he loved. For nature then
(The coarser pleasures of my boyish days
And their glad animal movements all gone by)   75
To me was all in all.—I cannot paint
What then I was. The sounding cataract
Haunted me like a passion; the tall rock,
The mountain, and the deep and gloomy wood,
Their colours and their forms, were then to me   80
An appetite: a feeling and a love,
That had no need of a remoter charm
By thought supplied, or any interest
Unborrowed from the eye.—That time is past,
And all its aching joys are now no more,   85
And all its dizzy raptures. Not for this
Faint I, nor mourn nor murmur; other gifts
Have followed, for such loss, I would believe,
Abundant recompense. For I have learned
To look on nature, not as in the hour   90
Of thoughtless youth, but hearing oftentimes
The still, sad music of humanity,
Nor harsh nor grating, though of ample power
To chasten and subdue. And I have felt
A presence that disturbs me with the joy   95
Of elevated thoughts: a sense sublime
Of something far more deeply interfused,

Whose dwelling is the light of setting suns,
And the round ocean and the living air,
And the blue sky, and in the mind of man;　　100
A motion and a spirit, that impels
All thinking things, all objects of all thought,
And rolls through all things.—Therefore am I still
A lover of the meadows and the woods
And mountains; and of all that we behold　　105
From this green earth; of all the mighty world
Of eye and ear, both what they half create
And what perceive; well pleased to recognise
In nature and the language of the sense
The anchor of my purest thoughts, the nurse,　　110
The guide, the guardian of my heart, and soul
Of all my moral being.

　　　　　　　　Nor, perchance,
If I were not thus taught, should I the more
Suffer my genial spirits to decay:
For thou art with me, here, upon the banks　　115
Of this fair river; thou, my dearest friend,
My dear, dear friend, and in thy voice I catch
The language of my former heart, and read
My former pleasures in the shooting lights
Of thy wild eyes. Oh! yet a little while　　120
May I behold in thee what I was once,
My dear, dear sister! And this prayer I make,
Knowing that Nature never did betray
The heart that loved her; 'tis her privilege,
Through all the years of this our life, to lead　　125
From joy to joy: for she can so inform
The mind that is within us, so impress
With quietness and beauty, and so feed
With lofty thoughts, that neither evil tongues,
Rash judgments, nor the sneers of selfish men,　　130
Nor greetings where no kindness is, nor all

The dreary intercourse of daily life,
Shall e'er prevail against us, or disturb
Our cheerful faith that all which we behold
Is full of blessings. Therefore let the moon   135
Shine on thee in thy solitary walk;
And let the misty mountain winds be free
To blow against thee: and, in after years,
When these wild ecstasies shall be matured
Into a sober pleasure, when thy mind   140
Shall be a mansion for all lovely forms,
Thy memory be as a dwelling-place
For all sweet sounds and harmonies; oh! then,
If solitude, or fear, or pain, or grief
Should be thy portion, with what healing thoughts   145
Of tender joy wilt thou remember me,
And these my exhortations! Nor, perchance,
If I should be where I no more can hear
Thy voice, nor catch from thy wild eyes these gleams
Of past existence, wilt thou then forget   150
That on the banks of this delightful stream
We stood together; and that I, so long
A worshipper of Nature, hither came
Unwearied in that service: rather say
With warmer love, oh! with far deeper zeal   155
Of holier love. Nor wilt thou then forget
That after many wanderings, many years
Of absence, these steep woods and lofty cliffs,
And this green pastoral landscape, were to me
More dear, both for themselves and for thy sake.   160

LYRICAL BALLADS,

WITH

PASTORAL

AND OTHER

POEMS.

IN TWO VOLUMES.

BY W. WORDSWORTH.

Quam nihil ad genium, Papiniane, tuum!

VOL. II.

FOURTH EDITION.

LONDON:

PRINTED FOR LONGMAN, HURST, REES, AND ORME,

By R. Taylor and Co. 38, Shoe-Lane.

1805.

HART-LEAP WELL

Hart-Leap Well is a small spring of water about five miles from Richmond in Yorkshire, and near the side of the road which leads from Richmond to Askrigg. Its name is derived from a remarkable chase, the memory of which is preserved by the monuments spoken of in the second part of the following poem, which monuments do now exist as I have there described them.

The knight had ridden down from Wensley moor
With the slow motion of a summer's cloud;
He turned aside towards a vassal's door,
And 'Bring another horse!' he cried aloud.

'Another horse!'—That shout the vassal heard,   5
And saddled his best steed, a comely grey;
Sir Walter mounted him; he was the third
Which he had mounted on that glorious day.

Joy sparkled in the prancing courser's eyes;
The horse and horseman are a happy pair;   10
But, though Sir Walter like a falcon flies,
There is a doleful silence in the air.

A rout this morning left Sir Walter's hall,
That as they galloped made the echoes roar;
But horse and man are vanished, one and all;   15
Such race, I think, was never seen before.

Sir Walter, restless as a veering wind,
Calls to the few tired dogs that yet remain;
Brach, Swift, and Music, noblest of their kind,
Follow, and up the weary mountain strain.   20

The knight hallooed, he chid and cheered them on
With suppliant gestures and upbraidings stern;
But breath and eyesight fail; and one by one
The dogs are stretched among the mountain fern.

Where is the throng, the tumult of the race?   25
The bugles that so joyfully were blown?
This chase it looks not like an earthly chase;
Sir Walter and the hart are left alone.

The poor hart toils along the mountain side;
I will not stop to tell how far he fled,   30
Nor will I mention by what death he died;
But now the knight beholds him lying dead.

Dismounting then, he leaned against a thorn;
He had no follower, dog, nor man, nor boy:
He neither smacked his whip, nor blew his horn, 35
But gazed upon the spoil with silent joy.

Close to the thorn on which Sir Walter leaned,
Stood his dumb partner in this glorious act;
Weak as a lamb the hour that it is yeaned,
And foaming like a mountain cataract.   40

Upon his side the hart was lying stretched:
His nose half-touched a spring beneath a hill,
And with the last deep groan his breath had
     fetched
The waters of the spring were trembling still.

And now, too happy for repose or rest   45
(Was never man in such a joyful case!),
Sir Walter walked all round, north, south, and
     west,
And gazed and gazed upon that darling place.

And climbing up the hill (it was at least
Nine roods of sheer ascent) Sir Walter found   50
Three several hoof-marks which the hunted
    beast
Had left imprinted on the verdant ground.

Sir Walter wiped his face and cried, 'Till now
Such sight was never seen by living eyes:
Three leaps have borne him from this lofty   55
    brow,
Down to the very fountain where he lies.

'I'll build a pleasure-house upon this spot,
And a small arbour, made for rural joy;
'Twill be the traveller's shed, the pilgrim's cot,
A place of love for damsels that are coy.   60

'A cunning artist will I have to frame
A basin for that fountain in the dell;
And they who do make mention of the same
From this day forth, shall call it HART-LEAP WELL.

'And, gallant brute! to make thy praises known,   65
Another monument shall here be raised:
Three several pillars, each a rough-hewn stone,
And planted where thy hoofs the turf have
    grazed.

'And in the summer-time when days are long,
I will come hither with my paramour;   70
And with the dancers, and the minstrel's song,
We will make merry in that pleasant bower.

'Till the foundations of the mountains fail
My mansion with its arbour shall endure:
The joy of them who till the fields of Swale,   75
And them who dwell among the woods of Ure!'

Then home he went, and left the hart, stone-
    dead,
With breathless nostrils stretched above the
    spring.
And soon the knight performed what he had said,
The fame whereof through many a land did ring.   80

Ere thrice the moon into her port had steered,
A cup of stone received the living well;
Three pillars of rude stone Sir Walter reared,
And built a house of pleasure in the dell.

And near the fountain, flowers of stature tall   85
With trailing plants and trees were intertwined,
Which soon composed a little sylvan hall,
A leafy shelter from the sun and wind.

And thither, when the summer-days were long,
Sir Walter journeyed with his paramour;   90
And with the dancers and the minstrel's song
Made merriment within that pleasant bower.

The knight, Sir Walter, died in course of time,
And his bones lie in his paternal vale.—
But there is matter for a second rhyme,   95
And I to this would add another tale.

PART SECOND

The moving accident is not my trade:
To freeze the blood I have no ready arts:
'Tis my delight, alone in summer shade,
To pipe a simple song to thinking hearts.   100

As I from Hawes to Richmond did repair,
It chanced that I saw standing in a dell
Three aspens at three corners of a square,
And one, not four yards distant, near a well.

What this imported I could ill divine: 105
And, pulling now the rein my horse to stop,
I saw three pillars standing in a line,
The last stone pillar on a dark hill-top.

The trees were grey, with neither arms nor head;
Half-wasted the square mound of tawny green; 110
So that you just might say, as then I said,
'Here in old time the hand of man has been.'

I looked upon the hills both far and near,
More doleful place did never eye survey;
It seemed as if the spring-time came not here, 115
And Nature here were willing to decay.

I stood in various thoughts and fancies lost,
When one, who was in shepherd's garb attired,
Came up the hollow. Him did I accost,
And what this place might be I then enquired. 120

The shepherd stopped, and that same story told
Which in my former rhyme I have rehearsed.
'A jolly place,' said he, 'in times of old!
But something ails it now; the spot is cursed.

'You see these lifeless stumps of aspen wood— 125
Some say that they are beeches, others elms—
These were the bower; and here a mansion stood;
The finest palace of a hundred realms!

'The arbour does its own condition tell;
You see the stones, the fountain, and the   130
    stream,
But as to the great lodge! you might as well
Hunt half a day for a forgotten dream.

'There's neither dog nor heifer, horse nor sheep
Will wet his lips within that cup of stone;
And oftentimes, when all are fast asleep,   135
This water doth send forth a dolorous groan.

'Some say that here a murder has been done,
And blood cries out for blood; but for my part,
I've guessed, when I've been sitting in the sun,
That it was all for that unhappy hart.   140

'What thoughts must through the creature's brain
      have passed!
From the stone upon the summit of the steep
Are but three bounds—and look, sir, at this last—
O master! it has been a cruel leap.

'For thirteen hours he ran a desperate race;   145
And in my simple mind we cannot tell
What cause the hart might have to love this place,
And come and make his death-bed near the well.

'Here on the grass perhaps asleep he sank,
Lulled by this fountain in the summer-tide;   150
This water was perhaps the first he drank
When he had wandered from his mother's side.

'In April here beneath the scented thorn
He heard the birds their morning carols sing;
And he, perhaps, for aught we know was born   155
Not half a furlong from that self-same spring.

'But now here's neither grass nor pleasant shade;
The sun on drearier hollow never shone;
So will it be, as I have often said,
Till trees, and stones, and fountain all are gone.'   160

'Grey-headed shepherd, thou hast spoken well;
Small difference lies between thy creed and mine:
This beast not unobserved by Nature fell;
His death was mourned by sympathy divine.

'The Being that is in the clouds and air, 165
That is in the green leaves among the groves,
Maintains a deep and reverential care
For them the quiet creatures whom he loves.

'The pleasure-house is dust; behind, before,
This is no common waste, no common gloom; 170
But Nature, in due course of time, once more
Shall here put on her beauty and her bloom.

'She leaves these objects to a slow decay,
That what we are, and have been, may be
    known;
But at the coming of the milder day, 175
These monuments shall all be overgrown.

'One lesson, shepherd, let us two divide,
Taught both by what she shows, and what
    conceals,
Never to blend our pleasure or our pride
With sorrow of the meanest thing that feels.' 180

'THERE WAS A BOY'

There was a boy, ye knew him well, ye cliffs
And islands of Winander! Many a time,
At evening, when the stars had just begun
To move along the edges of the hills,
Rising or setting, would he stand alone,   5
Beneath the trees, or by the glimmering lake;
And there, with fingers interwoven, both hands
Pressed closely palm to palm and to his mouth
Uplifted, he, as through an instrument,
Blew mimic hootings to the silent owls   10
That they might answer him. And they would shout
Across the watery vale, and shout again
Responsive to his call, with quivering peals,
And long halloos, and screams, and echoes loud
Redoubled and redoubled; concourse wild   15
Of mirth and jocund din! And, when it chanced
That pauses of deep silence mocked his skill,
Then, sometimes, in that silence, while he hung
Listening, a gentle shock of mild surprise
Has carried far into his heart the voice   20
Of mountain torrents; or the visible scene
Would enter unawares into his mind
With all its solemn imagery, its rocks,
Its woods, and that uncertain heaven, received
Into the bosom of the steady lake.   25

This boy was taken from his mates, and died
In childhood, ere he was full ten years old.
Fair are the woods, and beauteous is the spot,
The vale where he was born; the churchyard hangs
Upon a slope above the village school,   30
And there, along that bank, when I have passed
At evening, I believe that oftentimes
A full half-hour together I have stood
Mute—looking at the grave in which he lies.

THE BROTHERS

A PASTORAL POEM

'These tourists, Heaven preserve us! needs must live
A profitable life: some glance along,
Rapid and gay, as if the earth were air
And they were butterflies, to wheel about
Long as their summer lasted; some, as wise,   5
Upon the forehead of a jutting crag
Sit perched, with book and pencil on their knee,
And look and scribble, and scribble on and look,
Until a man might travel twelve stout miles,
Or reap an acre of his neighbour's corn.   10
But, for that moping son of idleness,
Why can he tarry *yonder?*—In our churchyard
Is neither epitaph nor monument,
Tombstone nor name—only the turf we tread,
And a few natural graves.' To Jane, his wife,   15
Thus spake the homely priest of Ennerdale.
It was a July evening; and he sat
Upon the long stone-seat beneath the eaves
Of his old cottage, as it chanced, that day
Employed in winter's work. Upon the stone   20
His wife sat near him, teasing matted wool,
While from the twin cards toothed with glittering wire
He fed the spindle of his youngest child,
Who turned her large round wheel in the open air
With back and forward steps. Towards the field   25
In which the parish chapel stood alone,
Girt round with a bare ring of mossy wall,
While half an hour went by, the priest had sent
Many a long look of wonder, and at last,
Risen from his seat, beside the snow-white ridge   30
Of carded wool which the old man had piled
He laid his implements with gentle care,

Each in the other locked; and down the path
Which from his cottage to the churchyard led
He took his way, impatient to accost   35
The stranger, whom he saw still lingering there.

'Twas one well-known to him in former days,
A shepherd lad; who ere his thirteenth year
Had changed his calling, with the mariners
A fellow-mariner, and so had fared   40
Through twenty seasons; but he had been reared
Among the mountains, and he in his heart
Was half a shepherd on the stormy seas.
Oft in the piping shrouds had Leonard heard
The tones of waterfalls, and inland sounds   45
Of caves and trees; and when the regular wind
Between the tropics filled the steady sail,
And blew with the same breath through days and
        weeks,
Lengthening invisibly its weary line
Along the cloudless main, he in those hours   50
Of tiresome indolence would often hang
Over the vessel's side, and gaze and gaze,
And while the broad green wave and sparkling foam
Flashed round him images and hues that wrought
In union with the employment of his heart,   55
He, thus by feverish passion overcome,
Even with the organs of his bodily eye
Below him in the bosom of the deep
Saw mountains, saw the forms of sheep that grazed
On verdant hills, with dwellings among trees,   60
And shepherds clad in the same country grey
Which he himself had worn.

                        And now at length
From perils manifold, with some small wealth
Acquired by traffic in the Indian isles,
To his paternal home he is returned,   65

With a determined purpose to resume
The life which he lived there; both for the sake
Of many darling pleasures, and the love
Which to an only brother he has borne
In all his hardships, since that happy time   70
When, whether it blew foul or fair, they two
Were brother shepherds on their native hills.
—They were the last of all their race: and now
When Leonard had approached his home, his heart
Failed in him; and, not venturing to enquire   75
Tidings of one whom he so dearly loved,
Towards the churchyard he had turned aside,
That as he knew in what particular spot
His family were laid, he thence might learn
If still his brother lived, or to the file   80
Another grave was added.—He had found
Another grave, near which a full half-hour
He had remained; but as he gazed, there grew
Such a confusion in his memory
That he began to doubt, and he had hopes   85
That he had seen this heap of turf before:
That it was not another grave, but one
He had forgotten. He had lost his path,
As up the vale he came that afternoon,
Through fields which once had been well known   90
     to him.
And oh! what joy the recollection now
Sent to his heart! He lifted up his eyes,
And looking round, he thought that he perceived
Strange alteration wrought on every side
Among the woods and fields, and that the rocks   95
And the eternal hills themselves were changed.

By this the priest, who down the field had come
Unseen by Leonard, at the churchyard gate
Stopped short, and thence, at leisure, limb by limb

He scanned him with a gay complacency.   100
Ay, thought the vicar, smiling to himself,
'Tis one of those who needs must leave the path
Of the world's business to go wild alone:
His arms have a perpetual holiday;
The happy man will creep about the fields   105
Following his fancies by the hour, to bring
Tears down his cheeks, or solitary smiles
Into his face, until the setting sun
Write *Fool* upon his forehead. Planted thus
Beneath a shed that over-arched the gate   110
Of this rude churchyard, till the stars appeared
The good man might have communed with himself,
But that the stranger, who had left the grave,
Approached; he recognised the priest at once,
And after greetings interchanged, and given   115
By Leonard to the vicar as to one
Unknown to him, this dialogue ensued.

LEONARD

You live, sir, in these dales a quiet life:
Your years make up one peaceful family;
And who would grieve and fret if, welcome come   120
And welcome gone, they are so like each other
They cannot be remembered? Scarce a funeral
Comes to this churchyard once in eighteen months;
And yet, some changes must take place among you:
And you, who dwell here, even among these rocks   125
Can trace the finger of mortality,
And see that with our threescore years and ten
We are not all that perish.—I remember,
For many years ago I passed this road,
There was a foot-way all along the fields   130
By the brook-side—'tis gone; and that dark cleft!
To me it does not seem to wear the face
Which then it had.

PRIEST

             Why, sir, for aught I know,
The chasm is much the same—

LEONARD

                  But, surely, yonder—

PRIEST

Ay, there, indeed, your memory is a friend   135
That does not play you false. On that tall pike
(It is the loneliest place of all these hills)
There were two springs which bubbled side by side,
As if they had been made that they might be
Companions for each other; ten years back,   140
Close to those brother fountains, the huge crag
Was rent with lightning: one is dead and gone,
The other, left behind, is flowing still.
For accidents and changes such as these,
Why, we have store of them! a water-spout   145
Will bring down half a mountain; what a feast
For folks that wander up and down like you
To see an acre's breadth of that wide cliff
One roaring cataract! A sharp May storm
Will come with loads of January snow,   150
And in one night send twenty score of sheep
To feed the ravens; or a shepherd dies
By some untoward death among the rocks;
The ice breaks up and sweeps away a bridge;
A wood is felled—and then, for our own homes!   155
A child is born or christened, a field ploughed,
A daughter sent to service, a web spun,
The old house-clock is decked with a new face;
And hence, so far from wanting facts or dates
To chronicle the time, we all have here   160
A pair of diaries, one serving, sir,
For the whole dale, and one for each fire-side.
Yours was a stranger's judgment: for historians,
Commend me to these valleys.

LEONARD

       Yet your churchyard
Seems, if such freedom may be used with you, 165
To say that you are heedless of the past.
An orphan could not find his mother's grave:
Here's neither head- nor foot-stone, plate of brass,
Cross-bones or skull, type of our earthly state
Or emblem of our hopes: the dead man's home 170
Is but a fellow to that pasture-field.

PRIEST

Why, there, sir, is a thought that's new to me.
The stone-cutters, 'tis true, might beg their bread
If every English churchyard were like ours:
Yet your conclusion wanders from the truth. 175
We have no need of names and epitaphs;
We talk about the dead by our fire-sides,
And then, for our immortal part—*we* want
No symbols, sir, to tell us that plain tale:
The thought of death sits easy on the man 180
Who has been born and dies among the mountains.

LEONARD

Your dalesmen, then, do in each other's thoughts
Possess a kind of second life: no doubt
You, sir, could help me to the history
Of half these graves?

PRIEST

      For eight-score winters past, 185
With what I've witnessed, and with what I've heard,
Perhaps I might; and on a winter's evening,
If you were seated at my chimney's nook,
By turning o'er these hillocks one by one
We two could travel, sir, through a strange round, 190
Yet all in the broad highway of the world.
Now there's a grave—your foot is half upon it,
It looks just like the rest; and yet that man
Died broken-hearted.

LEONARD

        'Tis a common case.
We'll take another: who is he that lies   195
Beneath yon ridge, the last of those three graves?
It touches on that piece of native rock
Left in the churchyard wall.

PRIEST

            That's Walter Ewbank.
He had as white a head and fresh a cheek
As ever were produced by youth and age   200
Engendering in the blood of hale fourscore.
For five long generations had the heart
Of Walter's forefathers o'erflowed the bounds
Of their inheritance, that single cottage—
You see it yonder!—and those few green fields.   205
They toiled and wrought, and still, from sire to son,
Each struggled, and each yielded as before
A little—yet a little—and old Walter,
They left to him the family heart, and land
With other burthens than the crop it bore.   210
Year after year the old man still kept up
A cheerful mind, and buffeted with bond,
Interest and mortgages; at last he sank,
And went into his grave before his time.
Poor Walter! whether it was care that spurred him   215
God only knows, but to the very last
He had the lightest foot in Ennerdale:
His pace was never that of an old man:
I almost see him tripping down the path
With his two grandsons after him—but you,   220
Unless our landlord be your host tonight,
Have far to travel, and in these rough paths
Even in the longest days of midsummer—

LEONARD

But these two orphans!

PRIEST

        Orphans! Such they were—
Yet not while Walter lived: for though their parents 225
Lay buried side by side as now they lie,
The old man was a father to the boys,
Two fathers in one father; and if tears,
Shed when he talked of them where they were not,
And hauntings from the infirmity of love,   230
Are aught of what makes up a mother's heart,
This old man in the day of his old age
Was half a mother to them.—If you weep, sir,
To hear a stranger talking about strangers,
Heaven bless you when you are among your kindred! 235
Ay. You may turn that way: it is a grave
Which will bear looking at.

LEONARD

        These boys—I hope
They loved this good old man?

PRIEST

        They did—and truly:
But that was what we almost overlooked,
They were such darlings of each other. For   240
Though from their cradles they had lived with Walter,
The only kinsman near them in the house,
Yet he being old, they had much love to spare,
And it all went into each other's hearts.
Leonard, the elder by just eighteen months,   245
Was two years taller: 'twas a joy to see,
To hear, to meet them! from their house the school
Was distant three short miles; and in the time
Of storm and thaw, when every water-course
And unbridged stream, such as you may have   250
    noticed
Crossing our roads at every hundred steps,
Was swollen into a noisy rivulet,

Would Leonard then, when elder boys perhaps
Remained at home, go staggering through the fords
Bearing his brother on his back. I've seen him   255
On windy days, in one of those stray brooks,
Ay, more than once I've seen him mid-leg deep,
Their two books lying both on a dry stone
Upon the hither side; and once I said,
As I remember, looking round these rocks   260
And hills on which we all of us were born,
That God who made the great book of the world
Would bless such piety—

LEONARD
It may be then—

PRIEST
Never did worthier lads break English bread!
The finest Sunday that the autumn saw,   265
With all its mealy clusters of ripe nuts,
Could never keep these boys away from church,
Or tempt them to an hour of sabbath breach.
Leonard and James! I warrant, every corner
Among these rocks, and every hollow place   270
Where foot could come, to one or both of them
Was known as well as to the flowers that grow there.
Like roebucks they went bounding o'er the hills;
They played like two young ravens on the crags;
Then they could write, ay and speak too, as well   275
As many of their betters; and for Leonard!
The very night before he went away,
In my own house I put into his hand
A Bible, and I'd wager twenty pounds
That if he is alive, he has it yet.   280

LEONARD
It seems these brothers have not lived to be
A comfort to each other.

PRIEST
        That they might
Live to that end, is what both old and young
In this our valley all of us have wished,
And what, for my part, I have often prayed: 285
But Leonard—

LEONARD
        Then James still is left among you?

PRIEST
'Tis of the elder brother I am speaking:
They had an uncle, he was at that time
A thriving man, and trafficked on the seas;
And but for this same uncle, to this hour   290
Leonard had never handled rope or shroud.
For the boy loved the life which we lead here;
And though a very stripling, twelve years old,
His soul was knit to this his native soil.
But as I said, old Walter was too weak   295
To strive with such a torrent: when he died
The estate and house were sold, and all their sheep,
A pretty flock, and which for aught I know
Had clothed the Ewbanks for a thousand years.
Well—all was gone, and they were destitute.   300
And Leonard, chiefly for his brother's sake,
Resolved to try his fortune on the seas.
'Tis now twelve years since we had tidings from him.
If there was one among us who had heard
That Leonard Ewbank was come home again,   305
From the Great Gavel down by Leeza's banks,
And down the Enna far as Egremont
The day would be a very festival,
And those two bells of ours, which there you see
Hanging in the open air—but, O good sir!   310
This is sad talk—they'll never sound for him
Living or dead. When last we heard of him
161

He was in slavery among the Moors
Upon the Barbary coast. 'Twas not a little
That would bring down his spirit, and no doubt   315
Before it ended in his death the lad
Was sadly crossed. Poor Leonard! When we parted,
He took me by the hand and said to me,
If ever the day came when he was rich,
He would return, and on his father's land   320
He would grow old among us.

LEONARD

If that day
Should come, 'twould needs be a glad day for him;
He would himself, no doubt, be happy then
As any that should meet him—

PRIEST

Happy! Sir,—

LEONARD

You said his kindred all were in their graves,   325
And that he had one brother—

PRIEST

That is but
A fellow tale of sorrow. From his youth
James, though not sickly, yet was delicate;
And Leonard being always by his side
Had done so many offices about him   330
That, though he was not of a timid nature,
Yet still the spirit of a mountain boy
In him was somewhat checked; and when his brother
Was gone to sea and he was left alone,
The little colour that he had was soon   335
Stolen from his cheek, he drooped, and pined and
     pined—

LEONARD

But these are all the graves of full-grown men!

162

PRIEST

Ay, sir, that passed away: we took him to us.
He was the child of all the dale—he lived
Three months with one, and six months with   340
   another;
And wanted neither food, nor clothes, nor love:
And many, many happy days were his.
But whether blithe or sad, 'tis my belief
His absent brother still was at his heart.
And when he lived beneath our roof, we found   345
(A practice till this time unknown to him)
That often, rising from his bed at night,
He in his sleep would walk about, and sleeping
He sought his brother Leonard.—You are moved!
Forgive me, sir: before I spoke to you   350
I judged you most unkindly.

LEONARD

          But this youth,
How did he die at last?

PRIEST

         One sweet May morning,
It will be twelve years since when spring returns,
He had gone forth among the new-dropped lambs,
With two or three companions whom it chanced   355
Some further business summoned to a house
Which stands at the dale-head. James, tired perhaps,
Or from some other cause, remained behind.
You see yon precipice—it almost looks
Like some vast building made of many crags;   360
And in the midst is one particular rock
That rises like a column from the vale,
Whence by our shepherds it is called the Pillar.
James pointed to its summit, over which
They all had purposed to return together,   365
And told them that he there would wait for them:

They parted, and his comrades passed that way
Some two hours after, but they did not find him
Upon the Pillar at the appointed place.
Of this they took no heed: but one of them,   370
Going by chance at night into the house
Which at that time was James's home, there learned
That nobody had seen him all that day:
The morning came, and still he was unheard of:
The neighbours were alarmed, and to the brook   375
Some went, and some towards the lake: ere noon
They found him at the foot of that same rock—
Dead, and with mangled limbs. The third day after
I buried him, poor lad, and there he lies.

LEONARD

And that then *is* his grave?—Before his death   380
You said that he saw many happy years?

PRIEST

Ay, that he did—

LEONARD

And all went well with him—

PRIEST

If he had one, the lad had twenty homes.

LEONARD

And you believe, then, that his mind was easy—

PRIEST

Yes, long before he died, he found that time   385
Is a true friend to sorrow; and unless
His thoughts were turned on Leonard's luckless
    fortune,
He talked about him with a cheerful love.

LEONARD

He could not come to an unhallowed end?

PRIEST

Nay, God forbid! You recollect I mentioned   390
A habit which disquietude and grief
Had brought upon him; and we all conjectured
That as the day was warm, he had lain down
Upon the grass and, waiting for his comrades,
He there had fallen asleep; that in his sleep   395
He to the margin of the precipice
Had walked, and from the summit had fallen
    headlong,
And so no doubt he perished; at the time
We guess that in his hands he must have had
His shepherd's staff: for midway in the cliff   400
It had been caught; and there for many years
It hung, and mouldered there.

                    The priest here ended;
The stranger would have thanked him, but he felt
Tears rushing in. Both left the spot in silence;
And Leonard, when they reached the churchyard   405
    gate,
As the priest lifted up the latch, turned round,
And, looking at the grave, he said, 'My brother.'
The vicar did not hear the words; and now,
Pointing towards the cottage, he entreated
That Leonard would partake his homely fare;   410
The other thanked him with a fervent voice,
But added that, the evening being calm,
He would pursue his journey. So they parted.

It was not long ere Leonard reached a grove
That overhung the road; he there stopped short,   415
And, sitting down beneath the trees, reviewed
All that the priest had said: his early years
Were with him in his heart; his cherished hopes
And thoughts which had been his an hour before

All pressed on him with such a weight, that now 420
This vale, where he had been so happy, seemed
A place in which he could not bear to live:
So he relinquished all his purposes.
He travelled on to Egremont; and thence,
That night, he wrote a letter to the priest 425
Reminding him of what had passed between them;
And adding, with a hope to be forgiven,
That it was from the weakness of his heart
He had not dared to tell him who he was.

This done, he went on shipboard, and is now 430
A seaman, a grey-headed mariner.

ELLEN IRWIN

OR, THE BRAES OF KIRTLE

Fair Ellen Irwin, when she sate
Upon the braes of Kirtle,
Was lovely as a Grecian maid
Adorned with wreaths of myrtle.
Young Adam Bruce beside her lay; 5
And there did they beguile the day
With love and gentle speeches,
Beneath the budding beeches.

From many knights and many squires
The Bruce had been selected; 10
And Gordon, fairest of them all,
By Ellen was rejected.
Sad tidings to that noble youth!
For it may be proclaimed with truth,
If Bruce hath loved sincerely, 15
The Gordon loves as dearly.

But what is Gordon's beauteous face?
And what are Gordon's crosses
To them who sit by Kirtle's braes
Upon the verdant mosses?   20
Alas that ever he was born!
The Gordon, couched behind a thorn,
Sees them and their caressing,
Beholds them blest and blessing.

Proud Gordon cannot bear the thoughts   25
That through his brain are travelling,
And starting up, to Bruce's heart
He launched a deadly javelin!
Fair Ellen saw it when it came,
And stepping forth to meet the same,   30
Did with her body cover
The youth her chosen lover.

And, falling into Bruce's arms,
Thus died the beauteous Ellen,
Thus from the heart of her true-love   35
The mortal spear repelling.
And Bruce, as soon as he had slain
The Gordon, sailed away to Spain;
And fought with rage incessant
Against the Moorish crescent.   40

But many days, and many months,
And many years ensuing,
This wretched knight did vainly seek
The death that he was wooing:
And coming back across the wave,   45
Without a groan on Ellen's grave
His body he extended,
And there his sorrow ended.

Now ye, who willingly have heard
The tale I have been telling,   50
May in Kirkonnel churchyard view
The grave of lovely Ellen;
By Ellen's side the Bruce is laid;
And, for the stone upon his head,
May no rude hand deface it,   55
And its forlorn HIC JACET!

'STRANGE FITS OF PASSION
I HAVE KNOWN'

Strange fits of passion I have known:
And I will dare to tell,
But in the lover's ear alone,
What once to me befell.

When she I loved was strong and gay   5
And like a rose in June,
I to her cottage bent my way,
Beneath the evening moon.

Upon the moon I fixed my eye,
All over the wide lea;   10
My horse trudged on—and we drew nigh
Those paths so dear to me.

And now we reached the orchard plot;
And, as we climbed the hill,
Towards the roof of Lucy's cot   15
The moon descended still.

In one of those sweet dreams I slept,
Kind Nature's gentlest boon!
And, all the while, my eyes I kept
On the descending moon.   20

My horse moved on; hoof after hoof
He raised, and never stopped:
When down behind the cottage roof
At once the planet dropped.

What fond and wayward thoughts will slide   25
Into a lover's head—
'O mercy!' to myself I cried,
'If Lucy should be dead!'

'SHE DWELT AMONG TH' UNTRODDEN WAYS'

She dwelt among th' untrodden ways
    Beside the springs of Dove,
A maid whom there were none to praise,
    And very few to love.

A violet by a mossy stone   5
    Half-hidden from the eye!
—Fair as a star, when only one
    Is shining in the sky.

She lived unknown, and few could know
    When Lucy ceased to be;   10
But she is in her grave, and oh!
    The difference to me.

'A SLUMBER DID MY SPIRIT SEAL'

A slumber did my spirit seal;
    I had no human fears:
She seemed a thing that could not feel
    The touch of earthly years.

No motion has she now, no force;   5
    She neither hears nor sees,
Rolled round in earth's diurnal course
    With rocks and stones and trees.

THE WATERFALL AND
THE EGLANTINE

'Begone, thou fond presumptuous elf,'
Exclaimed a thundering voice,
'Nor dare to thrust thy foolish self
Between me and my choice!'
A falling water swollen with snows   5
Thus spake to a poor briar-rose,
That, all bespattered with his foam,
And dancing high, and dancing low,
Was living, as a child might know,
In an unhappy home.   10

'Dost thou presume my course to block?
Off, off! or, puny thing,
I'll hurl thee headlong with the rock
To which thy fibres cling.'
The flood was tyrannous and strong;   15
The patient briar suffered long,
Nor did he utter groan or sigh,
Hoping the danger would be past:
But seeing no relief, at last
He ventured to reply.   20

'Ah!' said the briar, 'blame me not;
Why should we dwell in strife?
We who in this, our natal spot,
Once lived a happy life!
You stirred me on my rocky bed—   25
What pleasure through my veins you spread!
The summer long from day to day
My leaves you freshened and bedewed;
Nor was it common gratitude
That did your cares repay.   30

'When spring came on with bud and bell,
Among these rocks did I
Before you hang my wreath, to tell
That gentle days were nigh!
And in the sultry summer hours   35
I sheltered you with leaves and flowers;
And in my leaves, now shed and gone,
The linnet lodged, and for us two
Chanted his pretty songs, when you
Had little voice or none.   40

'But now proud thoughts are in your breast—
What grief is mine you see.
Ah! would you think, even yet how blest
Together we might be!
Though of both leaf and flower bereft,   45
Some ornaments to me are left—
Rich store of scarlet hips is mine,
With which I in my humble way
Would deck you many a winter's day,
A happy eglantine!'   50

What more he said I cannot tell.
The stream came thundering down the dell,
And galloped loud and fast;
I listened, nor aught else could hear,
The briar quaked—and much I fear   55
Those accents were his last.

THE OAK AND THE BROOM

A PASTORAL

His simple truths did Andrew glean
Beside the babbling rills;
A careful student he had been
Among the woods and hills.

One winter's night when through the trees 5
The wind was thundering, on his knees
His youngest born did Andrew hold:
And while the rest, a ruddy choir,
Were seated round their blazing fire,
This tale the shepherd told. 10

'I saw a crag, a lofty stone
As ever tempest beat!
Out of its head an oak had grown,
A broom out of its feet.
The time was March, a cheerful noon— 15
The thaw-wind with the breath of June
Breathed gently from the warm south-west;
When, in a voice sedate with age,
This oak, half giant and half sage,
His neighbour thus addressed: 20

' "Eight weary weeks, through rock and clay,
Along this mountain's edge
The frost hath wrought both night and day,
Wedge driving after wedge.
Look up! and think, above your head 25
What trouble surely will be bred;
Last night I heard a crash—'tis true,
The splinters took another road,
I see them yonder—what a load
For such a thing as you! 30

' "You are preparing as before
To deck your slender shape;
And yet, just three years back—no more—
You had a strange escape.
Down from yon cliff a fragment broke, 35
It came, you know, with fire and smoke
And hitherward it bent its way.

This ponderous block was caught by me,
And o'er your head, as you may see,
'Tis hanging to this day!   40

' "The thing had better been asleep,
Whatever thing it were,
Or breeze, or bird, or dog, or sheep,
That first did plant you there.
For you and your green twigs decoy   45
The little witless shepherd-boy
To come and slumber in your bower;
And trust me, on some sultry noon,
Both you and he, Heaven knows how soon!
Will perish in one hour.   50

' "From me this friendly warning take—"
The broom began to doze,
And thus to keep herself awake
Did gently interpose:
"My thanks for your discourse are due;   55
That it is true, and more than true,
I know, and I have known it long;
Frail is the bond by which we hold
Our being, be we young or old,
Wise, foolish, weak or strong.   60

' "Disasters, do the best we can,
Will reach both great and small;
And he is oft the wisest man
Who is not wise at all.
For me, why should I wish to roam?   65
This spot is my paternal home,
It is my pleasant heritage;
My father many a happy year
Here spread his careless blossoms, here
Attained a good old age.   70

  ' "Even such as his may be my lot.
What cause have I to haunt
My heart with terrors? Am I not
In truth a favoured plant?
The spring for me a garland weaves   75
Of yellow flowers and verdant leaves;
And when the frost is in the sky
My branches are so fresh and gay,
That you might look at me and say,
This plant can never die.   80

  ' "The butterfly, all green and gold,
To me hath often flown,
Here in my blossoms to behold
Wings lovely as his own.
When grass is chill with rain or dew,   85
Beneath my shade the mother ewe
Lies with her infant lamb; I see
The love they each to other make,
And the sweet joy which they partake,
It is a joy to me."   90

  'Her voice was blithe, her heart was light;
The broom might have pursued
Her speech, until the stars of night
Their journey had renewed.
But in the branches of the oak   95
Two ravens now began to croak
Their nuptial song, a gladsome air;
And to her own green bower the breeze
That instant brought two stripling bees
To feed and murmur there.   100

  'One night the wind came from the north
And blew a furious blast;
At break of day I ventured forth,
And near the cliff I passed.

The storm had fallen upon the oak   105
And struck him with a mighty stroke,
And whirled and whirled him far away;
And in one hospitable cleft
The little careless broom was left
To live for many a day.'   110

THE COMPLAINT OF A FORSAKEN INDIAN WOMAN

[*When a Northern Indian, from sickness, is unable to continue his journey with his companions, he is left behind, covered over with deer-skins; and is supplied with water, food, and fuel, if the situation of the place will afford it. He is informed of the track which his companions intend to pursue, and if he is unable to follow or overtake them he perishes alone in the desert, unless he should have the good fortune to fall in with some other tribes of Indians. The females are equally, or still more, exposed to the same fate. See that very interesting work, Hearne's* Journey from Hudson's Bay to the Northern Ocean. *In the high northern latitudes, as the same writer informs us, when the Northern Lights vary their position in the air they make a rustling and a crackling noise. This circumstance is alluded to in the first stanza of the following poem.*]

Before I see another day,
Oh let my body die away!
In sleep I heard the northern gleams;
The stars they were among my dreams;
In sleep did I behold the skies;   5
I saw the crackling flashes drive;
And yet they are upon my eyes,
And yet I am alive.
Before I see another day,
Oh let my body die away!   10

My fire is dead: it knew no pain;
Yet it is dead, and I remain.
All stiff with ice the ashes lie;
And they are dead, and I will die.
When I was well I wished to live,   15
For clothes, for warmth, for food and fire;
But they to me no joy can give,
No pleasure now, and no desire.
Then here contented will I lie!
Alone I cannot fear to die.   20

Alas! you might have dragged me on
Another day, a single one!
Too soon despair o'er me prevailed;
Too soon my heartless spirit failed;
When you were gone my limbs were stronger;   25
And oh, how grievously I rue
That afterwards, a little longer,
My friends, I did not follow you!
For strong and without pain I lay,
My friends, when you were gone away.   30

My child! they gave thee to another,
A woman who was not thy mother.
When from my arms my babe they took,
On me how strangely did he look!
Through his whole body something ran,   35
A most strange something did I see—
As if he strove to be a man,
That he might pull the sledge for me.
And then he stretched his arms, how wild!
Oh mercy! like a little child.   40

My little joy! my little pride!
In two days more I must have died.
Then do not weep and grieve for me;

I feel I must have died with thee.
Oh wind, that o'er my head art flying   45
The way my friends their course did bend,
I should not feel the pain of dying,
Could I with thee a message send!
Too soon, my friends, you went away;
For I had many things to say.   50

I'll follow you across the snow;
You travel heavily and slow:
In spite of all my weary pain,
I'll look upon your tents again.
—My fire is dead, and snowy white   55
The water which beside it stood;
The wolf has come to me tonight,
And he has stolen away my food.
For ever left alone am I,
Then wherefore should I fear to die?   60

My journey will be shortly run,
I shall not see another sun;
I cannot lift my limbs to know
If they have any life or no.
My poor forsaken child! if I   65
For once could have thee close to me,
With happy heart I then should die,
And my last thoughts would happy be.
I feel my body die away,
I shall not see another day.   70

LUCY GRAY

Oft I had heard of Lucy Gray:
And, when I crossed the wild,
I chanced to see at break of day
The solitary child.

No mate, no comrade Lucy knew;   5
She dwelt on a wide moor—
The sweetest thing that ever grew
Beside a human door!

You yet may spy the fawn at play,
The hare upon the green;   10
But the sweet face of Lucy Gray
Will never more be seen.

'Tonight will be a stormy night;
You to the town must go,
And take a lantern, child, to light   15
Your mother through the snow.'

'That, father, will I gladly do;
'Tis scarcely afternoon:
The Minster clock has just struck two,
And yonder is the moon.'   20

At this the father raised his hook
And snapped a faggot-band;
He plied his work, and Lucy took
The lantern in her hand.

Not blither is the mountain roe: 25
With many a wanton stroke
Her feet disperse the powdery snow,
That rises up like smoke.

The storm came on before its time:
She wandered up and down;   30
And many a hill did Lucy climb,
But never reached the town.

The wretched parents all that night
Went shouting far and wide;
But there was neither sound nor sight   35
To serve them for a guide.

At daybreak on a hill they stood
That overlooked the moor;
And thence they saw the bridge of wood,
A furlong from their door.   40

And now they homeward turned, and cried
'In Heaven we all shall meet!'
—When in the snow the mother spied
The print of Lucy's feet.

Then downward from the steep hill's edge   45
They tracked the footmarks small;
And through the broken hawthorn-hedge,
And by the long stone-wall:

And then an open field they crossed:
The marks were still the same;   50
They tracked them on, nor ever lost;
And to the bridge they came.

They followed from the snowy bank
The footmarks, one by one,
Into the middle of the plank;   55
And further there was none.

—Yet some maintain that to this day
She is a living child;
That you may see sweet Lucy Gray
Upon the lonesome wild.   60

O'er rough and smooth she trips along,
And never looks behind;
And sings a solitary song
That whistles in the wind.

''TIS SAID, THAT SOME HAVE DIED FOR LOVE'

'Tis said, that some have died for love:
And here and there a churchyard grave is found
In the cold North's unhallowed ground,
Because the wretched man himself had slain,
His love was such a grievous pain.   5
And there is one whom I five years have known:
He dwells alone
Upon Helvellyn's side;
He loved—the pretty Barbara died,
And thus he makes his moan: 10
Three years had Barbara in her grave been laid
When thus his moan he made:

'Oh move, thou cottage, from behind that oak!
Or let the aged tree uprooted lie,
That in some other way yon smoke   15
May mount into the sky!
The clouds pass on; they from the heavens depart:
I look—the sky is empty space;
I know not what I trace;
But, when I cease to look, my hand is on my heart.   20

'Oh! what a weight is in these shades! Ye leaves,
When will that dying murmur be suppressed?
Your sound my heart of peace bereaves,
It robs my heart of rest.
Thou thrush, that singest loud and loud and free,   25
Into yon row of willows flit,
Upon that alder sit;
Or sing another song, or choose another tree.

'Roll back, sweet rill! back to thy mountain bounds,
And there for ever be thy waters chained!   30
For thou dost haunt the air with sounds
That cannot be sustained;
If still beneath that pine-tree's ragged bough
Headlong yon waterfall must come,
Oh let it then be dumb!   35
Be any thing, sweet rill, but that which thou art now.

'Thou eglantine, whose arch so proudly towers
(Even like the rainbow spanning half the vale),
Thou one fair shrub, oh! shed thy flowers,
And stir not in the gale.   40
For thus to see thee nodding in the air,
To see thy arch thus stretch and bend,
Thus rise and thus descend,
Disturbs me, till the sight is more than I can bear.'

The man who makes this feverish complaint   45
Is one of giant stature, who could dance
Equipped from head to foot in iron mail.
Ah gentle Love! if ever thought was thine
To store up kindred hours for me, thy face
Turn from me, gentle Love! nor let me walk   50
Within the sound of Emma's voice, or know
Such happiness as I have known today.

THE IDLE SHEPHERD-BOYS

OR

DUNGEON-GILL FORCE*

A PASTORAL

I

The valley rings with mirth and joy;
Among the hills the echoes play
A never never ending song
To welcome in the May.
The magpie chatters with delight;   5
The mountain raven's youngling brood
Have left the mother and the nest,
And they go rambling east and west
In search of their own food;
Or through the glittering vapours dart   10
In very wantonness of heart.

II

Beneath a rock, upon the grass,
Two boys are sitting in the sun;
It seems they have no work to do,
Or that their work is done.   15
On pipes of sycamore they play
The fragments of a Christmas hymn;
Or with that plant which in our dale
We call stag-horn, or fox's-tail,
Their rusty hats they trim: 20
And thus, as happy as the day,
Those shepherds wear the time away.

Gill in the dialect of Cumberland and Westmorland is a short and, for the most part, a steep narrow valley, with a stream running through it. *Force* is the word universally employed in these dialects for *waterfall*. [Wordsworth's note.]

20. *rusty:* shabby, worn or faded

III

Along the river's stony marge
The sand-lark chants a joyous song;
The thrush is busy in the wood,   25
And carols loud and strong.
A thousand lambs are on the rocks,
All newly-born! Both earth and sky
Keep jubilee; and more than all,
Those boys with their green coronal;   30
They never hear the cry,
The plaintive cry! which up the hill
Comes from the depth of Dungeon-Gill.

IV

Said Walter, leaping from the ground,
'Down to the stump of yon old yew   35
We'll for our whistles run a race.'
Away the shepherds flew.
They leapt—they ran—and when they came
Right opposite to Dungeon-Gill,
Seeing that he should lose the prize,   40
'Stop!' to his comrade Walter cries—
James stopped with no good will;
Said Walter then, 'Your task is here,
'Twill keep you working half a year.

V

'Now cross where I shall cross—come on,   45
And follow me where I shall lead.'
The other took him at his word,
But did not like the deed.
It was a spot which you may see
If ever you to Langdale go: 50
Into a chasm a mighty block
Hath fallen, and made a bridge of rock;
The gulf is deep below,
And in a basin black and small
Receives a lofty waterfall.   55

VI

With staff in hand across the cleft
The challenger began his march;
And now, all eyes and feet, hath gained
The middle of the arch.
When list! he hears a piteous moan—⠀⠀⠀⠀⠀60
Again! his heart within him dies,
His pulse is stopped, his breath is lost,
He totters, pale as any ghost,
And looking down, he spies
A lamb, that in the pool is pent⠀⠀⠀⠀⠀65
Within that black and frightful rent.

VII

The lamb had slipped into the stream,
And safe without a bruise or wound
The cataract had borne him down
Into the gulf profound.⠀⠀⠀⠀⠀70
His dam had seen him when he fell,
She saw him down the torrent borne;
And while with all a mother's love
She from the lofty rocks above
Sent forth a cry forlorn,⠀⠀⠀⠀⠀75
The lamb, still swimming round and round,
Made answer to that plaintive sound.

VIII

When he had learnt what thing it was
That sent this rueful cry, I ween
The boy recovered heart, and told⠀⠀⠀⠀⠀80
The sight which he had seen.
Both gladly now deferred their task;
Nor was there wanting other aid—
A poet, one who loves the brooks
Far better than the sages' books,⠀⠀⠀⠀⠀85
By chance had hither strayed;
And there the helpless lamb he found
By those huge rocks encompassed round.

IX

He drew it gently from the pool,
And brought it forth into the light: 90
The shepherds met him with his charge,
An unexpected sight!
Into their arms the lamb they took,
Said they, 'He's neither maimed nor scarred.'
Then up the steep ascent they hied,   95
And placed him at his mother's side;
And gently did the bard
Those idle shepherd-boys upbraid,
And bade them better mind their trade.

POOR SUSAN

At the corner of Wood Street, when daylight appears,
There's a thrush that sings loud, it has sung for three
    years:
Poor Susan has passed by the spot, and has heard
In the silence of morning the song of the bird.

'Tis a note of enchantment; what ails her? She sees   5
A mountain ascending, a vision of trees;
Bright volumes of vapour through Lothbury glide,
And a river flows on through the vale of Cheapside.

Green pastures she views in the midst of the dale,
Down which she so often has tripped with her pail;   10
And a single small cottage, a nest like a dove's,
The one only dwelling on earth that she loves.

She looks, and her heart is in heaven: but they fade,
The mist and the river, the hill and the shade;
The stream will not flow, and the hill will not rise,   15
And the colours have all passed away from her eyes.

INSCRIPTION

If thou in the dear love of some one friend
Hast been so happy, that thou know'st what thoughts
Will sometimes in the happiness of love
Make the heart sick, then wilt thou reverence
This quiet spot. St. Herbert hither came,   5
And here for many seasons, from the world
Removed, and from the affections of the world,
He dwelt in solitude. But he had left
A fellow-labourer, whom the good man loved
As his own soul. And when within his cave   10
Alone he knelt before the crucifix,
While o'er the lake the cataract of Lodore
Pealed to his orisons, and when he paced
Along the beach of this small isle and thought
Of his companion, he would pray that both   15
Might die in the same moment. Nor in vain
So prayed he: as our chronicles report,
Though here the hermit numbered his last days
Far from St. Cuthbert his beloved friend,
Those holy men both died in the same hour.   20

LINES

WRITTEN WITH A PENCIL UPON A STONE IN THE WALL OF
THE HOUSE (AN OUT-HOUSE) ON THE ISLAND AT GRASMERE.

Rude is this edifice, and thou hast seen
Buildings, albeit rude, that have maintained
Proportions more harmonious, and approached
To somewhat of a closer fellowship
With the ideal grace. Yet as it is   5

Do take it in good part; for he, the poor
Vitruvius of our village, had no help
From the great city; never on the leaves
Of red morocco folio saw displayed
The skeletons and pre-existing ghosts   10
Of beauties yet unborn, the rustic box,
Snug cot, with coach-house, shed and hermitage.
It is a homely pile, yet to these walls
The heifer comes in the snow-storm, and here
The new-dropped lamb finds shelter from the wind. 15
And hither does one poet sometimes row
His pinnace, a small vagrant barge, up-piled
With plenteous store of heath and withered fern
(A lading which he with his sickle cuts
Among the mountains), and beneath this roof   20
He makes his summer couch, and here at noon
Spreads out his limbs, while, yet unshorn, the sheep
Panting beneath the burthen of their wool
Lie round him, even as if they were a part
Of his own household: nor, while from his bed   25
He through that door-place looks toward the lake
And to the stirring breezes, does he want
Creations lovely as the work of sleep,
Fair sights, and visions of romantic joy.

TO A SEXTON

Let thy wheelbarrow alone.
Wherefore, Sexton, piling still
In thy bone-house bone on bone?
'Tis already like a hill
In a field of battle made,   5
Where three thousand skulls are laid.
These died in peace each with the other,
Father, sister, friend, and brother.

187

Mark the spot to which I point!
From this platform eight feet square   10
Take not even a finger-joint:
Andrew's whole fire-side is there.
Here, alone, before thine eyes
Simon's sickly daughter lies,
From weakness now and pain defended,   15
Whom he twenty winters tended.

Look but at the gardener's pride:
How he glories, when he sees
Roses, lilies, side by side,
Violets in families!   20
By the heart of man, his tears,
By his hopes and by his fears,
Thou, old greybeard! art the warden
Of a far superior garden.

Thus then, each to other dear,   25
Let them all in quiet lie,
Andrew there and Susan here,
Neighbours in mortality.
And, should I live through sun and rain
Seven widowed years without my Jane,   30
O sexton, do not then remove her,
Let one grave hold the loved and lover!

ANDREW JONES

'I hate that Andrew Jones: he'll breed
His children up to waste and pillage.
I wish the press-gang or the drum
With its tantara sound, would come
And sweep him from the village!'   5

I said not this because he loves
Through the long day to swear and tipple;
But for the poor dear sake of one
To whom a foul deed he had done,
A friendless man, a travelling cripple.   10

For this poor crawling helpless wretch
Some horseman who was passing by
A penny on the ground had thrown;
But the poor cripple was alone,
And could not stoop; no help was nigh.   15

Inch-thick the dust lay on the ground,
For it had long been droughty weather:
So with his staff the cripple wrought
Among the dust till he had brought
The halfpennies together.   20

It chanced that Andrew passed that way
Just at the time; and there he found
The cripple in the mid-day heat
Standing alone, and at his feet
He saw the penny on the ground.   25

He stooped and took the penny up:
And when the cripple nearer drew,
Quoth Andrew, 'Under half-a-crown,
What a man finds is all his own,
And so, my friend, good-day to you.'   30

And *hence* I said, that Andrew's boys
Will all be trained to waste and pillage;
And wished the press-gang, or the drum
With its tantara sound, would come
And sweep him from the village!   35

RUTH

When Ruth was left half-desolate
Her father took another mate;
And Ruth, not seven years old,
A slighted child, at her own will
Went wandering over dale and hill,   5
In thoughtless freedom bold.

And she had made a pipe of straw,
And from that oaten pipe could draw
All sounds of winds and floods;
Had built a bower upon the green,   10
As if she from her birth had been
An infant of the woods.

Beneath her father's roof, alone
She seemed to live; her thoughts her own;
Herself her own delight: 15
Pleased with herself, nor sad nor gay,
She passed her time; and in this way
Grew up to woman's height.

There came a youth from Georgia's shore:
A military casque he wore   20
With splendid feathers dressed;
He brought them from the Cherokees;
The feathers nodded in the breeze,
And made a gallant crest.

From Indian blood you deem him sprung: 25
Ah, no! he spake the English tongue,
And bore a soldier's name;
And when America was free
From battle and from jeopardy,
He 'cross the ocean came.   30

With hues of genius on his cheek
In finest tones the youth could speak;
While he was yet a boy,
The moon, the glory of the sun,
And streams that murmur as they run,   35
Had been his dearest joy.

He was a lovely youth! I guess
The panther in the wilderness
Was not so fair as he;
And when he chose to sport and play,   40
No dolphin ever was so gay
Upon the tropic sea.

Among the Indians he had fought;
And with him many tales he brought
Of pleasure and of fear;   45
Such tales as, told to any maid
By such a youth in the green shade,
Were perilous to hear.

He told of girls, a happy rout!
Who quit their fold with dance and shout,   50
Their pleasant Indian town,
To gather strawberries all day long,
Returning with a choral song
When daylight is gone down.

He spake of plants divine and strange   55
That every hour their blossoms change,
Ten thousand lovely hues!
With budding, fading, faded flowers
They stand the wonder of the bowers
From morn to evening dews.   60

Of march and ambush, siege and fight,
Then did he tell; and with delight
The heart of Ruth would ache;
Wild histories they were, and dear:
But 'twas a thing of heaven to hear   65
When of himself he spake!

Sometimes most earnestly he said:
'Oh Ruth! I have been worse than dead;
False thoughts, thoughts bold and vain,
Encompassed me on every side   70
When I, in confidence and pride,
Had crossed the Atlantic main.

'It was a fresh and glorious world,
A banner bright that was unfurled
Before me suddenly: 75
I looked upon those hills and plains,
And seemed as if let loose from chains
To live at liberty.

'But wherefore speak of this? for now,
Sweet Ruth! with thee, I know not how,   80
I feel my spirit burn;
Even as the east when day comes forth,
And to the west, and south, and north,
The morning doth return.

'It is a purer, better mind: 85
O maiden innocent and kind,
What sights I might have seen!
Even now upon my eyes they break!'
—And he again began to speak
Of lands where he had been.   90

He told of the magnolia, spread
High as a cloud, high overhead!
The cypress and her spire;
Of flowers that with one scarlet gleam
Cover a hundred leagues, and seem   95
To set the hills on fire.

The youth of green savannahs spake,
And many an endless, endless lake,
With all its fairy crowds
Of islands, that together lie   100
As quietly as spots of sky
Among the evening clouds.

And then he said, 'How sweet it were
A fisher or a hunter there,
A gardener in the shade,   105
Still wandering with an easy mind
To build a household fire, and find
A home in every glade!

'What days and what sweet years! Ah me!
Our life were life indeed, with thee   110
So passed in quiet bliss,
And all the while,' said he, 'to know
That we were in a world of woe,
On such an earth as this!'

And then he sometimes interwove   115
Dear thoughts about a father's love;
'For there,' said he, 'are spun
Around the heart such tender ties,
That our own children to our eyes
Are dearer than the sun.   120

'Sweet Ruth! and could you go with me
My helpmate in the woods to be,
Our shed at night to rear;
Or run, my own adopted bride,
A sylvan huntress at my side,   125
And drive the flying deer!

'Beloved Ruth!'—No more he said.
Sweet Ruth alone at midnight shed
A solitary tear.
She thought again—and did agree   130
With him to sail across the sea,
And drive the flying deer.

'And now, as fitting is and right,
We in the church our faith will plight,
A husband and a wife.'   135
Even so they did; and I may say
That to sweet Ruth that happy day
Was more than human life.

Through dream and vision did she sink,
Delighted all the while to think   140
That on those lonesome floods
And green savannahs, she should share
His board with lawful joy, and bear
His name in the wild woods.

But, as you have before been told,   145
This stripling, sportive, gay and bold,
And with his dancing crest
So beautiful, through savage lands
Had roamed about with vagrant bands
Of Indians in the west.   150

194

The wind, the tempest roaring high,
The tumult of a tropic sky,
Might well be dangerous food
For him, a youth to whom was given
So much of earth, so much of Heaven,   155
And such impetuous blood.

Whatever in those climes he found
Irregular in sight or sound
Did to his mind impart
A kindred impulse, seemed allied   160
To his own powers, and justified
The workings of his heart.

Nor less to feed voluptuous thought
The beauteous forms of nature wrought,
Fair trees and lovely flowers;   165
The breezes their own languor lent;
The stars had feelings, which they sent
Into those magic bowers.

Yet, in his worst pursuits, I ween
That sometimes there did intervene   170
Pure hopes of high intent;
For passions linked to forms so fair
And stately, needs must have their share
Of noble sentiment.

But ill he lived, much evil saw   175
With men to whom no better law
Nor better life was known;
Deliberately and undeceived
Those wild men's vices he received,
And gave them back his own.   180

His genius and his moral frame
Were thus impaired, and he became
The slave of low desires:
A man who without self-control
Would seek what the degraded soul   185
Unworthily admires.

And yet he with no feigned delight
Had wooed the maiden, day and night
Had loved her, night and morn:
What could he less than love a maid   190
Whose heart with so much nature played?
So kind and so forlorn?

But now the pleasant dream was gone;
No hope, no wish remained, not one,
They stirred him now no more;   195
New objects did new pleasure give,
And once again he wished to live
As lawless as before.

Meanwhile, as thus with him it fared,
They for the voyage were prepared,   200
And went to the sea-shore;
But when they thither came, the youth
Deserted his poor bride, and Ruth
Could never find him more.

'God help thee, Ruth!'—Such pains she had   205
That she in half a year was mad,
And in a prison housed;
And there, exulting in her wrongs,
Among the music of her songs
She fearfully caroused.   210

Yet sometimes milder hours she knew,
Nor wanted sun, nor rain, nor dew,
Nor pastimes of the May—
They all were with her in her cell;
And a wild brook with cheerful knell   215
Did o'er the pebbles play.

When Ruth three seasons thus had lain
There came a respite to her pain,
She from her prison fled;
But of the vagrant none took thought;   220
And where it liked her best she sought
Her shelter and her bread.

Among the fields she breathed again:
The master-current of her brain
Ran permanent and free;   225
And coming to the banks of Tone,
There did she rest; and dwell alone
Under the greenwood tree.

The engines of her pain, the tools
That shaped her sorrow, rocks and pools,   230
And airs that gently stir
The vernal leaves, she loved them still,
Nor ever taxed them with the ill
Which had been done to her.

A barn her *winter* bed supplies;   235
But till the warmth of summer skies
And summer days is gone
(And all do in this tale agree),
She sleeps beneath the greenwood tree,
And other home hath none.   240

An innocent life, yet far astray!
And Ruth will long before her day
Be broken down and old.
Sore aches she needs must have! but less
Of mind, than body's wretchedness,   245
From damp and rain and cold.

If she is pressed by want of food,
She from her dwelling in the wood
Repairs to a road-side;
And there she begs at one steep place,   250
Where up and down with easy pace
The horsemen-travellers ride.

That oaten pipe of hers is mute,
Or thrown away; but with a flute
Her loneliness she cheers: 255
This flute, made of a hemlock stalk,
At evening in his homeward walk
The Quantock woodman hears.

I, too, have passed her on the hills
Setting her little water-mills   260
By spouts and fountains wild;
Such small machinery as she turned
Ere she had wept, ere she had mourned,
A young and happy child!

Farewell! and when thy days are told,   265
Ill-fated Ruth! in hallowed mould
Thy corpse shall buried be;
For thee a funeral bell shall ring,
And all the congregation sing
A Christian psalm for thee.   270

LINES

WRITTEN WITH A SLATE-PENCIL UPON A STONE, THE LARGEST OF A HEAP LYING NEAR A DESERTED QUARRY, UPON ONE OF THE ISLANDS AT RYDALE.

Stranger! this hillock of misshapen stones
Is not a ruin of the ancient time,
Nor, as perchance thou rashly deem'st, the cairn
Of some old British chief: 'tis nothing more
Than the rude embryo of a little dome   5
Or pleasure-house, once destined to be built
Among the birch-trees of this rocky isle.
But as it chanced, Sir William having learned
That from the shore a full-grown man might wade,
And make himself a freeman of the spot   10
At any hour he chose, the knight forthwith
Desisted, and the quarry and the mound
Are monuments of his unfinished task.
The block on which these lines are traced, perhaps,
Was once selected as the corner-stone   15
Of the intended pile, which would have been
Some quaint odd plaything of elaborate skill,
So that, I guess, the linnet and the thrush,
And other little builders who dwell here,
Had wondered at the work. But blame him not,   20
For old Sir William was a gentle knight
Bred in this vale, to which he appertained
With all his ancestry. Then peace to him,
And for the outrage which he had devised
Entire forgiveness! But if thou art one   25
On fire with thy impatience to become
An inmate of these mountains, if, disturbed
By beautiful conceptions, thou hast hewn
Out of the quiet rock the elements

Of thy trim mansion destined soon to blaze   30
In snow-white glory, think again, and, taught
By old Sir William and his quarry, leave
Thy fragments to the bramble and the rose;
There let the vernal slow-worm sun himself,
And let the redbreast hop from stone to stone.   35

'IF NATURE, FOR A FAVOURITE CHILD'

In the school of —— is a tablet on which are inscribed, in gilt letters, the names of the several persons who have been schoolmasters there since the foundation of the school, with the time at which they entered upon and quitted their office. Opposite one of those names the author wrote the following lines.

If Nature, for a favourite child
In thee hath tempered so her clay,
That every hour thy heart runs wild,
Yet never once doth go astray,

Read o'er these lines; and then review   5
This tablet, that thus humbly rears
In such diversity of hue
Its history of two hundred years.

When through this little wreck of fame,
Cypher and syllable! thine eye   10
Has travelled down to Matthew's name,
Pause with no common sympathy.

And if a sleeping tear should wake,
Then be it neither checked nor stayed:
For Matthew a request I make   15
Which for himself he had not made.

Poor Matthew, all his frolics o'er,
Is silent as a standing pool;
Far from the chimney's merry roar,
And murmur of the village school.   20

The sighs which Matthew heaved were sighs
Of one tired out with fun and madness;
The tears which came to Matthew's eyes
Were tears of light, the oil of gladness.

Yet sometimes, when the secret cup   25
Of still and serious thought went round,
It seemed as if he drank it up—
He felt with spirit so profound.

Thou soul of God's best earthly mould!
Thou happy soul! and can it be   30
That these two words of glittering gold
Are all that must remain to thee?

THE TWO APRIL MORNINGS

We walked along, while bright and red
Uprose the morning sun;
And Matthew stopped, he looked, and said
'The will of God be done!'

A village schoolmaster was he,   5
With hair of glittering grey;
As blithe a man as you could see
On a spring holiday.

And on that morning, through the grass
And by the steaming rills,   10
We travelled merrily, to pass
A day among the hills.

'Our work,' said I, 'was well begun;
Then from thy breast what thought,
Beneath so beautiful a sun,   15
So sad a sigh has brought?'

A second time did Matthew stop;
And fixing still his eye
Upon the eastern mountain-top,
To me he made reply: 20

'Yon cloud with that long purple cleft
Brings fresh into my mind
A day like this, which I have left
Full thirty years behind.

'And just above yon slope of corn   25
Such colours and no other
Were in the sky that April morn,
Of this the very brother.

'With rod and line my silent sport
I plied by Derwent's wave;   30
And coming to the church, stopped short
Beside my daughter's grave.

'Nine summers had she scarcely seen,
The pride of all the vale;
And then she sung; she would have been   35
A very nightingale.

'Six feet in earth my Emma lay;
And yet I loved her more,
For so it seemed, than till that day
I e'er had loved before.   40

'And turning from her grave, I met
Beside the churchyard yew
A blooming girl, whose hair was wet
With points of morning dew.

'A basket on her head she bare;45
Her brow was smooth and white:
To see a child so very fair,
It was a pure delight!

'No fountain from its rocky cave
E'er tripped with foot so free;50
She seemed as happy as a wave
That dances on the sea.

'There came from me a sigh of pain
Which I could ill confine;
I looked at her and looked again:55
—And did not wish her mine.'

Matthew is in his grave, yet now
Methinks I see him stand,
As at that moment, with his bough
Of wilding in his hand.60

60. *wilding:* wild apple-tree, crab-tree

THE FOUNTAIN

A CONVERSATION

We talked with open heart, and tongue
Affectionate and true;
A pair of friends, though I was young,
And Matthew seventy-two.

We lay beneath a spreading oak,5
Beside a mossy seat;
And from the turf a fountain broke,
And gurgled at our feet.

'Now, Matthew! let us try to match
This water's pleasant tune   10
With some old Border song, or catch
That suits a summer's noon.

'Or of the church-clock and the chimes
Sing here beneath the shade,
That half-mad thing of witty rhymes   15
Which you last April made!'

In silence Matthew lay, and eyed
The spring beneath the tree;
And thus the dear old man replied,
The grey-haired man of glee: 20

'Down to the vale this water steers,
How merrily it goes!
'Twill murmur on a thousand years,
And flow as now it flows.

'And here, on this delightful day,   25
I cannot choose but think
How oft, a vigorous man, I lay
Beside this fountain's brink.

'My eyes are dim with childish tears,
My heart is idly stirred,   30
For the same sound is in my ears
Which in those days I heard.

'Thus fares it still in our decay:
And yet the wiser mind
Mourns less for what age takes away   35
Than what it leaves behind.

'The blackbird in the summer trees,
The lark upon the hill,
Let loose their carols when they please,
Are quiet when they will.   40

'With Nature never do *they* wage
A foolish strife; they see
A happy youth, and their old age
Is beautiful and free:

'But we are pressed by heavy laws;   45
And often, glad no more,
We wear a face of joy, because
We have been glad of yore.

'If there is one who need bemoan
His kindred laid in earth,   50
The household hearts that were his own,
It is the man of mirth.

'My days, my friend, are almost gone,
My life has been approved,
And many love me; but by none   55
Am I enough beloved.'

'Now both himself and me he wrongs,
The man who thus complains!
I live and sing my idle songs
Upon these happy plains,   60

'And, Matthew, for thy children dead
I'll be a son to thee!'
At this he grasped his hands, and said
'Alas! that cannot be.'

We rose up from the fountain-side;   65
And down the smooth descent
Of the green sheep-track did we glide;
And through the wood we went;

And, ere we came to Leonard's Rock,
He sang those witty rhymes   70
About the crazy old church clock
And the bewildered chimes.

NUTTING

It seems a day
(I speak of one from many singled out),
One of those heavenly days which cannot die,
When forth I sallied from our cottage-door,
And with a wallet o'er my shoulder slung,   5
A nutting crook in hand, I turned my steps
Towards the distant woods, a figure quaint,
Tricked out in proud disguise of beggar's weeds
Put on for the occasion, by advice
And exhortation of my frugal dame.   10
Motley accoutrement! of power to smile
At thorns, and brakes, and brambles, and in truth
More ragged than need was. Among the woods
And o'er the pathless rocks I forced my way,
Until at length I came to one dear nook   15
Unvisited, where not a broken bough
Drooped with its withered leaves, ungracious sign
Of devastation, but the hazels rose
Tall and erect, with milk-white clusters hung,
A virgin scene!—A little while I stood,   20
Breathing with such suppression of the heart
As joy delights in; and with wise restraint
Voluptuous, fearless of a rival, eyed
The banquet, or beneath the trees I sate
Among the flowers, and with the flowers I played;   25
A temper known to those who, after long
And weary expectation, have been blessed
With sudden happiness beyond all hope.
Perhaps it was a bower beneath whose leaves
The violets of five seasons reappear   30
And fade, unseen by any human eye;
Where fairy water-breaks do murmur on
For ever, and I saw the sparkling foam,

32. *water-breaks:* small springs

And with my cheek on one of those green stones
That, fleeced with moss, beneath the shady trees   35
Lay round me scattered like a flock of sheep,
I heard the murmur and the murmuring sound,
In that sweet mood when pleasure loves to pay
Tribute to ease; and, of its joy secure,
The heart luxuriates with indifferent things,   40
Wasting its kindliness on stocks and stones,
And on the vacant air. Then up I rose,
And dragged to earth both branch and bough, with crash
And merciless ravage; and the shady nook
Of hazels, and the green and mossy bower,   45
Deformed and sullied, patiently gave up
Their quiet being: and, unless I now
Confound my present feelings with the past,
Even then, when from the bower I turned away
Exulting, rich beyond the wealth of kings,   50
I felt a sense of pain when I beheld
The silent trees and the intruding sky.

   Then, dearest maiden! move along these shades
In gentleness of heart; with gentle hand
Touch,—for there is a spirit in the woods.   55

'THREE YEARS SHE GREW IN SUN AND SHOWER'

   Three years she grew in sun and shower,
   Then Nature said, 'A lovelier flower
    On earth was never sown;
   This child I to myself will take;
   She shall be mine, and I will make   5
    A lady of my own.

   'Myself will to my darling be
   Both law and impulse; and with me

The girl, in rock and plain,
In earth and heaven, in glade and bower,   10
Shall feel an overseeing power
To kindle or restrain.

'She shall be sportive as the fawn
That wild with glee across the lawn
Or up the mountain springs;   15
And hers shall be the breathing balm,
And hers the silence and the calm
Of mute insensate things.

'The floating clouds their state shall lend
To her; for her the willow bend;   20
Nor shall she fail to see
Even in the motions of the storm
Grace that shall mould the maiden's form
By silent sympathy.

'The stars of midnight shall be dear   25
To her; and she shall lean her ear
In many a secret place
Where rivulets dance their wayward round,
And beauty born of murmuring sound
Shall pass into her face.   30

'And vital feelings of delight
Shall rear her form to stately height,
Her virgin bosom swell;
Such thoughts to Lucy I will give
While she and I together live   35
Here in this happy dell.'

Thus Nature spake. The work was done—
How soon my Lucy's race was run!
She died, and left to me
This heath, this calm and quiet scene;   40
The memory of what has been,
And never more will be.

THE PET LAMB

A PASTORAL

The dew was falling fast, the stars began to blink;
I heard a voice, it said, 'Drink, pretty creature, drink!'
And looking o'er the hedge, before me I espied
A snow-white mountain lamb with a maiden at its side.

No other sheep were near, the lamb was all alone,   5
And by a slender cord was tethered to a stone;
With one knee on the grass did the little maiden kneel
While to that mountain lamb she gave its evening meal.

The lamb while from her hand he thus his supper took
Seemed to feast with head and ears; and his tail with 10
    pleasure shook.
'Drink, pretty creature, drink,' she said in such a tone
That I almost received her heart into my own.

'Twas little Barbara Lewthwaite, a child of beauty rare!
I watched them with delight, they were a lovely pair.
Now with her empty can the maiden turned away;   15
But ere ten yards were gone her footsteps did she stay.

Towards the lamb she looked; and from that shady place
I unobserved could see the workings of her face:
If Nature to her tongue could measured numbers
    bring,
Thus, thought I, to her lamb that little maid might 20
    sing.

'What ails thee, young one? What? Why pull so at thy
    cord?
Is it not well with thee? Well both for bed and board?
Thy plot of grass is soft, and green as grass can be;
Rest, little young one, rest; what is't that aileth thee?

209

'What is it thou wouldst seek? What is wanting to 25
    thy heart?
Thy limbs are they not strong? And beautiful thou
    art;
This grass is tender grass; these flowers they have no
    peers;
And that green corn all day is rustling in thy ears!

'If the sun be shining hot, do but stretch thy woollen
    chain,
This beech is standing by, its covert thou canst gain; 30
For rain and mountain storms! the like thou needst
    not fear—
The rain and storm are things which scarcely can
    come here.

'Rest, little young one, rest; thou hast forgot the day
When my father found thee first in places far away;
Many flocks were on the hills, but thou wert owned 35
    by none;
And thy mother from thy side for evermore was gone.

'He took thee in his arms, and in pity brought thee
    home:
A blessed day for thee! then whither wouldst thou
    roam?
A faithful nurse thou hast, the dam that did thee yean
Upon the mountain tops no kinder could have been. 40

'Thou know'st that twice a day I have brought thee in
    this can
Fresh water from the brook as clear as ever ran;
And twice in the day when the ground is wet with
    dew
I bring thee draughts of milk, warm milk it is and
    new.

'Thy limbs will shortly be twice as stout as they   45
    are now,
Then I'll yoke thee to my cart like a pony in the
    plough;
My playmate thou shalt be; and when the wind is cold
Our hearth shall be thy bed, our house shall be thy
    fold.

'It will not, will not rest!—poor creature, can it be
That 'tis thy mother's heart which is working so in   50
    thee?
Things that I know not of belike to thee are dear,
And dreams of things which thou canst neither see
    nor hear.

'Alas, the mountain tops that look so green and fair!
I've heard of fearful winds and darkness that come
    there;
The little brooks that seem all pastime and all play,   55
When they are angry, roar like lions for their prey.

'Here thou needst not dread the raven in the sky;
Night and day thou art safe—our cottage is hard by.
Why bleat so after me? Why pull so at thy chain?
Sleep—and at break of day I will come to thee   60
    again!'

As homeward through the lane I went with lazy feet,
This song to myself did I oftentimes repeat;
And it seemed, as I retraced the ballad line by line,
That but half of it was hers, and one half of it was mine.

Again, and once again did I repeat the song;   65
'Nay,' said I, 'more than half to the damsel must
    belong,
For she looked with such a look, and she spake with
    such a tone,
That I almost received her heart into my own.'

WRITTEN IN GERMANY

*I must apprise the reader that the stoves in North Germany
generally have the impression of a galloping horse upon them,
this being part of the Brunswick arms.*

A fig for your languages, German and Norse!
Let me have the song of the kettle;
And the tongs and the poker, instead of that horse
That gallops away with such fury and force
On this dreary dull plate of black metal.   5

Our Earth is no doubt made of excellent stuff;
But her pulses beat slower and slower;
The weather in 'forty was cutting and rough,
And then, as Heaven knows, the glass stood
   low enough;
And *now* it is four degrees lower.   10

Here's a fly, a disconsolate creature, perhaps
A child of the field, or the grove;
And, sorrow for him! this dull treacherous heat
Has seduced the poor fool from his winter retreat,
And he creeps to the edge of my stove.   15

Alas! how he fumbles about the domains
Which this comfortless oven environ!
He cannot find out in what track he must crawl,
Now back to the tiles, and now back to the wall,
And now on the brink of the iron.   20

Stock-still there he stands like a traveller bemazed;
The best of his skill he has tried;
His feelers methinks I can see him put forth

To the east and the west, and the south and the
    north;
But he finds neither guide-post nor guide.   25

See! his spindles sink under him, foot, leg and
    thigh;
His eyesight and hearing are lost;
Between life and death his blood freezes and
    thaws;
And his two pretty pinions of blue dusky gauze
Are glued to his sides by the frost.   30

No brother, no friend has he near him—while I
Can draw warmth from the cheek of my love;
As blest and as glad in this desolate gloom,
As if green summer grass were the floor of my
    room,
And woodbines were hanging above.   35

Yet, God is my witness, thou small helpless thing!
Thy life I would gladly sustain
Till summer comes up from the south, and with
    crowds
Of thy brethren a march thou shouldst sound
    through the clouds,
And back to the forests again.   40

THE CHILDLESS FATHER

'Up, Timothy, up with your staff and away!
Not a soul in the village this morning will stay;
The hare has just started from Hamilton's grounds,
And Skiddaw is glad with the cry of the hounds.'

Of coats and of jackets grey, scarlet and green,   5
On the slopes of the pastures all colours were seen;
With their comely blue aprons, and caps white as snow,
The girls on the hills made a holiday show.

The basin of box-wood,* just six months before,
Had stood on the table at Timothy's door;   10
A coffin through Timothy's threshold had passed;
One child did it bear, and that child was his last.

Now fast up the dell came the noise and the fray,
The horse and the horn, and the hark! hark away!
Old Timothy took up his staff, and he shut   15
With a leisurely motion the door of his hut.

Perhaps to himself at that moment he said,
'The key I must take, for my Ellen is dead.'
But of this in my ears not a word did he speak,
And he went to the chase with a tear on his cheek.   20

---

*In several parts of the north of England, when a funeral takes
place, a basin full of sprigs of box-wood is placed at the door of
the house from which the coffin is taken up, and each person who
attends the funeral ordinarily takes a sprig of this box-wood and
throws it into the grave of the deceased. [Wordsworth's note.]

THE OLD CUMBERLAND BEGGAR

A DESCRIPTION

I saw an aged beggar in my walk,
And he was seated by the highway side
On a low structure of rude masonry
Built at the foot of a huge hill, that they
Who lead their horses down the steep rough road   5
May thence remount at ease. The aged man

Had placed his staff across the broad smooth stone
That overlays the pile, and from a bag
All white with flour, the dole of village dames,
He drew his scraps and fragments, one by one,⠀⠀⠀⠀⠀10
And scanned them with a fixed and serious look
Of idle computation. In the sun,
Upon the second step of that small pile,
Surrounded by those wild unpeopled hills,
He sat, and ate his food in solitude;⠀⠀⠀⠀⠀15
And ever, scattered from his palsied hand,
That still attempting to prevent the waste
Was baffled still, the crumbs in little showers
Fell on the ground, and the small mountain birds,
Not venturing yet to peck their destined meal,⠀⠀⠀⠀⠀20
Approached within the length of half his staff.

Him from my childhood have I known; and then
He was so old, he seems not older now;
He travels on, a solitary man,
So helpless in appearance that for him⠀⠀⠀⠀⠀25
The sauntering horseman-traveller does not throw
With careless hand his alms upon the ground,
But stops, that he may safely lodge the coin
Within the old man's hat; nor quits him so,
But still when he has given his horse the rein⠀⠀⠀⠀⠀30
Towards the aged beggar turns a look,
Sidelong and half-reverted. She who tends
The toll-gate, when in summer at her door
She turns her wheel, if on the road she sees
The aged beggar coming, quits her work,⠀⠀⠀⠀⠀35
And lifts the latch for him that he may pass.
The post-boy, when his rattling wheels o'ertake
The aged beggar in the woody lane,
Shouts to him from behind, and if perchance
The old man does not change his course, the boy⠀⠀⠀⠀⠀40
Turns with less noisy wheels to the road-side,

And passes gently by, without a curse
Upon his lips, or anger at his heart.
He travels on, a solitary man;
His age has no companion. On the ground   45
His eyes are turned, and as he moves along
They move along the ground; and, evermore,
Instead of common and habitual sight
Of fields with rural works, of hill and dale,
And the blue sky, one little span of earth   50
Is all his prospect. Thus from day to day,
Bowbent, his eyes for ever on the ground,
He plies his weary journey; seeing still,
And never knowing that he sees, some straw,
Some scattered leaf, or marks which, in one track,   55
The nails of cart or chariot wheel have left
Impressed on the white road, in the same line,
At distance still the same. Poor traveller!
His staff trails with him; scarcely do his feet
Disturb the summer dust; he is so still   60
In look and motion, that the cottage curs
Ere he have passed the door will turn away,
Weary of barking at him. Boys and girls,
The vacant and the busy, maids and youths
And urchins newly breeched, all pass him by: 65
Him even the slow-paced waggon leaves behind.

But deem not this man useless.—Statesmen! ye
Who are so restless in your wisdom, ye
Who have a broom still ready in your hands
To rid the world of nuisances; ye proud,   70
Heart-swoll'n, while in your pride ye contemplate
Your talents, power and wisdom, deem him not
A burthen of the earth. 'Tis Nature's law
That none, the meanest of created things,
Of forms created the most vile and brute,   75
The dullest or most noxious, should exist

Divorced from good: a spirit and pulse of good,
A life and soul to every mode of being
Inseparably linked. While thus he creeps
From door to door, the villagers in him   80
Behold a record which together binds
Past deeds and offices of charity
Else unremembered, and so keeps alive
The kindly mood in hearts which lapse of years,
And that half-wisdom half-experience gives,   85
Make slow to feel, and by sure steps resign
To selfishness and cold oblivious cares.
Among the farms and solitary huts,
Hamlets and thinly-scattered villages,
Where'er the aged beggar takes his rounds,   90
The mild necessity of use compels
To acts of love; and habit does the work
Of reason; yet prepares that after joy
Which reason cherishes. And thus the soul,
By that sweet taste of pleasure unpursued,   95
Doth find itself insensibly disposed
To virtue and true goodness. Some there are,
By their good works exalted, lofty minds
And meditative, authors of delight
And happiness, which to the end of time   100
Will live, and spread, and kindle; minds like these,
In childhood, from this solitary being,
This helpless wanderer, have perchance received
(A thing more precious far than all that books
Or the solicitudes of love can do!)   105
That first mild touch of sympathy and thought
In which they found their kindred with a world
Where want and sorrow were. The easy man
Who sits at his own door and, like the pear
Which overhangs his head from the green wall,   110
Feeds in the sunshine; the robust and the young,
The prosperous and unthinking, they who live

Sheltered, and flourish in a little grove
Of their own kindred, all behold in him
A silent monitor, which on their minds   115
Must needs impress a transitory thought
Of self-congratulation, to the heart
Of each recalling his peculiar boons,
His charters and exemptions; and perchance
Though he to no one give the fortitude   120
And circumspection needful to preserve
His present blessings, and to husband up
The respite of the season, he at least
(And 'tis no vulgar service) makes them felt.

Yet further. Many, I believe, there are   125
Who live a life of virtuous decency,
Men who can hear the Decalogue and feel
No self-reproach; who of the moral law
Established in the land where they abide
Are strict observers; and not negligent,   130
Meanwhile, in any tenderness of heart
Or act of love to those with whom they dwell,
Their kindred, and the children of their blood.
Praise be to such, and to their slumbers peace!
—But of the poor man ask, the abject poor,   135
Go and demand of him if there be here,
In this cold abstinence from evil deeds
And these inevitable charities,
Wherewith to satisfy the human soul?
No: man is dear to man; the poorest poor   140
Long for some moments in a weary life
When they can know and feel that they have been
Themselves the fathers and the dealers-out
Of some small blessings, have been kind to such
As needed kindness, for this single cause,   145
That we have all of us one human heart.

127. *the Decalogue:* the Ten Commandments

Such pleasure is to one kind being known:
My neighbour, when with punctual care, each week
Duly as Friday comes, though pressed herself
By her own wants, she from her chest of meal   150
Takes one unsparing handful for the scrip
Of this old mendicant, and from her door
Returning with exhilarated heart,
Sits by her fire and builds her hope in heaven.

Then let him pass, a blessing on his head!   155
And while in that vast solitude to which
The tide of things has led him, he appears
To breathe and live but for himself alone,
Unblamed, uninjured let him bear about
The good which the benignant law of Heaven   160
Has hung around him; and while life is his
Still let him prompt the unlettered villagers
To tender offices and pensive thoughts.
Then let him pass, a blessing on his head!
And, long as he can wander, let him breathe   165
The freshness of the valleys; let his blood
Struggle with frosty air and winter snows;
And let the chartered wind that sweeps the heath
Beat his grey locks against his withered face.
Reverence the hope whose vital anxiousness   170
Gives the last human interest to his heart.
May never HOUSE, misnamed OF INDUSTRY,
Make him a captive! For that pent-up din,
Those life-consuming sounds that clog the air,
Be his the natural silence of old age!   175
Let him be free of mountain solitudes;
And have around him, whether heard or not,
The pleasant melody of woodland birds.
Few are his pleasures: if his eyes, which now
Have been so long familiar with the earth,   180
No more behold the horizontal sun

Rising or setting, let the light at least
Find a free entrance to their languid orbs.
And let him, *where* and *when* he will, sit down
Beneath the trees, or by the grassy bank   185
Of highway side, and with the little birds
Share his chance-gathered meal; and finally,
As in the eye of Nature he has lived,
So in the eye of Nature let him die.

RURAL ARCHITECTURE

There's George Fisher, Charles Fleming, and Reginald
   Shore,
Three rosy-cheeked schoolboys, the highest not more
Than the height of a counsellor's bag;
To the top of Great How did it please them to climb;
And there they built up, without mortar or lime,   5
A man on the peak of the crag.

They built him of stones gathered up as they lay;
They built him and christened him all in one day,
An urchin both vigorous and hale;
And so without scruple they called him Ralph Jones.   10
Now Ralph is renowned for the length of his bones;
The Magog of Legberthwaite dale.

Just half a week after, the wind sallied forth
And, in anger or merriment, out of the north
Coming on with a terrible pother,   15
From the peak of the crag blew the giant away.
And what did these schoolboys? The very next day
They went and they built up another.

A POET'S EPITAPH

Art thou a statesman, in the van
Of public business trained and bred?
—First learn to love one living man;
Then may'st thou think upon the dead.

A lawyer art thou?—Draw not nigh;   5
Go, carry to some other place
The hardness of thy coward eye,
The falsehood of thy sallow face.

Art thou a man of purple cheer?
A rosy man, right plump to see?   10
Approach; yet, doctor, not too near:
This grave no cushion is for thee.

Art thou a man of gallant pride,
A soldier, and no man of chaff?
Welcome!—but lay thy sword aside,   15
And lean upon a peasant's staff.

Physician art thou? One, all eyes,
Philosopher? A fingering slave,
One that would peep and botanise
Upon his mother's grave?   20

Wrapped closely in thy sensual fleece,
O turn aside, and take, I pray,
That he below may rest in peace,
Thy pin-point of a soul away!

A moralist perchance appears,   25
Led, Heaven knows how, to this poor sod:
And he has neither eyes nor ears,
Himself his world, and his own God;

One to whose smooth-rubbed soul can cling
Nor form, nor feeling, great nor small; 30
A reasoning, self-sufficient thing,
An intellectual all-in-all!

Shut close the door; press down the latch;
Sleep in thy intellectual crust;
Nor lose ten tickings of thy watch 35
Near this unprofitable dust.

But who is he, with modest looks
And clad in homely russet brown?
He murmurs near the running brooks
A music sweeter than their own. 40

He is retired as noontide dew,
Or fountain in a noonday grove;
And you must love him, ere to you
He will seem worthy of your love.

The outward shows of sky and earth, 45
Of hill and valley, he has viewed;
And impulses of deeper birth
Have come to him in solitude.

In common things that round us lie
Some random truths he can impart— 50
The harvest of a quiet eye
That broods and sleeps on his own heart.

But he is weak, both man and boy
Hath been an idler in the land;
Contented if he might enjoy 55
The things which others understand.

Come hither in thy hour of strength;
Come, weak as is a breaking wave!
Here stretch thy body at full length;
Or build thy house upon this grave. 60

A FRAGMENT

Between two sister moorland rills
There is a spot that seems to lie
Sacred to flowerets of the hills,
And sacred to the sky.
And in this smooth and open dell   5
There is a tempest-stricken tree;
A corner-stone by lightning cut,
The last stone of a cottage hut;
And in this dell you see
A thing no storm can e'er destroy,   10
The shadow of a Danish boy.

In clouds above the lark is heard,
He sings his blithest and his best;
But in this lonesome nook the bird
Did never build his nest.   15
No beast, no bird hath here his home;
The bees borne on the breezy air
Pass high above those fragrant bells
To other flowers, to other dells,
Nor ever linger there.   20
The Danish boy walks here alone:
The lovely dell is all his own.

A spirit of noon day is he,
He seems a form of flesh and blood;
Nor piping shepherd shall he be,   25
Nor herd-boy of the wood.
A regal vest of fur he wears,
In colour like a raven's wing;
It fears not rain, nor wind, nor dew;
But in the storm 'tis fresh and blue   30
As budding pines in spring;
His helmet has a vernal grace,
Fresh as the bloom upon his face.

A harp is from his shoulder slung:
He rests the harp upon his knee;   35
And there in a forgotten tongue
He warbles melody.
Of flocks upon the neighbouring hills
He is the darling and the joy;
And often, when no cause appears,   40
The mountain ponies prick their ears—
They hear the Danish boy,
While in the dell he sits alone
Beside the tree and corner-stone.

There sits he: in his face you spy   45
No trace of a ferocious air,
Nor ever was a cloudless sky
So steady or so fair.
The lovely Danish boy is blest
And happy in his flowery cove: 50
From bloody deeds his thoughts are far;
And yet he warbles songs of war;
They seem like songs of love,
For calm and gentle is his mien;
Like a dead boy he is serene.   55

* * * * *

POEMS ON THE NAMING OF PLACES

By persons resident in the country and attached to rural objects, many places will be found unnamed or of unknown names where little incidents will have occurred, or feelings been experienced, which will have given to such places a private and peculiar interest. From a wish to give some sort of record to such incidents, or renew the gratification of such feelings, names have been given to places by the author and some of his friends, and the following poems written in consequence.

I

It was an April morning: fresh and clear
The rivulet, delighting in its strength,
Ran with a young man's speed; and yet the voice
Of waters which the winter had supplied
Was softened down into a vernal tone.   5
The spirit of enjoyment and desire,
And hopes and wishes, from all living things
Went circling, like a multitude of sounds.
The budding groves appeared as if in haste
To spur the steps of June; as if their shades   10
Of *various* green were hindrances that stood
Between them and their object: yet meanwhile
There was such deep contentment in the air
That every naked ash, and tardy tree
Yet leafless, seemed as though the countenance   15
With which it looked on this delightful day
Were native to the summer. Up the brook
I roamed in the confusion of my heart,
Alive to all things and forgetting all.
At length I to a sudden turning came   20
In this continuous glen, where down a rock
The stream, so ardent in its course before,
Sent forth such sallies of glad sound, that all

Which I till then had heard appeared the voice
Of common pleasure: beast and bird, the lamb,   25
The shepherd's dog, the linnet and the thrush
Vied with this waterfall, and made a song
Which, while I listened, seemed like the wild growth
Or like some natural produce of the air
That could not cease to be. Green leaves were here,   30
But 'twas the foliage of the rocks—the birch,
The yew, the holly, and the bright green thorn,
With hanging islands of resplendent furze:
And on a summit, distant a short space,
By any who should look beyond the dell   35
A single mountain cottage might be seen.
I gazed and gazed, and to myself I said,
'Our thoughts at least are ours; and this wild nook,
My EMMA, I will dedicate to thee.'
—Soon did the spot become my other home,   40
My dwelling and my out-of-doors abode.
And, of the shepherds who have seen me there,
To whom I sometimes in my idle talk
Have told this fancy, two or three, perhaps,
Years after we are gone and in our graves,   45
When they have cause to speak of this wild place
May call it by the name of EMMA'S DELL.

II

TO JOANNA

Amid the smoke of cities did you pass
Your time of early youth; and there you learned,
From years of quiet industry, to love
The living beings by your own fire-side
With such a strong devotion, that your heart   5
Is slow towards the sympathies of them
Who look upon the hills with tenderness,
And make dear friendships with the streams and groves.

Yet we, who are transgressors in this kind,
Dwelling retired in our simplicity   10
Among the woods and fields, we love you well,
Joanna! and I guess, since you have been
So distant from us now for two long years,
That you will gladly listen to discourse
However trivial, if you thence are taught   15
That they with whom you once were happy talk
Familiarly of you and of old times.

While I was seated, now some ten days past,
Beneath those lofty firs that overtop
Their ancient neighbour, the old steeple tower,   20
The vicar from his gloomy house hard by
Came forth to greet me; and when he had asked,
'How fares Joanna, that wild-hearted maid?
And when will she return to us?' he paused;
And after short exchange of village news   25
He with grave looks demanded for what cause,
Reviving obsolete idolatry,
I, like a runic priest, in characters
Of formidable size had chiselled out
Some uncouth name upon the native rock   30
Above the Rotha, by the forest side.
Now, by those dear immunities of heart
Engendered betwixt malice and true love,
I was not loth to be so catechised,
And this was my reply: 'As it befell,   35
One summer morning we had walked abroad
At break of day, Joanna and myself.
'Twas that delightful season when the broom,
Full-flowered, and visible on every steep,
Along the copses runs in veins of gold.   40
Our pathway led us on to Rotha's banks:
And when we came in front of that tall rock
Which looks towards the east, I there stopped short,

And traced the lofty barrier with my eye
From base to summit; such delight I found   45
To note in shrub and tree, in stone and flower,
That intermixture of delicious hues
Along so vast a surface, all at once
In one impression, by connecting force
Of their own beauty imaged in the heart.   50
When I had gazed perhaps two minutes' space,
Joanna, looking in my eyes, beheld
That ravishment of mine, and laughed aloud.
The rock, like something starting from a sleep,
Took up the lady's voice, and laughed again: 55
That ancient woman seated on Helm Crag
Was ready with her cavern; Hammar Scar
And the tall steep of Silver How sent forth
A noise of laughter; southern Loughrigg heard,
And Fairfield answered with a mountain tone: 60
Helvellyn far into the clear blue sky
Carried the lady's voice—old Skiddaw blew
His speaking-trumpet—back out of the clouds
Of Glaramara southward came the voice;
And Kirkstone tossed it from his misty head.   65
Now whether (said I to our cordial friend,
Who in the heyday of astonishment
Smiled in my face) this were in simple truth
A work accomplished by the brotherhood
Of ancient mountains, or my ear was touched   70
With dreams and visionary impulses,
Is not for me to tell: but sure I am
That there was a loud uproar in the hills.
And, while we both were listening, to my side
The fair Joanna drew, as if she wished   75
To shelter from some object of her fear.
—And hence, long afterwards, when eighteen moons
Were wasted, as I chanced to walk alone
Beneath this rock, at sunrise, on a calm

And silent morning, I sat down, and there   80
In memory of affections old and true
I chiselled out in those rude characters
Joanna's name upon the living stone.
And I, and all who dwell by my fireside,
Have called the lovely rock JOANNA'S ROCK.'   85

III

There is an eminence, of these our hills
The last that parleys with the setting sun.
We can behold it from our orchard seat;
And when at evening we pursue our walk
Along the public way, this cliff, so high   5
Above us, and so distant in its height,
Is visible, and often seems to send
Its own deep quiet to restore our hearts.
The meteors make of it a favourite haunt;
The star of Jove, so beautiful and large   10
In the mid-heavens, is never half so fair
As when he shines above it. 'Tis in truth
The loneliest place we have among the clouds.
And she who dwells with me, whom I have loved
With such communion that no place on earth   15
Can ever be a solitude to me,
Hath said, this lonesome peak shall bear my name.

IV

A narrow girdle of rough stones and crags,
A rude and natural causeway interposed
Between the water and a winding slope
Of copse and thicket, leaves the eastern shore
Of Grasmere safe in its own privacy.   5
And there myself and two beloved friends
One calm September morning, ere the mist
Had altogether yielded to the sun,
Sauntered on this retired and difficult way.

229

Ill suits the road with one in haste, but we 10
Played with our time; and, as we strolled along,
It was our occupation to observe
Such objects as the waves had tossed ashore,
Feather, or leaf, or weed, or withered bough,
Each on the other heaped along the line 15
Of the dry wreck. And in our vacant mood
Not seldom did we stop to watch some tuft
Of dandelion-seed or thistle's beard,
Which, seeming lifeless half, and half impelled
By some internal feeling, skimmed along 20
Close to the surface of the lake that lay
Asleep in a dead calm—ran closely on
Along the dead calm lake, now here, now there,
In all its sportive wanderings all the while
Making report of an invisible breeze 25
That was its wings, its chariot and its horse,
Its very playmate, and its moving soul.
And often, trifling with a privilege
Alike indulged to all, we paused, one now
And now the other, to point out, perchance 30
To pluck, some flower or water-weed, too fair
Either to be divided from the place
On which it grew, or to be left alone
To its own beauty. Many such there are,
Fair ferns and flowers, and chiefly that tall fern 35
So stately, of the queen Osmunda named;
Plant lovelier in its own retired abode
On Grasmere's beach, than Naiad by the side
Of Grecian brook, or lady of the mere
Sole-sitting by the shores of old romance. 40
So fared we that sweet morning: from the fields
Meanwhile a noise was heard, the busy mirth
Of reapers, men and women, boys and girls.
Delighted much to listen to those sounds,
And in the fashion which I have described 45

Feeding unthinking fancies, we advanced
Along the indented shore; when suddenly,
Through a thin veil of glittering haze, we saw
Before us on a point of jutting land
The tall and upright figure of a man   50
Attired in peasant's garb, who stood alone
Angling beside the margin of a lake.
That way we turned our steps; nor was it long
Ere, making ready comments on the sight
Which then we saw, with one and the same voice   55
We all cried out that he must be indeed
An idle man, who thus could lose a day
Of the mid-harvest, when the labourer's hire
Is ample, and some little might be stored
Wherewith to cheer him in the winter-time.   60
Thus talking of that peasant, we approached
Close to the spot where with his rod and line
He stood alone; whereat he turned his head
To greet us—and we saw a man worn down
By sickness, gaunt and lean, with sunken cheeks   65
And wasted limbs, his legs so long and lean
That, for my single self, I looked at them
Forgetful of the body they sustained.
Too weak to labour in the harvest-field,
The man was using his best skill to gain   70
A pittance from the dead unfeeling lake
That knew not of his wants. I will not say
What thoughts immediately were ours, nor how
The happy idleness of that sweet morn,
With all its lovely images, was changed   75
To serious musing and to self-reproach.
Nor did we fail to see within ourselves
What need there is to be reserved in speech,
And temper all our thoughts with charity.
Therefore, unwilling to forget that day,   80
My friend, myself, and she who then received

The same admonishment, have called the place
By a memorial name, uncouth indeed
As e'er by mariner was given to bay
Or foreland on a new-discovered coast,   85
And POINT RASH-JUDGMENT is the name it bears.

V

TO M. H.

Our walk was far among the ancient trees;
There was no road, nor any woodman's path;
But the thick umbrage, checking the wild growth
Of weed and sapling, on the soft green turf
Beneath the branches of itself had made   5
A track, which brought us to a slip of lawn
And a small bed of water in the woods.
All round this pool both flocks and herds might drink
On its firm margin even as from a well,
Or some stone basin which the herdsman's hand   10
Had shaped for their refreshment; nor did sun
Or wind from any quarter ever come,
But as a blessing, to this calm recess,
This glade of water and this one green field.
The spot was made by Nature for herself: 15
The travellers know it not, and 'twill remain
Unknown to them: but it is beautiful;
And if a man should plant his cottage near,
Should sleep beneath the shelter of its trees,
And blend its waters with his daily meal,   20
He would so love it that in his death hour
Its image would survive among his thoughts:
And therefore, my sweet MARY, this still nook
With all its beeches we have named for you.

LINES

WRITTEN WHEN SAILING IN A BOAT AT EVENING

How rich the wave in front, impressed
With evening twilight's summer hues,
While facing thus the crimson west
The boat her silent course pursues!
And see how dark the backward stream!   5
A little moment past, so smiling!
And still, perhaps, with faithless gleam
Some other loiterer beguiling.

Such views the youthful bard allure;
But, heedless of the following gloom,   10
He deems their colours shall endure
Till peace go with him to the tomb.
—And let him nurse his fond deceit,
And what if he must die in sorrow?
Who would not cherish dreams so sweet,   15
Though grief and pain may come tomorrow?

REMEMBRANCE OF COLLINS

WRITTEN UPON THE THAMES NEAR RICHMOND

Glide gently, thus for ever glide,
O Thames! that other bards may see
As lovely visions by thy side
As now, fair river! come to me.
O glide, fair stream! for ever so,   5
Thy quiet soul on all bestowing,
Till all our minds for ever flow
As thy deep waters now are flowing.

Vain thought! . . . Yet be as now thou art,
That in thy waters may be seen   10
The image of a poet's heart,
How bright, how solemn, how serene!
Such as did once the poet bless
Who, pouring here a later ditty,*
Could find no refuge from distress   15
But in the milder grief of pity.

Now let us, as we float along,
For *him* suspend the dashing oar;
And pray that never child of song
May know that poet's sorrows more.   20
How calm! How still! the only sound
The dripping of the oar suspended!
—The evening darkness gathers round
By virtue's holiest Powers attended.

a later ditty: 'Collins's *Ode on the Death of Thomson,* the last written, I believe, of the poems which were published during his lifetime. This Ode is also alluded to in the next stanza.' [Wordsworth's note.]

THE TWO THIEVES

OR

THE LAST STAGE OF AVARICE

O now that the genius of Bewick were mine,
And the skill which he learned on the banks of the Tyne!
Then the Muses might deal with me just as they chose,
For I'd take my last leave both of verse and of prose.

What feats would I work with my magical hand!   5
Book-learning and books should be banished the land;
And for hunger and thirst and such troublesome calls,
Every ale-house should then have a feast on its walls.

The traveller would hang his wet clothes on a chair;
Let them smoke, let them burn, not a straw would he 10
    care:
For the Prodigal Son, Joseph's Dream and his Sheaves,
Oh, what would they be to my tale of two thieves?

Little Dan is unbreeched, he is three birthdays old;
His grandsire, that age more than thirty times told;
There are ninety good seasons of fair and foul 15
    weather
Between them, and both go a-stealing together.

With chips is the carpenter strewing his floor?
Is a cartload of peats at an old woman's door?
Old Daniel his hand to the treasure will slide;
And his grandson's as busy at work by his side. 20

Old Daniel begins, he stops short—and his eye
Through the last look of dotage is cunning and sly.
'Tis a look which at this time is hardly his own,
But tells a plain tale of the days that are flown.

Dan once had a heart that was moved by the wires 25
Of manifold pleasures and many desires:
And what if he cherished his purse? 'Twas no more
Than treading a path trod by thousands before.

'Twas a path trod by thousands; but Daniel is one
Who went something further than others have gone; 30
And now with old Daniel you see how it fares;
You see to what end he has brought his grey hairs.

The pair sally forth hand in hand; ere the sun
Has peered o'er the beeches their work is begun:
And yet, into whatever sin they may fall, 35
This child but half knows it, and that not at all.

They hunt through the streets with deliberate tread,
And each in his turn is both leader and led;
And, wherever they carry their plots and their wiles,
Every face in the village is dimpled with smiles.   40

Neither checked by the rich nor the needy they roam;
For grey-headed Dan has a daughter at home,
Who will gladly repair all the damage that's done;
And three, were it asked, would be rendered for one.

Old man! whom so oft I with pity have eyed,   45
I love thee, and love the sweet boy at thy side:
Long yet mayst thou live! for a teacher we see
That lifts up the veil of our nature in thee.

'A WHIRL-BLAST FROM BEHIND THE HILL'

A whirl-blast from behind the hill
Rushed o'er the wood with startling sound:
Then all at once the air was still,
And showers of hailstones pattered round.
Where leafless oaks towered high above,   5
I sat within an undergrove
Of tallest hollies, tall and green;
A fairer bower was never seen.
From year to year the spacious floor
With withered leaves is covered o'er,   10
You could not lay a hair between:
And all the year the bower is green.
But see! where'er the hailstones drop
The withered leaves all skip and hop;
There's not a breeze—no breath of air—   15
Yet here, and there, and everywhere
Along the floor, beneath the shade
By those embowering hollies made,

The leaves in myriads jump and spring,
As if with pipes and music rare   20
Some Robin Goodfellow were there,
And all those leaves, that jump and spring,
Were each a joyous, living thing.

Oh! grant me, Heaven, a heart at ease,
That I may never cease to find,   25
Even in appearances like these,
Enough to nourish and to stir my mind!

SONG FOR THE WANDERING JEW

Though the torrents from their fountains
Roar down many a craggy steep,
Yet they find among the mountains
Resting-places calm and deep.

Though almost with eagle pinion   5
O'er the rocks the chamois roam,
Yet he has some small dominion
Which, no doubt, he calls his home.

If on windy days the raven
Gambol like a dancing skiff,   10
Not the less he loves his haven
On the bosom of the cliff.

Though the sea-horse in the ocean
Own no dear domestic cave;
Yet he slumbers without motion   15
On the calm and silent wave.

Day and night my toils redouble!
Never nearer to the goal,
Night and day I feel the trouble
Of the Wanderer in my soul.   20

MICHAEL

A PASTORAL POEM

If from the public way you turn your steps
Up the tumultuous brook of Green-head Gill,
You will suppose that with an upright path
Your feet must struggle; in such bold ascent
The pastoral mountains front you, face to face.　　　5
But courage! for beside that boisterous brook
The mountains have all opened out themselves,
And made a hidden valley of their own.
No habitation there is seen; but such
As journey thither find themselves alone　　　10
With a few sheep, with rocks and stones, and kites
That overhead are sailing in the sky.
It is in truth an utter solitude;
Nor should I have made mention of this dell
But for one object which you might pass by,　　　15
Might see and notice not. Beside the brook
There is a straggling heap of unhewn stones:
And to that place a story appertains
Which, though it be ungarnished with events,
Is not unfit, I deem, for the fireside,　　　20
Or for the summer shade. It was the first,
The earliest of those tales that spake to me
Of shepherds, dwellers in the valleys, men
Whom I already loved, not verily
For their own sakes, but for the fields and hills　　　25
Where was their occupation and abode.
And hence this tale, while I was yet a boy
Careless of books, yet having felt the power
Of nature, by the gentle agency
Of natural objects led me on to feel　　　30
For passions that were not my own, and think
(At random and imperfectly indeed)
On man, the heart of man, and human life.

Therefore, although it be a history
Homely and rude, I will relate the same   35
For the delight of a few natural hearts,
And, with yet fonder feeling, for the sake
Of youthful poets who among these hills
Will be my second self when I am gone.

Upon the forest-side in Grasmere Vale   40
There dwelt a shepherd, Michael was his name,
An old man, stout of heart, and strong of limb.
His bodily frame had been from youth to age
Of an unusual strength; his mind was keen,
Intense and frugal, apt for all affairs,   45
And in his shepherd's calling he was prompt
And watchful more than ordinary men.
Hence he had learned the meanings of all winds,
Of blasts of every tone; and oftentimes
When others heeded not, he heard the South   50
Make subterraneous music, like the noise
Of bagpipers on distant Highland hills;
The shepherd, at such warning, of his flock
Bethought him, and he to himself would say,
'The winds are now devising work for me!'   55
And truly, at all times the storm, that drives
The traveller to a shelter, summoned him
Up to the mountains: he had been alone
Amid the heart of many thousand mists,
That came to him and left him on the heights.   60
So lived he till his eightieth year was past.

And grossly that man errs, who should suppose
That the green valleys and the streams and rocks
Were things indifferent to the shepherd's thoughts.
Fields, where with cheerful spirits he had breathed   65
The common air; the hills, which he so oft
Had climbed with vigorous steps; which had impressed
So many incidents upon his mind

Of hardship, skill or courage, joy or fear;
Which like a book preserved the memory   70
Of the dumb animals whom he had saved,
Had fed or sheltered, linking to such acts,
So grateful in themselves, the certainty
Of honourable gain; these fields, these hills,
Which were his living being, even more   75
Than his own blood—what could they less?—had laid
Strong hold on his affections, were to him
A pleasurable feeling of blind love,
The pleasure which there is in life itself.

He had not passed his days in singleness.   80
He had a wife, a comely matron, old—
Though younger than himself full twenty years.
She was a woman of a stirring life,
Whose heart was in her house; two wheels she had
Of antique form, this large for spinning wool,   85
That small for flax; and if one wheel had rest,
It was because the other was at work.
The pair had but one inmate in their house,
An only child, who had been born to them
When Michael telling o'er his years began   90
To deem that he was old—in shepherd's phrase,
With one foot in the grave. This only son,
With two brave sheep-dogs tried in many a storm,
The one of an inestimable worth,
Made all their household. I may truly say,   95
That they were as a proverb in the vale
For endless industry. When day was gone,
And from their occupations out of doors
The son and father were come home, even then
Their labour did not cease; unless when all   100
Turned to their cleanly supper-board, and there,
Each with a mess of pottage and skimmed milk,
Sat round their basket piled with oaten cakes,

And their plain home-made cheese. Yet when their meal
Was ended, Luke (for so the son was named)   105
And his old father both betook themselves
To such convenient work as might employ
Their hands by the fireside; perhaps to card
Wool for the housewife's spindle, or repair
Some injury done to sickle, flail or scythe,   110
Or other implement of house or field.

Down from the ceiling by the chimney's edge,
Which in our ancient uncouth country style
Did with a huge projection overbrow
Large space beneath, as duly as the light   115
Of day grew dim the housewife hung a lamp;
An aged utensil, which had performed
Service beyond all others of its kind.
Early at evening did it burn and late,
Surviving comrade of uncounted hours,   120
Which going by from year to year had found
And left the couple neither gay perhaps
Nor cheerful, yet with objects and with hopes,
Living a life of eager industry.
And now, when Luke was in his eighteenth year,   125
There by the light of this old lamp they sat,
Father and son, while late into the night
The housewife plied her own peculiar work,
Making the cottage through the silent hours
Murmur as with the sound of summer flies.   130
The light was famous in its neighbourhood,
And was a public symbol of the life
The thrifty pair had lived. For, as it chanced,
Their cottage on a plot of rising ground
Stood single, with large prospect, north and south,   135
High into Easedale, up to Dunmal Raise,
And westward to the village near the lake;
And from this constant light, so regular

And so far seen, the house itself, by all
Who dwelt within the limits of the vale,   140
Both old and young, was named THE EVENING STAR.

Thus living on through such a length of years,
The shepherd, if he loved himself, must needs
Have loved his help-mate; but to Michael's heart
The son of his old age was yet more dear—   145
Effect which might perhaps have been produced
By that instinctive tenderness, the same
Blind spirit, which is in the blood of all;
Or that a child, more than all other gifts,
Brings hope with it, and forward-looking thoughts,   150
And stirrings of inquietude when they
By tendency of nature needs must fail.
From such and other causes, to the thoughts
Of the old man his only son was now
The dearest object that he knew on earth.   155
Exceeding was the love he bare to him,
His heart and his heart's joy! For oftentimes
Old Michael, while he was a babe in arms,
Had done him female service, not alone
For dalliance and delight, as is the use   160
Of fathers, but with patient mind enforced
To acts of tenderness; and he had rocked
His cradle with a woman's gentle hand.

And in a later time, ere yet the boy
Had put on boy's attire, did Michael love,   165
Albeit of a stern unbending mind,
To have the young one in his sight when he
Had work by his own door, or when he sat
With sheep before him on his shepherd's stool
Beneath that large old oak, which near their door   170
Stood, and from its enormous breadth of shade
Chosen for the shearer's covert from the sun,
Thence in our rustic dialect was called

The CLIPPING TREE, a name which yet it bears.
There, while they two were sitting in the shade   175
With others round them, earnest all and blithe,
Would Michael exercise his heart with looks
Of fond correction and reproof bestowed
Upon the child, if he disturbed the sheep
By catching at their legs, or with his shouts   180
Scared them, while they lay still beneath the shears.

And when by Heaven's good grace the boy grew up
A healthy lad, and carried in his cheek
Two steady roses that were five years old,
Then Michael from a winter coppice cut   185
With his own hand a sapling, which he hooped
With iron, making it throughout in all
Due requisites a perfect shepherd's staff,
And gave it to the boy; wherewith equipped
He as a watchman oftentimes was placed   190
At gate or gap, to stem or turn the flock;
And to his office prematurely called
There stood the urchin, as you will divine,
Something between a hindrance and a help;
And for this cause not always, I believe,   195
Receiving from his father hire of praise,
Though nought was left undone which staff or voice,
Or looks, or threatening gestures could perform.
But soon as Luke, full ten years old, could stand
Against the mountain blasts, and to the heights,   200
Not fearing toil, nor length of weary ways,
He with his father daily went, and they
Were as companions—why should I relate
That objects which the shepherd loved before
Were dearer now? that from the boy there came   205
Feelings and emanations, things which were
Light to the sun and music to the wind;
And that the old man's heart seemed born again.

Thus in his father's sight the boy grew up;
And now when he had reached his eighteenth year,   210
He was his comfort and his daily hope.

While in the fashion which I have described
This simple household thus were living on
From day to day, to Michael's ear there came
Distressful tidings. Long before the time   215
Of which I speak, the shepherd had been bound
In surety for his brother's son, a man
Of an industrious life and ample means;
But unforeseen misfortunes suddenly
Had pressed upon him; and old Michael now   220
Was summoned to discharge the forfeiture,
A grievous penalty, but little less
Than half his substance. This unlooked-for claim,
At the first hearing, for a moment took
More hope out of his life than he supposed   225
That any old man ever could have lost.
As soon as he had gathered so much strength
That he could look his trouble in the face,
It seemed that his sole refuge was to sell
A portion of his patrimonial fields.   230
Such was his first resolve: he thought again,
And his heart failed him. 'Isabel,' said he,
Two evenings after he had heard the news,
'I have been toiling more than seventy years,
And in the open sunshine of God's love   235
Have we all lived; yet if these fields of ours
Should pass into a stranger's hand, I think
That I could not lie quiet in my grave.
Our lot is a hard lot: the sun itself
Has scarcely been more diligent than I,   240
And I have lived to be a fool at last
To my own family. An evil man
That was, and made an evil choice, if he

Were false to us; and if he were not false,
There are ten thousand to whom loss like this   245
Had been no sorrow. I forgive him—but
'Twere better to be dumb than to talk thus.
When I began, my purpose was to speak
Of remedies and of a cheerful hope.
Our Luke shall leave us, Isabel; the land   250
Shall not go from us, and it shall be free;
He shall possess it, free as is the wind
That passes over it. We have, thou knowest,
Another kinsman: he will be our friend
In this distress. He is a prosperous man,   255
Thriving in trade; and Luke to him shall go,
And with his kinsman's help and his own thrift
He quickly will repair this loss, and then
May come again to us. If here he stay,
What can be done? Where every one is poor   260
What can be gained?' At this the old man paused,
And Isabel sat silent, for her mind
Was busy, looking back into past times.
There's Richard Bateman, thought she to herself,
He was a parish-boy: at the church-door   265
They made a gathering for him, shillings, pence,
And halfpennies, wherewith the neighbours bought
A basket, which they filled with pedlar's wares;
And with this basket on his arm the lad
Went up to London, found a master there,   270
Who out of many chose the trusty boy
To go and overlook his merchandise
Beyond the seas; where he grew wondrous rich,
And left estates and moneys to the poor,
And at his birth-place built a chapel floored   275
With marble, which he sent from foreign lands.
These thoughts, and many others of like sort,
Passed quickly through the mind of Isabel,
And her face brightened. The old man was glad,

And thus resumed: 'Well, Isabel! this scheme   280
These two days has been meat and drink to me.
Far more than we have lost is left us yet.
We have enough—I wish indeed that I
Were younger—but this hope is a good hope.
Make ready Luke's best garments, of the best   285
Buy for him more, and let us send him forth
Tomorrow, or the next day, or tonight—
If he could go, the boy should go tonight.'
Here Michael ceased, and to the fields went forth
With a light heart. The housewife for five days   290
Was restless morn and night, and all day long
Wrought on with her best fingers to prepare
Things needful for the journey of her son.
But Isabel was glad when Sunday came
To stop her in her work: for when she lay   295
By Michael's side, she for the two last nights
Heard him, how he was troubled in his sleep;
And when they rose at morning she could see
That all his hopes were gone. That day at noon
She said to Luke, while they two by themselves   300
Were sitting at the door, 'Thou must not go:
We have no other child but thee to lose,
None to remember—do not go away,
For if thou leave thy father he will die.'
The lad made answer with a jocund voice;   305
And Isabel, when she had told her fears,
Recovered heart. That evening her best fare
Did she bring forth, and all together sat
Like happy people round a Christmas fire.

Next morning Isabel resumed her work;   310
And all the ensuing week the house appeared
As cheerful as a grove in spring; at length
The expected letter from their kinsman came,
With kind assurances that he would do

His utmost for the welfare of the boy;   315
To which requests were added that forthwith
He might be sent to him. Ten times or more
The letter was read over; Isabel
Went forth to show it to the neighbours round;
Nor was there at that time on English land   320
A prouder heart than Luke's. When Isabel
Had to her house returned, the old man said,
'He shall depart tomorrow.' To this word
The housewife answered, talking much of things
Which if at such short notice he should go   325
Would surely be forgotten. But at length
She gave consent, and Michael was at ease.

Near the tumultuous brook of Green-head Gill,
In that deep valley, Michael had designed
To build a sheep-fold; and, before he heard   330
The tidings of his melancholy loss,
For this same purpose he had gathered up
A heap of stones, which close to the brook side
Lay thrown together, ready for the work.
With Luke that evening thitherward he walked;   335
And soon as they had reached the place he stopped,
And thus the old man spake to him: 'My son,
Tomorrow thou wilt leave me: with full heart
I look upon thee, for thou art the same
That wert a promise to me ere thy birth,   340
And all thy life hast been my daily joy.
I will relate to thee some little part
Of our two histories; 'twill do thee good
When thou art from me, even if I should speak
Of things thou canst not know of. After thou   345
First cam'st into the world, as it befalls
To new-born infants, thou didst sleep away
Two days, and blessings from thy father's tongue
Then fell upon thee. Day by day passed on,

And still I loved thee with increasing love.⠀⠀⠀⠀⠀350
Never to living ear came sweeter sounds
Than when I heard thee by our own fireside
First uttering, without words, a natural tune:
When thou, a feeding babe, didst in thy joy
Sing at thy mother's breast. Month followed month,⠀355
And in the open fields my life was passed
And in the mountains, else I think that thou
Hadst been brought up upon thy father's knees.
But we were playmates, Luke: among these hills,
As well thou know'st, in us the old and young⠀⠀⠀360
Have played together, nor with me didst thou
Lack any pleasure which a boy can know.'
Luke had a manly heart; but at these words
He sobbed aloud. The old man grasped his hand,
And said, 'Nay, do not take it so—I see⠀⠀⠀⠀⠀365
That these are things of which I need not speak.
Even to the utmost I have been to thee
A kind and a good father: and herein
I but repay a gift which I myself
Received at others' hands; for, though now old⠀⠀⠀370
Beyond the common life of man, I still
Remember them who loved me in my youth.
Both of them sleep together: here they lived,
As all their forefathers had done; and when
At length their time was come, they were not loth⠀⠀375
To give their bodies to the family mould.
I wished that thou shouldst live the life they lived.
But 'tis a long time to look back, my son,
And see so little gain from sixty years.
These fields were burthened when they came to me;⠀380
Till I was forty years of age, not more
Than half of my inheritance was mine.
I toiled and toiled; God blessed me in my work,
And till these three weeks past the land was free.
—It looks as if it never could endure⠀⠀⠀⠀⠀385

Another master. Heaven forgive me, Luke,
If I judge ill for thee, but it seems good
That thou shouldst go.' At this the old man paused;
Then, pointing to the stones near which they stood,
Thus, after a short silence, he resumed: 390
'This was a work for us; and now, my son,
It is a work for me. But, lay one stone—
Here, lay it for me, Luke, with thine own hands.
Nay, boy, be of good hope—we both may live
To see a better day. At eighty-four   395
I still am strong and stout; do thou thy part,
I will do mine. I will begin again
With many tasks that were resigned to thee;
Up to the heights, and in among the storms,
Will I without thee go again, and do   400
All works which I was wont to do alone
Before I knew thy face. Heaven bless thee, boy!
Thy heart these two weeks has been beating fast
With many hopes—it should be so—yes—yes—
I knew that thou couldst never have a wish   405
To leave me, Luke: thou hast been bound to me
Only by links of love: when thou art gone,
What will be left to us!—But I forget
My purposes. Lay now the corner-stone,
As I requested; and hereafter, Luke,   410
When thou art gone away, should evil men
Be thy companions, think of me, my son,
And of this moment; hither turn thy thoughts,
And God will strengthen thee; amid all fear
And all temptation, Luke, I pray that thou   415
May'st bear in mind the life thy fathers lived,
Who, being innocent, did for that cause
Bestir them in good deeds. Now, fare thee well—
When thou return'st, thou in this place will see
A work which is not here; a covenant   420
'Twill be between us. But whatever fate

Befall thee, I shall love thee to the last,
And bear thy memory with me to the grave.'

The shepherd ended here; and Luke stooped down,
And, as his father had requested, laid   425
The first stone of the sheep-fold. At the sight
The old man's grief broke from him, to his heart
He pressed his son, he kisséd him and wept;
And to the house together they returned.

Next morning, as had been resolved, the boy   430
Began his journey, and when he had reached
The public way, he put on a bold face;
And all the neighbours as he passed their doors
Came forth with wishes and with farewell prayers,
That followed him till he was out of sight.   435

A good report did from their kinsman come
Of Luke and his well-doing; and the boy
Wrote loving letters, full of wondrous news,
Which, as the housewife phrased it, were throughout
The prettiest letters that were ever seen.   440
Both parents read them with rejoicing hearts.
So, many months passed on: and once again
The shepherd went about his daily work
With confident and cheerful thoughts; and now
Sometimes when he could find a leisure hour   445
He to that valley took his way, and there
Wrought at the sheep-fold. Meantime Luke began
To slacken in his duty; and at length
He in the dissolute city gave himself
To evil courses: ignominy and shame   450
Fell on him, so that he was driven at last
To seek a hiding-place beyond the seas.

There is a comfort in the strength of love;
'Twill make a thing endurable, which else

Would break the heart: old Michael found it so.   455
I have conversed with more than one who well
Remember the old man, and what he was
Years after he had heard this heavy news.
His bodily frame had been from youth to age
Of an unusual strength. Among the rocks   460
He went, and still looked up upon the sun,
And listened to the wind; and as before
Performed all kinds of labour for his sheep,
And for the land his small inheritance.
And to that hollow dell from time to time   465
Did he repair, to build the fold of which
His flock had need. 'Tis not forgotten yet
The pity which was then in every heart
For the old man—and 'tis believed by all
That many and many a day he thither went,   470
And never lifted up a single stone.

There, by the sheep-fold, sometimes was he seen
Sitting alone, with that his faithful dog,
Then old, beside him, lying at his feet.
The length of full seven years from time to time   475
He at the building of this sheep-fold wrought,
And left the work unfinished when he died.
Three years, or little more, did Isabel
Survive her husband; at her death the estate
Was sold, and went into a stranger's hand.   480
The cottage which was named THE EVENING STAR
Is gone—the ploughshare has been through the
      ground
On which it stood; great changes have been wrought
In all the neighbourhood: yet the oak is left
That grew beside their door; and the remains   485
Of the unfinished sheep-fold may be seen
Beside the boisterous brook of Green-head Gill.

Appendix[1]

See Preface, page 38—'by what is usually called poetic diction.'

As PERHAPS I have no right to expect from a reader of an introduction to a volume of poems that attentive perusal without which it is impossible, imperfectly as I have been compelled to express my meaning, that
5 what I have said in the preface should throughout be fully understood, I am the more anxious to give an exact notion of the sense in which I use the phrase *poetic diction*; and for this purpose I will here add a few words concerning the origin of the phraseology
10 which I have condemned under that name. The earliest poets of all nations generally wrote from passion excited by real events; they wrote naturally, and as men; feeling powerfully as they did, their language was daring and figurative. In succeeding times poets, and
15 men ambitious of the fame of poets, perceiving the influence of such language, and desirous of producing the same effect without having the same animating passion, set themselves to a mechanical adoption of those figures of speech; and made use of them some-
20 times with propriety, but much more frequently applied them to feelings and ideas with which they had no natural connection whatsoever. A language was thus insensibly produced differing materially from the real language of men in *any situation*. The reader or
25 hearer of this distorted language found himself in a perturbed and unusual state of mind; when affected by the genuine language of passion he had been in a perturbed and unusual state of mind also; in both cases he was willing that his common judgment and
30 understanding should be laid asleep, and he had no

[1]Added by Wordsworth in 1802.

instinctive and infallible perception of the true to make
him reject the false: the one served as a passport for
the other. The agitation and confusion of mind were
in both cases delightful, and no wonder if he con-
founded the one with the other and believed them both 5
to be produced by the same or similar causes. Besides,
the poet spake to him in the character of a man to be
looked up to, a man of genius and authority. Thus,
and from a variety of other causes, this distorted
language was received with admiration; and poets, it 10
is probable, who had before contented themselves for
the most part with misapplying only expressions which
at first had been dictated by real passion, carried the
abuse still further, and introduced phrases composed
apparently in the spirit of the original figurative 15
language of passion, yet altogether of their own invention, and distinguished by various degrees of wanton
deviation from good sense and nature.

It is indeed true that the language of the earliest
poets was felt to differ materially from ordinary 20
language, because it was the language of extraordinary
occasions; but it was really spoken by men, language
which the poet himself had uttered when he had been
affected by the events which he described, or which
he had heard uttered by those around him. To this 25
language it is probable that metre of some sort or
other was early superadded. This separated the
genuine language of poetry still further from common
life, so that whoever read or heard the poems of these
earliest poets felt himself moved in a way in which he 30
had not been accustomed to be moved in real life, and
by causes manifestly different from those which acted
upon him in real life. This was the great temptation
to all the corruptions which have followed: under the
protection of this feeling succeeding poets constructed 35
a phraseology which had one thing, it is true, in com-

mon with the genuine language of poetry, namely that
it was not heard in ordinary conversation: that it was
unusual. But the first poets, as I have said, spake a
language which though unusual was still the language
5 of men. This circumstance, however, was disregarded
by their successors: they found that they could please
by easier means; they became proud of a language
which they themselves had invented, and which was
uttered only by themselves; and with the spirit of a
10 fraternity they arrogated it to themselves as their own.
In process of time metre became a symbol or promise
of this unusual language, and whoever took upon him
to write in metre, according as he possessed more or
less of true poetic genius, introduced less or more of
15 this adulterated phraseology into his compositions,
and the true and the false become so inseparably interwoven that the taste of men was gradually perverted;
and this language was received as a natural language;
and at length, by the influence of books upon men, did
20 to a certain degree really become so. Abuses of this
kind were imported from one nation to another, and
with the progress of refinement this diction became
daily more and more corrupt, thrusting out of sight
the plain humanities of nature by a motley masquerade
25 of tricks, quaintnesses, hieroglyphics and enigmas.

It would be highly interesting to point out the
causes of the pleasure given by this extravagant and
absurd language, but this is not the place: it depends
upon a great variety of causes, but upon none perhaps
30 more than its influence in impressing a notion of the
peculiarity and exaltation of the poet's character, and
in flattering the reader's self-love by bringing him
nearer to a sympathy with that character; an effect
which is accomplished by unsettling ordinary habits
35 of thinking, and thus assisting the reader to approach
to that perturbed and dizzy state of mind in which if

he does not find himself, he imagines that he is *baulked* of a peculiar enjoyment which poetry can and ought to bestow.

The sonnet which I have quoted from Gray in the preface, except the lines printed in italics, consists of little else but this diction, though not of the worst kind; and indeed, if I may be permitted to say so, it is far too common in the best writers both ancient and modern. Perhaps I can in no way, by positive example, more easily give my reader a notion of what I mean by the phrase *poetic diction* than by referring him to a comparison between the metrical paraphrases we have of passages in the Old and New Testament, and those passages as they exist in our common translation. See Pope's *Messiah* throughout, Prior's 'Did sweeter sounds adorn my flowing tongue,' etc., etc., 'Though I speak with the tongues of men and of angels,' etc., etc. See 1st Corinthians, chapter xiiith. By way of immediate example, take the following of Dr. Johnson:

> Turn on the prudent Ant thy heedless eyes,
> Observe her labours, Sluggard, and be wise;
> No stern command, no monitory voice,
> Prescribes her duties, or directs her choice;
> Yet, timely provident, she hastes away
> To snatch the blessings of a plenteous day;
> When fruitful Summer loads the teeming plain,
> She crops the harvest and she stores the grain.
> How long shall sloth usurp thy useless hours,
> Unnerve thy vigour, and enchain thy powers?
> While artful shades thy downy couch enclose,
> And soft solicitation courts repose,
> Amidst the drowsy charms of dull delight,
> Year chases year with unremitted flight,
> Till want now following, fraudulent and slow,
> Shall spring to seize thee, like an ambushed foe.

From this hubbub of words pass to the original. 'Go to the ant, thou sluggard, consider her ways, and be wise: which having no guide, overseer, or ruler, provideth her meat in the summer, and gathereth her food 5 in the harvest. How long wilt thou sleep, O sluggard? when wilt thou arise out of thy sleep? Yet a little sleep, a little slumber, a little folding of the hands to sleep. So shall thy poverty come as one that travaileth, and thy want as an armed man.' Proverbs, chap. vith.

10 One more quotation and I have done. It is from Cowper's *Verses supposed to be written by Alexander Selkirk*:

> Religion! what treasure untold
> Resides in that heavenly word!
> 15 More precious than silver and gold,
> Or all that this earth can afford.
> But the sound of the church-going bell
> These valleys and rocks never heard,
> Ne'er sighed at the sound of a knell,
> 20 Or smiled when a sabbath appeared.
>
> Ye winds, that have made me your sport,
> Convey to this desolate shore
> Some cordial endearing report
> Of a land I must visit no more.
> 25 My friends, do they now and then send
> A wish or a thought after me?
> O tell me I yet have a friend,
> Though a friend I am never to see.

I have quoted this passage as an instance of three 30 different styles of composition. The first four lines are poorly expressed: some critics would call the language prosaic; the fact is it would be bad prose, so bad that it is scarcely worse in metre. The epithet 'church-going' applied to a bell, and that by so chaste a writer as Cowper, is an instance of the strange abuses which poets have introduced into their language till they and their readers take them as matters of course, if they do not single them out expressly as objects of admiration. The two lines 'Ne'er sighed at the sound,' etc., are in my opinion an instance of the language of passion wrested from its proper use and, from the mere circumstance of the composition being in metre, applied upon an occasion that does not justify such violent expressions; and I should condemn the passage, though perhaps few readers will agree with me, as vicious poetic diction. The last stanza is throughout admirably expressed: it would be equally good whether in prose or verse, except that the reader has an exquisite pleasure in seeing such natural language so naturally connected with metre. The beauty of this stanza tempts me here to add a sentiment which ought to be the pervading spirit of a system, detached parts of which have been imperfectly explained in the preface: namely, that in proportion as ideas and feelings are valuable, whether the composition be in prose or in verse, they require and exact one and the same language.

Notes

REFERENCES AND QUOTATIONS

'W.W., 1843' indicates a quotation from the series of notes on his poems dictated by Wordsworth in that year to Isabella Fenwick, which may be found in full in the *Poetical Works*, ed. E. de Selincourt and Helen Darbishire (O.U.P., 1940-9). All other abbreviations are shown in the Bibliography, pp. 420-7. The page numbers given for Coleridge's *Biographia Literaria* (*B.L.*) are those of the Everyman edition by George Watson (Dent, 1957); chapter references are also given for the benefit of readers using other editions. In quotations from this text Coleridge's original italic has been restored where this seemed helpful. Capitals, spelling and punctuation have been modernised throughout.

ORIGINS OF 'LYRICAL BALLADS'

One June 6th 1797 Coleridge paid a visit to Wordsworth and his sister Dorothy, who were then living at Racedown in Dorset. The two men were much of an age: each had published poems, each was at work on a blank-verse tragedy, each had been disappointed in his hopes of the French Revolution, each still took an unpatriotic view of the war. Above all, each recognised in the other a strong original mind, with differences of temperament that made exchanges all the more stimulating. They had met twice before, and already liked and admired each other; now they entered upon a period of intimate friendship, with Dorothy as an indispensable third. Coleridge's visit lasted three weeks, after which he took the Wordsworths back with him to his cottage at Nether Stowey, in Somerset. By the end of a fortnight a new home had been found for the Wordsworths at Alfoxden, a fair-sized country house four miles from Stowey. For a year the three friends were in almost daily contact, except for an interval from mid-December to mid-January when

Coleridge was at Shrewsbury and the Wordsworths in London. This year brought both men to maturity as poets, and its most immediate result was the publication of *Lyrical Ballads*.

On November 12th Wordsworth, Coleridge and Dorothy set out from Alfoxden on a walking-tour towards Watchet. Funds were low, and the two men agreed to pay the expenses of the trip by writing a poem that could be sold for five pounds to the *Monthly Magazine*, where verse by Coleridge had already appeared. This periodical had also published translations of German ballads on supernatural themes, such as Bürger's *Lenore*; and between them Wordsworth and Coleridge devised the story for a new supernatural ballad, *The Ancient Mariner*. (For Wordsworth's account of their collaboration see *P.W.*, i, 360-1; see also *M.M.*, i, 347-8.) The subject seized Coleridge's imagination: before long Wordsworth felt himself to be a 'clog' and withdrew. By November 20th the poem was 300 lines long (*C.L.*, i, 357), and the plan of printing it in a volume with some pieces by Wordsworth had already been considered (*E.L.W.*, p. 194). During the winter, however, this scheme lapsed. Coleridge worked intermittently at *The Ancient Mariner*, but in January he reverted to the plan of sending it to the *Monthly Magazine* (*C.L.*, i, 368). In February and again in mid-March he wrote to his publisher, Joseph Cottle of Bristol, discussing plans for an enlarged third edition of his *Poems on Various Subjects* (1796), in which it is clear that *The Ancient Mariner* would have been included (*C.L.*, i, 387, 399).

This third edition did not materialise, however, and shortly afterwards the scheme for including *The Ancient Mariner* in a joint publication with Wordsworth was revived. Coleridge brought the poem completed to Alfoxden on March 23rd, four days after Wordsworth had begun work on a very different kind of ballad, *The Thorn* (*D.W.J.*, i, 13). It seems likely that about this time they formed the dual plan described by Coleridge in *Biographia Literaria* (see below, p. 408). Their joint work was to include two complementary kinds of poem: those by Coleridge would deal with 'supernatural, or at least romantic' subjects, while those by Wordsworth would deal with subjects from ordinary life but in such a way as to 'excite a feeling analogous to the supernatural.' With this scheme, probably, in mind Wordsworth completed *The Thorn* and wrote a new long poem, *Peter Bell*, which bears signs of having been intended as a companion-piece for *The Ancient Mariner*. His *Goody Blake* and *The Idiot Boy* too were probably written in furtherance of this plan; and he gave Coleridge his own unfinished ballad on the theme of a mother's curse—*The Three Graves*—hoping that Coleridge would be able to complete it (*M.M.*, i, 317, 388-9). All these poems 'excite a feeling analogous to the supernatural' in a much more direct and obvious way than Coleridge's subsequent account suggests. Coleridge added two cantos to *The Three Graves* and also worked at his own more important 'supernatural' tale, *Christabel*; probably too at his *Ballad of the Dark Ladie* (*C.P.W.*, i, 213-26, 293-5). Unfortunately he was unable to finish any of these poems. *The Ancient Mariner*, which had been the nucleus of the joint work, now looked like becoming 'an interpolation of heterogeneous matter'; so indeed Coleridge described his own contributions in 1817.

Meanwhile a series of negotiations was taking place between the poets and the publisher, Cottle. About March 13th Coleridge had written offering him two publications: a volume containing his and Wordsworth's tragedies, and another containing Wordsworth's poems only (*C.L.*, i, 399-400). Cottle showed interest in Wordsworth's poems, visited Stowey in late March or early April, and seems to have written offering to publish the two men's work separately. But Wordsworth and Coleridge were now resolved on a joint anonymous publication, and about the end of April Coleridge replied: 'We deem that the volumes offered to you are to a certain degree *one work*, in *kind tho' not in degree*, as an ode is one work; and that our different poems are as stanzas, good relatively rather than absolutely' (*C.L.*, i, 412). (Griggs assigns this letter to the end of May, but seems to have been misled by the fact that Cottle visited the poets twice: cf. *M.M.*, i, 372, 396.) The word 'volumes' shows that Coleridge is describing a larger publication than *L.B.* (*1798*), such as would have been produced if the dual scheme had been fully carried out. By the last week in May, however, when Cottle visited Alfoxden, it was clear that this would not be the case. Most of the 'supernatural' poems had failed to materialise; Wordsworth needed money, and it must have seemed the best course to make up a single volume out of poems already written. From the final scheme, as drawn up during this visit, *Peter Bell* was excluded. The volume was to contain *The Ancient Mariner, The Thorn, Goody Blake, The Idiot Boy,* two excerpts from Coleridge's tragedy, a long excerpt from *Salisbury Plain*—a narrative poem at which Wordsworth had been working on and off since 1793—and upwards of a dozen shorter poems, most of which had been written by Wordsworth in the very creative period which had begun in March. For the copyright of Wordsworth's contributions Cottle gave thirty guineas; after his departure Dorothy wrote, on May 31st, 'William has sold his poems very advantageously' (*E.L.W.*, p. 219). Two more short poems, *Expostulation and Reply* and *The Tables Turned,* were probably added in June; and the finest of all Wordsworth's contributions, *Tintern Abbey,* was written in mid-July when *Lyrical Ballads* was already at the press.

Wordsworth's 'Advertisement' or preface to this volume (reprinted below, pp. 428-9) makes no mention of the plan for a twofold series of poems on contrasting themes. It announces instead that 'the majority of the following poems' are experiments in using the language of ordinary conversation for poetic purposes. Wordsworth had been working towards a simplification of diction since 1793, when reviewers had noted a 'laboured and artificial cast of expression' in *An Evening Walk* and *Descriptive Sketches*; and with his burst of poetic activity in the spring of 1798 this process had been intensified. Coleridge's development had in some respects been similar, with Cowper as an important influence. But within this broad pattern the poems of *L.B.* (*1798*) are astonishingly diverse: the first eight printed, for example, are all of quite different kinds (for a list of contents see below, p. 430). In his prefatory remarks Wordsworth is really explaining and defending poems like *Simon Lee* and *The Last of the Flock,* which deal with humble rustic themes in a deliberately simple, un-literary language. These remarks do not prepare us for *The Ancient Mariner* or *Tintern Abbey*; they are not particularly relevant even to poems like *Lines written in Early Spring*; and they are misleading in that they suggest that this miscellaneous and somewhat haphazardly assembled volume is the product of a critical programme. This said, it is true that *Lyrical Ballads* as a whole represents a movement away from ornate and conventionally figurative poetry towards a poetry refreshed, on the one hand, by the example of the traditional ballads, and on the other by contact with living speech.

EARLY REVIEWS AND EDITIONS

Cottle printed *Lyrical Ballads* during the summer of 1798, and circulated a few copies; but it is doubtful whether he ever put it on sale. For reasons that are still not wholly clear he transferred the impression to a London firm of booksellers, J. and A. Arch, who published the work on October 4th. (For the most recent discussion of these events see D. F. Foxon, 'The Printing of *Lyrical Ballads*, 1798,' *The Library*, ser. 5, ix (1954), 221-41.) The sale seems at first to have been slow, and the earliest reviews were discouraging: a predominantly unfavourable article by Southey in the *Critical Review* for October was followed in December by rather perfunctory notices in the *Analytical Review* and *Monthly Magazine*. But in June 1799 a long and, on the whole, kindly article appeared in the influential *Monthly Review*; and in the following October the *British Critic* gave the poems almost unqualified praise. (For texts or summaries of these reviews see Elsie Smith, *An Estimate of William Wordsworth by his Contemporaries* (Blackwell, 1932), pp. 29-41.) By the summer of 1799 the sales too had improved (see *E.L.W.*, pp. 264, 267). In April 1800 a short but very enthusiastic notice appeared in the *Antijacobin Review* (v, 434). It seems clear that after a slow start *Lyrical Ballads* was winning a good deal of favour both from critics and from the public. The reviewers were not outraged by Wordsworth's 'experiments,' which on a superficial view at least were not the first of their kind (see Robert Mayo, 'The Contemporaneity of the *Lyrical Ballads*,' *P.M.L.A.*, lxix (1954), 486-522). *The Thorn, Goody Blake, The Idiot Boy* and *Simon Lee* all received their share of praise; but four reviewers complained of the obscurity of *The Ancient Mariner*. Wordsworth wrote to Cottle in June 1799:

> From what I can gather it seems that The Ancyent Marinere has upon the whole been an injury to the volume, I mean that the old words and the strangeness of it have deterred readers from going on. If the volume should come to a second edition I would put in its place some little things which would be more likely to suit the common taste. (*E.L.W.*, p. 264.)

By June 1800 the first edition had sold out, and Wordsworth and Coleridge were preparing a second, in two volumes. For the copyright of this edition Longman paid £80. Coleridge renewed his efforts at *Christabel* and completed the second part, but in October the decision was taken to exclude it. On October 9th Coleridge wrote that

> . . . the poem was in direct opposition to the very purpose for which the *Lyrical Ballads* were published—viz., an experiment to see how far those passions which alone give any value to extraordinary incidents were capable of interesting, in and for themselves, in the incidents of common life.
>
> (*C.L.*, i, 631.)

As this incident suggests, Wordsworth's influence predominated in the new edition even more than 1798. The title-page bore his name alone—an arrangement probably urged by Coleridge, who was unreasonably modest about his own poems and anxious to make Wordsworth's name known. The first volume began with Wordsworth's long Preface, a statement of the conclusions about poetry to which his rejection of poetic diction had now led him. This was followed by all the poems of *L.B.* (*1798*) except Wordsworth's *The Convict*, which was replaced by Coleridge's *Love*; but these poems were rearranged so that *The Ancient Mariner* appeared last instead of first, the Preface being followed by *Expostula-*

tion and Reply. The second volume consisted of forty-one
new poems by Wordsworth. As we should expect, this volume
corresponds more closely to the theories put forward in the
Preface than does the miscellaneous first volume; and it concludes with *Michael*, an achievement as impressive in its own
way as *The Ancient Mariner* or *Tintern Abbey*. Though this
edition bears the date 1800 it did not appear until January
1801, owing to delays in the writing of the Preface and
Michael. Within two months of publication a very favourable
review had appeared from the pen of John Stoddart, who
admired both poets and had visited them while the second
volume was being prepared (see R. S. Woof, 'John Stoddart,
Michael and *Lyrical Ballads*,' *Ariel* (April 1970), pp. 7-22).
In March Coleridge wrote: 'The character of the *Lyrical
Ballads* is very great, and will increase daily. They have
extolled them in the *British Critic*' (*C.L.*, ii, 707-8).

This season of calm weather ended in October 1802, with
the opening number of the *Edinburgh Review*. Francis
Jeffrey and his collaborators were out to produce a lively first
issue; they needed a butt, and Wordsworth, Coleridge and
Southey were by now well enough known to be worth
attacking. In the course of reviewing Southey's *Thalaba*
(1801) Jeffrey created the collective caricature of the 'Lake
School of Poetry,' which was to provide him with a useful
Aunt Sally for the next twenty years (*Edinburgh Review*, i,
63-83). Jeffrey had seen *L.B. (1798)* and knew something of
the poems Southey had published between 1797 and 1800:
he ridiculed the sentimental humanitarian poems represented in *Lyrical Ballads* by *The Convict* and *The Dungeon*,
and the attempt, which Southey also had made, to write
poems in a language based on that of common conversation.
For the purposes of this review he invokes a rather old-
fashioned Augustanism (see the extract printed below, pp.
410-12); but on the whole his attacks should be seen as
journalistic entertainments rather than as expressions of a
genuine critical reaction to the new poetry. They reached an
unprecedentedly wide public, however, and in a period
when critical standards were uncertain they had a good deal
of influence. Smaller journals followed the lead of the *Edinburgh Review*; and it was in the face of much derision and

hostility that Wordsworth and Coleridge finally established themselves as the major poets of their generation.

A third edition of *Lyrical Ballads* appeared in the summer of 1802, before Jeffrey's attack was in print. For this edition Wordsworth again revised and rearranged the poems, omitting two of the weaker ones, and made substantial additions to the Preface. In the fourth and final edition of 1805 the poems appeared in the same order but with a few changes of text, while the Preface remained unaltered except in punctuation. It is on the text of this edition that the present volume is based. Details follow of four poems which appeared in some earlier editions, but not in that of 1805:

(1) Coleridge's *Lewti* (*C.P.W.*, i, 253-6). This poem had appeared in the *Morning Post* for April 13th 1798 and was widely known to be by Coleridge. It was to have been included in *L.B.* (*1798*), but was withdrawn after the sheets had actually been printed, probably because to have included it would have revealed Coleridge as one of the authors of the volume. *The Nightingale* was printed in its place. (*Lewti* is an expanded and adapted version of Wordsworth's early *Beauty and Moonlight*: see *P.W.*, i, 263-4, 367; ii, 531.)

(2) Wordsworth's *The Convict* (*P.W.*, i, 312-14). This poem too had appeared in the *Morning Post* (December 14th, 1797), sent probably by Coleridge, who had just begun to contribute to that newspaper. It was included in *L.B.* (*1798*), but never afterwards reprinted by Wordsworth.

(3) Coleridge's *The Dungeon* (*C.P.W.*, i, 185). An excerpt from *Osorio*, included in *L.B.* (*1798*) and *L.B.* (*1800*) but not afterwards reprinted by Coleridge as a separate poem. The decision to withdraw this poem and *The Convict* may have been influenced by the *Monthly Review*'s complaint of excessive tenderness shown towards criminals (see E. Smith, pp. 36-7).

(4) Wordsworth's *A Character* (*P.W.*, iv, 58-9). Included in *L.B.* (*1800*), but not reprinted by Wordsworth until 1836.

NOTES ON THE TITLE PAGE

The title suggests a crossing of two literary *genres*. The
main function of the ballad was to tell a story in a comparatively simple style, usually in quatrains; of the lyric, to express emotion. F. W. Bateson suggests that the title is meant to convey that where these poems tell a story, 'the emphasis is not on the story . . . but on the emotions embodied in the story' (*Wordsworth: A Re-interpretation* (Longmans, 1954), pp. 137-8). The title was probably felt to cover verse dialogues such as *Expostulation and Reply*, and even poems like *Lines written in Early Spring*, which express the poet's thoughts and feelings directly but are written in the ballad stanza. The 'other poems' are the blank-verse pieces and *The Female Vagrant*, written in the elaborate Spenserian stanza. Few of the poems are 'lyrical' or 'ballads' in the sense of being suitable for singing.

Admiration for the traditional ballad had been steadily increasing in England since Thomas Percy published his *Reliques of Ancient English Poetry* in 1765 (a fourth edition, much enlarged, had appeared in 1794). Wordsworth paid tribute to Percy's collection in 1815 in his *Essay Supplementary to the Preface*:

> I have already stated how much Germany is indebted to this latter work; and for our own country, its poetry has been absolutely redeemed by it. I do not think that there is an able writer in verse of the present day who would not be proud to acknowledge his obligations to the *Reliques*; I know that it is so with my friends; and for myself, I am happy in this occasion to make a public avowal of my own. (*P.W.*, ii, 424-5.)

Helen Darbishire writes: 'It is hard to see in the *Lyrical Ballads* any literary influence at all except that of the [traditional] ballads' (*The Poet Wordsworth* (O.U.P., 1958), p. 46). This is clearly an overstatement, but the influence of the *Reliques* was certainly important. Wordsworth found in these ballads the directness of language and the appeal to common human feeling that he wanted

17 to achieve in his own poetry; Coleridge found in some of them the 'supernatural, or at least romantic' themes which best stimulated his imagination.

WITH PASTORAL AND OTHER POEMS 1802-5; WITH A FEW OTHER POEMS 1798; WITH OTHER POEMS 1800.

BY W. WORDSWORTH 1800-5; see above, p. 266.

Quam nihil ad genium, Papiniane, tuum! This motto first appeared in 1800 and means 'How utterly unsuited to your taste, Papinianus!' It was probably taken from John Selden's prefatory letter to Michael Drayton's poem *Poly-Olbion* (1612-22): this work was included in Robert Anderson's *Complete Edition of the Poets of Great Britain* (13 vols., Edinburgh, 1792-5), a set of which was in Wordsworth's possession during 1800 (see *M.M.*, i, 515). Selden's own source is unknown to us, and may well have been unknown to Wordsworth and Coleridge. Aemilius Papinianus was an eminent Roman jurist, executed by Caracalla in A.D. 212. Selden is voicing his scorn for ignorant critics, and his use of this quotation suggests that for him Papinianus represents the true learning which despises their 'barbarous glosses.' But in its new context the sentence must refer to the *Lyrical Ballads* themselves, and 'Papinianus' seems to stand for the unsympathetic persons who are here warned that the poems will not be to their liking. The motto may also have been meant as a private joke against the lawyer and political writer Sir James Mackintosh (1765-1832). Coleridge greatly disliked this man, whom he regarded as a superficial time-server. Apparently Mackintosh had disparaged Wordsworth in Coleridge's presence, whereupon Coleridge had remarked: 'He strides on so far before you, that he dwindles in the distance!' (See William Hazlitt, 'My First Acquaintance with Poets,' *Works*, ed. P. P. Howe (Dent, 1930-34), xvii, 111; *cf. C.L.*, ii, 737.) Coleridge certainly connected this motto with Mackintosh on March 4th 1805, when he described in his notebook a nightmare and added: 'Quam nihil ad genium, Papiliane [sic], tuum! i.e., this Mackintosh would prove to be non-sense by a Scotch smile' (*C.N.*, ii, 2468).

GENERAL NOTE ON THE PREFACE

Lyrical Ballads originally appeared in 1798 with no intro- 18
duction but the short 'Advertisement' reproduced on
pp. 426-7. Wordsworth began writing the long Preface in
the summer of 1800 and had completed it by the end of
September (*M.M.*, i, 492). Coleridge claimed in 1802
that it was 'half a child of my own brain,' since many of
its ideas had originated in discussions between the two
poets; and he may have given further help by making
notes on these topics (see *C.L.*, ii, 811, 830). Nevertheless it was Wordsworth who finally shaped this material
and in doing so assimilated it to his own way of thinking.
With several of his formulations Coleridge subsequently
came to disagree. The essay first appeared with *L.B.*
(*1800*); for the edition of 1802 Wordsworth made revisions
and some additions, the most important of which runs
from p. 29 to p. 38. No significant changes were made in
1805, but further revisions occurred in later years when
Wordsworth reprinted the essay as an appendix to his
poems.

Considered as the introduction to a collection of poems,
the Preface is not a tactful piece of writing. Forty pages
of none-too-easy prose seem as likely to have deterred
readers at the outset as Coleridge's *Ancient Mariner*,
which Wordsworth had just removed from the beginning
to the end of Volume I. Those who persevered ran some
risk of being alienated either by the extreme form in
which Wordsworth states some of his doctrines, or by his
tone, which is sometimes pedantic, sometimes arrogant
and sometimes absurdly self-protective. Wordsworth
makes bold claims for his poems, such as not all of
them will bear; declares that to accommodate them
drastic revaluations of earlier poetry will be necessary;
and cautions the reader interminably as to how they must
and must not be read. Despite this care the account he
gives of the poems is misleading, since they are much
more diverse than the Preface suggests. Coleridge may
have been right to conclude that it was this Preface
which provoked the hostility of critics from 1802 on-

18 wards. Nevertheless, it is probably the most important
single document in the history of English criticism. It
helped substantially to bring about the reforms Wordsworth most wanted; it gave valuable new insights into
the nature, scope and function of poetry, and into the
creative process; above all, it set new standards for the
discussion of such matters by its intense seriousness and
by its grasp of inward experience. By comparison with
Wordsworth's Preface all previous writings on poetry are
apt to seem superficial.

The theme Wordsworth pursues most consistently is
his argument against 'poetic diction.' The immediate
objects of his attack were the 'gaudiness and inane phraseology' of poets like the Della Cruscans and Erasmus
Darwin, forgotten now but esteemed in the 1790's and
an influence upon Wordsworth's own earlier writing.
More generally, Wordsworth is arguing against what
F. W. Bateson calls a 'positive theory of poetic diction,'
current throughout the eighteenth century: the belief not
only that some modes of diction were best avoided in
poetry, but that other modes were specially suitable.
Thus a poet might write 'reddening Phoebus' instead of
'rising sun,' and 'green attire' for 'grass,' with no particular intention but that of increasing the elegance of his
lines. This theory and practice fell into discredit during
the early nineteenth century, partly because of Wordsworth's growing prestige and influence. Wordsworth's
fundamental objection to what he elsewhere calls a
'vague, glossy and unfeeling language' is that to separate
poetry from ordinary speech is to separate it from human
life. For him the great value of poetry is that it permits
the sharing of experience, the communication of truths
'carried alive into the heart by passion.' Characteristically
he prefers to compare poetry with prose, thus emphasising
its communicative power, rather than to draw the traditional parallel with painting, which emphasised its
aesthetic qualities (p. 28); and as an example of 'poetic
diction' he chooses a sonnet by Gray which expresses
very little, but resembles, one might say, a small decorous
monument. The view of poetry as communication is

not confined to one period or movement; but it has 18 never been so forcefully expressed as in the great passage Wordsworth added in 1802, foreshadowed by his earlier sentence:

> Poetry sheds no tears 'such as angels weep,' but natural and human tears; she can boast of no celestial ichor that distinguishes her vital juices from those of prose; the same human blood circulates through the veins of them both.

Though Wordsworth's argument against poetic diction is forceful and cogent, its terms are often inexact. His phrase 'the real language of men' begs important questions; and by using the word 'language' synonymously with 'diction' he obscures the fact that language involves the organisation as well as the choice of words. Moreover, he runs some risk of setting up an opposite but equally false standard for poetry whereby none but commonplace words shall be used. His theoretical preference for the language as well as the themes of 'low and rustic life' obviously owes something to the contemporary tendency to idealise peasants, savages, and others who might have escaped the corrupting influence of civilisation. Had Wordsworth really used rustic language, however 'purified,' in his poetry, the poetry would have been impoverished; but as Coleridge points out (*B.L.*, chapt. xviii, p. 202), his practice is sounder than his precept. The usual modern view would be that no words are in themselves either specially fit or unfit for poetry, and that they must be judged by their effectiveness where they occur. Coleridge goes some way towards formulating this view in chapters xvii and xviii of *Biographia Literaria*, which provide the earliest and best commentary on Wordsworth's discussion of poetic diction. (For other accounts of this discussion see F. W. Bateson, 'Poetic Diction and the Sublime,' *English Critical Essays: Twentieth Century*, Series 2 (O.U.P., 1958), pp. 169-80; Geoffrey Tillotson, *On the Poetry of Pope* (O.U.P., 2nd edn., 1950), pp. 63-104 and *Augustan Studies* (Athlone Press, 1961), chaps. i-iii; Donald Davie, *Purity of Diction in English Verse* (Chatto, 1952).)

18   Wordsworth's view of the scope of poetry is even less
restricted than his view of its language. 'It is the honourable characteristic of poetry,' he wrote in 1798, 'that its
materials are to be found in every subject which can
interest the human mind'; and this attitude underlies the
whole Preface. Several passages of 1800 can be seen as
amplifications of the same idea, as for example the statement that 'the feeling . . . gives importance to the action
and situation, and not the action and situation to the
feeling' (p. 24). Subjects no more than words are poetic
or unpoetic in themselves: a slight incident of village
life may be material not merely for verse of the pastoral
or burlesque kind but for serious poetry, if the poet can
make it meaningful; nor need it detract from this seriousness to mention such undignified matters as round
shoulders and swollen ankles. To some extent this view
was already implicit in the work of poets as different as
Burns and Cowper. But until 1798 it had not been decis-
ively stated: critical theory was still dominated by the neoclassical *genres*, each with its appropriate subject-matter,
method and status. In 1802 Wordsworth extends his own
theory of poetry into the future in a striking passage which
foresees the possible transformation of men's environment
by science. Should this occur, he writes, scientific
matters which cannot now be brought into poetry simply
because they are not generally understood will become
available for the poet's use; and by using them the poet
will help other men to become more fully and imaginatively aware of them (pp. 35-6). Since 1800 science has of
course both transformed our environment and provided
material for many poems. A comparison of Wordsworth's
treatment of this topic with that of C. Day Lewis in 1947
(see below, pp. 294-5) gives the effect of two contemporaries conversing, though in slightly different
idioms.

By emphasising the communicative power of poetry
Wordsworth raises the question of what it communicates.
The traditional formula had been that poetry should both
teach and delight; and Wordsworth analyses both processes in terms of the system of psychology set forth by

David Hartley (1705-57) in his *Observations on Man* **18**
(1749). Some knowledge of Hartley's doctrines is necessary to a full understanding both of the Preface and of
several of Wordsworth's poems. Like modern behaviour-
ists, Hartley taught that character is evolved by continuous and largely automatic processes of conditioning (or
'association'), all of which begin with the experience of
the senses. From earliest childhood we learn to associate
certain sights, sounds, tastes, etc., with pleasant or painful
feelings. As more and more associations are formed they
build themselves into increasingly complex systems of
responses which together make up the whole of our personality, 'imagination' being the first faculty thus developed and the 'moral sense' the last. Hartley assumed
that nature (i.e. the created universe) was rationally
organised for a benevolent purpose. From this it followed
that the general tendency of nature's conditioning must
be to lead men to happiness and virtue. Just as we come
to know wholesome food by associating it with pleasure
(and bad food by associating it with pain), so by more
intricate but essentially similar processes we learn the
pleasures of self-approval, sympathy for our fellow-
creatures, and the love of God (and the pains of the
opposite states). While apparently scientific in character,
Hartley's system could be felt to confirm that sense of a
living relationship between men and the material universe
which it had become increasingly difficult to preserve in
a century dominated by mathematics and Newtonian
physics. Coleridge showed his admiration by naming his
eldest son 'David Hartley' in 1796, and Wordsworth too
was strongly influenced by Hartley's ideas during the
period when most of the *Lyrical Ballads* were being
written.

Hartley's optimism may seem shallow to modern
readers, but it suited and supported Wordsworth's growing happiness at this time. Furthermore, Hartley's asso-
ciationist psychology showed Wordsworth the importance
of unconscious processes in our mental and emotional life
and gave him terms in which to describe them. It is with
Hartley's help that Wordsworth redefines the poet's

18 'teaching' rôle on pp. 22-3, lines 16-14. The latter part of this passage describes in Hartleian terms the process by which a poet acquires what we should now call 'values' and communicates them to others. Wordsworth sees that this process need not be a matter of explicit moralising but of the poet's unconsciously ('blindly and mechanically') expressing his own habits of mind. Thus the poet 'teaches' whenever he gives himself fully to the theme he is engaged on—though it be only the story of an old man cutting wood. What is 'taught' depends on the quality of his response to this theme. Wordsworth assumes (as Hartley would have done) that both processes are normally for the better and that the values acquired and imparted are healthy ones; though he does glance at the possibility that the reader (and the poet too, p. 43, line 36 to p. 44, line 4) may form false standards. Once allowances have been made for what is obsolete in Hartley, Wordsworth's treatment of these points is surprisingly modern. So too is his declaration (p. 25) that urban life and work have reduced men to a state in which they read little but newspapers and sensational fiction, and that poetry is all the more necessary if the 'discriminating powers of the mind' are to be preserved. These comments may indeed apply more closely to our own world than to that of 1800, when England was far less industrialised and many 'gross and violent stimulants' had yet to be devised.

Poetry with such uses deserves to be taken seriously. Wordsworth felt this strongly, and writes with scorn of cultivated persons 'who talk of poetry as of a matter of amusement and idle pleasure; who will converse with us as gravely about a *taste* for poetry, as they express it, as if it were a thing as indifferent as a taste for rope-dancing, or Frontiniac, or sherry.' Not content with describing specific functions of poetry, Wordsworth attempts in the long passage added in 1802 to sketch a general theory of poetic activity that will put it on an equal footing with science and show that poetic truth has the same objective validity as scientific truth. This attempt fails, chiefly because the universe in which Wordsworth places his poet is the somewhat hypothetical 'system of benevolence' **18** described by Hartley. What does emerge from the passage is a conception of the poet as (so to speak) the scientist of human experience in general, observing daily life with the same vigilance that the scientist brings to his specialised concerns, trying to see the whole behind the part, and continually refreshed (as the scientist cannot be) by a sense of contact with his fellow-men and of the *immediate* human value of his work.

One last topic illuminated by the Preface is the process by which Wordsworth produced his own major poetry. His account of poetic creation has to be pieced together from several passages in the Preface (mainly from p. 22, l. 19 to p. 23, l. 14 and p. 42, ll. 5-18) and each part of it needs to be read in its context. Thus the memorable and misleading statement that 'all good poetry is the spontaneous overflow of powerful feelings' should not be taken too literally: nothing could be further from Wordsworth's mind than to equate poetry with a rapid gush of emotion. The statement occurs twice (pp. 22, 42), each time in a context which describes intense mental as well as emotional activity. For Wordsworth the process characteristically begins in a state of calm with the remembering of some past emotional experience. Excitement gradually increases until the poet is almost reliving the experience—yet with a difference: the present emotion is 'kindred to,' not identical with, that of the past (p. 42). The difference is that the emotion has now been modified by thought, and related to many past thoughts and feelings (p. 22, l. 31 to p. 23, l. 14). The germinal experience has in fact been or is in the process of being understood and evaluated, and it is by this means that the ensuing poem acquires its 'worthy purpose.' Thought and emotion, conscious and unconscious elements continue their intimate interaction until the 'spontaneous overflow' begins: that is, until these elements are ready to combine in a poem and begin the work of shaping it. 'Spontaneous' seems to imply both that the shaping process cannot be begun at will and that once begun it is to some extent self-directing. This does not mean that the

18 poet's active intelligence has to be switched off: like the more passive and intuitive faculties it plays its part in the 'selecting' and 'composing,' and one of the pleasures experienced by the poet at work is 'the sense of difficulty overcome.' Finally the poem is complete, and if all has gone well it will achieve 'the complex end which the poet proposes to himself.' This account could not be expected to apply to the writing of all poetry, nor even to all of Wordsworth's: but as a description of the process behind the intensely-felt, deeply-meditated writing found in *Tintern Abbey* and in much of Wordsworth's other work of this period it is completely convincing, and shows something of the same searching self-awareness as the poems themselves.

Lamb wrote to Wordsworth in January 1801 commenting on the volumes which had just appeared:

> I could . . . have wished the critical preface had appeared in a separate treatise. All its dogmas are true and just, and most of them new, *as* criticism. But they associate a *diminishing* idea with the poems which follow, as having been written for *experiment* on the public taste, more than having sprung (as they must have done) from living and daily circumstances.
>
> (*Lamb*, i, 240.)

On the publication of *L.B.* (*1802*) Coleridge wrote to Southey:

> In the new edition of the *L. Ballads* there is a valuable appendix, which I am sure you must like, and in the Preface itself considerable additions, one on the dignity and nature of the office and character of a poet that is very grand, and of a sort of Verulamian power and majesty—but it is in parts (and this is the fault, *me judice*, of all the latter half of that Preface) obscure beyond any necessity; and the extreme elaboration and almost constrainedness of the diction contrasted (to my feelings) somewhat harshly with the general style of the poems to which the Preface is an introduction. Sara . . . said with some acuteness that she wished all that part of the Preface to have been in blank verse—and *vice versa*. (*C.L.*, ii 830.)

As to the views set out in the Preface, Coleridge seems 18 at first to have identified himself with them unreservedly. Soon after the essay was completed he wrote to Daniel Stuart: 'The Preface contains our joint opinions on poetry' (*C.L.*, i, 627). By July 1802, however, he had begun to suspect 'that somewhere or other there is a radical difference in our theoretical opinions respecting poetry' (see the letter to Southey quoted above; *cf. C.L.*, i, 812). Coleridge's attempt to 'go to the bottom' of this difference was to bear fruit fifteen years later in the *Biographia Literaria*. Wordsworth too continued to develop and refine his conceptions of poetry and his view of its history, notably in the *Essay Supplementary to the Preface* of 1815 (*P.W.*, ii, 409-30). Though appended to a different Preface, this essay forms a valuable supplement to the one of 1800-5.

18 1-2. *The first volume . . . perusal*, i.e. in 1798.

19-20. *I was induced . . . friend.* This seems to imply that Wordsworth first planned the 'experiment' and then invited Coleridge's contributions. In fact the original nucleus of *Lyrical Ballads* was Coleridge's *Ancient Mariner* (see above, pp. 262-5).

19 26. *revolutions*, cycles of change, not necessarily rapid or violent.

20 3-4. *exponent or symbol.* An 'exponent' in algebra (now more commonly called an 'index') is a figure or symbol showing the power to which some other figure or symbol is to be raised. Wordsworth means that metre is felt to lift discourse on to another plane, where only certain kinds of word and theme are appropriate.

15-22. *They who have been . . . assume that title.* This sentence from the 'Advertisement' of 1798 was inserted here in 1802.

16-7. *the gaudiness and inane phraseology of many modern writers.* Wordsworth refers to poets now generally forgotten, such as the 'Della Cruscans,' who had been in vogue from 1788 to 1791 and whose mannered style had influenced Wordsworth's own early work. Some examples of their diction are given by Thomas Pearne in a review of Robert Merry's poem *The Laurel of Liberty* (1790):

> When Mr. Merry calls the sun *the lord of lustre*, and talks of *lawny vales, gleamy meteors, streamy warblings, paly shrouds, pearly panoplies* and *lightless crowds*, we do not approve; but when he soars a flight higher and entertains us with *tissued rays, gauzy zephyrs, filmy rains* and *gossamery tears*, we do not understand. . . . This pretty tinsel excites no ideas in our minds; nor, we believe, in any minds, but such as run away with sound and conceive it to be sense.
>
> (*Monthly Review*, Ser. 2, iv (1791), 60.)

The adjective 'paly' occurs in the 1793 version of

Wordsworth's *An Evening Walk* (*P.W.*, i, 32, line 335). **20**
For other contemporary criticisms of Della Cruscan
diction see William Gifford, *The Baviad* (1791), and a
review of this work in the *English Review*, xix (1792),
349-53, which refers to their 'pompous and glittering
phraseology.' Another poet Wordsworth may have had
in mind is Erasmus Darwin, author of *The Botanic
Garden* (1789-91). A friendly reviewer of *L.B.* (*1798*)
preferred 'the simplicity, even of the most unadorned
tale in this volume, to all the meretricious frippery of
the *Darwinian* taste'; and Henry Crabb Robinson wrote
in 1802 that he would 'rather have written *The Thorn*
than all the tinsel gaudy lines of Darwin's *Botanic
Garden*' (see E. Smith, pp. 38, 60).

35. *The principal object,* etc. The first sentence of this
paragraph, as it stood in 1800, agrees with Coleridge's
account of the original twofold scheme whereby Wordsworth's poems were to deal with ordinary themes from
village life (see below, pp. 408-9). But Wordsworth
goes on to give reasons for preferring these themes to
others, and for using a language too that would be
founded on rustic speech. From these views Coleridge
subsequently dissented; he also objected to the phrase
'the language really used by men,' which Wordsworth
introduced in 1802 (see following note). For Coleridge's
criticism of this paragraph see *B.L.*, chaps. xvii-xviii,
esp. pp. 188-202.

36. *to choose incidents and situations . . . to make the
incidents and situations interesting* 1802; *to make the
incidents of common life interesting* 1800. The expanded
version introduces for the first time the phrase 'a
selection of the language really used by men.'

7-9. *by tracing . . . laws of our nature.* Poems such **21**
as *Simon Lee* and *The Two April Mornings* differ
strikingly from earlier treatments of village life in that
they do not merely reproduce the accepted characteristics
of a class, but sensitively record the speech and behaviour
(often unexpected) of individuals. Nevertheless Wordsworth does not, like Browning, seek the picturesquely
idiosyncratic. His concern is to reveal a humanity

21   common to villagers and to educated middle-class persons, and to divest his reader 'of the pride that induces him to dwell upon those points wherein men differ from each other, to the exclusion of those in which all men are alike, or the same' (*Essay Supplementary to the Preface* (1815), *P.W.*, ii, 426).

9-11. *chiefly . . . excitement*. Following Hartley, Wordsworth regards 'association' as the key to all human behaviour: see notes, pp. 274-5.

11. *Low and rustic life was generally chosen*, etc. In this paragraph Wordsworth suggests that country communities show human nature in a pure state, whereas in cities it tends to become distorted or disguised. There is also an implication that rural life encourages virtue ('a better soil,' etc.), though of course Wordsworth knows that not all peasants are good. His attitude is influenced by contemporary 'primitivism,' i.e. the tendency to idealize unsophisticated people. For an introduction to this subject see C. B. Tinker, *Nature's Simple Plan* (Princeton Univ. Press and O.U.P., 1922).

11. *Low* 1800-27; *Humble* 1832.

16. *co-exist* 1802; *exist* 1800.

19-24. *because the manners of rural life . . . forms of nature*. *Cf.* a letter written by Wordsworth to Coleridge in February 1799:

> I do not so ardently desire character in poems like Bürger's as manners, not transitory manners reflecting the wearisome unintelligible obliquities of city life, but manners connected with the permanent objects of nature and partaking of the simplicity of those objects. Such pictures must interest when the original shall cease to exist.   (*E.L.W.*, p. 255.)

'Manners' here means all behaviour characteristic of a society or class, not only forms of politeness.

24-34. *The language, too . . . unelaborated expressions*. To this Coleridge replies

> that a rustic's language, purified from all provincialism

and grossness, and so far reconstructed as to be made **21**
consistent with the rules of grammar, . . . will not
differ from the language of any other man of common
sense, however learned or refined he may be, except
as far as the notions which the rustic has to convey
are fewer and more indiscriminate.

(B.L., chapt. xvii, p. 196.)

It is not, however, essential to Wordsworth's main
argument that a poet's language should be based on
rustic speech: his chief concern is that it should be in
touch with the rest of life and with 'the plain humanities
of nature' (p. 254).

36. *philosophical.* At this period 'philosophy' was a
very general term covering the methodical pursuit of
almost any kind of knowledge. The more exact names
for its branches were 'metaphysical philosophy,' 'moral
philosophy' and 'natural philosophy.' Most of what we
now call 'science' came under this last heading, and
'philosophical' in this passage means, approximately,
'scientific.'

8-12. *the present outcry . . . compositions.* Jeffrey's **22**
first attack on 'the Lake School of poetry' was not yet
in print when Wordsworth wrote this. Coleridge himself had satirised the forced simplicity of language he
had detected in some of his own early poems, and in
those of his friends, in a sonnet published in the *Monthly
Magazine* in November 1797:

> O! I do love thee, meek *Simplicity*!
> For of thy lays the lulling simpleness
> Goes to my heart and soothes each small distress,
> Distress though small, yet haply great to me! . . .

(See *C.P.W.*, i, 210-11; *C.L.*, i, 357-8; *B.L.*, chapt. i,
pp. 14-15.) It is more likely, however, that Wordsworth
is thinking of the critical reception given to Southey's
experiments with humble subjects and conversational
language, in his *Poems* of 1797-9 and in pieces published
in the *Annual Anthology* (1799-1800). Reviewers had
complained of 'too much colloquial familiarity,' of

22 prosaisms, and of 'vulgar simplicity.' Of *The Last of the Family* John Ferriar had written: 'Mr. S has proved so very correct in his imitation of the gossipping style of Farmer James and Farmer Gregory that he has taken off much from the gravity, as well as the interest, of the piece' (*Monthly Review*, Ser. 2, xxxi (April 1800), 361). See also *Analytical Review*, Ser. 2, i (April 1799), 403-6; *Critical Review*, Ser. 2, xxvi (June 1799), 161-4; *Monthly Review*, Ser. 2, xxxi (March 1800), 261-7. Wordsworth probably knew of these reviews even if he had not seen them: all were in print before he had finished writing his Preface.

19-23, 14. *Not that . . . affections ameliorated.* See above, pp. 275-6.

26-7. *all good poetry is the spontaneous overflow of powerful feelings.* See above, pp. 277-8.

23 **15-24**, 22. *I have said . . . the latter poem.* Unless the preceding passage is kept in mind this paragraph may give the impression that Wordsworth wrote his poems according to a scientific programme. Some of the objectives he here assigns to them seem rather forced, and it seems likely that in most cases he wrote the poem first and fitted it into a scheme afterwards. In 1845 the whole paragraph is reduced to:

> It has been said that each of these poems has a purpose. Another circumstance must be mentioned which distinguishes these poems from the popular poetry of the day: it is this, that the feeling therein developed gives importance to the action and situation, and not the action and situation to the feeling.

33-4. *fraternal or . . . moral attachment.* Wordsworth seems to imply that the love between Leonard and James has developed to the point of involving the moral sense, and that this development is due at least in part to the influence of mountain scenery. This would be quite consistent with Wordsworth's interpretation of Hartley (see above, p. 275).

24 **6-7.** *The Two April Mornings, The Fountain.* These titles were added in 1802.

8-9. *characters . . . belonging rather to nature than to*   **24**
manners, i.e. examples of 'human nature' little modified
by society (*cf.* p. 21, line 11 and note). But if Matthew
and Daniel had been born in Samoa or among the
Kwakiutl Indians they would have become very different
people. Not until our own century has it been realised
how much of what has traditionally passed for 'human
nature' is in fact the result of social environment: for
some striking illustrations of this fact see Ruth Benedict,
Patterns of Culture (Routledge, 1935).

16-18. *the feeling therein developed . . . the feeling.* This
important point follows logically from Wordsworth's
discussion of 'purpose' in the preceding paragraph (see
too above, pp. 275-6). The reverse of what Wordsworth intends may be seen in some of Southey's
poems, e.g. *The Soldier's Wife* and *The Widow.* The
situations presented by these poems are dramatic and
pathetic, but for want of any real insight into the kind
of experience described the poems themselves remain
trivial.

20-21. *Poor Susan . . . The Childless Father.* The version
of *Poor Susan* to which this sentence originally referred
included a fifth stanza, subsequently deleted (see notes,
p. 373). What matters about these poems, Wordsworth
implies, is not that they present a 'poor outcast' and a
'bereaved father,' but that they contain true perceptions
of the way human beings think and feel—developed in
each case from a tiny imagined incident.

28. *excited,* made active; without the modern implication of tension or emotion at a high pitch.

7. *great national events.* Several effects of the French   **25**
Revolution and the ensuing war may be relevant: the
general atmosphere of rumours and sensational 'intelligence'; the brutalising effect of apparently endless
violence reported, not only from the battlefields, but
from Paris, the Vendée, Ireland and the Nore; and the
hysteria of the anti-Jacobin reaction in England, which
drove a mob to burn Priestley's house and library in
1791 and was to harry liberals for another thirty years.
Wordsworth's reference to 'national events' is under-

25 standably cautious: in 1797 he and Coleridge had been under surveillance by a Home Office spy (see *M.M.*, i, 329-31).

11. *intelligence*, news.

17. *frantic novels*. The last quarter of the eighteenth century saw a great increase in the volume of prose fiction, much of it manufactured quickly to meet a rising demand. By 1800 the gentler kind of 'Gothic' romance written by Charlotte Smith and Ann Radcliffe was being driven out by cruder and more terrifying stories translated or imitated from the German. Of these the best-known is *Ambrosio, or The Monk* (1796), by M. G. Lewis, a frank exploitation of sex and sadism.

17. *sickly and stupid German tragedies*. More than twenty plays by A. F. von Kotzebue were translated into English between 1796 and 1800. One of the most popular, *Das Kind der Liebe*, was adapted by Elizabeth Inchbald under the title *Lover's Vows*; this version is printed as an appendix to R. W. Chapman's edition of Jane Austen's *Mansfield Park* (O.U.P., 1923).

18. *idle and extravagant stories in verse*. Wordsworth is probably thinking of works like M. G. Lewis's *Tales of Terror* (1799).

26 2-14. *The reader will find . . . by prescription* 1802; 1800—

> Except in a very few instances the reader will find no personifications of abstract ideas in these volumes, not that I mean to censure such personifications; they may be well fitted for certain sorts of composition, but in these poems I propose to myself to imitate, and as far as possible to adopt, the very language of men, and I do not find that such personifications make any regular or natural part of that language.

In the earlier version Wordsworth's criticism of personification is less emphatic and his disclaimer ('Not that I mean to censure,' etc.) more prominent than in 1802; but in neither version does he condemn personification outright as he does poetic diction. One reason may be that Coleridge used personification freely at this period, especially in his political poetry. Words-

worth too uses it in *The Female Vagrant*, line 122 (p. 81); **26**
see also the cancelled stanza on p. 319.

9-10. *They are, indeed . . . prompted by passion.*
Wordsworth's belief that a man, say, in a rage might
utter personifications like those in Gray's *Elegy* is based
on tradition rather than experience. The tradition begins
with Longinus, who, though he does not specifically
mention personification, assumes in his treatise *On the
Sublime* that passion naturally gives rise to figurative
speech (see especially his treatment of 'images' or
'visualisations' in section xv, and of metaphor in
section xxxii). This opinion was repeated by eighteenth-
century English writers on aesthetics, including Harris,
Blackwell, Blair and Kames. See René Wellek, *The Rise
of English Literary History* (University of North Carolina
Press, 1941), pp. 86-9.

21. *poetic diction:* the conventionally refined phraseology
which led even a realistic poet like Crabbe to write of
'the finny tribe' when he meant 'fish' (see above, pp. 272-
3).

32. *to look steadily at my subject*, i.e. not at the traditions
and conventions of literature. Part of Wordsworth's
conception of poetry is that it should reveal general
truths about human nature through an *accurate* observation of particular experiences (*cf.* Preface, p. 21, lines
15-18 and p. 23, line 15ff., and notes). His customary
sobriety of style and his preference for real occurrences
as themes are in accord with this aim.

12. *If in a poem*, etc. For Coleridge's commentary on **27**
the following three paragraphs and on Gray's sonnet see
B.L., chapt. xviii, pp. 202-21; only a few of his points
can be included in these notes.

13. *language.* By this Wordsworth means, largely, the
choice of words; Coleridge points out that the order of
words is also part of language, and that the word-order
of poetry often differs from that of prose.

22-30. *And it would be . . . well written.* Coleridge's
reply is that though some language is equally fit
for poetry and prose, other language is to be found
which is fit for one and not for the other (*B.L.*, chapt.

27 xviii, pp. 205-6). Poetry in particular imposes special requirements, even apart from the obvious demands of metre, which not all language can satisfy. As examples of poetry which fails solely because of its 'prosaic' language Coleridge quotes passages by Daniel and by Wordsworth himself (*ibid.*, pp. 213-17).

34-5. *a short composition of Gray*, etc. This is his *Sonnet on the Death of Mr. Richard West*. If Gray's tribute fails it is not through insincerity, since he and West had been close friends. Gray's belief in the value of 'poetic diction' was quite explicit: to West himself he had written in 1742 that 'the language of the age is never the language of poetry' (*Correspondence*, ed. Paget Toynbee and L. Whibley (O.U.P., 1935), i, 192-3).

28 18-23. *It will easily be perceived . . . that of prose.* Coleridge comments:

> In Mr. Wordsworth's criticism of Gray's sonnet, the reader's sympathy with his praise or blame of the different parts is taken for granted rather perhaps too easily. He has not, at least, attempted to win or compel it by argumentative analysis. In *my* conception at least, the lines rejected as of no value do, with the exception of the two first, differ as much and as little from the language of common life as those which he has printed in italics as possessing genuine excellence. Of the five lines thus honourably distinguished, two of them differ from prose even more widely than the lines which either precede or follow, in the *position* of the words.
>
> *A different object do these eyes require;*
> My lonely anguish melts no heart but mine;
> And in my breast the imperfect joys expire.
>
> But were it otherwise, what would this prove but a truth of which no man ever doubted?—videlicet, that there are sentences which would be equally in their place both in verse and prose. Assuredly it does not prove the point which alone requires proof, namely, that there are not passages which would suit the one and not suit the other. . . . The second line,
> And reddening Phoebus lifts his golden fire,

has indeed almost as many faults as words. But then **28**
it is a bad line, not because the language is distinct
from that of prose, but because it conveys incongruous
images; because it confounds the cause and the effect,
the real thing with the personified representative of
the thing; in short, because if differs from the language
of good sense! (*B.L.*, chapt. xviii, pp. 212-13.)

24-31. *By the foregoing quotation ... metrical composition* 1802; 1800—

Is there then, it will be asked, no essential difference
between the language of prose and metrical composition? I answer that there neither is nor can be any
essential difference.

31-3. *We are fond of tracing the resemblance between poetry and painting.* The classical source for this analogy
is Horace, *Art of Poetry*, lines 1-13, 19-21, 378-82. In
England the idea had been most fully developed by
Dryden in *A Parallel of Poetry and Painting* (see *Essays*,
ed. W. P. Ker (O.U.P., 1900), ii, 115-53); it also occurs
in Sidney's *Defence of Poesy*, in Jonson's *Discoveries*, in
Pope's *Essay on Criticism* (lines 293-6, 484-93), and in
Johnson's *Idler*, no. 34. For a discussion of the implications of this parallel see Mark van Doren, *The Poetry of
John Dryden* (1931), pp. 54-60; see also Jean Hagstrum,
The Sister Arts (Chicago Univ. Press, 1958).

33-4. *but where shall we find bonds,* etc. Here and in the
next paragraph Wordsworth emphasises all that poetry
and prose have in common, and finds no difference
between the two arts except that in poetry metre is
'superadded.' This difference, he implies, is comparatively unimportant: the fundamental distinction to
be made is that between imaginative writing and factual
or scientific writing. His discussion probably owes
something to an essay, 'Is Verse essential to Poetry?' in
the *Monthly Magazine* for July 1796 (ii, 453-6). The
writer (?John Aikin) finds 'that the terms *poetry* and
prose are incorrectly opposed to each other. *Verse* is, properly, the contrary of *prose*; ... and writing should
be divided, not into poetry and prose, but into *poetry*
and *philosophy.*'

29 *Footnote.* So 1802-5; 1800 omits *matter of fact, or* and stops after *prose is metre*; editions after 1805 omit the note altogether.

4-5. *tears 'such as angels weep'*; see *Paradise Lost*, Bk. i, line 620.

6. *ichor:* in classical mythology, an ethereal fluid which ran in the veins of the gods instead of blood.

13. *other artificial distinctions* 1802; *other distinctions* 1800.

14-38, 9. *I answer that the language . . . remind the reader.* This passage of nine pages was added in 1802. Though it contains some of the most acute perceptions in the Preface, and some of the most impressive writing, its insertion at this point certainly obscures the course of Wordsworth's argument.

30 34. *What is a poet?* etc. Wordsworth is still at this point concerned to combat the notion that a poet is a being apart, practising a unique activity which needs a special language. As might have been expected, his description of a poet is one that could apply equally well to a novelist or a prose dramatist (*cf.* note to p. 28, lines 33-4). Nor in his view is the writer, of whatever kind, 'essentially' different from other men: he shares their world, though he is more intensely aware of it and better able to communicate his experience of it.

36. *a man speaking to men.* This seems to imply that poetry communicates by a mode basically similar to that of ordinary conversation or prose exposition. But the distinction between expository or scientific writing and imaginative or artistic writing is a fundamental one, as Wordsworth himself recognises (see footnote to p. 29). The author of a novel is obviously not 'speaking to men' in the same direct sense as is the author of a newspaper article. The same is true of plays, and of all poems which do not take the form of direct personal statement. And poems which do take this form have a dramatic aspect which the poet may exploit in various ways: it is often unwise to equate the 'I' of a poem with the historical Donne or Yeats. Even a poem which consists of literally accurate statements affects us differently

from a prose exposition of the same facts, because of **30**
the greater importance of formal elements in the work
as a whole. Thus the 'loop in time' movement of
Tintern Abbey adds something to the total effect, and
therefore to the total meaning, of the poem, that is not
part of ordinary autobiography. For a full elaboration
of these ideas illustrated by critical essays see Cleanth
Brooks, *The Well-Wrought Urn: Studies in the Structure
of Poetry* (Dennis Dobson, London, 1949).

1. *endued* 1802-32; *endowed* 1836 (the meanings of the **31**
two words are identical in this context).

2-5. *more enthusiasm and tenderness . . . mankind.* Not
every poet, of course, has all these qualities: Wordsworth seems for the moment to be describing the poets
he values most rather than poets in general. But it is
consistent with his attitude throughout the Preface that
he puts the writer's human endowment first (tenderness,
understanding of human nature, etc.), his imaginative
power second and his technical skill last.

26-32, 6. *But whatever portion . . . his own feelings
with theirs.* That is, the language of a writer describing
an imaginary scene of grief is bound to be less expressive
than that of a man actually grieving. Wordsworth puts
forward this very doubtful statement as though it were
an obvious truth. Here as on p. 26, lines 9-10 he
shows the influence of a critical tradition going back to
Longinus, who frequently advises the orator to imitate
the language of impassioned men (see for example *On
the Sublime*, sections xix-xxii).

36. *Frontiniac* or Frontignac, a wine made from the **32**
muscat grapes of Frontignan in France.

1-2. *Aristotle . . . hath said that poetry is the most* **33**
philosophic of all writing. Aristotle did say that poetry
was more philosophic than history. The statement
comes in his discussion of what plots are suitable for
tragedy. See *Poetics*, trans. John Warrington (Everyman's Library, Dent, 1963):

It is clear . . . that the poet's function is to describe
not what *has* happened, but the kind of thing that

33 *might* happen, i.e. what is possible as being probable or necessary. . . . Poetry therefore is more philosophic and of greater significance than history, for its statements are of the nature rather of universals, whereas those of history are particulars. A universal statement declares what such or such a kind of man will probably or necessarily say or do; and that is the aim of poetry, though it affixes proper names to the characters. (p. 17)

Wordsworth believed that poetry, like science, should reveal general truths, particularly truths about human nature: *cf.* Preface, p. 21, ll. 6-11 and p. 23, l. 15 to p. 24, l. 12. Here he was on common ground not only with Aristotle but with the English neoclassical critics (for a summary of their position see Johnson's *Rasselas*, chapt. x). Wordsworth differs from these in wishing to arrive at general truths through a close study of particular experiences, as in *Simon Lee* or, on a different scale, in *The Prelude*.

4. *operative*, influential and effective. *Cf.* Sir William Davenant's preface to *Gondibert* (1652): 'Truth narrative and past is the idol of historians (who worship a dead thing), and truth operative, and by effects continually alive, is the mistress of poets' (quoted by E. de Selincourt, *P.W.*, ii, 395).

5. *carried alive into the heart by passion.* Poetry has more powerful means than prose of reinforcing statement by feeling; and it can command the kind of conviction that results, not from viewing evidence ('external testimony'), but from participating in experience. The phrase also suggests the compressed kind of poetry that conveys intact ('alive into the heart') a complex state of mind or feeling, the effect of which would be dissipated in a prose exposition.

6. *strength and divinity* 1802-32; *competence and confidence* 1836.

7. *the tribunal to which it appeals*: presumably, the heart and mind of the reader.

9-12. *The obstacles . . . by the poet.* The truth of

history must be tried by documents and other 'external **33**
testimony'; the truth of poetry can be tried by human
beings themselves, since it should be 'the image of man
and nature.' *Cf.* Pope's description of 'wit' in *An Essay
on Criticism* (1711):

> Something, whose truth convinced at sight we find,
> That give us back the image of our mind.
>
> (lines 299-300)

Pope gives a supporting quotation from Quintilian.
23. *Nor let this necessity,* etc. The theoretical basis of
this paragraph is supplied by Hartley (see above, pp.
274-7). Hartley believed that by Providential design
the instinctive tendency to seek pleasure and avoid pain
operated as the mainspring of all human behaviour,
including all intellectual and moral development, in a
generally progressive system. The idea of this 'grand
elementary principle' excited Wordsworth's imagination, as can be felt from the impressive movement of the
first part of this paragraph. But the reader may subsequently feel bewildered on being dropped from the
heights of rhetoric ('What then does the poet?') into
a long abstract sentence which turns out to be a summary
of Hartley's account of men's relations with their
environment. These relations, however, are presented
as the poet's true subject. Wordsworth's conception of
the poet as (so to speak) the scientist of everyday life is
already in his mind, though not made explicit until
the next paragraph. Thus the question 'What then does
the poet?' means in effect 'What then is the poet's
proper field of study?' (as compared with those of the
chemist, mathematician etc. just mentioned). The
answer is 'Man is his own nature and in his ordinary
life,' placed in an environment as well adapted to him
as he to it. It is therefore natural for the poet to take
pleasure in his work, and for his poems to give men the
same 'overbalance of enjoyment' that they find, according to Hartley, in all normal experiences.

34   27. *nature* here and in line 30 includes the whole of man's environment and not merely the landscape.

       29. *qualities* 1802-32; *properties* 1836.

35   11-14. *Poetry is the breath . . . all science.* The ardent pursuit of any truth felt as important in direct relation to human beings is an activity resembling the poet's

       15-16. '*that he looks before and after.*' *Hamlet*, IV.iv. 36-9:

> Sure, he that made us with such large discourse,
> Looking before and after, gave us not
> That capability and god-like reason
> To fust in us unused.

       16. *the rock of defence of human nature*: because it is in poetry that wisdom and insight into human experience are kept alive from one age into another.

       18-24. *In spite of difference . . . all time.* Anyone who has deeply enjoyed a Latin, a mediæval or a Chinese poem (even in translation) will feel the force of this majestic sentence. Nevertheless, differences of culture can affect human beings more fundamentally than it was possible to realise in 1800 (see above, p. 285), and Wordsworth's last eight words are not strictly true. For a novel which takes this problem as its theme see André Malraux, *The Walnut Trees of Altenburg*, trans. A. W. Fielding (Lehmann, 1952), esp. pp. 98-114.

       26-8. *yet he will follow . . . his wings.* Abstract ideas are fit subject-matter for poetry if they are such as to interest men's feelings, not as scientists or scholars, but as men (see below, and *cf.* p. 33, lines 13-22).

       29-36, 14. *If the labours of men of science . . . household of man.* In *The Poetic Image* (Cape, 1947) C. Day Lewis suggests that the modern answer to the question 'How far can the poet successfully make use of objects like aeroplanes and engines in metaphor?' is:

> No object is inherently un-poetical; whether a poet can create an image from any given object depends first upon the imaginative strength of his own response to it, and secondly upon the extent to which this

object has been assimilated by the general conscious- **35**
ness.
(pp. 89-90)

This 'modern' attitude corresponds almost exactly with
Wordsworth's.

11-12. *the poet will lend his divine spirit to aid the trans-* **36**
figuration. This 'transfiguration' is discussed by C. Day
Lewis (*op. cit.,* pp. 107-8), who distinguishes between the
'general consciousness' mentioned above and the 'general
imagination':

> Telegraph poles became a part of the general
> consciousness when they had become a normal part
> of the landscape . . . but for them to enter the general
> imagination, we must have experienced them poetically
> —seen the forest tree in the stripped pole, heard
> along the wire the voices of crisis and commonplace.
> Now it is the poet's job, certainly, to make the
> telegraph poles poetic for us in this way. But this
> particular job is more difficult for him today, because
> he gets no help from the general imagination and
> therefore his images have to start from cold. The
> Greeks would have seen a telegraph pole both from a
> utilitarian and a poetic point of view, . . . as an
> upright wooden object with wires attached but also
> as a receptacle and transmitter of spirit.

23-5. *but especially . . . his characters.* This seems to
refer back to p. 29, l. 25–p. 30, l. 13 and p. 31, l .26–p.
32, l. 18 rather than to anything in the last two paragraphs. Wordsworth has obviously had some difficulty in
incorporating his deeper meditations on the nature and
scope of poetry into his earlier argument about poetic
diction.

32-3. *But poets do not write for poets alone, but for men.* **37**
Because of his insistence on poetry as communication,
Wordsworth sometimes seems to be reverting to the
early Augustan view that a poet should keep the needs
of ordinary readers constantly in mind. He shows no
undue deference towards his own readers, however,
implying more than once that they must do their share

37 of the work if his poems are to be properly appreciated (see p. 44, lines 24-34 and p. 46, lines 13-35). At bottom his attitude seems to be the Romantic (and modern) one, that though a poet naturally wishes to be understood he must above all things remain faithful to his own imaginative conceptions.

38 10-16. *the distinction of metre . . . connect with the passion.* After quoting this passage, Coleridge asks:

> But is this a *poet*, of whom a poet is speaking? No, surely! rather of a fool or madman: or at best of a vain or ignorant phantast! And might not brains so wild and so deficient make just the same havoc with rhymes and metres as they are supposed to effect with modes and figures of speech? How is the reader at the *mercy* of such men? If he continue to read their nonsense, is it not his own fault?'
>
> (*B.L.*, chapt. xviii, p. 217.)

Coleridge objects to Wordsworth's attempt to lay down general principles about the diction a poet should use. In his view the wording of a poem should be governed only by its particular needs; and these are to be determined by the poet's creative imagination, which coordinates the work of his intelligence, his sense of language and all his other resources. Where these are adequate, rules about diction are unnecessary; where they are not, rules are of little help (*loc. cit.*, pp. 217-19). 10. *the distinction of metre* 1802; *the distinction of rhyme and metre* 1800.

24-5. *Why . . . have I written in verse?* Wordsworth's answer to this question is the weakest part of his argument: the paragraph which follows amounts to little more than 'Well, why not?' He is in fact more successful in pointing out the similarities between poetry and prose than in accounting for their differences. This, together with some pedestrian passages in the poems, laid Wordsworth open to Byron's gibe that he

> both by precept and example shows
>
> That prose is verse, and verse is merely prose.

(*English Bards and Scotch Reviewers* (1809), lines 241-2.)

35. *supposing* 1802; *granting* 1800. The original wording **38** may have suggested too strongly that Wordsworth was, in fact, granting this.

36-40, 2. *The end of poetry is to produce excitement in co-* **39** *existence with an over-balance of pleasure.* This statement leaves out of account the moral function of poetry, which Wordsworth has already discussed. It is obvious too that imaginative prose as well as verse must somehow compensate the reader for any distress it inflicts on him, if it is to be read. But the rest of this paragraph makes it clear that Wordsworth is not "thinking of the total effect of a poem or a novel, but only of the sensations it creates from moment to moment. He contends that these can never be so purely painful with verse as they can with prose, because of the modifying effects of the metre and the unconscious pleasure it gives.

1. *excitement*: activity of mind or feelings, not necessarily extreme activity as implied by modern usage.

11-13. *something to which . . . in a less excited state.* Wordsworth's tendency to explain all psychological effects in terms of 'association' is probably a handicap to him here, as also on p. 43, line 36 to p. 44, line 4.

12-13. *in various moods and in a less excited state* 1802; *when in an unexcited or in a less excited state* 1800.

15-29. *and of feeling not strictly . . . similar instances will be found in them.* This passage, introducing the idea that metre throws 'a sort of half-consciousness of unsubstantial existence' over what we read and appealing to 'the old ballads,' was added in 1802.

17-25. *though the opinion . . . than in prose.* It seems true that one effect of metre, as of rhyme and other poetic devices, is to make the reader more conscious that it is art and not 'real life' to which he is responding. But to complete the paradox Wordsworth needs to add that the same devices may simultaneously intensify the reader's response, increasing the pain as well as the pleasure that he feels.

29-35. *This opinion . . . bounds of pleasure.* Not all readers would agree; but even if the statement is true,

40 the comparison is unfair. Wordsworth might instead have compared the mad scenes in *King Lear* (in prose) with the scene of Gloucester's blinding (in verse).

32-3. *Clarissa Harlowe*. Samuel Richardson's masterpiece was published in 1748 and remained the most powerfully harrowing novel in English for a hundred years.

33. *The Gamester*: a popular tragedy published in 1753 by Edward Moore (1712-57). It attacks the vice of gambling, 'through which the weak creature Beverley is lured to ruin and death by the villain Stukeley' (*Oxford Companion to English Literature*, ed. Paul Harvey, O.U.P., 1932).

36-41, 1. *which, in a much greater degree than might at first be imagined, is* 1802; *which is in a great degree* 1800.

41 17-18. *the theory upon which these poems are written.* See note-p. 23, line 15 to p. 41, line 22.

42 5-18. *I have said . . . state of enjoyment.* This account of poetic activity complements that on p. 22, line 19-p. 23, line 14. Here Wordsworth describes the sensations of writing poetry, whereas in the earlier passage he attempts to reconstruct the process (not necessarily conscious) by which a poet's 'values' find expression in his work. Both passages describe an interaction of thought and feeling in what is virtually one creative process: feeling is modified by thought, which represents past feeling; emotion is recollected in tranquillity, which begets a kindred emotion. (See above, pp. 277-8.)

25-36. *Now the music . . . deeper passions.* This sentence describes the experience of the reader, not of the poet; 'the sense of difficulty overcome' refers to the pleasure and admiration with which the reader participates in the writer's achievement.

27. *blind,* involuntary and unconscious: *cf.* Preface, p. 23, line 8 and *Michael*, p. 240, line 78, and notes.

29-32. *an indistinct perception . . . differing from it so widely.* Added in 1802.

43 7-11. *of two descriptions . . . is read once.* This must mean, not that more persons will read the verse descrip-

tion, but that a person who has read both will return **43**
to the verse description more often. Whether this is so
depends of course on the descriptions, and on who is
reading them: the comparison as it stands is rather too
hypothetical.

11-26. *We see that Pope . . . usual in ballads.* Omitted
in 1845.

36-44, 4. *I am sensible . . . unworthy subjects.* Wordsworth's reading of Hartley (see above, pp. 274-6),
leads him to regard the human environment as an
educational system in which there is, so to speak, a
normal course to be followed: here he apologises for
any instances in which he has learned the wrong lessons
from experience by forming eccentric 'associations'.

3-4. *sometimes from diseased impulses* omitted 1836. **44**

12-33. *Such faulty expressions . . . lightly and carelessly.*
Many poets before Wordsworth must have felt themselves better judges than the public where their own
work was concerned: few had expressed this conviction
so fully.

25. *reader* 1800-32; *critic* 1836.

27-8. *in saying that it is not probable he* 1800-32; *in
saying of most readers that it is not probable they* 1836.

4. *I put my hat upon my head,* etc. Johnson was apt **45**
to ridicule contemporary imitations of the ballads, and
this stanza was probably meant for a parody of Thomas
Percy's *Hermit of Warkworth* (1771). But it was often
taken, as Wordsworth seems to take it, for a parody of
the genuine ballads Percy had collected. Wordsworth's
version does not agree with any earlier printed text
that is known, but does agree, unaccountably, with the
earliest MS. See *Poems of Samuel Johnson,* ed. D. Nichol
Smith and E. Laming McAdam (O.U.P., 1941), pp.
156-8.

10. *These pretty babes,* etc. The stanza is from a street
ballad of the late sixteenth century, printed in *Reliques,*
iii, 169-76. Wordsworth's title and text differ slightly
from Percy's, and it is possible that he knew a 'broadside'
version. On this ballad Coleridge remarks:

We all willingly throw ourselves back for a while into

45   the feelings of childhood. . . . But I am not convinced by the collation of facts that 'The Children in
the Wood' owes either its preservation or its popu-
larity to its metrical form. . . . [The prose tales of]
'Tom Hickathrift,' 'Jack the Giant-Killer,' 'Goody
Two-Shoes' and 'Little Red Riding-Hood' are
formidable rivals.   (*B.L.*, chapt. xviii, p. 208.)
Here Coleridge gently hints that Wordsworth had over-
rated this ballad. See also Wordsworth's *Lucy Gray*
(p. 178-80), especially lines 29-36, and notes, p. 372.
20-1. *Whence arises this difference? . . . not a man?*
Coleridge agrees that Johnson's stanza is trivial because
of its trivial content, but cites cases in which

> . . . the sense shall be good and weighty, the language
> correct and dignified, the subject interesting and
> treated with feeling; and yet the style shall, not-
> withstanding all these merits, be justly blamable as
> *prosaic*, and solely because the words and the order
> of the words . . . are not suitable to metrical
> composition.   (*B.L.*, chapt. xviii, p. 215.)

34-5. *Why take pains . . . that he is not a man?* Cf.
An Essay on Man, Epistle ii, lines 31-4, where Pope
supposes that 'superior beings' such as angels might
have 'showed a Newton as we show an ape.'

46   23-35. *for an* accurate *taste in poetry . . . necessarily
will be so.* This passage is reproduced from the 'Advertisement' of 1798 (see pp. 426-7), with minor changes
('severe thought' is now softened to 'thought'). Reynolds
said in his seventh Discourse (1776):

> We may . . . conclude that the real substance, as it
> may be called, of what goes under the name of taste
> is fixed and established in the nature of things; that
> there are certain and regular causes by which the
> imagination and passions of men are affected; and
> that the knowledge of these causes is acquired by a
> laborious and diligent investigation of nature, and
> by the same slow progress as wisdom or knowledge
> of any kind, however instantaneous its operations
> may appear when thus acquired.

                      (*Literary Works* (1870), i, 426-7.)

And again:

> To form this just taste is undoubtedly in your own
> power, but it is to reason and philosophy that you
> must have recourse; from them you must borrow the
> balance by which is to be weighed and estimated the
> value of every pretension that intrudes itself on your
> notice. *(Ibid.,* i, 436.)

Although Wordsworth makes scornful use of the word
'taste' earlier in the Preface (p. 32, line 29), he has not
yet repudiated the eighteenth-century conception of
taste here presented. For Reynolds 'taste' is a generally
valid standard, difficult to codify but based none the less
on permanent and universal facts of art and experience.
But whereas for Reynolds 'taste' had coincided with the
ruling opinions of his day, for Wordsworth it does not:
he clearly anticipates resistance to his poetry both from
critics and from ordinary readers. To a limited extent
he can and does represent his work as a return to the
true 'taste' of earlier periods. But the real conclusion
to be drawn is that 'taste' is not, after all, 'fixed and
established,' but in a state of continuous development.
Wordsworth had drawn this conclusion (apparently with
Coleridge's assistance) by 1807, when he wrote to Lady
Beaumont

> that every great and original writer, in proportion as
> he is great or original, must himself create the taste
> by which he is to be relished; he must teach the art
> by which he is to be seen.
> *(The Letters of William and Dorothy Wordsworth:*
> *The Middle Years,* ed. E. de Selincourt, revd. Mary
> Moorman (O.U.P., 1969), i, 150.)

He restates this idea in 1815 in his *Essay Supplementary
to the Preface (P.W.,* ii, 426), where he also points out
that 'taste' is a misleading term since it suggests passive
reception: a full response to poetry involves 'the exertion
of a co-operating *power* in the mind of the reader'
(p. 427).

46 Reynolds's advice is addressed to painters: he would probably not have urged upon his patrons the same attentiveness and diligent research that Wordsworth here commends to his readers. Though Wordsworth saw the poet as essentially 'a man speaking to men,' he did not expect such communication always to be easy and saw that it might demand an effort on both sides.

47 21-4. *I am willing to allow . . . ordinarily enjoyed.* Wordsworth does not make it clear what poetry should be displaced in favour of that which he recommends. To give up all poetry not written in 'a selection of language really used by men' would mean abandoning much of Shakespeare and still more of Milton. But Wordsworth is probably thinking for the most part of verse encumbered by conventional 'poetic diction' of the kind illustrated on p. 28.

49 This half-title first appeared in 1800. The motto is taken from Quintilian, *Institutio Oratoria*, X.vii. 15, and means:

> It is feeling and force of imagination that make us eloquent; it is for this reason that even the uneducated have no difficulty in finding words to express their meaning, if only they are stirred by some strong emotion.

(H. E. Butler's translation, in the Loeb Classical Library edition of Quintilian (Heinemann, 1922), iv, 141.) *Cf.* Wordsworth's Preface, p. 26, lines 9-10 and p. 31, line 26 to p. 32, line 18, and notes.

This poem and its companion-piece, *The Tables Turned*, are closely related to *Lines written at a Small Distance from my House* (p. 76). All three poems were written in the spring or early summer of 1798; each claims that 'nature' (here, primarily, the countryside) gives not only pleasure and health, but also wisdom. Wordsworth believed this to be literally true; and Hartley's philosophy (see above, pp. 274-7) gave him a means of explaining and justifying this belief. In Hartleian terms,

> What Wordsworth here asserts is simply that it is our senses which furnish us with the primary data out of which we build up our intellectual and moral life, and that from time to time it is well to return to the data of our senses for information and control upon our higher processes of thought.   (Beach, p. 136.)

For Wordsworth the sights, sounds, etc., of the unspoiled countryside were the most important kinds of sense-experience, and the chief instruments of 'nature's education.'

Wordsworth's belief in the educative value of concrete experience and the danger of replacing it by books probably owes something to Rousseau's *Emile* (1762), at first or second hand, as well as to Hartley. He and Dorothy put this belief into practice when little Basil Montagu, the son of a friend, made his home with them for some years. In 1797, when Basil was four, Dorothy wrote:

> We teach him nothing at present but what he learns from the evidence of his senses. He has an insatiable curiosity which we are always careful to satisfy to the best of our ability. It is directed to everything he sees, the sky, the fields, trees, shrubs, corn, the making of tools, carts, etc., etc. He knows his letters, but we have not attempted any further step in the path of *book learning*. Our grand study has been to make him *happy*, in which we have not been altogether disappointed: he is certainly the most contented child I ever saw. . . .   (*E.L.W.*, p. 180.)

50 15. *my good friend Matthew*. 'Matthew' is usually associated with Wordsworth's schooldays at Hawkshead, 'by Esthwaite lake,' and in later poems he is represented as a schoolmaster. But in the 'Advertisement' of 1798 Wordsworth mentions that this poem and its sequel 'arose out of conversation with a friend who was somewhat unreasonably attached to modern books of moral philosophy'; and this friend is traditionally identified as Hazlitt, who 'got into a metaphysical argument with Wordsworth' on June 6th, 1798 (see *M.M.*, i, 379-81, 399). Probably 'Matthew' is a composite figure, here as in later poems. His rôle in these lines is simply to put the case for purposeful intellectual activity, as 'William' does for fruitful unreasoning passivity. William has the last word, but the debate is not a sham.

21-2. *Nor less I deem that there are powers/Which of themselves our minds impress*. The phrasing is deliberately tentative: 'William' is not seeking to define these powers, but to express his intuitive awareness of their existence. Several kinds of 'powers' may be relevant: (1) the power of external objects, in the psychology of Locke and Hartley, to imprint 'ideas' of themselves on the mind; (2) the power of natural objects to communicate with one another and with men—

> All beings have their properties which spread
> Beyond themselves, a power by which they make
> Some other being conscious of their life. . . .

> (MS. of 1798-9, *P.W.*, v, 286, *app. crit.*)—

and (3) nature-spirits, addressed as 'Powers' in some lines written for *Nutting* (see below, pp. 383-4).

51   THE TABLES TURNED

To the theme of 'nature's education,' this poem adds two others anticipated in line 14 of *Expostulation and Reply*: confidence in spontaneous pleasure, and a mistrust of 'the meddling intellect.' The speaker's mood of vigorous, careless confidence is as much a part of the poem as the statements he makes, which are appropriately exaggerated and simplified: 'dull and endless strife' should not be taken as Wordsworth's final verdict upon literature.

21-4. *One impulse . . . can.* 'That is, to speak in prose, 51
real knowledge gained from experience is better than all
the ready-made knowledge in the world' (Beatty, p. 126).

25. *Sweet is the lore that nature brings.* Wordsworth could
regard the delight he took in nature as proof of her
beneficent teaching, since according to Hartley it is only
by pursuing the pleasures appropriate to each stage of our
development that we arrive at wisdom and the 'moral
sense.' *Cf.* 'We have no knowledge . . . but what has
been built up by pleasure, and exists in us by pleasure
alone' (Wordsworth's Preface, pp. 33-4).

26-8. *Our meddling intellect . . . dissect.* These famous lines 52
are consistent with Wordsworth's Hartleian beliefs in that
they suggest that our primary knowledge of the world
should come through our senses, and that the intellect
'meddles' if it usurps this function. But the passage also
suggests an intuitive grasp of truths not to be found in
Hartley, though they feature in the work of many
Romantic writers besides Wordsworth. One is that the
'beauteous forms' that nature presents to our senses are
more important to us, *as men*, than the intellectual
abstractions we use for understanding them: it is better
to be able to enjoy the beauty and scent of a flower than
only to classify it. Another is that the habit of intellectual
analysis may interfere with the natural responses of our
senses and feelings, and perhaps destroy our capacity for
spontaneous living.

30. *these barren leaves.* The phrase suggests a contrast
between the 'leaves' of books (dry, dead and fruitless)
and the living 'leaves' of the vernal wood.

ANIMAL TRANQUILLITY AND DECAY 52

This poem is referred to in the Preface (p. 24) as *The Old
Man Travelling*, the title it bore in *L.B.* (*1798*). Most of
lines 1-14 are found in early MSS. of *The Old Cumberland Beggar* (see p. 214), a poem based on recollections
from Wordsworth's childhood. 'The present poem has
split off as a study of the inward state of the Old Man
expressed in his outward form: "resigned to quietness"
in the margin of lines 7-8 [i.e. in MS.] expresses the

52 spiritual core of it.' (E. de Selincourt and Helen Darbishire, *P.W.*, iv, 448.) Wordsworth began writing *The Old Cumberland Beggar* at Racedown (i.e. after September 26th 1795), and completed it at Alfoxden.

15-20. *I asked . . . hospital.* These lines were added in 1798, presumably in an attempt to convert the fragment into a self-contained poem. They were not reprinted after 1805. Critics have differed about their merits: certainly the loss they describe seems incompatible with 'perfect peace.'

53   GOODY BLAKE AND HARRY GILL

Wordsworth probably wrote this poem in the early spring of 1798, at a time when he and Coleridge were planning a double series of poems—those by Coleridge dealing with supernatural or romantic themes, and those by Wordsworth dealing with ordinary subjects in such a way as to 'excite a feeling analogous to the supernatural' (see pp. 262-3, 408-9). Either Wordsworth or, more likely, Coleridge had previously come across the story of 'Goody Blake' in Erasmus Darwin's *Zoönomia* (1794-6), and now realised that a poem on this subject would fit admirably into the scheme. Darwin explains the apparently supernatural effects of Goody's curse in psychological terms, as the result of a powerful 'suggestion,' and Wordsworth accepts this explanation (see Preface, p. 43). He asks Cottle urgently for the loan of Darwin's book in a letter written in late February or early March 1798 (*E.L.W.*, p. 98). The book was returned to Cottle in May. For the relevant passage from *Zoönomia* see *P.W.*, iv, 439-40.

F. W. Bateson makes some good comments on this poem in *Wordsworth: a Re-interpretation* (Longmans, 1954), pp. 16-21:

Wordsworth has identified himself to a quite remarkable degree with this simple old woman and her lifelong struggle to keep warm. . . . What is so admirable is Wordsworth's attitude to Goody Blake. There is not a trace of condescension in it. . . . Goldsmith and Cowper would either have sentimentalised the old woman

or turned her ever so slightly into a figure of fun. **53**
1-2. *Oh! . . . Gill?* The dramatic questioning and frequent
repetitions, which occur elsewhere in *Lyrical Ballads*,
are devices found in traditional ballads such as Wordsworth had met with in Thomas Percy's *Reliques of
Ancient English Poetry*. The double-quatrain form is used
in, for example, *Sir Andrew Barton* (*Reliques*, ii, 188-201).
9. *July*. Eighteenth-century pronunciation could make
this word rhyme with 'truly' in line 11; cf. *The Brothers*,
line 17.
29-32. *This woman dwelt . . . tide*. After 1820 these lines
were altered more than once.
39. *canty*. Originally printed in italic. The word occurs **54**
in Burns and in some Scottish ballads (e.g. *The Gaber-
lunyie Man*, in *Reliques*, ii, 69).

THE LAST OF THE FLOCK **57**

Written in 1798. 'The incident occurred in the village of
Holford, close by Alfoxden' (W.W., 1843). The weeping
man may have been a victim of the 'Speenhamland
system' of supplementing agricultural wages from local
poor-rates. The consequent high rates impoverished
many small property-owners, who were unable themselves to claim relief while savings or property remained.
In Bk. viii, chapt. ii of *Political Justice* (1793), a work
which strongly influenced Wordsworth's views until late
in 1795, William Godwin maintained that the accumulation of private property was one of the greatest sources of
evil. Wordsworth's poem suggests that in some cases at
least it produces good: the pride and pleasure taken by
the owner in his flock have, by association, strengthened
his self-respect and his love for his family, and its loss
does him real harm. (The theme recurs in *Michael*.)

LINES LEFT UPON A SEAT IN A YEW-TREE **60**

Wordsworth began this poem at Hawkshead, probably
while still at school; he was still working on it in 1797,
perhaps also in 1798 (see *P.W.*, i, 329). The core of the
poem is Wordsworth's own response to a real scene, at a
spot he remembered as 'my favourite walk in the even-

60 ings during the latter part of my school-time.' His conception of this poem probably changed more than once during the long period of its composition. The melancholy, sensitive man, contemplating nature in solitude, was an admired figure in the literature of 'sensibility' (*cf.* Gray's *Elegy*), and Wordsworth's original attempt may have been to assimilate his own real experience to the kind of reverie expected from such a figure. In the years when Wordsworth was actively concerned with politics he probably came to disapprove of the recluse's withdrawn attitude: thus the poem contrasts his wasted life with the cheerful 'labours of benevolence,' and traces his motives to shallow misanthropy and egotism. Lastly, we may guess, Wordsworth returned to the poem with a renewed interest in the possibility of a valid communion between men and nature, by the light of which he might interpret his own earlier experience. Hence, for example, the line 'When Nature had subdued him to herself,' which seems really to belong to a different poem. In the final section Coleridge's presence makes itself felt: see Jonathan Wordsworth, *The Music of Humanity* (Harper, 1969), pp. 206-7 n.; Stephen Parrish, *The Art of the Lyrical Ballads* (Harvard Univ. Press, 1973), pp. 66-70.

3. *verdant herb.* This passage seems to have been written before Wordsworth's quarrel with poetic diction; note also the combination of inverted word-order and rhetorical question in the following line, which in 1832 Wordsworth altered to 'What if the bee love not these barren boughs?'

21-2. *wherefore he at once . . . away* so 1805; 1800—

> . . . he was like a plant
> Fair to the sun, the darling of the winds,
> But hung with fruit which no one that passed by
> Regarded, and, his spirit damped at once,
> With indignation did he turn away.

61 32. *An emblem of his own unfruitful life*: because of the yew's 'barren boughs.'

48-9. *the holy forms/Of young imagination.* H. W. Piper explains these as 'natural forms which passed into the child's mind associated with deep feeling' (*The Active Universe* (Athlone Press, 1962), p. 110).

THE FOSTER-MOTHER'S TALE 62

An excerpt from Coleridge's tragedy *Osorio*, Act IV, lines 169-234 (*C.P.W.*, ii, 572-4). Coleridge began writing this play in March 1797 and brought the unfinished manuscript with him when he first visited Wordsworth in June. In October he sent the completed play to Drury Lane theatre, but it was rejected because of the 'obscurity of the last three acts' (*ibid.*, p. 518 n.). In February he contemplated printing two scenes 'as fragments' in a new edition of his *Poems on Various Subjects* (*C.L.*, i, 387). He probably decided to include the present excerpt in *Lyrical Ballads* at a time when his rôle was to supply poems on 'supernatural, or at least romantic' subjects. To Cottle he wrote: 'The extract from my tragedy will have no sort of reference to my tragedy, but is a tale in itself, as *The Ancient Mariner*. The tragedy will not be mentioned' (*C.L.*, i, 412). In *L.B.* (*1798*) the excerpt began at line 154 of the play. Subsequent editions omit the first speech-heading.

A narration in dramatic blank verse 1800; *A dramatic fragment* 1798.

53/4. After '*Tis a sweet tale* 1798 has: *Such as would lull* 63 *a listening child to sleep,/His rosy face besoiled with unwiped tears.*

THE THORN 64

'Arose out of my observing on the ridge of Quantock Hill, on a stormy day, a thorn which I had often passed in calm and bright weather without noticing it. I said to myself, "Cannot I by some invention do as much to make this thorn permanently an impressive object, as the storm has made it to my eyes at this moment?" I began the poem accordingly, and composed it with great rapidity.' (W.W., 1843.) *Cf.* Coleridge's remarks on 'the poetry of nature,' quoted below, p. 408. The poem was probably begun on March 19th 1798, when Dorothy noted: 'William wrote some lines describing a stunted thorn' (*D.W.J.*, i, 13).

64 Wordsworth's method of making the thorn impressive was to use it as the focus of a tale about a betrayed girl and her murdered child. Such themes were fairly common in the traditional ballads and in their eighteenth-century imitations. A fragment printed in David Herd's *Ancient and Modern Scottish Songs* (1769, reprinted 1776, 1791) begins:

> And there she's leaned her back to a thorn,
>> Oh, and alas-a-day! Oh, and alas-a-day!
> And there she has her baby born,
>> Ten thousand times good night, and be wi' thee.
>
> She has houked a grave ayont the sun,
>> Oh, and alas-a-day! Oh, and alas-a-day!
> And there she has buried the sweet babe in,
>> Ten thousand times good night, and be wi' thee.

Wordsworth copied a version of this fragment into a commonplace book, which does not seem to have been used before 1800 (see *P.W.*, ii, 514; *M.M.*, i, 387-8). Another ballad which offers some close parallels is *Des Pfarrers Tochter von Taubenheim*, by G. A. Bürger; Wordsworth probably knew of William Taylor's translation, published in the *Monthly Magazine* in 1796 under the title *The Lass of Fair Wone*. This poem opens and closes by describing a barren spot near a 'pond of toads,' and the supernatural effects to be seen there. The spot is the murdered child's grave.

It may have been the contrast between *The Thorn* and *The Ancient Mariner* which suggested to Wordsworth and Coleridge their original scheme for a twofold series of poems (see above, pp. 262-3). Wordsworth's rôle was to deal with themes from village life, but in such a way as 'to excite a feeling analogous to the supernatural.' In *The Thorn*, as in *Goody Blake* and *Peter Bell*, Wordsworth describes 'supernatural' effects which can be accounted for by natural causes—in this case by the superstitious credulity of the narrator and the other villagers. This credulity is emphasised in the following note appended by Wordsworth in 1800-5:

'This poem ought to have been preceded by an intro-

ductory poem, which I have been prevented from writing **64**
by never having felt myself in a mood when it was probable that I should write it well. The character which I
have here introduced speaking is sufficiently common. The
reader will perhaps have a general notion of it if he has
ever known a man, the captain of a small trading vessel
for example, who, being past the middle age of life, had
retired upon an annuity or small independent income to
some village or country town of which he was not a
native, or in which he had not been accustomed to live.
Such men, having little to do, become credulous and
talkative from indolence; and from the same cause, and
other predisposing causes by which it is probable that
such men may have been affected, they are prone to
superstition. On which account it appeared to me proper
to select a character like this to exhibit some of the
general laws by which superstition acts upon the mind.
Superstitious men are almost always men of slow faculties and deep feelings; their minds are not loose, but
adhesive; they have a reasonable share of imagination, by
which word I mean the faculty which produces impressive
effects out of simple elements; but they are utterly
destitute of fancy, the power by which pleasure and surprise are excited by sudden varieties of situation and an
accumulated imagery.

'It was my wish in this poem to show the manner in
which such men cleave to the same ideas; and to follow
the turns of passion, always different, yet not palpably
different, by which their conversation is swayed. I had
two objects to attain: first, to represent a picture which
should not be unimpressive, yet consistent with the character that should describe it; secondly, while I adhered to
the style in which such persons describe, to take care that
words which in their minds are impregnated with passion
should likewise convey passion to readers who are not
accustomed to sympathise with men feeling in that
manner or using such language. It seemed to me that this
might be done by calling in the assistance of lyrical and
rapid metre. It was necessary that the poem, to be
natural, should in reality move slowly; yet I hoped that,

64 by the aid of the metre, to those who should at all enter into the spirit of the poem it would appear to move quickly. The reader will have the kindness to excuse this note, as I am sensible that an introductory poem is necessary to give this poem its full effect.

'Upon this occasion I will request permission to add a few words closely connected with *The Thorn* and many other poems in these volumes. There is a numerous class of readers who imagine that the same words cannot be repeated without tautology; this is a great error: virtual tautology is much oftener produced by using different words when the meaning is exactly the same. Words, a poet's words more particularly, ought to be weighed in the balance of feeling, and not measured by the space which they occupy upon paper. For the reader cannot be too often reminded that poetry is passion: it is the history or science of feelings; now every man must know that an attempt is rarely made to communicate impassioned feelings without something of an accompanying consciousness of the inadequateness of our own powers, or the deficiencies of language. During such efforts there will be a craving in the mind, and as long as it is unsatisfied the speaker will cling to the same words, or words of the same character. There are also various other reasons why repetition and apparent tautology are frequently beauties of the highest kind. Among the chief of these reasons is the interest which the mind attaches to words, not only as symbols of the passion, but as *things*, active and efficient, which are of themselves part of the passion. And further, from a spirit of fondness, exultation and gratitude, the mind luxuriates in the repetition of words which appear successfully to communicate its feelings. The truth of these remarks might be shown by innumerable passages from the Bible, and from the impassioned poetry of every nation. 'Awake, awake, Deborah!' etc. Judges, chap. v, verses 12th, 27th, and part of 28th. See also the whole of that tumultuous and wonderful poem.'

(*P.W.*, ii, 512-3.)

Wordsworth's attempt to present *The Thorn* as a study in the psychology of superstition is not very convincing:

most of the reader's attention goes to the story rather than **64** to the narrator, whose voice and manner are not very unlike what we find in *Goody Blake* and *The Idiot Boy*. Byron parodied Wordsworth's note on the supposed story-teller in his cancelled Preface to *Don Juan*; and Tennyson's comment was 'such hammering to set a scene for so small a drama' (quoted in Hallam Tennyson's *Life*, chapt. vi). Recent criticism, however, has taken a more favourable view of the poem and of its narrative or dramatic method. See John Danby, *The Simple Wordsworth* (Routledge, 1960), pp. 57-72; Helen Darbishire, *The Poet Wordsworth*, pp. 36-44; A. S. Gérard, 'Of Trees and Men,' *Essays in Criticism*, xiv (1964), pp. 237-55; Stephen Parrish, *The Art of the Lyrical Ballads*, pp. 97-114.

27-33. *Not five yards . . . two feet wide.* These lines were **65** probably more ridiculed than any others in *Lyrical Ballads*. In 1815 Wordsworth maintained that 'they ought to be liked' (E. Smith, p. 213); but in 1820 he changed lines 32-3 to read *Though but of compass small, and bare/To thirsty suns and parching air*. A precedent for the exact measurements of the original version is to be found in *The Lass of Fair Wone*, stanza xlv:

> Hard by the bower her gibbet stands;
>   Her skull is still to show;
> It seems to eye the barren grave,
>   Three spans in length below.

67-77. Of this seventh stanza Coleridge wrote: **66**

> . . . when I . . . compare this with the language of ordinary men, or with that which I can conceive as at all likely to proceed in real life from such a narrator as is supposed in the note to the poem; compare it either in the succession of the images or of the sentences; . . . I reflect with delight how little a mere theory, though of his own workmanship, interferes with the processes of genuine imagination in a man of true poetic genius . . .
> (*B.L.*, chapt. xviii, p. 202.)

72 WE ARE SEVEN

Written in 1798, but based on a conversation Wordsworth had had with a little girl in 1793 (see *P.W.*, i, 360). The incident recalled his early sense of his own immortality: 'Nothing was more difficult for me in childhood than to admit the notion of death as a state applicable to my own being' (*P.W.*, iv, 463). See also Preface, p. 23.

1. *A simple . . . Jim* so 1798-1805; *A simple child* 1815. According to Wordsworth's note of 1843 this prefatory stanza was extemporised by Coleridge and 'Jim' was originally 'Jem,' a reference to their Bristol friend James Tobin.

74 ANECDOTE FOR FATHERS

Based on a conversation between Wordsworth and little Basil Montagu, the son of a friend, who had made his home with the Wordsworths since 1795. In 1796 Wordsworth had complained that Basil lied 'like a little devil,' and Mary Moorman suggests that '. . . at Alfoxden, after a particularly long catechism, Wordsworth at last realised that it was himself, and not Basil, who was to blame' (*M.M.*, i, 289). Many years afterwards Wordsworth explained that the poem was intended '. . . to point out the injurious effects of putting inconsiderate questions to children, and urging them to give answers upon matters either uninteresting to them, or upon which they had no decided opinion' (*The Letters of William and Dorothy Wordsworth: The Later Years*, ed. E. de Selincourt (O.U.P., 1939), i, 253).

Showing . . . taught. This sub-title was replaced in 1845 by a quotation from Eusebius, *Retine vim istam, falsa enim dicam, si coges* (*Restrain your strength, for if you compel me I will tell lies*)—Apollo's reply to those who tried to extort an answer from his oracle by force. W. J. B. Owen cites *Præparatio Evangelica*, vi. 5.

3. *His limbs are cast in beauty's mould.* Cf. *The Children in the Wood*, lines 17-20 (*Reliques*, iii, 172):

> The one a fine and pretty boy,
>   Not passing three yeares olde;
> The other a girl more young than he,

And fram'd in beautyes molde.

As Helen Darbishire points out (*The Poet Wordsworth*, p. 47), 'cast in beauty's mould' is in its way an example of poetic diction.

47. *five times* 1798-36; *three times* 1845.   **75**

LINES WRITTEN AT A SMALL DISTANCE   **76**
FROM MY HOUSE

Later called *To my Sister*; probably the earliest of the group which also includes *Expostulation and Reply* and *The Tables Turned*. Joy at the return of spring and a sense of man's sharing in nature's rebirth have of course been themes for poetry from Chaucer's 'Whan that Aprill . . .' to Auden's 'May with its light behaving/Stirs vessel, eye, and limb.' Wordsworth treats these themes simply but sensitively, and at the same time expresses his conviction that the natural order is not only harmonious and benevolent, but also instructive. Joseph Warren Beach (pp. 178-80) quotes passages from Thomson's *Seasons* which are worth comparing with Wordsworth's poem for the similarity of ideas and difference of treatment: these are *Spring*, lines 582-5, 867-72 and *Hymn*, lines 111-16.

5-8. *There is a blessing . . . field.* For Wordsworth's interest in the belief that natural objects have some kind of life and feeling see *Lines written in Early Spring* (p. 85) and notes.

13. *Edward* is Basil Montagu (see note to previous poem).   **77**

14. *Put on with speed your woodland dress.* This line illustrates Coleridge's point that even where the words chosen are simple and common, the 'language' may still be very different from that 'really used by men.'

26. *fifty years of reason* 1798-1832; *years of toiling reason* 1837.

27-8. *Our minds shall drink at every pore . . . season.* Not only metaphorically but literally, since it is through the body and its senses that the minds are to be fed.

29-30. *Some silent laws . . . obey.* That is, the pure pleasures we enjoy now may contribute to the growth of our minds and characters (see above, pp. 304-5).

78 THE FEMALE VAGRANT

An extract from a much longer poem, first called *Salisbury Plain* or *A Night on Salisbury Plain*, which Wordsworth began during his own journey on foot across the Plain in 1793. (Possibly even earlier material is included: Wordsworth noted in 1843 that 'much of the "Female Vagrant's" story was composed at least two years before,' i.e. in 1791-92, but his dating is unreliable. See *P.W.*, i, 330.) In the original version (extant in a MS. copy made by Dorothy in 1794) a traveller on the Plain endures a stormy night, sees visions of Druids, meets the Vagrant and hears her story. Wordsworth thoroughly revised the poem in 1795-6 and in this new version, called *Adventures on Salisbury Plain*, the traveller is himself an outcast—a sailor who, driven by poverty to despair, has committed robbery and murder and fled his home. *The Female Vagrant* is an excerpt from this version. The complete poem was not printed until 1842, when after further revisions it was called *Guilt and Sorrow*. For summaries and comparisons of the different texts see *P.W.*, i, 94-127 and 330-41; for a critical study see Enid Welsford, *Wordsworth's 'Salisbury Plain'* (Blackwell, 1966).

Salisbury Plain was conceived as a protest against war and social injustice. Six months before beginning it Wordsworth had returned from France an ardent humanitarian and a republican. Since then he had read Godwin's *Political Justice* and had written the *Letter to the Bishop of Llandaff* (not published until after his death), a passionate indictment of the English social order. France declared war on England on February 1st, 1793, and a few months later Wordsworth watched with 'melancholy forebodings' as the English fleet prepared for sea off Spithead.

The American war was still fresh in memory. The struggle which was beginning, and which many thought would be brought to a speedy close by the irresistible arms of Great Britain being added to those of the Allies, I was assured in my own mind would be of long continuance, and productive of distress and misery beyond all possible calculation. This conviction was pressed upon me by having been a witness, during a long residence in revolutionary France, of the spirit **78** which prevailed in that country.

('Advertisement' to *Guilt and Sorrow*, *P.W.*, i, 94-95.) In this mood Wordsworth set out on his journey across the Plain and began his poem. The story of *Salisbury Plain* seems designed to illustrate as many as possible of the evils condemned by English radicals: poverty amidst affluence, the irresponsible use of wealth and power, enclosures, the press-gang, conditions on board the king's ships, the degrading effects of soldiering, the cruelty of war, the hardship it inflicts on the poor, neglect of servicemen and their dependents, inadequate public hospitals, the penal laws. In his successive revisions Wordsworth attempted to reduce the element of protest and to lighten the sombre mood of the poem.

Wordsworth soon became critical of *The Female Vagrant*. In 1801 he wrote: 'The diction of that poem is often vicious, and the descriptions are often false, giving proofs of a mind inattentive to the true nature of the subject on which it was employed' (*E.L.W.*, p. 328). In 1814 he remarked that '. . . it was addressed to coarse sympathies, and had little or no imagination about it, or invention as to story' (*P.W.*, i, 334). Coleridge praised *Adventures on Salisbury Plain* for

the union of deep feeling with profound thought; the fine balance of truth in observing, with the imaginative faculty in modifying, the objects observed; and above all the original gift of spreading the tone, the *atmosphere*, and with it the depth and height of the ideal world, around forms, incidents and situations of which, for the common view, custom had bedimmed all the lustre, had dried up the sparkle and the dew drops.

(*B.L.*, chapt. iv, pp. 48-9.)

Here, however, Coleridge is remembering a reading of the poem that must have taken place twenty years earlier (perhaps misremembering it: see Bateson, p. 15 n.), and his phrases seem much more applicable to Wordsworth's mature poetry. Apart from the rather obtrusive Spenserian stanzas, much of *The Female Vagrant* seems little different from other humanitarian propaganda in verse

78 that was being written at this period. Nevertheless passages occur (e.g. lines 100-8) in which Wordsworth succeeds in making contact with genuine experience of his own, or in imaginatively apprehending that of the humble people and outcasts with whom he sought in those years to identify himself.

1-9. Three additional stanzas describing the Vagrant's girlhood appear in versions from 1794 to 1800. In 1798 they were printed as follows: preceding line 1—

> By Derwent's side my father's cottage stood
> (The woman thus her artless story told),
> One field, a flock, and what the neighbouring flood
> Supplied, to him were more than mines of gold.
> Light was my sleep; my days in transport rolled:
> With thoughtless joy I stretched along the shore
> My father's nets, or watched, when from the fold
> High o'er the cliffs I led my fleecy store,
> A dizzy depth below! his boat and twinkling oar.

Between lines 9 and 10—

> Can I forget what charms did once adorn
> My garden, stored with peas, and mint, and thyme,
> And rose and lily for the sabbath morn?
> The sabbath bells, and their delightful chime;
> The gambols and wild freaks at shearing-time;
> My hen's rich nest through long grass scarce espied;
> The cowslip-gathering at May's dewy prime;
> The swans, that when I sought the water-side
> From far to meet me came, spreading their snowy pride.
>
> The staff I yet remember which upbore
> The bending body of my active sire;
> His seat beneath the honeyed sycamore
> When the bees hummed, and chair by winter fire;
> When market-morning came, the neat attire
> With which, though bent on haste, myself I decked;
> My watchful dog, whose starts of furious ire,
> When stranger passed, so often I have checked;
> The redbreast, known for years, which at my casement pecked.

These stanzas are rather conventional and bear traces of

'poetic diction' in 'fleecy store' and 'snowy pride' (line 3 of **78**
the 1794 MS. has 'finny flood'); but without them the
opening is disproportionately rapid, and Wordsworth
restored the latter two in 1820.

12. *a stately hall*, etc. In the 1794 MS. the father's misfortunes are attributed to 'cruel chance and wilful wrong'
and to 'oppression.' In 1798 Wordsworth refers more
specifically to the greedy master of 'a mansion proud,'
which in 1800 becomes 'a stately hall.' *Guilt and Sorrow*
refers vaguely to 'severe mischance and cruel wrong.' For
Wordsworth the oppressive magnate was something more
than a stock figure of fiction: Sir James Lowther, Earl of
Lonsdale, evaded paying a large debt owed to Wordsworth's father (who died in 1783) until his own death
in 1802. As a result the young Wordsworths were brought
up in straitened and sometimes humiliating circumstances.

66-7. *the noisy drum/Beat round*, i.e. to recruit men for **80**
the American War of Independence (1775-83).

90/91. A stanza condemning soldiering appeared here in
versions from 1794 to 1800:

> Oh! dreadful price of being, to resign
> All that is dear *in* being! Better far
> In Want's most lonely cave till death to pine,
> Unseen, unheard, unwatched by any star;
> Or in the streets and walks where proud men are,
> Better our dying bodies to obtrude,
> Than dog-like, wading at the heels of war,
> Protract a curs'd existence, with the brood
> That lap (their very nourishment!) their brother's
>   blood.

91-144. *The pains and plagues*, etc. 'All that relates to
[the Vagrant's sufferings] in America, and her condition
of mind during her voyage home, were faithfully taken
from the report made to me of her own case by a friend
who had been subjected to the same trials and affected
in the same way' (Wordsworth's note, *P.W.*, i, 330).

181-9. *My heart is touched . . . overflowed*. This stanza **83**
was omitted from all editions after 1805. De Selincourt
suggests that 'the praise accorded to the gipsies, as rebels
to society,' has been 'smoothed away' (*P.W.*, i, 333).

85   LINES WRITTEN IN EARLY SPRING

This apparently simple poem unites several important beliefs and experiences: Hartley's philosophy and psychology, Darwin's belief in the sensibility of plants, Wordsworth's joyous response to the spring weather, his sense of a kinship between men and nature, and his disappointed humanitarianism. As in *Lines written at a small Distance from my House* the speaker delights not only in the outdoor scene, but in his sense of participating in a benevolent and harmonious natural order. Pleasure is the law of life, guiding men to their own good (see note to line 25 of *The Tables Turned*, p. 305) as it guides the birds and perhaps also the plants; 'sad thoughts' arise from the reflection that men so often refuse this kindly guidance and are less happy and good than nature intends. For a full account of the thought of this poem, taking into account several possible modern objections, see Beach, pp. 180-7.

1-3. *notes . . . thoughts.* Wordsworth spoke with a Cumberland burr and pronounced 'notes' to rhyme with 'thoughts'; in one letter he writes 'nought' meaning a banknote (see Helen Darbishire, *The Poet Wordsworth*, pp. 8-9).

5-6. *To her fair works . . . ran.* The 'link' is that of association: Hartley's system is invoked to explain Wordsworth's intense feeling, in moments like these, that man and nature are 'essentially adapted to each other' (Preface, p. 34, lines 27-8).

7-8. *And much . . . of man.* Society has taught men different lessons from the kindly ones of nature. The phrasing here recalls Burns's 'Man's inhumanity to man/ Makes countless thousands mourn' (*Man was Made to Mourn*, stanza vii).

11-12. *And 'tis my faith . . . breathes.* 'It is probable that Wordsworth meant seriously and literally to attribute pleasure to the budding twigs as well as to the birds at play' (Beach, p. 182); though, as Beach recognises, he puts the belief forward as a matter of faith and not of scientific certainty. His interest in this idea had recently been stimulated by Erasmus Darwin's *Zoönomia* (1794-

6), which 'attributes to vegetable life not merely sensi- **85**
bility, but some degree of voluntary power and even of
conscious thought' (Beach, p. 183). Wordsworth borrowed this book in the spring of 1798 (see *M.M.*, i, 284,
383). A fragment Wordsworth wrote in his notebook
early in 1798 explicitly connects 'man's inhumanity to
man' with his inability to communicate with other forms
of life:

> And never for each other shall we feel
> As we may feel, till we have sympathy
> With nature in her forms inanimate,
> With objects such as have no power to hold
> Articulate language. In all forms of things
> There is a mind. (*P.W.*, v, 340.)

But as early as 1794 he had expressed similar notions in
his MS. corrections to *An Evening Walk* (*P.W.*, i, 10,
app. crit.). H. W. Piper suggests that Wordsworth
learned this doctrine of 'the active principle' from certain French writers and from Radicals and Unitarians
with whom he associated in 1792-3: see *The Active
Universe* (Athlone Press, 1962), chapt. iii.

17-18. *spread . . . catch*. Wordsworth's phrasing, while **86**
strictly accurate, momentarily animates and even
humanises the tree.

21-2. *If I these thoughts . . . plan* so 1798-1815; *If this
belief from heaven be sent,/If such be Nature's holy plan*
1837.

SIMON LEE, THE OLD HUNTSMAN **86**

'This old man had been huntsman to the Squires of
Alfoxden, which at the time we occupied it belonged to
a minor. The old man's cottage stood upon the common,
a little way from the entrance to Alfoxden Park. . . . It
is unnecessary to add, the fact was as mentioned in the
poem; and I have, after an interval of forty-five years,
the image of the old man as fresh before my eyes as if I
had seen him yesterday. The expression when the
hounds were out, "I dearly love their voices," was word
for word from his own lips.' (W.W., 1843.)

Comparatively few poems in *L.B.* (*1798*) fulfil the
complete programme laid down in the Preface of 1800,

86 i.e. of treating simple incidents from 'low and rustic life' in a language close to common speech: of these *Simon Lee* is probably the most successful. The poem is perhaps best understood as a stratagem to 'ruffle the perfect manners of the frozen heart.' Wordsworth relates the facts of Simon Lee's active youth and decrepit age in terms so homely as to appear at first naïve: 'For still, the more he works, the more/His poor old ankles swell.' Ridicule is checked, not only because the facts claim our compassion, but because the language is so authentic; banal, unpretentious, pathetic, it belongs to no literary convention but is the language Simon or old Ruth might use. The 'gentle reader' does not laugh, but arrives at the final incident still in doubt as to whether Simon Lee (or the poem) really deserves his serious attention. The last stanzas compel him to put aside his dignity and accept Simon Lee on the footing of common humanity which the previous stanzas have so trustfully assumed. For a sensitive reading see Danby, pp. 38-47.

Between 1798 and 1845 Wordsworth often revised this poem, making its language more dignified and grouping its facts tidily into 'past' and 'present.' Only changes made between 1798 and 1805 are noted here.

87 3-4. *An old man . . . tall.* 'The ludicrous, if we like, is brought teasingly near the surface. It is as though the reader were being challenged to recognise his first impulse to laugh, get over it at the outset, and dismiss it for the rest of the poem' (Danby, p. 40).

14. *running huntsman.* The physical prowess needed by such men is well shown by the note on Thomas Ridge in Joseph Hunter's *History of Hallamshire* (revd. A. Gatty, 1869), pp. 13-14. Ridge was huntsman of the Ecclesfield harriers for forty years.

25-48. In 1798 stanzas 4-6 appeared in the order 6, 4, 5.

26. *dwindled* 1800-45; *little* 1798.

39. *chiming hounds.* A pack of hounds in full cry creates harmony from the blending of differently-pitched voices; huntsmen would take pride in a well-matched 'cry.'

88 69-80. *My gentle reader*, etc. Wordsworth recognises the reader's suspense and artfully prolongs it for another 12

lines. Note the shifting implications of *gentle*, which in **88**
line 69 is primarily a formal mode of address (=gentle-
manly), but by line 75 has become an appeal to the
reader's tenderness and humanity.

89. *good Simon Lee*. Despite the friendly offer of help,
the form of address recognises social differences: Simon
would not have addressed the speaker as 'good William
Wordsworth.'

101-4. *I've heard . . . mourning*. The cryptic close (the
last word of the poem is a surprise) comes with special
force after the relaxed, almost garrulous narrative. A
remark ascribed to Scott in 1818 makes the main point
more explicitly. 'We occasionally hear complaints of how
thankless men are for favours bestowed upon them; but
when I consider that we are all of the same flesh and
blood, it grieves me more to see slight acts of kindness
acknowledged with such humility and deep sense of
obligation' (H. J. C. Grierson, *Sir Walter Scott, Bart.*
(Constable, 1938), pp. 296-7).

THE NIGHTINGALE   **90**

Though this poem was written in April 1798, the
decision to include it in *Lyrical Ballads* was not made
until the sheets of the volume had already been printed.
It was substituted for *Lewti*, which might have revealed
Coleridge as one of the authors (see above, p. 268).

The Nightingale belongs to the group of directly
autobiographical poems in blank verse by Coleridge
which also includes *The Eolian Harp, This Lime-Tree
Bower my Prison*, and *Frost at Midnight*. Like Wordsworth's 'experiments,' these poems represent a movement away from conventional poetic rhetoric: they seek
the effect of direct and intimate, though heightened,
speech. Humphry House shows in *Coleridge* (Hart-
Davis, 1962), pp. 70-83, that the point of departure for
this kind of development was Cowper's *The Task* (1785).
The Nightingale is probably the best poem of the group
after *Frost at Midnight*. Though slightly marred in
places by an over-effusive and exclamatory manner—

90 which may be contrasted with the steady self-assured tone of Wordsworth's *Tintern Abbey*—it conveys Coleridge's joy in the friendship of the Wordsworths and in their evening walks in the spring of 1798. Coleridge seems to have been satisfied with the beginning and middle of the poem, but not with the ending: see the humorous verses which accompanied the copy he sent to Wordsworth on May 10th (*C.L.*, i, 406).

In 1798 *The Nightingale* was sub-titled *A Conversational Poem*, and in 1828-34 *A Conversation Poem*.

13. '*Most musical, most melancholy*': Milton, *Il Penseroso*, line 62. Coleridge adds a footnote:

This passage in Milton possesses an excellence far superior to that of mere description: it is spoken in the character of the melancholy man, and has therefore a *dramatic* propriety. The author makes this remark to rescue himself from the charge of having alluded with levity to a line in Milton: a charge than which none could be more painful to him, except perhaps that of having ridiculed his Bible.

(So 1798-1829; in 1834 the last phrase, 'a charge . . . Bible,' was omitted.)

23-49. *And many a poet . . . all its music!* Wordsworth and Coleridge took this passage seriously as illustrating the difference between first-hand contact with nature and contact through literature, especially conventional literature. Wordsworth thought *The Nightingale* would do something to rectify men's feelings in this respect (see his letter to John Wilson, *E.L.W.*, p. 296).

25-34. *When he . . . like nature!* That nature is our best teacher if we are willing to absorb impressions through our senses in a 'wise passiveness' was of course one of Wordsworth's favourite doctrines at this period: *cf. Expostulation and Reply, The Tables Turned* and related poems.

91 39. *Philomela*: a princess of Greek legend who was ravished and mutilated by Tereus, the husband of her sister Procne. Subsequently she was changed into a nightingale and Procne into a swallow: the story explains the supposedly plaintive songs of these two birds. Cole-

ridge's lines are aimed at readers who know more about **91**
the nightingales of legend and convention than about
real ones.

40. *My friend, and my friend's sister!* 1798-1805; *My
friend, and thou, our sister!* 1817. These persons are of
course Wordsworth and Dorothy.

50. *a castle huge*: Enmore Castle, near Stowey, the seat
of Lord Egmont; the 'gentle maid' in line 64 is Ellen
Cruikshank. Her brother, John Cruikshank, was Lord
Egmont's agent and Coleridge was on friendly terms
with both Cruikshanks.

64. *Forget it was not day.*/*A most gentle maid* so 1800-5;
1798—

> Forget it was not day! On moonlight bushes,
> Whose dewy leafits are but half disclosed,
> You may perchance behold them on the twigs,
> Their bright, bright eyes, their eyes both bright
>   and full,
> Glistening, while many a glow-worm in the shade
> Lights up her love-torch.
>   A most gentle maid, etc.

Coleridge restored these lines in 1817, but with 'leaflets'
for 'leafits.'

79. *blosmy* 1798-1817; *blossomy* 1828. Coleridge probably **92**
found the form 'blosmy' in Chaucer: see *Troilus and
Criseyde*, Bk. ii, l. 821, and *Parlement of Foules*, l. 183.

81. *tipsy Joy*. Coleridge did not share Wordsworth's
distaste for personifications (see Preface, p. 26, and note).

86. *My dear babe:* David Hartley Coleridge, who was
about eighteen months old when this poem was written.

93-100. *once, when he awoke . . . yellow moonbeam. Cf.* an
entry in Coleridge's notebook, written late in 1797 or
early in 1798:

> Hartley fell down and hurt himself—I caught him up
> crying and screaming—and ran out of doors with him.
> The moon caught his eye—he ceased crying immedi-
> ately—and his eyes and the tears in them, how they
> glittered in the moonlight!   (*C.N.*, i, 219.)

Cf. also *Frost at Midnight* for Coleridge's wish to bring
the child up under the influences of nature.

93

THE IDIOT BOY

'Alfoxden, 1798. The last stanza—"The cocks did crow
to-whoo, to-whoo, and the sun did shine so cold"—was
the foundation of the whole. The words were reported
to me by my dear friend Thomas Poole; but I have since
heard the same repeated of other idiots. Let me add that
this long poem was composed in the groves of Alfoxden, almost extempore; not a word, I believe, being
corrected, though one stanza was omitted. I mention
this in gratitude to those happy moments, for in truth I
never wrote anything with so much glee.' (W.W., 1843.)
That 'Johnny,' if not his story, had an equivalent in real
life is shown by a letter Wordsworth wrote in 1802:
'The boy whom I had in my mind was by no means disgusting in his appearance, quite the contrary' (*E.L.W.*,
p. 357).

When Wordsworth wrote *The Idiot Boy* he and Coleridge were probably still intending to produce the double
series of poems described in *Biographia Literaria* (see
below, pp. 408-9). Wordsworth's rôle was to create
'feelings analogous to the supernatural' by dealing with
ordinary incidents of village life. Here the episode in
which Susan Gale is 'as if by magic cured' illustrates
the power of mind over body, which is also a theme of
Goody Blake. Lines 323-66, especially 357-66, seem to
invite comparison with the intended companion-pieces
by Coleridge and with other 'supernatural' poems, in
the same way that the preamble to *Peter Bell* does.

Many critics have disliked this poem. On its first
appearance Southey wrote: 'No tale less deserved the
labour that appears to have been bestowed upon this.
It resembles a Flemish picture in the worthlessness of
its design and the excellence of its execution' (see E.
Smith, p. 31; for similar comments by John Wilson see
ibid., pp. 57-8). Though Coleridge refers to *The Idiot
Boy* as a 'fine poem,' he describes Betty Foy as 'an
impersonation of an instinct abandoned by judgment,'
and adds that the following two criticisms are 'not
wholly groundless':

The one is that the author has not, in the poem itself,

taken sufficient care to preclude from the reader's **93**
fancy the disgusting images of *ordinary morbid idiocy*,
which yet it was by no means his intention to represent. He has even, by the 'burr, burr, burr,' un-
counteracted by any preceding description of the
boy's beauty, assisted in recalling them. The other is
that the idiocy of the *boy* is so evenly balanced by the
folly of the *mother*, as to present to the general reader
rather a laughable burlesque on the blindness of anile
dotage, than an analytic display of maternal affection
in its ordinary workings. (*B.L.*, chapt. xvii, p. 194.)
Swinburne thought the piece a 'doleful example of
eccentricity in dullness,' and Dowden and Hutchinson
viewed it as a clumsy frolic.

In 1802 Wordsworth defended his choice of subject
in a letter to John Wilson, who had warmly praised
Lyrical Ballads as a whole but had been 'disgusted' by
the idiot boy and by the 'excessive fondness' of Betty:

... the loathing and disgust which many people have
at the sight of an idiot is a feeling ... owing in a great
measure to a false delicacy, and, if I may say it without
rudeness, a certain want of comprehensiveness of
thinking and feeling. Persons in the lower classes
of society have little or nothing of this: if an idiot is born
in a poor man's house it must be taken care of, and
cannot be boarded out as it would be by gentlefolks, or
sent to a public or private asylum for such unfortunate
beings. [Poor people,] seeing frequently among their
neighbours such objects, easily [forget] whatever there
is of natural disgust about them, and have [therefore]
a sane state, so that without pain or suffering they [per-
form] their duties towards them. ... I have often
applied to idiots, in my own mind, that sublime expression of Scripture, that *their life is hidden with
God*. ... I have, indeed, often looked upon the conduct
of fathers and mothers of the lower classes of society
towards idiots as the great triumph of the human
heart. It is there that we see the strength, disinter-
estedness, and grandeur of love; nor have I ever been
able to contemplate an object that calls out so many

93   excellent and virtuous sentiments without finding it hallowed thereby, and having something in me which bears down before it, like a deluge, every feeble sensation of disgust and aversion. (*E.L.W.*, pp. 356-7.)

Johnny's affliction is not concealed or softened as Coleridge would have wished, nor is it dwelt on as a source of misery—it is rather one of a mysterious happiness. Wordsworth treats the boy naturally, without repulsion, embarrassment or sentimentality, at times with a kindly humour. The reader with enough 'comprehensiveness of thinking and feeling' to accept this will probably enjoy the poem. It might best be approached in the first instance, not as a study of maternal passion or of moral grandeur, but as a comic ballad numbering among its ancestors Cowper's *John Gilpin*. It has as good a story and as many amusing touches as that poem, and Betty's visit to the doctor has nearly the same kind of narrative humour. But Wordsworth surpasses Cowper by the sympathy and insight he brings to his figures:

> She is uneasy everywhere,
> Her limbs are all alive with joy.

His attitude has not that touch of condescension, as of a gentleman observing the pursuits of 'citizens,' that lingers in Cowper's poem: it is approximately that of a neighbour. The poem is enriched too by Wordsworth's evocations of the serene, owl-haunted, 'long blue night.' For interesting readings see Roger Murray, 'Betty Foy: an early Mental Traveler,' *Journal of English and Germanic Philology*, lxx (1971), 51-61; Mary Jacobus, 'The Idiot Boy,' in *Bicentenary Wordsworth Studies*, ed. Jonathan Wordsworth (Cornell Univ. Press, 1970), pp. 238-65.

97   125-6. *Yet for his life . . . upon his back. Cf.* Cowper's *John Gilpin*, stanza xxiv:

> His horse, who never in that sort
> Had handled been before,
> What thing upon his back had got
> Did wonder more and more.

102 288-91. *road . . . abroad*. Wordsworth probably pro-

nounced 'road' to rhyme with 'abroad': *cf. Lines written* **102**
in Early Spring (p. 85), lines 1-3 and note, p. 320.

372. *Your pony's worth his weight in gold.* A popular ex-   **105**
pression (still current) of the kind Wordsworth liked to
use in his ballad poetry. *Cf.* 'That beast is worth his
weight in gold,' in stanza xv of *Market Night*, by the
shoemaker-poet Robert Bloomfield (first published in
Rural Tales, Ballads and Songs, 1802).

LOVE   **108**

Written in 1799, soon after Coleridge had met and begun
to fall in love with Sara Hutchinson. A version was
published in the *Morning Post* on December 21st, 1799
(see *C.P.W.*, ii, 1052-9 for this text). At first Coleridge
intended the poem to be an introduction, or rather a
'sister-tale,' to his *Ballad of the Dark Ladie*, begun the
previous year but never completed: the *Morning Post*
version bears the title *Introduction to the Tale of the Dark
Ladie*, and is set in a frame of seven stanzas whose
function is to link it with the other ballad. The present
version first appeared in *L.B.* (*1800*), where it replaced
Coleridge's *The Dungeon*.

44/45. Between these lines comes another stanza in 1799: **110**

> And how he crossed the woodman's paths
> Though briars and swampy mosses beat,
> How boughs rebounding scourged his limbs,
> And low stubs gored his feet.

(In 1799 the narrative clauses are uniformly introduced
by 'how' where *L.B.* has 'that.')

80/81. Between these lines comes another stanza in 1799: **111**

> I saw her bosom heave and swell,
> Heave and swell with inward sighs—
> I could not choose but love to see
> Her gentle bosom rise.

The next stanza then begins 'Her wet cheek glowed.'

THE MAD MOTHER   **112**

Later called *Her Eyes are Wild*. 'Alfoxden, 1798. The
subject was reported to me by a lady of Bristol who had
seen the poor creature' (W.W., 1843). Here Wordsworth

112 shows an unusually direct debt to Percy's *Reliques* (see above, pp. 269-70). *Lady Anne Bothwell's Lament* (*Reliques*, ii, 209-13) is also an address by a deserted mother to her baby, and Wordsworth's poem resembles this ballad not only in its general theme and form but in some details of its treatment. Note for example the similarity of the stanza, and the internal rhyme in the penultimate line:

> Bairne, sin thy cruel father is gane,
> Thy winsome smiles maun eise my pain;
> My babe and I'll together live,
> He'll comfort me when cares doe grieve;
> My babe and I right saft will ly,
> And quite forget man's cruelty.
>> Balow, etc.

But Wordsworth's poem is not an imitation: his aim is to keep the vigour, simplicity and pathos of the ballad while developing it as a psychological study. The poem traces 'the manner in which we associate ideas in a state of excitement,' in this case of madness (Preface, p. 21). *The Mad Mother* was singled out for praise both by Coleridge and by Lamb (*C.L.*, i, 652; *Lamb*, i, 240) and was one of the most popular poems in the collection, being several times reprinted in magazines.

39-40. *The breeze I see . . . my babe and me.* Coleridge praises this 'fine transition . . . so expressive of that deranged state in which from the increased sensibility the sufferer's attention is abruptly drawn off by every trifle and in the same instant plucked back again by the one despotic thought, and bringing home with it, by the blending, fusing power of imagination and passion, the alien object to which it had been so abruptly diverted, no longer an alien but an ally and an inmate' (*B.L.*, chapt. xxii, p. 270).

115 THE ANCIENT MARINER

This poem was planned and partly written during a walking-tour made by Coleridge and the Wordsworths in November 1797 (see above, p. 262; *P.W.*, i, 360-1; *M.M.*, i, 347-9). Coleridge's imagination seems to have been set to work by hearing of his friend John

Cruikshank's strange dream about 'a skeleton ship with **115** figures in it' (see A. Dyce's note reprinted in Coleridge's *Poetical Works*, ed. James Dykes Campbell (1893), p. 594; also *P.W.*, i, 361). This dream probably combined in Coleridge's mind with some version of the legend of Falkenberg, a guilty seaman doomed to sail forever accompanied by two spectral figures playing at dice for his soul (see notes to lines 183-92). To convert these elements into a story, 'some crime' was needed 'which should bring upon the Old Navigator . . . the spectral persecution'; this crime Wordsworth supplied, by suggesting that the Mariner should shoot an albatross and suffer punishment accordingly (see his note, *P.W.*, i, 361). Wordsworth also contributed the idea of the Mariner's ship being worked by dead men. For a while the poem was planned as a joint production: but after supplying a few lines Wordsworth felt himself to be a 'clog' and left the writing of the poem to Coleridge. A version was complete by March 23rd 1798 (see *D.W.J.*, i, 13), and as *The Rime of the Ancyent Marinere* it provided the nucleus of *Lyrical Ballads*.

Coleridge had resolved to treat this supernatural sea-story in 'the *style* as well as . . . the spirit of the elder poets.' His general intention was to produce a ballad something like those in Percy's *Reliques* (see pp. 269-70); one of these in particular, *Sir Cauline*, supplied him with some unusual variations of the ballad stanza and with archaisms such as *sterte* and *swound* (*Reliques*, i, 61-76). His treatment was also influenced by some recent imitations of the ballads, notably those of Gottfried August Bürger (1747-94). Bürger had specialised in the supernatural themes which occur in relatively few of Percy's ballads, and had dealt with them in a macabre and horrific fashion. In his most famous ballad, *Lenore*, Death visits a girl in the likeness of her dead lover and bears her to the grave on horseback, while ghosts and animated corpses play minor parts. *Lenore* was introduced to English readers by William Taylor, whose free translation appeared in the *Monthly Magazine* in March 1796. Taylor gave his version an authentic

115 air by introducing several ballad-phrases from the
Reliques and by using archaic spellings and forms
such as *sowne* for sound, *eyne* for eyes and *ble* for com-
plexion. Coleridge admired Taylor's *Ellenore* (*C.L.*, i,
565-6), and it is not surprising that he should have tried
to write something similar for the same magazine.
(For texts of *Ellenore* and another gruesome ballad
Coleridge knew—*Alonzo the Brave*, by M. G. Lewis—
see *The Literary Ballad*, ed. Anne Henry Ehrenpreis
(Arnold, 1966), pp. 64-97.)

Another German poem, C. M. Wieland's *Oberon*
(1780), set a precedent for more elaborate supernatural
machinery. Oberon here is a powerful nature-spirit or
dæmon who controls the elements; he first befriends
the hero Huon, then persecutes him for a sin committed
during a sea voyage, and finally allows him to expiate
the sin after great suffering and deprivation. A detailed
synopsis of *Oberon* had appeared in the *Monthly
Review* for August/September 1797 (xxiii, 576-84), and
about 20 November Coleridge was apparently attempting to translate this poem from the German (*C.L.*,
i, 357). For Wieland's influence see W. W. Beyer, *The
Enchanted Forest* (Blackwell, 1963).

The Mariner's course to the Pacific equator, which he
reaches in line 103, follows that of Drake and the other
navigators who sailed the world westwards. Coleridge
had not yet been to sea; but he had read the narratives
of many famous voyages (e.g. those edited in the early
seventeenth century by Samuel Purchas), and what
he read he intensely experienced. His descriptions, for
example of the icefields or of tropical calms, give the
essence of all such descriptions in the Voyages. J.
Livingston Lowes has shown in *The Road to Xanadu*
(Constable, 1927) how much the phrasing of these
passages owes to Coleridge's conscious or unconscious
memories of his reading, and points out that the idiom
of the poem as a whole—concise, concrete, vivid,
sometimes homely—owes a debt to the kind of narrative
Coleridge found in Purchas. Stanzas inspired by the
Voyages—

The breezes blew, the white foam flew,
The furrow followed free;
We were the first that ever burst
Into that silent sea—

tend to be more memorable than those describing the
spectre crew, or reporting the conversation of dæmons.

The force with which the Mariner's thirst, fear, loneliness and homesickness are conveyed also owes something to the Voyages. But Coleridge had experienced
these sensations for himself, and others too which
appear less often in seamen's narratives: feelings of
social isolation, worthlessness, guilt, self-contempt and
weariness of life. The most deeply moving phase of the
poem is Part IV, which expresses these feelings, and
ends with the temporary release from torment that
follows an outgoing impulse of love. Here Coleridge is
obviously presenting his own inward experience, more
poignantly than in any other poem except *Dejection*: yet
he does so without moving away from the situation of
the Mariner or from the concrete imagery the tale demands. Indeed, one of the shaping forces behind the
poem as a whole is Coleridge's need to express his
emotional nature through a pattern that would include
guilt, submission and partial expiation. From this point
of view it is right that dreadful retribution should follow
the apparently trivial act of shooting the albatross, since
Coleridge's own guilt was of the irrational kind that
bears no relation to crimes really performed. Thus the
Mariner's story is 'a fiction which permits the expression of real experience' (D. W. Harding, 'The Theme of
The Ancient Mariner,' *Scrutiny*, ix, (1941), 338). We need
not, of course, suppose that every detail of the poem has
this kind of significance. For some effects of fear and
horror Coleridge seems to have drawn upon the experience of nightmares: see especially some passages
omitted after 1798—

And I quak'd to think of my own voice,
How frightful it would be! . . .
Thought I, I am as thin as air,
They cannot me behold.

115 Indeed the whole poem, with its swift, apparently inconsequential transitions from one state of intense feeling to another, has something of the character of a dream, as Lamb observed (see below, p. 337).

There is a long-standing dispute as to whether the poem has a 'moral,' and if so what it is. Coleridge gave his own view in a conversation which must have taken place about 1802:

Mrs. Barbauld once told me that she admired *The Ancient Mariner* very much, but that there were two faults in it—it was improbable, and had no moral. As for the probability, I owned that that might admit some question; but as to the want of a moral, I told her that in my own judgment the poem had too much; and that the only or chief fault, if I might say so, was the obtrusion of the moral sentiment so openly on the reader as a principle or cause of action in a work of such pure imagination. It ought to have had no more moral than the Arabian Nights' tale of the merchant's sitting down to eat dates by the side of the well, and throwing the shells aside, and lo! a genie starts up, and says he *must* kill the aforesaid merchant *because* one of the date shells had, it seems, put out the eye of the genie's son. (*Table-Talk*, quoted by House, p. 90.)

Poets are not necessarily the best interpreters of their own work, however, and some good modern critics believe that *The Ancient Mariner* has 'a very serious moral and spiritual bearing upon human life' (see House, p. 92). Taken at face value, the punishment inflicted on the Mariner and his shipmates for the shooting of a seabird seems excessive by any standards: so that to find a satisfying moral meaning in the poem involves seeking moral as well as psychological symbolism. A detailed interpretation is offered by Robert Penn Warren ('A Poem of Pure Imagination,' *Kenyon Review*, viii (1946), 391-427), who finds in the poem the twin themes of 'the One Life' and the creative imagination. Thus the shooting of the albatross represents both the violation of a sacramental bond between man and nature, and the subjection of the imagination to the workaday 'under-

334

standing'; and other features of the poem, notably the 115
sun, moon and weather, are associated in one way or
another with the same two groups of ideas. Such associations may well have been present in Coleridge's mind,
but House rightly warns us against too 'technical and
diagrammatic' a reading of the poem. *The Ancient
Mariner* is a remarkable synthesis of very different
materials and motives, and it would be too much to
expect mathematical consistency of the kind found in
simpler allegories. Variations in imaginative intensity
and poetic achievement should also be recognised. These
are inevitable in any long poem, but are rarely as extreme as here, where magnificent passages give place to
stanzas that seem merely macabre or even slightly
ludicrous.

For *L.B.* (*1800*) Coleridge thoroughly revised the
poem, removing many of the more obvious archaisms
(e.g. *Ancyent Marinere* became *Ancient Mariner*, *ne . . .
ne* became *nor . . . nor* and *Pheere* became *mate*). Further
improvements were made when the poem was published
in *Sibylline Leaves* (1817). The 'gloss' or prose
commentary too first appeared in 1817, though it
may have been written considerably earlier. It is
modelled on the editorial gloss to the seamen's narratives in *Purchas his Pilgrimage* (1617) and *Purchas his
Pilgrims* (1625): see Lowes, pp. 324-5. Huntington
Brown points out that just as the 'rime' purports
to be the work of a minstrel of the late fifteenth or
early sixteenth century, so the gloss is written in the
character of a pious antiquarian of c. 1600-1660 ('The
Gloss to *The Rime of the Ancient Mariner*,' *Mod. Lang.
Quart.*, vi (1945), 319-24). It should not be mistaken
for an authorial commentary by Coleridge. More subtly
than the archaisms of 1798, the gloss creates an illusory
historical perspective which makes the poem seem both
mysterious and authentic. The imaginary editor's inter-
pretations are not always to be accepted as final, and his
note at line 436 can mislead; but on some points, e.g. the
identification of Life-in-Death, his information is indispensable. And at times his prose rises to an 'astounding

115 beauty' (House, p. 101). For these reasons the gloss of 1817 has here been printed alongside the text of 1805, within square brackets. For contrasting views of the successive revisions see B. R. McElderry Jr., 'Coleridge's Revision of *The Ancient Mariner*,' *Stud. Phil.*, xxix (1932), 68-94; W. Empson and D. Pirie, eds. *Coleridge's Verse: A Selection* (Faber, 1972).

The Ancient Mariner not only provided a nucleus for *Lyrical Ballads* but is the longest, and certainly one of the finest, poems in the collection. Yet it was the one least appreciated by contemporaries. Southey, who in 1798 was on bad terms with Coleridge, wrote impatiently:

> Many of the stanzas are laboriously beautiful; but in connection they are absurd or unintelligible. . . . We do not sufficiently understand the story to analyse it. It is a Dutch attempt at German sublimity. Genius has here been employed in producing a poem of little merit. (E. Smith, p. 31.)

Another reviewer echoed Southey: 'In our opinion it has more of the extravagance of a mad German poet, than of the simplicity of our ancient ballad writers' (*op. cit.*, p. 33). Dr. Charles Burney, whose criticism is quoted on p. 417, changed the emphasis slightly by finding 'poetical touches of an exquisite kind' among the 'rhapsody of unintelligible wildness.' The *British Critic* reviewer of 1799 was more favourable, but still not very perceptive (E. Smith, pp. 38-9). Even Wordsworth's appreciation seems at this time to have been very limited. Not only was *The Ancient Mariner* harming the reception of *Lyrical Ballads*, but it was irrelevant to his programme for dealing with humble and rustic themes in 'the real language of men.' He seems to have contemplated omitting the poem from the second edition (*E.L.W.*, pp. 63-4), and when it did reappear in 1800 added a note pointing out its 'great defects':

> first, that the principal person has no distinct character, either in his profession of mariner or as a human being who, having been long under the control of super-

natural impressions, might be supposed himself to **115**
partake of something supernatural; secondly, that he
does not act, but is continually acted upon; thirdly,
that the events, having no necessary connection, do not
produce each other; and lastly, that the imagery is
somewhat too laboriously accumulated. Yet the poem
contains many delicate touches of passion, and indeed
the passion is everywhere true to nature; a great number
of the stanzas present beautiful images, and are expressed with unusual felicity of language; and the
versification, though the metre is itself unfit for long
poems, is harmonious and artfully varied, exhibiting
the utmost powers of that metre, and every variety of
which it is capable.

Wordsworth withdrew this note in 1802 after an
admonition by Lamb, who was certainly the most appre-
ciative contemporary reader of the poem:

For me, I was never so affected with any human
tale. After first reading it, I was totally possessed with
it for many days. I dislike all the miraculous part of
it, but the feelings of the man under the operations
of such scenery dragged me along like Tom Piper's
magic whistle. I totally differ from your idea that the
Marinere should have had a character and profession.
This is a beauty in *Gulliver's Travels*, where the mind
is kept in a placid state of little wonderments; but
the Ancient Marinere undergoes such trials as over-
whelm and bury all individuality and memory of what
he was, like the state of a man in a bad dream, one
terrible peculiarity of which is: that all consciousness
of personality is gone. Your other observation is I
think as well a little unfounded: the Marinere from
being conversant in supernatural events *has* acquired
a supernatural and strange cast of *phrase*, eye, appearance, etc., which frighten the wedding guest. You
will excuse my remarks, because I am hurt and vexed
that you should think it necessary with a prose apology
to open the eyes of dead men that cannot see.

(*Lamb*, i, 240, dated January 30th, 1801.)

115 Title so 1802-5; *The Rime of the Ancyent Marinere, in Seven Parts* 1798; *The Ancient Mariner, a Poet's Reverie* 1800; *The Rime of the Ancient Mariner, in Seven Parts* 1817. The sub-title *A Poet's Reverie* seems intended to offer puzzled readers a possible approach to the poem. Lamb condemned it:

> ... it is as bad as Bottom the weaver's declaration that he is not a lion but only the scenical representation of a lion. What new idea is gained by this title, but one subversive of all credit, which the tale should force upon us, of its truth? (*Lamb*, i, 240.)

It was deleted from the printer's copy for *L.B.* (*1802*), but by an oversight was allowed to stand in the separate half-title which there preceded this poem; so also in 1805.

The following 'Argument' was prefixed in 1798:

> How a Ship having passed the Line was driven by Storms to the cold Country towards the South Pole; and how from thence she made her course to the tropical Latitude of the Great Pacific Ocean; and of the strange things that befell; and in what manner the Ancyent Marinere came back to his own Country.

In 1800 this became:

> How a Ship, having first sailed to the Equator, was driven by Storms to the cold Country towards the South Pole; how the Ancient Mariner cruelly and in contempt of the laws of hospitality killed a Sea-bird and how he was followed by many and strange Judgements: and in what manner he came back to his own Country.

Neither 'Argument' was reprinted by Coleridge after 1800; from 1817 onwards they were superseded by the continuous gloss (see notes, above).

An epigraph from Thomas Burnet's *Archæologiæ Philosophicæ* (1692) was also added in 1817:

> Facile credo, plures esse Naturas invisibiles quam visibiles in rerum universitate. Sed horum omnium familiam quis nobis enarrabit, et gradus et cognationes et discrimina et singulorum munera? Quid agunt? quæ loca habitant? Harum rerum notitiam semper

ambivit ingenium humanum, nunquam attigit. Juvat, **115**
interea, non diffiteor, quandoque in animo, tanquam
in tabula, majoris et melioris mundi imaginem con-
templari: ne mens assuefacta hodiernæ vitæ minutiis
se contrahat nimis, et tota subsidat in pusillas cogita-
tiones. Sed veritati interea invigilandum est, modus-
que servandus, ut certa ab incertis, diem a nocte,
distinguamus.—T. Burnet, *Archæol. Phil.*, p. 68.

This may be approximately translated:

I can readily believe that in the sum of existing things
there are more invisible beings than visible. But who
will explain this great family to us—their ranks, their
relationships, their differences, and their respective
duties? What do they do, and where do they live?
Man's intelligence has always sought knowledge of
these matters, but has never attained it. Meanwhile,
I do not deny that it pleases me sometimes to contemplate in my mind, as in a picture, the idea of a
greater and better world: lest the mind, grown used
to dealing with the small matters of everyday life, should
dwindle and be wholly submerged in petty thoughts.
Nevertheless we should be vigilant of truth and keep
a sense of proportion, so that we may discriminate
between things certain and things uncertain, daylight
and darkness.

Coleridge has omitted from the end of Burnet's first
sentence a clause which translated reads 'and that there
are more angels in heaven than there are fishes in the
sea'; and the third sentence ('What do they do,' etc.)
seems to be his own interpolation. By these changes
Burnet's discussion of angels is adapted to serve as an
introduction to a story of dæmons and spectres. For the
Latin of the original see *C.P.W.*, i, 186.

1. *ancient Mariner* 1800; *ancyent Marinere* 1798 (and so
throughout).

3. *and thy glittering* 1798-1805; *and glittering* 1817.

4. *stoppest* 1798-1805; *stopp'st thou* 1817.

9-16. so 1798-1805; in 1817 one stanza, thus:

> He holds him with his skinny hand,
> 'There was a ship,' quoth he.

115   'Hold off! unhand me, grey-beard loon!'
          Eftsoons his hand dropt he.

15. *Loon:* rogue, idler, boor.

17. The Mariner's hypnotic eye owes something to popular treatments of another guilt-laden traveller, the Wandering Jew (see below, pp. 398-9). For this parallel and for contemporary interest in mesmerism see Lowes, pp. 252-4.

19-20. These lines were contributed by Wordsworth: see *P.W.*, i, 361.

gloss 29-34. *the line:* the equator.

116 34. The overhead sun at noon shows that the ship has now reached the equator in her southward voyage. As Lowes points out, the interruption from the bassoon helps to cover the rapid geographical transitions from the home port to the equator and again to the Antarctic.

45-8. so 1800-5; in 1798 thus:

> Listen, Stranger! Storm and Wind,
>   A Wind and Tempest strong!
> For days and weeks it play'd us freaks—
>   Like Chaff we drove along.

And in 1817 two stanzas, thus:

> And now the STORM-BLAST came, and he
> Was tyrannous and strong;
> He struck with his o'ertaking wings,
> And chased us south along.
>
> With sloping masts and dipping prow,
> As who pursued with yell and blow
> Still treads the shadow of his foe,
> And forward bends his head,
> The ship drove fast, loud roared the blast,
> And southward aye we fled.

49. so 1800; *Listen, Stranger! Mist and Snow* 1798.

50-2. *cold . . . Emerald* 1800; *cauld . . . Emerauld* 1798.

117 53. *drifts:* floating ice. *clifts:* either clefts or cliffs, the word being used in both senses in the Voyages. 'Snowy clifts' may describe the enormous snow-filled fissures in black rock depicted in Frederick Martens's *Voyage into Spitzbergen and Greenland* (1694), a work Coleridge

knew: see Lowes, pp. 143-5 and accompanying photo- **117**
graph.

54. *a dismal sheen.* The 'blink,' or reflection of light
from ice or snow, can be seen for many miles and forms
a characteristic feature of polar landscapes (see Lowes,
pp. 142-3).

55. *Nor* . . . *nor* 1800; *Ne* . . . *ne* 1798 (and so throughout).

59-60. *It cracked and growled* . . . *sound.* Polar ice does
make this kind of noise: see Lowes, pp. 146-7.

60. *A wild and ceaseless sound* 1800-5; *Like noises of a
swound* 1798; *Like noises in a swound* 1817. 'Swound'
means 'swoon.'

61-80. More than forty years after the poem was written,
Wordsworth claimed that it was he who had suggested the
shooting of the albatross:

> I had been reading in Shelvocke's *Voyages* a day or
> two before that while doubling Cape Horn they fre-
> quently saw albatrosses in that latitude, the largest
> sort of sea-fowl, some extending their wings twelve or
> thirteen feet. 'Suppose,' said I, 'you represent him as
> having killed one of these birds on entering the South
> Sea, and that the tutelary spirits of those regions take
> upon them to avenge the crime.' The incident was
> thought fit for the purpose and adopted accordingly.
> (*P.W.*, i, 361.)

In *A Voyage Round the World by Way of the Great South
Sea* (1726), George Shelvocke describes the 'wandering
albatross' in terms very similar to Wordsworth's. A bird
of this size could not, however, have been fed on biscuit-
worms (line 65) or hung round the Mariner's neck
(lines 137-8). Coleridge may have been thinking of the
much smaller 'sooty albatross.' On another page Shelvocke relates that 'a disconsolate black albatross . . .
accompanied us for several days,' and that an officer,
taking it for a bird of ill omen, shot it in the hope of
getting a wind. For relevant extracts and a discussion
see Lowes, pp. 224-7.

63-4. *As if it had been . . . God's name.* The 'Christian'

117 aspect of the albatross appears elsewhere in the poem, e.g. lines 74, 137-8, 393.

63. *As if it had been* 1800; *And an it were* 1798.

65. *The Mariners gave it biscuit-worms* 1798-1805; *It ate the food it ne'er had eat* 1817.

118 81-4. The change in the sun's position shows that Cape Horn has been doubled and the ship is sailing northwards.

81. *The Sun now rose* 1800; *The Sun came up* 1798.

83. *so* 1800; *And broad as a weft upon the left* 1798. A weft is an ensign rolled up and hoisted as a signal of distress (see Lowes, pp. 261-9).

92/3. Two lines were added here in 1817:

> Ah wretch! said they, the bird to slay,
> That made the breeze to blow!

93. *Like an Angel's head* 1800-5; *Like God's own head* 1798, 1817. A reviewer of 1799 had called the original simile one 'which makes a reader shudder . . . with religious disapprobation' (see E. Smith, pp. 38-9).

99. *The breezes blew* 1798-1805; *The fair breeze blew* 1817. The 'Brises' were easterly winds, and Lowes argues (pp. 128-9) that this stanza and the next refer specifically to the south-easterly Trade Winds.

100. So all edns. except 1817, which has *The furrow streamed off free* and a footnote by Coleridge:

> In the former editions the line was 'The furrow followed free'; but I had not been long on board a ship before I perceived that this was the image as seen by a spectator from the shore, or from another vessel. From the ship itself the wake appears like a brook flowing off from the stern.

107-10. The ship is now becalmed at the equator in the Pacific; the sun is diminished and discoloured by heat haze (*cf.* passages quoted by Lowes, pp. 157-60).

119 119. *deeps* 1798-1805; *deep* 1817.

122. *the slimy Sea.* Cf. James Cook's *Voyage to the Pacific Ocean* (1784), ii, 257: 'During a calm . . . some parts of the sea seemed covered with a kind of slime' (quoted by Lowes, p. 46; for other instances of the sea's 'corruption,' see Lowes, pp. 87-9).

124. *the Death-fires.* Usually, wandering fires that hover **119** above graveyards (*cf.* Coleridge's *Ode to the Departing Year*, line 59, *C.P.W.*, i, 163). Here Coleridge transfers the name and nature of these fires to the St. Elmo's fire or *corpo santo*, which appears at the masts and in the rigging of ships. The next two lines give a similar sinister quality to the phosphorescence caused by tropical marine life.

gloss 127-30. *Josephus, and . . . Michael Psellus.* These references help to establish the character of the imaginary editor as a learned antiquarian. Coleridge owned a copy of a fifteenth-century compilation by Marsilio Ficino in which both these writers are represented. The volume, 'a *vade mecum* of Neoplatonic dæmonology,' includes Psellus's *De Dæmonibus* and a summary of Josephus's account of the Essenes, which centres upon their doctrine of departed souls (see Lowes, pp. 229-40).

135. *well-a-day* 1800; *wel-a-day* 1798.

137-8. *Instead of the Cross . . . hung.* This visible emblem of guilt connects the Mariner with the Wandering Jew and with Cain, two figures which were in Coleridge's mind at about this time (see Lowes, pp 242-60; see also Coleridge's prose fragment *The Wanderings of Cain* with its prefatory note, *C.P.W.*, i, 285-92). In M. G. Lewis's romance *The Monk* (1796), a work Coleridge had reviewed, the Jew appears with 'a burning cross impressed upon his brow.'

139-46. so 1800-5; in 1798 one six-line stanza— **120**

> I saw a something in the Sky
> No bigger than my fist;
> At first it seem'd a little speck, etc.

In 1817 'So passed' in line 139 becomes 'There passed,' and two more lines are inserted after line 140:

> A weary time! a weary time!
> How glazed each weary eye.

148. *ner'd and ner'd* 1798-1805; *neared and neared* 1817 (so also *neres* becomes *nears* in line 176, and throughout).

149. *And as if* 1800-17; *And, an* 1798; *As if* 1828.

151-5. so 1800-5; 1798—

343

120 With throat unslack'd, with black lips bak'd
   Ne could we laugh, ne wail:
   Then while thro' drouth all dumb they stood
   I bit my arm and suck'd the blood
      And cry'd, A sail! a sail!

The final version (1828) follows the present text but *throats* for *throat*, *drought* for *drouth*, *stood!* for *stood*, and at line 154 *I bit my arm, I sucked the blood.*
156. *throat unslaked* 1800-5; *throat unslack'd* 1798; *throats unslaked* 1817.
161-4. so 1800; 1798—

      She doth not tack from side to side—
         Hither to work us weal
      Withouten wind, withouten tide
         She steddies with upright keel.

(The form 'steddies' is retained until 1828.)
163-4. Several traditional sea stories of phantom ships that sail independently of wind and tide, usually at sunset, are mentioned by Lowes (pp. 275-6).
121 171. *straight* 1805; *strait* 1798-1802.
175-80. The Mariner apparently recognises and dreads the phantom ship; hence the italicised *her* in lines 177, 179, which refers to the ship and not (as in lines 188-9) to the spectre-woman Life-in-Death.
178. *restless gossameres.* A gossamer is a film of cobwebs floating in the air in calm clear weather. *Cf.* Dorothy Wordsworth's description of a heath on February 8th, 1798: 'Its surface restless and glittering with the motion of the scattered piles of withered grass, and the waving of the spiders' threads' (*D.W.J.*, i, 7).
179-82. so 1800-5; 1798—

      Are those *her* naked ribs, which fleck'd
         The sun that did behind them peer?
      And are these two all, all the crew,
         That woman and her fleshless Pheere?

('Pheere' is presumably the archaic *fere*, a mate, companion or wife.) In 1817 lines 181-2 became:

344

> And is that Woman all her crew? **121**
> Is that a DEATH? and are there two?
> Is DEATH that woman's mate?

183-92. His *bones were black*, etc. The episode of the phantom ship has a close parallel in the legend of Falkenberg, who in punishment for a murder was doomed to sail the sea for ever accompanied by two spectral forms, one black and the other white, who played at dice for his soul (see Lowes, p. 277).

183-7. His *bones . . . purple and green* so 1798 (but *They're* for *They were*), 1800-5; omitted 1817. It is here and in lines 197-200 that the poem comes closest to the crudely horrific effects used by M. G. Lewis and Bürger. *Cf. Alonzo the Brave*, lines 59-61:

> The worms they crept in, and the worms they crept out,
> And sported his eyes and his temples about,
>   While the spectre addressed Imogine.

Cf. also Taylor's *Ellenore*, lines 237-48, or the last stanza but three of Scott's *William and Helen* (also based on *Lenore*):

> The eyes desert the naked skull,
>   The mould'ring flesh the bone,
> Till Helen's lily arms entwine
>   A ghastly skeleton.

188-92. Her *lips were red . . . air cold* so 1798 (but verbs in present tense), 1800-5. In 1817 lines 191-2 became:

> The Night-mare LIFE-IN-DEATH was she,
> Who thicks man's blood with cold.

The name 'Life-in-Death' is first introduced in 1817.

194. *playing* 1798-1805; *casting* 1817. **122**

196. *whistled thrice* 1798-1805; *whistles thrice* 1817.

197-209. *A gust of wind . . . with his ee* so 1798 (but *atween* in line 205), 1800-5. This passage was rewritten in 1817, with the charnel horrors of lines 197-200 omitted and effective new material added:

> The Sun's rim dips; the stars rush out:
> At one stride comes the dark;
> With far-heard whisper, o'er the sea,
> Off shot the spectre-bark.

122

We listened and looked sideways up!
Fear at my heart, as at a cup,
My life-blood seemed to sip!
The stars were dim, and thick the night,
The steersman's face by his lamp gleamed
    white;
From the sails the dew did drip—
Till clomb above the eastern bar
The hornéd Moon, with one bright star
Within the nether tip.

One after one, by the star-dogged Moon,
Too quick for groan or sigh,
Each turned his face with a ghastly pang,
And cursed me with his eye.

Opposite 'The Sun's rim dips . . . the dark' an addition
was later made to the gloss: 'No twilight within the
courts of the Sun.' This comment was not printed until
1828, but was extant in manuscript from 1817 (see
Lowes, pp. 164-8).

211. so 1798-1805; (*And I heard nor sigh nor groan*) 1817.
214. *Their souls* 1798-1805; *The souls* 1817.

123 220-1. *And thou . . . ribbed Sea-sand.* Coleridge adds a
note in editions from 1817: 'For the last two lines of this
stanza I am indebted to Mr. Wordsworth. It was on a
delightful walk from Nether Stowey to Dulverton with
him and his sister, in the autumn of 1797, that this poem
was planned and in part composed.'

226-46. D. W. Harding writes: 'The human experience
around which Coleridge centres the poem is surely the
depression and the sense of isolation and unworthiness
which the Mariner describes in Part IV. The suffering
he describes is of a kind which is perhaps not found
except in slightly pathological conditions, but which,
pathological or not, has been felt by a great many people.
He feels isolated to a degree that baffles expression and
reduces him to the impotent, repetitive emphasis which
becomes doggerel in schoolroom reading [lines 226-7].
At the same time he is not just physically isolated but is
socially abandoned, even by those with the greatest

obligations [228-9]. With this desertion the beauty of the **123**
ordinary world has been taken away [230-1]. All that is
left, and especially, centrally, oneself, is disgustingly
worthless [232-3]. With the sense of worthlessness
there is also guilt. When he tried to pray

> A wicked whisper came, and made
> My heart as dry as dust.

And enveloping the whole experience is the sense of
sapped energy, oppressive weariness [244-6]. This, the
central experience, comes almost at the middle of the
poem. It is the nadir of depression to which the earlier
stanzas sink; the rest of the poem describes what is in
part recovery and in part aftermath. You need not have
been a mariner in a supernatural Pacific in order to have
felt this mood. Coleridge knew it well, and *Dejection*
and *The Pains of Sleep* deal with closely related experiences.' ('The Theme of *The Ancient Mariner*,'
Scrutiny, ix (1941), 335-6.)

227. *the wide* 1798-1805; *a wide* 1817.

228. *Christ would take no pity* 1798-1805; *never a saint
took pity* 1817.

232. *million million* 1798-1805; *thousand thousand* 1817.

236. *ghastly* 1800-5; *eldritch* 1798; *rotting* 1817.

243. *Till* 1798-1805; *And* 1817.

254. *the curse* 1798-1817, 1834; *a curse* 1828-9.   **124**

262. *April hoar-frost spread* 1800; *morning frosts yspread*
1798.

266-85. Here again Coleridge is expressing feelings that
were probably recurrent in his own experience. What
happens in terms of the ballad story is that the Mariner's
love for the water-snakes partly atones for his killing of
the bird; while the 'blessing' and the intervention of the
'kind saint' suggest that this sequence of guilt and expiation is controlled by a divine order in the universe. But
this sequence also represents a psychological process.
Just as the Mariner's sin was mysterious and unmoti-
vated, and his punishment apparently disproportionate,
so the movement that releases him takes place 'unaware.' Harding writes:

It begins with the momentary rekindling of simple

124   pleasure in the things around him, at the very moment
when he has touched bottom in apathy. . . . When he
was in the depths the only beauty he would consent
to see was beauty dead and spoilt; the beauty still
present in the world he denied.

(op. cit., pp. 339-40.)

Yet the Mariner has first to be *enabled* to love and bless
the water-snakes; he does not understand this prelimin-
ary step, but guesses that it was brought about by his
'kind saint' (lines 280-1). The detail is true to experience,
for in such depressed states the sufferer can take no
pleasure from the external world until some inner transformation has made him ready to receive it. Coleridge's
own explicit statement of this truth occurs in *Dejection*,
stanzas ii-iv (*C.P.W.*, i, 364-5).

125 288. *Mary-queen* 1798-1805; *Mary Queen* 1817. *given*
1800; *yeven* 1798.

291. *silly buckets*. The meanings of 'sely,' from which
'silly' is derived, are: happy, blessed; innocent, good,
kind; poor, wretched, hapless. Besides the Mariner's
gratitude for the filled buckets, Coleridge may be intending to convey a sense of the joy derived from the
humblest objects in certain states of mind, e.g. in con-
valescence.

gloss 303-6. *the element*, i.e. the air.

303. so 1800; *The roaring wind! it roar'd far off* 1798.

126 307-11. *The upper air burst into life*, etc. A display of the
Aurora Borealis, through which the stars are visible (see
Lowes, pp. 187-90).

307-320. *The upper air . . . steep and wide* so 1800; all
verbs in the present tense in 1798.

311. *The wan stars danced* 1800; *The stars dance on* 1798.

312-17. so 1800; 1798—

> The coming wind doth roar more loud;
> > The sails do sigh, like sedge;
> The rain pours down from one black cloud
> > And the Moon is at its edge.
>
> Hark! hark! the thick black cloud is cleft,
> > And the Moon is at its side.

348

318-20. *Like waters shot . . . wide. Cf.* William Bartram's **126** description of a hurricane in Florida: '. . . every object was totally obscured, excepting the continual streams or rivers of lightning pouring from the clouds.' Bartram's *Travels through North and South Carolina, Georgia,* etc., first appeared in 1791 and was known to both Coleridge and Wordsworth. The passage quoted appears on p. 133 of the reprint edited by Mark van Doren (Dover Publications, New York, 1928); see also Lowes, pp. 186-7.

gloss 321-4. *inspired* 1828; *inspirited* 1817. The original reading announces (prematurely, perhaps) the presence of spirits: the later suggests only that some form of life has been 'breathed into' the bodies.

321-2. so 1800; *The strong wind reach'd the ship: it roar'd/And dropp'd down, like a stone!* 1798.

338. *But he said nought to me.* In 1798 only, two addi- **127** tional lines followed: *And I quak'd to think of my own voice/How frightful it would be!*

339-43. *I fear thee . . . Spirits blest.* This stanza was added in 1800.

gloss 341-7. *dæmons* 1817-29; *demons* 1834 (and so throughout). The spelling 'demon' usually indicates an evil spirit: 'dæmon' is neutral and more often used of tutelary spirits, or of the intermediate beings between gods and men discussed by Michael Psellus and others. The change of 1834 is probably an unnecessary piece of editing and is silently corrected by E. H. Coleridge in *C.P.W.*, i, 200 *ff.*

344. *For when it dawned* 1800; *The day-light dawn'd* 1798.

352-6. *Cf.* the Chaucerian *Romaunt of the Rose*, lines 661-716:

> There mightin men se many flockes
> Of Turtels and of Laverockes. . . .
> Thei song ther song, as faire and wel
> As angels don espirituell. . . .
> Layis of love ful wel souning
> Thei songin in ther jargoning.

(Quoted by Lowes, p. 334, from the text used by

127 Coleridge.) The parallel is closer between the *Romaunt* and Coleridge's original version (see following note).

353. *Sky-lark* 1800; *Lavrock* 1798. A 'lavrock' is a skylark.

366/7. *a quiet tune./Till noon.* The following four stanzas appeared here in 1798 only:

> Listen, O listen, thou Wedding-guest!
>   'Marinere! thou hast thy will:
> For that, which comes out of thine eye, doth make
>   My body and soul to be still.'

> Never sadder tale was told
>   To a man of woman born:
> Sadder and wiser thou wedding-guest!
>   Thou'lt rise tomorrow morn.

> Never sadder tale was heard
>   By a man of woman born:
> The Marineres all return'd to work
>   As silent as beforne.

> The Marineres all 'gan pull the ropes,
>   But look at me they n'old:
> Thought I, I am as thin as air—
>   They cannot me behold.

128 367. *silently* 1798-1805; *quietly* 1817.

gloss 371-6. *as far as the Line.* It is less easy to trace the Mariner's course in the latter part of the poem—as Lowes remarks, he is brought home by magic. But this comment suggests that he has rounded the Cape of Good Hope and sailed northward to the Atlantic equator.

386. *into* 1798-1805; *down in* 1817.   *swound:* swoon.

130 417. *Without or wave* 1800; *Withouten wave* 1798.

434-5. *eyes . . . Nor* 1800; *een . . . Ne* 1798.

436-9. so 1800; 1798—

> And in its time the spell was snapt,
>   And I could move my een:
> I look'd far-forth, but little saw
>   Of what might else be seen.

E. M. W. Tillyard takes the breaking of this spell to

mean the fulfilment of the further penance promised in **130**
line 403, and comments: '. . . the final expiation in line
[436] comes in very casually' (*Poetry and Its Background* (Chatto, 1955), p. 68). But it seems that the
curse which is expiated at this point is 'the curse in a
dead man's eye,' and the 'spell' which is snapped is the
mesmeric effect of their stony stare. The Mariner may
have purged his guilt towards the dead crew, but his
larger guilt must still be atoned for by 'the penance of
life' (see gloss to lines 568–75); and this is the further
penance promised by the dæmon in line 403. It is true
that the snapping of the 'spell' here is perfunctory,
especially by comparison with the water-snakes episode.

440. *lonesome* 1800; *lonely* 1798.

455. *she sailed softly*. *Cf.* 'We sailed softly west-north-
west,' *Purchas his Pilgrims*, ii, 273, quoted by Lowes,
p. 324.

469/70. *shadow of the moon./The rock shone bright*. Five **132**
additional stanzas appeared here in 1798 only:

> The moonlight bay was white all o'er,
>   Till rising from the same,
> Full many shapes, that shadows were,
>   Like as of torches came.
>
> A little distance from the prow
>   Those dark-red shadows were;
> But soon I saw that my own flesh
>   Was red as in a glare.
>
> I turn'd my head in fear and dread,
>   And by the holy rood,
> The bodies had advanc'd, and now
>   Before the mast they stood.
>
> They lifted up their stiff right arms,
>   They held them strait and tight;
> And each right-arm burnt like a torch,
>   A torch that's borne upright.
> Their stony eyeballs glitter'd on
>   In the red and smoky light.

132   I pray'd and turn'd my head away
                Forth looking as before.
             There was no breeze upon the bay,
             No wave against the shore.

133   494. *But soon* 1800; *Eftsones* 1798.
      497/8. *a boat appear.*/*The pilot.* The following stanza
appeared here in 1798:
             Then vanish'd all the lovely lights;
                The bodies rose anew:
             With silent pace, each to his place,
                Came back the ghastly crew.
             The wind, that shade nor motion made,
                On me alone it blew.
      511. *Mariners* 1800; *Marineres* 1798.
      512. *countrée* 1800; *Contrée* 1798.
134   527. *The skeletons* 1798-1805; *Brown skeletons* 1817.
135   571. *manner of man* 1805; *manner man* 1798-1802.
      577-9. *That agony . . . burns* so 1800; 1798—
             Now oftimes and now fewer,
             That anguish comes and makes me tell
             My ghastly aventure.
136   580-1. *I pass, like night . . . speech.* Both the journeying
and the 'strange power of speech' suggest the influence
of popular treatments of the Wandering Jew (see Lowes,
pp. 242-54).
      582. *The moment* 1798-1805; *That moment* 1817.
      595-603. Several critics have been made uneasy by the
quietism of the Mariner's conclusion. E. M. W. Tillyard, discussing the 'rebirth theme' in the poem, writes:
        This theme is certainly present. It was only through
        the destruction of his old state of mind that the
        Mariner was able to achieve the new, enlarged state of
        mind that could include the water-snakes in its
        sympathies. But the *Ancient Mariner* is unlike the most
        satisfying works that render the theme, for instance the
        Oresteia or *Lycidas*, in that the renovation brought
        about is less powerful than the thing from whose
        destruction it has sprung. There is nothing to corres-
        pond to the thrust of energy that ends *Lycidas* with

Tomorrow to fresh woods, and pastures new.

The Ancient Mariner has been born again into a ghostly existence, not rejuvenated. And the haunting terror of the destructive experience remains the dominant theme of the poem:

O Wedding-Guest! this soul hath been
Alone on a wide wide sea.'

(*Poetry and its Background*, pp. 72-3.)

D. W. Harding finds the end of the poem consistent with his view that the shooting of the albatross represents the rejection of a social offering, and contrasts the Mariner's 'submissive sociability' here with the buoyant opening of his voyage:

Such a voyage . . . entails a self-reliant thrusting forth into the outer world and repudiates dependence on the comfort of ordinary social ties. But Coleridge's anxieties seem to have shown him this attitude taken beyond all bounds and leading to a self-sufficiency which would wantonly destroy the ties of affection. The albatross is killed, and then the penalty must be paid in remorse, dejection, and the sense of being a worthless social outcast. Only a partial recovery is possible; once the horrifying potentiality has been glimpsed in human nature Coleridge dare not imagine a return to self-reliant voyaging. Creeping back defeated into the social convoy, the Mariner is obviously not represented as having advanced through his suffering to a fuller life; and he no more achieves a full rebirth than Coleridge ever could. There is nothing but the crushed admission that he would, after all, have done better to have stayed at home in humble companionship. Even the vigour and excitement of the marriage feast are too daring for him. . . .

(*op. cit.*, p. 341.)

606-11. *He prayeth well . . . loveth all.* This passage may well have been in Coleridge's mind when he regretted 'the obtrusion of the moral sentiment so openly . . . in a work of such pure imagination' (see introductory note to poem, p. 334). The 'moral sentiment' is not irrelevant, even taken quite simply at its face value.

136 Coleridge believed 'that every thing has a life of its own, and that we are all *one Life*' (letter of 1802, *C.L.*, ii, 864); and the wanton destruction of a friendly creature is presented as an evil thing in itself, whatever further evil it may represent. But many readers have felt that the lines are too simple and too explicit after what has gone before; and that the context makes them appear a summary of the entire meaning of the poem, which is thus momentarily reduced to 'a tract for the prevention of cruelty to albatrosses.' For an opposite view, however, see House, pp. 91-2: '. . . coming in context, after the richness and terror of the poem, it is no more a banal moral apothegm, but a moral which has its meaning *because it has been lived.*'

138   LINES WRITTEN . . . ABOVE TINTERN ABBEY
Written between July 10th and 13th, 1798, when the rest of *Lyrical Ballads* was already at the press. 'No poem of mine was composed under circumstances more pleasant for me to remember than this. I began it upon leaving Tintern, after crossing the Wye, and concluded it just as I was entering Bristol in the evening, after a ramble of four or five days, with my sister. Not a line of it was altered, and not any part of it written down till I reached Bristol.' (W.W., 1843.) Wordsworth's earlier visit to the Wye had been made in July or August 1793, on his way from Salisbury Plain to North Wales.

One of Wordsworth's strongest needs was for a sense of continuity in his life. (A comparatively simple expression of this need is the well-known poem beginning 'My heart leaps up when I behold/A rainbow in the sky.') In *Tintern Abbey* Wordsworth's thought moves from his present pleasure in the landscape back to the intenser experiences of the past, returns through successive stages to the present, and casts a glance into the future, finding order and development in the whole. John Danby describes the movement of the poem as a 'loop in time,' and compares it with Coleridge's *Frost* **138** *at Midnight* (*C.P.W.*, i, 240-2) as 'a chapter of integrative autobiography' (Danby, pp. 91-7).

Wordsworth here interprets his past and present experiences of nature by means of theories of 'nature's education' already described in these notes. But the poem is far from being versified philosophy: the 'deep power of joy' is felt throughout, and Mary Moorman can describe the poem as 'a hymn of thanksgiving . . . at the end of an extraordinarily happy year' (*M.M.*, i, 403). Basil Willey writes in *The Eighteenth-Century Background* (Chatto, 1940):

> Nature's healing power, which for some may be merely an outworn doctrine, was for him a fact of experience; and the rapture of that experience, which glows through 'Tintern Abbey' and much of his best poetry, can be caught by any reader, without reference to the ethical and philosophical theories which Wordsworth evolved from it. (p. 283.)

Wordsworth's achievement here is in fact to combine deep feeling with analysis and mature reflection, in a way that completely illustrates and fulfils the account of poetic creation given in the Preface (pp. 22-3, 42). The language of the poem is impressively sober, truthful and accurate, but can be metaphorical and richly suggestive where a rare personal experience is being communicated ('with an eye made quiet by the power/Of harmony . . . /We see into the life of things'). This confident mastery of technical resources, and of his own experience, makes *Tintern Abbey* one of Wordsworth's finest performances.

4. *sweet* 1798-1836; *soft* 1845. *inland murmur:* 'The river is not affected by the tides a few miles above Tintern' (Wordsworth's note).

13-15. *Are clad . . . landscape* so 1802-43; *Among the woods and copses lose themselves,/Nor, with their green and simple hue, disturb/The wild green landscape* 1798-1800; *Are clad in one green hue, and lose themselves/ 'Mid groves and copses* 1845.

138 18-19. *Wreaths of smoke . . . trees.* The smoke was caused by charcoal-burners; its picturesque effect is mentioned in William Gilpin's *Tour of the Wye* (1771), a book which Wordsworth and Dorothy may have taken with them on their expedition (*M.M.*, i, 402).

23-50. *Though absent long . . . life of things.* In this passage Wordsworth analyses his debt to 'these forms of beauty,' making careful distinctions between known fact ('I have owed . . . restoration') and that which can only be conjectured ('such, perhaps . . . love'; 'Nor less, I trust . . . things'). At the same time the language and rhythm skilfully suggest to the reader the feelings that are being discussed, 'gently leading on' his 'affections' to the deeply moving climax at line 50.

23-4. *Though . . . beauty* so 1798-1820; *These beauteous forms,/Through a long absence* 1827.

139 33. *As may have had no trivial influence* 1798-1815; *As have no slight or trivial influence* 1820.

36-50. *Nor less, I trust . . . things.* Probably no English poetry written before 1798 conveys such intimately personal experience with such directness and power. Though the 'serene and blessed mood' is convincingly described, Wordsworth does not explain the conditions in which it has occurred: the 'affections' which 'lead on' to it may be any human feelings. Wordsworth trusts that the Wye's 'forms of beauty' may have played their part in making him capable of this mood; but he concedes that this may be a 'vain belief' (lines 50-1), and it seems that though memories of the Wye are cheering and refreshing they are not *directly* associated with the mood of harmony and insight. This mood is sometimes termed 'mystical,' but the passage need have no specifically religious reference: for some readers it exactly describes the state of feeling induced by certain music, e.g. Beethoven, Opus 135.

50-1. *If this/Be but a vain belief.* Syntactically 'this' refers back to 'I may have owed . . .' (line 37), and the clause concedes that Wordsworth cannot be sure just what part the Wye's 'forms' have played in creating the 'blessed mood' (see previous note). But from its position

in the rhythmic and emotive sequence of the passage **139**
the clause has also the effect of asking whether we really
do 'see into the life of things,' suggesting the doubt that
may follow the mood of assurance. From this double
doubt the poem returns to the known facts of relief and
refreshment, but with a sense of loss and diminution:
the introductory phrases 'If this . . .' and 'yet, oh! how
oft . . .' convey a weariness that reminds us of the unintelligible world and, by contrast, of the joy of the
moment when it had seemed intelligible. It is a mark of
Wordsworth's integrity that he should record both the
mood of insight and the doubt.

73-103. *For nature then . . . rolls through all things.* **140**
Wordsworth here seeks to describe and explain the contrast between the 'aching joys' and 'dizzy raptures' of
his first visit to the Wye at the age of twenty-three, and
the quieter, more thoughtful mood of five years later.
He distinguishes three successive phases in his response
to nature: (i) that of childhood, dominated by simple
sensation ('The coarser pleasures of my boyish days/
And their glad animal movements'); (ii) that of youth,
dominated by emotion (lines 76-86); (iii) that of
maturity, dominated by thought (lines 86-103). These
phases correspond broadly to stages in human development described by Hartley (see notes, p. 276; see also
Beatty, chapt. v). Between 1793 and 1798, Wordsworth believes, he has passed from the second phase
to the third. Nature's scenes are linked to the stages
of his own moral development, so that in beholding
them he now hears 'the still, sad music of humanity.'
Moreover, he is at moments aware of an active principle
working both in men and in the rest of nature (lines 94-
103). These two kinds of experience differ, but both
belong to maturity. The choice of verb in line 95 is
another example of the accuracy and integrity with which
Wordsworth describes his inner life.

98. *Whose dwelling is the light of setting suns.* 'The line **141**
. . . is almost the grandest in the English language,
giving the sense of the abiding in the transient' (Tennyson, quoted by his son Hallam in *Alfred Lord Tennyson:*

141 *A Memoir*, chapt. xiv). For other comments by Tennyson on this poem (not all favourable) see *ibid.*, pp. 475-6, 659.

106-8. *the mighty world/Of eye and ear, both what they half create/And what perceive.* According to Locke such 'secondary qualities' as colour and scent do not exist in external 'bodies' such as flowers, but only in our minds and senses (*An Essay Concerning Human Understanding*, Bk. II, chapt. viii). Thus the beauty of nature is in a sense conferred on it by the observer. Edward Young, in *The Complaint, or Night Thoughts* (1742-4), celebrates our

> . . . senses which inherit earth, and heavens;
> Enjoy the various riches Nature yields;
> Far nobler! *give* the riches they enjoy;
> Give taste to fruits, and harmony to groves;
> Their radiant beams to gold, and gold's bright
> fire;
> Take in, at once, the landscape of the world
> At a small inlet which a grain might close,
> And half create the wondrous world they see.
> Our senses, as our reason, are divine.
> But for the magic organ's powerful charm,
> Earth were a rude, uncoloured chaos still.
>
> (Night Sixth, lines 417-27.)

This passage must have been at the back of Wordsworth's mind when composing this part of *Tintern Abbey*, as his footnote shows: 'This line [107] has a close resemblance to an admirable line of Young, the exact expression of which I cannot recollect'—presumably the eighth of the lines quoted above. Some critics have taken Wordsworth's lines to mean that he was already following Coleridge in tracing 'a collaboration between man's imaginative faculty and external nature' (Beach, p. 142); but, as will be seen, they are much more restricted in scope and consistent with the most orthodox Hartleianism. The creative power referred to is not that of the imagination, but that of the 'eye and ear.'

117-22. *in thy voice I catch . . . sister!* Dorothy was only twenty months younger than Wordsworth, but in 1798 her response to nature still represented for him the **141** youthful phase to which, in this poem, he bids farewell. The address to the sister who had sharpened Wordsworth's awareness of country sights and sounds, and increased in many other ways his happiness at this period, fittingly concludes the poem.

HART-LEAP WELL   **144**

'Town End. [Early] 1800. Grasmere. The first eight stanzas were composed extempore one winter evening in the cottage; when, after having tired myself with labouring at an awkward passage in *The Brothers*, I started with a sudden impulse to this to get rid of the other, and finished it in a day or two. My sister and I had passed the place a few weeks before in our wild winter journey from Sockburn on the banks of the Tees to Grasmere. A peasant whom we met near the spot told us the story so far as concerned the name of the well, and the hart, and pointed out the stones.' (W.W., 1843.) Wordsworth also refers to this incident in some lines written for *The Recluse* (*P.W.*, ii, 514-15). Hearing the countryman's story, Wordsworth and Dorothy felt not only sorrow for men's past and present cruelties, but joyful anticipations of a 'milder day' when the spread of 'love and knowledge' would have made such deeds impossible.

Under 'Fox-Hound,' Bewick's *History of Quadrupeds* (1790) quotes an account of a long chase which began and ended at Whinfield Park, Westmorland. The stag died after a last mighty leap, and the event was commemorated by a trophy, the 'Hart-horn tree.' The same work reports that in 1788 Sir William Lowther (cousin of Sir James: see above, p. 319) paid 1,000 guineas for a pack of hounds.

Hart-Leap Well differs from *Goody Blake* and other poems written by Wordsworth in 1798 in that it seems to present the curse on the well as a genuine supernatural effect. The last sentence of Wordsworth's note (above) suggests that this curse did not form part of the countryman's story but was added by Wordsworth.

144 A ruthless hunter is punished by a curse in Burger's ballad *Der Wilde Jäger*, which was freely translated by Walter Scott in 1796. A voice of thunder pronounces sentence on 'Earl Walter':

> Go, hunt for ever through the wood;
> For ever roam th' affrighted wild;
> And let thy fate instruct the proud,
> God's meanest creature is his child.
>
> (Scott, *The Chase*.)

The 'moral' of Wordsworth's poem is very similar, and he contrives some eerie effects which recall Bürger's kind of ballad (e.g. 'This chase it looks not like an earthly chase,' line 27); but in general his restraint may be contrasted with the violence and horror of Bürger's treatment.

146 50. *Nine* 1800-36; *Four* 1845. 'Rood' is a local variant of 'rod,' strictly 5½ yards but sometimes more.

52. *verdant* 1800-15; *grassy* 1820.

147 97. *moving accident*, i.e. stirring event: from *Othello*, I. iii. 135, 'Of moving accidents by flood and field.'

98. *freeze* Errata 1800; *curl* 1800. 'Curl' may have been a misprint for 'curd' (='curdle').

151 'THERE WAS A BOY'

The first known draft of lines 1-25 appears in a note-book used at Goslar in the winter of 1798-9 for passages of autobiographical blank verse, most of which later found a place in Bk. i of *The Prelude* (see *Prelude*, p. xxvi; for text of this draft see *ibid.*, pp. 639-40). The second half of this version is written in the first person ('Responsive to my call,' etc.), and it is clear that the 'boy' is the young Wordsworth. Before publishing the lines in 1800 Wordsworth not only revised and improved them, but transposed them entirely into the third person and added the 'obituary conclusion' (lines 26-34). His main intention was probably to make the earlier passage seem more like a self-contained poem: *cf.* his treatment of the fragments which became *Animal Tranquillity and Decay* and *Andrew Jones*. But

the boy's death seems inconsequential, and as poetry **151**
the conclusion falls far short of the original twenty-five
lines—it is 'a piece of mere literary carpentry' (Bateson,
p. 24). The poem was later incorporated into *The
Prelude* (Bk. v, pp. 158-61) substantially as it is printed
here.

Lines 1-25 vividly re-create a scene from Wordsworth's
boyhood and the 'deep mindless happiness' which the
absorbed boy seems to share with the owls (see Aldous
Huxley's comments, quoted by Bateson, p. 22). They
also illustrate Wordworth's discovery that his senses and
feelings were particularly impressionable in the first
relaxed moments following an effort of concentration.
In later life he told De Quincey:

> I have remarked from my earliest days that if under
> any circumstances the attention is energetically
> braced up to an act of steady observation, or of steady
> expectation, then, if this intense condition of vigilance
> should suddenly relax, at that moment any beautiful,
> any impressive visual object, or collection of objects,
> falling upon the eye is carried to the heart with a
> power not known under other circumstances.

(See Thomas De Quincey, *Recollections of the Lake
Poets*, ed. E. Sackville-West (Lehmann, 1948), p. 144;
the passage and an illustrative anecdote are quoted by
Bateson, p. 25.) Wordsworth believed that such impressions served to develop the imagination, a belief which
fitted in with Hartley's theory that this and other
faculties are formed by processes of association. In the
preface to his *Poems* (1815) Wordsworth wrote:

> . . . in the series of poems placed under the head of
> Imagination, I have begun [i.e. in 'There was a boy']
> with one of the earliest processes of Nature in the
> development of this faculty. Guided by one of my
> own primary consciousnesses, I have represented a
> commutation and transfer of internal feelings co-
> operating with external accidents to plant, for immor-
> tality, images of sound and sight in the celestial soil
> of the imagination. The boy there introduced is
> listening, with something of a feverish and restless

151 anxiety, for the recurrence of the riotous sounds which he had previously excited; and at the moment when the intenseness of his mind is beginning to remit, he is surprised into a perception of the solemn and tranquillising images which the poem describes.
(*Prelude*, p. 547; *P.W.*, ii, 440 n.)

3. *stars had just begun* 1800-5; *earliest stars began* 1815.

16-25. *And, when it chanced . . . steady lake.* The movement of this sentence, with its sounds and rhythms, is as exquisitely fitted to its meaning as that of the finest passages of *Tintern Abbey*: note for example the suspense of '. . . hung/Listening . . .' The 'uncertain' effect of line 24 is created partly by the double pause, partly by the momentary uncertainty as to whether 'received' is a verb or a participle. (A further uncertainty, never quite resolved, is whether this word applies to the whole series of nouns which precede it, or only to 'heaven.') By contrast, the movement of line 25 is rapid and sure.

22. *unawares.* This adverb presumably applies, not to the immediate impact of these sights and sounds upon the boy (they strike him with 'a gentle shock'), but to the process by which they become a permanent part of his mind and '. . . plant, for immortality, images of sound and sight in the celestial soil of the imagination.'

24-5. *that uncertain heaven . . . lake.* Coleridge wrote to Wordsworth that he would have recognised this passage anywhere: '. . . had I met these lines running wild in the deserts of Arabia, I should have instantly screamed out "Wordsworth!" ' (*C.L.*, i, 452). The lake acts indirectly as a metaphor of the boy's unconscious mind, which takes in the scene passively and 'unawares' as the lake does.

26-34. *This boy was taken . . . in which he lies* so 1805; 1800-2 omit lines 26-7, and conclude:

. . . I believe that near his grave
A full half-hour together I have stood
Mute—for he died when he was ten years old.

27. *full* is not printed in 1805, but is inserted by Wordsworth in MS. in some copies and appears in all other MSS. and printed versions (see *Prelude*, pp. 158-9).

'This poem was intended to be the concluding poem of
a series of pastorals, the scene of which was laid among
the mountains of Cumberland and Westmorland. I
mention this to apologise for the abruptness with which
the poem begins' (Wordsworth's footnote, 1800-32).
Since the Renaissance the 'pastoral' had been a poetic
genre in which the conventional doings of unreal shepherds and shepherdesses (Damon, Chloë, etc.) had provided occasions for love-poetry or disguised satire.
Wordsworth revives the original meaning of the term
by applying it to *The Brothers* and *Michael*, poems
dealing with the lives of real English shepherds. His
interest in the Dalesmen had been greatly strengthened
by his move to Grasmere in December 1799. While
rejecting 'Arcadian dreams' of rural happiness and
virtue, he nevertheless regarded the conditions of these
men's lives as almost ideal: close to nature, linked with
a living past by memory and tradition, free members of
a small and genuine community, demoralised neither by
riches nor by extreme poverty. (See the fragment of
The Recluse written at this period, *P.W.*, v, 324-35, lines
309-468; see also the letter to Fox quoted below, pp.
399-400.)

The Brothers originated in a walking-tour through the
Lakes made by Wordsworth and Coleridge in November
1799. During the first few days they were accompanied
by Wordsworth's much-loved brother John, who, like
the Leonard of the poem, had gone to sea and hoped
to make a fortune large enough to support himself and
his brother (*M.M.*, i, 448-50, 471). John was now on
long leave between voyages. Soon after he had left them
Wordsworth and Coleridge walked through Ennerdale,
where they heard the story of a shepherd named Bowman who had died after a mountain accident. Bowman's
son died too:

This man's son broke his neck before this by falling
off a crag—supposed to have layed down and slept—
but walked in his sleep, and so came to this crag and
fell off. This was at Proud Knot on the mountain

152   called Pillar, up Ennerdale—his pike staff struck mid-way and stayed there till it rotted away.

(*C.N.*, i, 540.)

Elements of this story and of Wordsworth's own re-lationship with his brother are brought together in the poem. On December 24th 1799, four days after moving in at Grasmere, Wordsworth wrote to Coleridge: 'I have begun the pastoral of *Bowman*. . . . I am afraid it will have one fault, that of being too long' (*E.L.W.*, p. 277). *The Brothers* was completed in 1800. John Wordsworth began a long visit at Grasmere at the end of January, probably while the poem was still being written: Mary Moorman suggests that lines 74-7 may be a version of his 'shy and anxious' arrival (see *M.M.*, i, 471, 480; *E.L.W.*, p. 649).

153 38. *thirteenth* 1800-5; *sixteenth* 1815.

53-62. *And while the broad green wave . . . worn.* 'This description of the calenture is sketched from an imper-fect recollection of an admirable one in prose by Mr. Gilbert, author of *The Hurricane*' (Wordsworth's foot-note). The calenture is a tropical fever said to produce the hallucinations described in the poem. *The Hurricane*, by William Gilbert, was published in 1796.

53. *green* 1800-36; *blue* 1845.

156 136-43. *On that tall pike . . . flowing still.* 'The impressive circumstance here described actually took place some years ago in this country, upon an eminence called Kidstow Pike, one of the highest of the mountains that surround Haweswater. The summit of the pike was stricken by lightning; and every trace of one of the fountains disappeared, while the other continued to flow as before.' (Wordsworth's note, 1800-5.)

157 180-1. *The thought of death . . . mountains.* 'There is not anything more worthy of remark in the manners of the inhabitants of these mountains than the tranquillity, I might say indifference, with which they think and talk upon the subject of death. Some of the country church-yards, as here described, do not contain a single tomb-stone, and most of them have a very small number.' (Wordsworth's footnote, 1800-5.)

306-7. *From the Great Gavel*, etc. 'The Great Gavel— **161**
so called, I imagine, from its resemblance to the gable
end of a house—is one of the highest of the Cumberland
mountains. It stands at the head of the several vales of
Ennerdale, Wastdale and Borrowdale. The Leeza is a
river which flows into the Lake of Ennerdale; on issuing
from the lake it changes its name and is called the End,
Eyne, or Enna. It falls into the sea a little below Egremont.' (Wordsworth's footnote.) The country described
is that of Wordsworth and Coleridge's walking-tour of
November 1799; modern forms are *Great Gable*, *Liza*,
and *River Ehen*.

364-73. *James pointed . . . all that day.* Coleridge quotes **163**
this passage as it appeared in 1800 as an example of
prosaism, on the grounds that if it were transcribed as
prose it could not be recognized as verse by the ear
alone (*B.L.*, chapt. xviii, p. 217 n.). Wordsworth made
frequent alterations to these lines, and in 1827 finally
recast them as follows:

> Upon its aëry summit crowned with heath
> The loiterer, not unnoticed by his comrades,
> Lay stretched at ease; but, passing by the place
> On their return, they found that he was gone.
> No ill was feared; till one of them by chance
> Entering, when evening was far spent, the house
> Which at that time, etc.

404. *Tears rushing in . . . silence* so 1800-5; *A gushing* **165**
from his heart, that took away/The power of speech. Both
left the spot in silence 1815.

ELLEN IRWIN   166

'As there are Scotch poems on the subject in the
simple ballad strain, I thought it would be both presumptuous and superfluous to attempt treating it in
the same way; and accordingly I chose a construction
of stanza quite new in our language, in fact the same
as that of Bürger's *Leonora*, except that the first and
third line do not, in my stanzas, rhyme. At the outset
I threw out a classical image to prepare the reader for
the style in which I meant to treat the story, and so to

166 preclude all comparison.' (W.W., 1843.) Despite this disclaimer it may be useful to compare the poem either with a good ballad (e.g. *Helen of Kirkonell*) or with some of Wordsworth's own better work in the ballad style (e.g. *Goody Blake*). Wordsworth probably took the story from *Scottish Songs*, ed. Joseph Ritson (1794); the comfortably detached treatment does not suggest that he was deeply stirred by it.

The Braes of Kirtle. 'The Kirtle is a river in the southern part of Scotland, on the banks of which the events here related took place' (Wordsworth's footnote).

168   'STRANGE FITS OF PASSION I HAVE KNOWN'

This poem, the two which follow it, and a fourth, '*Three years she grew in sun and shower*' (p. 207), mention the death, real or imagined, of a girl who in three of these poems is named 'Lucy.' All four were written at Goslar near the Harz forest in Germany, where Wordsworth and Dorothy lived from October 1798 to April 1799. A 'Lucy' also appears in '*I travelled among unknown men,*' written probably in 1801, and in *The Glow-worm*, written in April 1802 (these two poems were not published until 1807). Standing somewhat apart from these poems is the ballad *Lucy Gray* (p. 178), written in 1799.

The name 'Lucy' had been used for rustic figures by other poets, e.g. William Collins ('*Song: the Sentiments borrowed from Shakespeare,*' stanza vi) and Samuel Rogers (*A Wish*, stanza iii, a passage Wordsworth seems to have recollected). A rustic 'Lucy Gray' is mourned by her 'lonely swain' in a song by Robert Anderson, published at Carlisle in 1798 (see F. W. Bateson, *English Poetry, a Critical Introduction* (Longmans, 2nd edn., 1966), p. 147). The rôle of Wordsworth's 'Lucy' varies widely from poem to poem, but in most cases she is adequately defined by the poem itself for its own purposes and there is no need to search for a biographical counterpart. The two most important of these poems ('*A slumber*' and '*She dwelt among th' untrodden ways*') do, however, present critical

366

problems which may lead us to ask whether a real person **168** was in Wordsworth's mind when he wrote them. So far as is known, no girl loved by Wordsworth had at this time died. The woman to whom he was most deeply attached in 1799-1800 was probably his sister. 'Lucy' certainly stands for Dorothy in *The Glow-worm* (see *P.W.*, ii, 466, 531-2), perhaps too in an unpublished fragment of *Nutting* written at Goslar (see Bateson, p. 152). Coleridge guessed that '*A slumber*' had arisen from Wordsworth's imagining the moment of his sister's death (see note, p. 369), and this guess seems the best of many that have been made; the same process may also have led to '*She dwelt among th' untrodden ways.*' But Dorothy and 'Lucy' cannot in every case be equated: the 'Lucy' of '*Three years she grew*' is tall and stately, while Dorothy was neither. For further discussion of 'Lucy' see Herbert Hartman, 'Wordsworth's "Lucy" Poems: Notes and Marginalia,' *P.M.L.A.*, xlix (1934), 134-42 (Hartman cites many other studies); Margoliouth, p. 52 *ff.*; Bateson, p. 150 *ff.*; *M.M.*, i, 423-6.

In '*Strange fits of passion*' the entranced lover unconsciously identifies the moon with his beloved (perhaps because she is to his thoughts what the moon is to his eyes; and he is riding towards them both). Hence the irrational fear which provides the surprise ending. In scene and mood the poem resembles *The Glow-worm*; possibly it too records an incident of the Racedown period, Wordsworth and Dorothy's very close relationship being transposed to that of lover and mistress. The MS. of 1799 omits lines 1-4 and has this additional stanza at the end:

> I told her this: her laughter light
> Is ringing in my ears:
> And when I think upon that night
> My eyes are dim with tears.

F. R. Leavis gives a short criticism of '*Strange fits of passion*' in *Revaluation* (Chatto, 1936), pp. 199-202, as an example of 'the highly idiosyncratic art of those short poems which are so characteristic of [Wordsworth's] genius.' He points out that what looks like

168 'uninspired matter-of-factness' in the middle stanzas
is a necessary preparation for the 'sudden awakening
surprise' of the close, and comments (p.202):

It is a poem such as only Wordsworth could have
written, and it belongs peculiarly to its period. It
seems to come close to his characteristic faults, but it
has his characteristic virtues. It is of its essence to be
in a mode remote from any form of 'wit.' It is completely successful, yet we feel that its poise is an
extremely delicate, almost a precarious one, and our
sense of its success is bound up with this feeling. Of
a number of Wordsworth's poems, it is relevant to
recall here, there is notoriously division of opinion
as to whether they succeed or not.

1. *I have* 1800-27; *have I* 1832.

169   'SHE DWELT AMONG TH' UNTRODDEN WAYS'
(See pp. 366-7 for general note on the 'Lucy' poems.)
The MS. of 1799 gives two additional stanzas for this
poem, one at the beginning—

My hope was one, from cities far,
    Nursed on a lonesome heath;
Her lips were red as roses are,
    Her hair a woodbine wreath—

the other between lines 8 and 9:

And she was graceful as the broom
    That flowers by Carron's side;
But slow distemper checked her bloom,
    And on the heath she died.

For a very close reading of this 'subtle and elusive'
poem see Bateson, pp. 30-5. Bateson points out the
recurrent verbal contradictions (e.g. 'untrodden ways'),
the merging of apparent opposites in stanza ii, and the
uncertain nature of Lucy herself, and concludes: 'The
total effect of these devices is to create in the reader's
mind the impression that Lucy exists on a plane of
reality to which such contradictory categories do not
apply.'

2. *the springs of Dove.* 'Wordsworth knew a river Dove **169**
in Derbyshire, in Yorkshire, and in Westmorland; and
it is impossible to say of which he was thinking' (E. de
Selincourt, *P.W.*, ii, 472).

5-8. The success of the poem springs from its being
able to reconcile two apparently contradictory metaphors for Lucy: the violet (unobtrusive, close, humble,
vulnerable) and the star (striking, remote, regal, secure).
'It looks as though the half-hidden violet is intended to
symbolise Lucy's insignificance in the public world, and
the single star to represent her supreme importance in
the private world. In the actual reading, however, the
images behave in a much less logical way' (Bateson, p.
33). For another reading of this stanza see Danby,
pp. 83-4.

9-11. *She lived . . . she is* so 1800; *Long time before her
head lay low/Dead to the world was she:/But now she's*
MS. 1799.

'A SLUMBER DID MY SPIRIT SEAL' **169**
(See note on the 'Lucy' poems, pp. 366-7.) Coleridge
wrote to Thomas Poole on April 6th, 1799: 'Some
months ago Wordsworth transmitted to me a most sublime epitaph—whether it had any reality, I cannot say.
Most probably in some gloomier moment he had fancied
the moment in which his sister might die' (*C.L.*, i, 479).
Coleridge then transcribes this poem, under the title
Epitaph. We do not know whether this was Wordsworth's original title for the piece, or whether it was
added by Coleridge.

As an 'epitaph' the poem is unusual in that almost
nothing is said about the dead woman. If lines 3-4
suggest those qualities in her which had seemed to defy
time, they do so very remotely; and even in those lines
she is 'a thing.' In lines 5-8 she seems always to have
been a part of the inanimate world. The real theme of
the poem seems to be the difficulty of grasping the fact
of death, whether as a future experience or as something that has actually occurred (*cf.* Wordsworth's note,

169 p. 314). Wordsworth's narrative form and poetic technique compel the reader to experience this difficulty. The first line—rhythmic, alliterated, powerful and obscure—creates a hypnotic effect which is never quite dispelled, and which distracts attention from what is being said. News of the death is obliquely conveyed: the reader is likely to feel disturbed by the changes of tense and diction in line 5 without at first taking in the full implications of the statement. Even when these implications have become clearer, a full response to the woman's death is prevented by the fact that we have been made so little aware of her as a living person. This may be part of the desired total effect, as though the speaker had said: 'I feel as if I never really knew her— and now I never shall.'

For a novel reading of this poem see Hugh Sykes Davies, 'Another New Poem by Wordsworth,' *Essays in Criticism*, xv (1965), 135-61.

5-6. *motion . . . force*. These abstract, scientific terms convey the sense that 'she' is now part of an impersonal world to which such language is appropriate. The effect of the following line is almost ironical.

7. *Rolled* all edns.; *Moved* Coleridge's letter.

170 THE WATERFALL AND THE EGLANTINE
The second volume of *Lyrical Ballads* includes seven light pieces later classified by Wordsworth as 'Poems of the Fancy': this poem, *The Oak and the Broom, To a Sexton, Andrew Jones, A Fragment, 'A whirl-blast from behind the hill,'* and *Song for the Wandering Jew*. This classification is not used for any poem in the first volume. The subjects for this and the following poem, *The Oak and the Broom*, occurred to Wordsworth 'upon the mountain pathway that leads from Upper Rydal to Grasmere' (W.W., 1843).

175 THE COMPLAINT OF A FORSAKEN INDIAN WOMAN
'Written at Alfoxden in 1798, where I read Hearne's Journey with deep interest. It was composed for the volume of Lyrical Ballads' (W.W., 1843). The poem was

published in 1798 and transferred to vol. ii of the two- **175**
volume edition in 1802. 'Hearne's Journey' is Samuel
Hearne's *A Journey from Prince of Wales's Fort in
Hudson's Bay to Northern Ocean 1769-1772, by order
of the Hudson's Bay Company* (1795). Chapt. vii tells of
a woman left behind by Indians who caught up with
them again three times: 'At length, poor creature, she
dropped behind, and no one attempted to go in search
of her' (quoted in *P.W.*, ii, 475). For a 45-line 'overflow
from this poem' see *P.W.*, *loc. cit.* Robert Mayo shows
that the themes of the deserted woman and the bereaved
mother were common in the magazine poetry of the
1790's, and that *The Forsaken Indian Woman* is not the
only poem on these themes with an exotic background.
'In comparison with Wordsworth's, most magazine
poems of this class seem hopelessly sentimental and
derivative, but they are not so much different in kind as
in degree. In both, for example, the suffering is rendered in terms of a kind of generalised human nature.'
('The Contemporaneity of the *Lyrical Ballads*,' *P.M.
L.A.*, lxix (1954), 497.)

LUCY GRAY   **178**

'Written at Goslar in Germany in 1799. It was founded
on a circumstance told me by my sister of a little girl
who, not far from Halifax in Yorkshire, was bewildered
in a snowstorm. Her footsteps were traced by her
parents to the middle of the lock of a canal, and no
other vestige of her, backward or forward, could be
traced. The body however was found in the canal. The
way in which the incident was treated, and the spiritualis-
ing of the character, might furnish hints for contrasting
the imaginative influences which I have endeavoured to
throw over common life with Crabbe's matter-of-fact
style of treating subjects of the same kind. This is not
spoken to his disparagement, far from it. . . .' (W.W.,
1843.) In the sense of 'incorporeal' (Bateson's word for
the poem, p. 12) Lucy Gray is certainly one of the most
'spiritualised' of Wordsworth's figures (*cf.* e.g. Simon

178 Lee). For the first three stanzas she resembles the Lucy of '*She dwelt among th' untrodden ways*' in her remoteness from normal human contacts and her ambiguous nature (lines 7-8 suggest a plant rather than a girl). In the narrative which follows she acquires parents and behaves more 'matter-of-factly,' until the last two stanzas remove her again from the human level. The 'frame' stanzas are more interesting as poetry than the pedestrian narrative stanzas, which recall the street-ballads Wordsworth admired.

Wordsworth told Henry Crabb Robinson in 1816 that he had 'removed from his poem all that pertained to art, and, it being his object to exhibit poetically entire *solitude*, [represented] his child as observing the day-*moon*, which no town or village girl would ever notice.' (*Henry Crabb Robinson on Books and their Writers*, ed. Edith J. Morley (Dent, 1938), i, 190.)

25-8. *Not blither . . . smoke*. This stanza continues the association of Lucy Gray with shy wild animals from lines 9-10, and is linked in other ways with the 'frame' stanzas of the poem.

179 29-32. *The storm . . . town. Cf.* the stanza from *The Babes in the Wood* quoted in Wordsworth's Preface, p. 45. The general influence of this street-ballad can be felt throughout the narrative part of *Lucy Gray*. (A version appears in Percy's *Reliques*, iii, 169-76; but the title and quotation given in Wordsworth's Preface are from a different text, possibly that of a popular 'broadside.') For a seventeenth-century burlesque of this type of ballad see *Three Children Sliding on the Ice*, in *The Oxford Dictionary of Nursery Rhymes*, ed. Iona and Peter Opie (1951), pp. 118-9.

180 ''TIS SAID, THAT SOME HAVE DIED FOR LOVE'
Written in 1800. Wordsworth uses many different poetic forms at this period, in this case one close to Augustan convention. The verse recalls imitations of the Pindaric ode by Gray and others in the wide variation of line length, and the language, though largely free from

cliché, is a literary language. The theme too at first **180**
appears conventional: but the details of Wordsworth's
treatment show his genuine interest in 'the manner in
which our feelings and ideas are associated in a state of
excitement' (Preface, p. 23).

51. *Emma.* The 'Emma' of some poems corresponds to **181**
Dorothy (e.g. '*It was an April morning*,' p. 225). Here it
seems used simply as a name for the speaker's sweetheart;
but see D. H. Reiman in *TLS.*, 13 Sept. 1974, pp. 979–80.

THE IDLE SHEPHERD-BOYS **182**

Written at Grasmere in 1800.

18-20. *Or with that plant . . . they trim.* 'When Coleridge
and Southey were walking together upon the fells,
Southey observed that if I wished to be considered a
faithful painter of rural manners I ought not to have
said that my shepherd-boys trimmed their rustic hats
as described in the poem. Just as the words had passed
his lips two boys appeared with the very plant entwined
round their hats.' (W.W., 1843.)

POOR SUSAN **185**

Later called *The Reverie of Poor Susan*. 'This arose
out of my observation of the affecting music of these
birds hanging in this way in the London streets during
the freshness and stillness of the spring morning'
(W.W., 1843). Wordsworth did not visit London in the
spring between 1794 and the publication of this poem
in 1800. In 1836 Wordsworth assigned the poem to
1797, and though his dating is unreliable it may have
been written during his winter visit of 1797-8.

In *L.B.* (*1800*) the poem has a fifth stanza:
Poor outcast! return—to receive thee once more
The house of thy father will open its door,
And thou once again, in thy plain russet gown,
May'st hear the thrush sing from a tree of its own.
Wordsworth omitted these lines from *L.B.* (*1802*) and
all subsequent editions. Lamb wrote perceptively:
Susan stood for the representative of poor *Rus in
Urbe.* . . . The last verse of Susan was to be got rid of

185   at all events. . . . Susan is a servant maid. I see her
trundling her mop and contemplating the whirling
phenomenon through blurred optics; but to term her
a poor outcast seems as much as to say that poor
Susan was no better than she should be, which I trust
was not what you meant to express. (*Lamb*, ii, 158.)

Lamb is here approving of a decision which he had
not noticed until he read Wordsworth's *Poems* (1815),
but which Wordsworth had made at least thirteen years
earlier. As Lamb noted, Susan is a country creature
imprisoned in a town: the caged thrush only revives
her memories but symbolises her plight.

It has been said (Parrish, p. 134) that this poem is
based on Bürger's *Des Armen Suschens Traum*; but
there is not much resemblance.

7. *bright volumes of vapour*: sunlit mist or cloud, seen
at ground level in mountain districts. *Cf.*

> . . . aloft above my head,
> Emerging from the silvery vapours, lo!
> A shepherd and his dog!
> (*Prelude*, p. 268: lines 93-5 of Bk. viii in 1805.)

186   INSCRIPTION

FOR THE SPOT WHERE THE HERMITAGE STOOD
Written in 1800. The 'inscription,' briefly expressing
the thoughts and feelings prompted by or appropriate
to a place, was a common poetic form of the period.
Southey wrote more than forty such pieces, including
one, *For the Apartment in Chepstow Castle*, which was
the subject of a famous parody in the *Anti-Jacobin*.
4. *sick* 1802-5; *sink* 1800, 1815.

186   LINES WRITTEN WITH A PENCIL
Written in 1800. In *L.B.* (*1800*) the poem is called
Inscription for the House (*an Out-house*), etc.

187   7. *Vitruvius*. Marcus Vitruvius Pollio wrote the only
book on architecture which has survived from classical
times, a work which was of great importance for
architects of the Renaissance.

TO A SEXTON 187

Written in Germany in 1799.

ANDREW JONES 188

Wordsworth wrote most of these stanzas in 1798 intending them to be part of *Peter Bell*. Later he converted them into a separate poem by adding the first and last stanzas, adapting the second, and changing 'Peter' to 'Andrew' in lines 21 and 28. (See *P.W.*, ii, 463-4, 531.) The poem was not republished after 1815.

RUTH 190

'Written in Germany 1799. Suggested by an account I had of a wanderer in Somersetshire' (W.W., 1843). For the American background Wordsworth drew upon William Bartram's *Travels through North and South Carolina, Georgia*, etc. (1791). 'Mr. E. H. Coleridge points out that the whole passage describing the flora of Georgian scenery is a close rendering of Bartram's narrative, and that the frontispiece of the book depicts a chieftain, whose feathers nod in the breeze just as did the military casque of the youth from Georgia's shore' (*P.W.*, ii, 510).

Ruth expresses a development in Wordsworth's ideas about 'Nature's education.' For him in 1798 'nature' had been a concept uniting his own experience of the English countryside, which had brought him peace and joy, with the universal 'system of benevolence' described by Hartley (see above, pp. 274-6). Thus poems like *Expostulation and Reply*, *The Tables Turned* and, above all, *Tintern Abbey* present nature as a purely beneficent influence: 'the nurse,/The guide, the guardian of my heart, and soul/Of all my moral being.' Critics from John Stuart Mill onwards have pointed out that this is far too optimistic a view of nature as a whole (see Beach, pp. 187-9); Aldous Huxley suggests that such a view is possible only in the 'tamed and temperate' regions Wordsworth knew, and that 'a few weeks in Malaya or Borneo would have undeceived him' ('Wordsworth in the Tropics,' *Collected Essays* (Chatto, 1960)

190 pp. 1-10.) In *Ruth* Wordsworth to some extent anticipates these criticisms by recognising that where nature is
violent and 'voluptuous' it may foster the same qualities
in men—as with Ruth's faithless lover. Nature can teach
evil lessons as well as good: a 'natural' environment
produces not only the hart and the Dalesmen, but also
the panther and the Cherokees. Wordsworth seems disturbed by these facts and uncertain how to fit them into
his earlier synthesis. Lines 169-74 maintain that where
nature is beautiful its moral influence must be at least
partly good; lines 157-62, however, suggest that nature
works on men chiefly by strengthening good or evil
tendencies that are already present. The poem also
glances towards religious orthodoxy in a way unusual
with Wordsworth at this period: the 'wild men's vices'
are attributable to their knowing no 'better law' (lines
175-80), and a Christian burial is predicted for Ruth at
the close.

Of the four stanzas which explicitly discuss the influence of 'tropic' nature, three (lines 156-74) were in
1802 recast in the first person and spoken by the youth
during his courtship. In 1805 they became third-person
commentary again, as in 1800. Partly to accommodate
these changes, a total of seven stanzas were added
between 1800 and 1805; for a full record of variants see
P.W., ii, 227-35.

13-18. *Beneath her father's . . . height*. This stanza was
added in 1802.

28-9. *when America was free/From battle*, i.e. after the
War of Independence (1775-83).

191 43. *Among the Indians he had fought*. The youth seems
to have fought in company with the Indians and on the
side of the Colonists; though the Cherokee were allies of
the Crown (see Clark Wissler, *Indians of the United
States* (Doubleday, New York, 1954), p. 127).

192 61-72. *Of march and ambush . . . Atlantic main*. These
two stanzas were added in 1802, and in that edition led
on to a first-person version of lines 157-74—'Whatever
in those climes *I* found,' etc.

73-8. *It was a fresh . . . liberty*. This stanza was added

in 1805, filling the gap left when the transposed version **192**
of lines 157-74 was removed (see previous note).

79-90. *But wherefore . . . he had been.* These two stanzas
were added in 1802; with lines 61-72, they 'frame' the
transposed passage.

91. *the magnolia.* 'Magnolia grandiflora' (Wordsworth's **193**
footnote, 1800-5). In *L.B.* (*1800*), and again in edns.
from 1815 onwards, the description of flowers and trees
continues uninterrupted from line 60 to line 91.

94. *flowers that with one scarlet gleam,* etc. 'The splendid
appearance of these scarlet flowers, which are scattered
with such profusion over the hills in the southern parts
of North America, is frequently mentioned by Bartram
in his *Travels*' (Wordsworth's footnote, 1800-5).

151-3. *The wind, the tempest . . . might well be dangerous* **195**
food. 'These lines are among the very few in which
Wordsworth shows any consciousness that Nature
sometimes does betray the heart that loves her, that she
often seems capricious, wild, and voluptuous, and may
encourage self-indulgence and lawlessness' (R. D.
Havens, *The Mind of a Poet* (Johns Hopkins Press,
Baltimore, 1941), p. 114).

163. *voluptuous* 1800, 1805; *unhallowed* 1802.

165. *lovely* 1800-43; *gorgeous* 1845.

168. *magic* 1800-5; *gorgeous* 1815-43; *favoured* 1845.

170. *sometimes* 1800, 1805; *often* 1802.

172-4. *For passions linked . . . sentiment.* The phrasing is
that regularly used by Wordsworth to describe nature's
influence through Hartleian association: *cf.* 'To her fair
works did Nature link/The human soul that through
me ran,' *Lines written in Early Spring*, p. 85, lines 5-6.
Havens comments: ' "Noble sentiment" this child of
nature had, but not much else, as Wordsworth clearly
saw' (*op. cit.*, p. 115).

172. *linked to* 1800, 1805; *amid* 1802.

173. *needs must have* 1800, 1805; *wanted not* 1802.

226. *the banks of Tone.* 'The Tone is a river of Somerset- **197**
shire at no great distance from the Quantock hills.
These hills, which are alluded to a few stanzas below,
are extremely beautiful, and in most places richly

197 covered with coppice woods.' (Wordsworth's footnote, 1800-5.)

229-34. *The engines of her pain . . . done to her.* Possibly Wordsworth means to present Ruth, like her lover, as a person for whom 'Nature's education' has been inadequate. Motherless and 'slighted' by her father, Ruth has grown up 'in thoughtless freedom' like 'an infant of the woods' (lines 1-12). Nature gives her much, but not the kind of guidance needed to save her from a rash marriage. The rocks, pools, etc., 'shaped her sorrow' by leaving her vulnerable to the Georgian youth. Another possible reading is that the rocks and pools are associated with her love, so that to see them now brings her pain by giving a shape to her sorrow.

229. *pain* 1802; *grief* 1800.

198 241-6. *An innocent life . . . cold.* This stanza was added in 1802.

241-2. *An innocent . . . will* 1805; *The neighbours grieve for her, and say/That she will* 1802.

199 LINES WRITTEN WITH A SLATE-PENCIL

Written in 1800.

8. *Sir William.* 'This would be Sir William Fleming of Rydal Hall, the first Baronet, *died* 1736' (E. de Selincourt, *P.W.*, iv, 443).

25-35. *But if thou art one . . . stone to stone.* In 1810 Wordsworth described some of the unwelcome changes brought about by the late eighteenth-century vogue for picturesque scenery. 'The lakes had now become celebrated; visitors flocked hither from all parts of England; the fancies of some were smitten so deeply that they became settlers; and the islands of Derwentwater and Winandermere, as they offered the strongest temptation, were the first places seized upon, and were instantly defaced by the intrusion.' (*A Guide through the District of the Lakes*, intro. W. M. Merchant (Hart-Davis, 1951), p. 104.)

200 31. *snow-white glory*: for Wordsworth's objections to white as a colour for buildings in this district see *ibid.*, pp. 113-17.

Later called *Matthew*. 'Such a tablet as is here spoken of continued to be preserved in Hawkshead School, though the inscriptions were not brought down to our time. This and other poems connected with Matthew would not gain by a literal detail of facts. Like the Wanderer in *The Excursion*, this schoolmaster was made up of several both of his class and men of other occupations. I do not ask pardon for what there is of untruth in such verses, considered strictly as matters of fact. It is enough if, being true and consistent in spirit, they move and teach in a manner not unworthy of a poet's calling.' (W.W., 1843.)

This and the following two 'Matthew' poems were written at Goslar in 1799. As Wordsworth's note makes clear, 'Matthew' is a composite figure; Mary Moorman suggests that his character is taken largely from that of a 'packman' or pedlar with whom Wordsworth was friendly during his schooldays at Hawkshead, and who later figures in *The Excursion* (*M.M.*, i, 51-3). He has sometimes been identified with William Taylor, headmaster of Hawkshead 1781-6, who died while Wordsworth was still at the school: but Taylor was only thirty-two when he died and so hardly corresponds with the 'Matthew' of *The Fountain*. Other poems concerning or mentioning 'Matthew' are *Expostulation and Reply* and *The Tables Turned* (pp. 50-2); also *Address to the Scholars of the Village School of* ——, written in 1798, and some other pieces written in the same year but unpublished in Wordsworth's lifetime (*P.W.*, iv, 256-8, 451-5). One of these includes the stanza:

> Learning will often dry the heart,
> The very bones it will distress,
> But Matthew had an idle art
> Of teaching love and happiness.

24. *oil* 1800-5; *dew* 1815.   201
32. *to thee* 1805; *of thee* 1800-2, 1815.

201 THE TWO APRIL MORNINGS

(See p. 379 for a general note on 'Matthew'.) This poem and the next follow a similar pattern; confident happiness is disturbed by a revelation of sorrow and human vulnerability which is all the more unexpected in that it comes from Matthew, the 'man of mirth.' The effect is not to belittle the happiness, but to convey a sense of the terms on which even a happy life is lived.

202 41-52. *And turning . . . on the sea.* The girl is vividly particularised, yet appearing as she does beside the grave and the yew, adorned with beauty, youth and light, she seems a symbol of life—endlessly renewed, like the fountain, yet in herself but one of countless impulses of energy, like the wave. For a discussion of lines 41-56 see Danby, pp. 85-7.

203 56. *And did not wish her mine.* The unexpected negative must mean, primarily, that Matthew would not risk another loss: that the risk of pain outweighs the joys of relationship. To the extent that the girl is felt to stand for life it may also suggest a larger refusal, reluctant but considered. Danby finds a further meaning, that Matthew is momentarily freed from possessiveness and self-regard. This agrees with the 'pure delight' of Matthew's vision, but less well with the 'sigh of pain' or with the general tenor of this and the following poem.

203 THE FOUNTAIN

(See general note on the 'Matthew' poems, p. 379, and on *The Two April Mornings*, above.) Like *Simon Lee*, this poem uses a stratagem to induce a fresh response to familiar facts. The opening presents a picture of simple happiness, youth and age meeting on equal terms. The reflections of the 'dear old man' at first seem conventional and undisturbing; but they soon show us that his 'glee' is not to be taken for granted, and lead into confessions of loneliness and egotism which in this context shock us. In face of the losses time brings, both friends are revealed as helpless (lines 61-4). Friendship remains, and a normal appearance of happiness is restored; but the close of the poem, though seemingly

as gay as its opening, evokes quite a different response **203**
in the reader.

34-6. *And yet the wiser . . . leaves behind.* What age leaves **204**
behind seems here to be the 'heavy laws' of self-
discipline and social habit, which compel men to seem
cheerful even after old age has taken away much which
had caused them to be so.

63. *his hands* 1800-5; *my hand* 1815. The earlier reading **205**
gives a stronger impression of distress and isolation.

69-72. *And, ere we came . . . chimes.* 'Is this Matthew
discovering again a genuine joy, or rehearsing again an
old one, or is it the old man indulging a boy's fancy?
Is the "man of mirth" lending his voice to a blitheness
as "childish" as the tears he shed by the fountain and
which can only exist in the willed dissociation that produces "a half-mad thing of witty rhymes," half madness
and half wit, something maybe similar in effect to
Wordsworth's own apparently dissociated quatrains,
their springy gaiety of movement jarring grotesquely
with the sombre overtones?' (Danby, pp. 82-3.)

NUTTING

206

Like '*There was a boy*' (p. 151) and other autobiographical passages of blank verse written at Goslar, this
piece was originally intended for *The Prelude*; Wordsworth noted in 1843 that it was 'struck out as not
being wanted there.' As R. D. Havens writes: 'Why it
was not wanted is a mystery, since it is greater poetry
and is more directly connected with the imagination
and with the growth of the poet's mind than hundreds
of passages that were retained' (*The Mind of a Poet*, p.
275). However, the idea that it should form part or
whole of an independent poem must have occurred to
Wordsworth at an early stage. Dorothy sent Coleridge
a version of these lines in December 1798 with the
comment: 'It is the conclusion of a poem of which the
beginning is not written' (*E.L.W.*, p. 238). Soon
afterwards Wordsworth wrote a 'beginning' of more
than fifty lines, which survives in a notebook of the
German period. In this version (printed in *P.W.*, ii,

206 504-6) the speaker and his 'beloved friend' Lucy are gathering hazel-nuts: he reproves her for handling the branches roughly, and explains that he has been

> early taught
> To look with feelings of fraternal love
> Upon those unassuming things which hold
> A silent station in this beauteous world.

After addressing the 'Powers' or spirits of the trees and describing the various ways in which they have ministered to him, he then relates a boyhood experience as in the present poem. Unlike the ending devised for '*There was a boy,*' this beginning is poetically effective and uses material which had been associated with the *Nutting* theme from an early stage (see Q^r of MS. JJ, *Prelude*, p. 641). Nevertheless Wordsworth excised it before publication and allowed the autobiographical fragment to stand by itself. Thus the dialogue with the 'dearest maiden' and the description of the tree-spirits survive only vestigially in lines 53-5. For a discussion of MSS. and of the poem's development see Reed, pp. 331-2.

For Wordsworth at twenty-eight the boy's 'ravage' represented not only the destruction of something beautiful, but an offence against 'fraternal' forms of life and a profanation of Nature's temple (see the passage from MS. 18*a* beginning 'I would not strike a flower,' *Prelude*, pp. 612-14). These views affect the perspective and detail of *Nutting*, but are not obtruded. Wordsworth's triumph is to have presented his two boyhood selves simultaneously and with such sympathy: the conventionally 'normal' boy bent on heroic enterprise, who sees the bower as a rich source of plunder, enjoys his 'merciless ravage' and swaggers home 'exulting'; and the sensitive, reflective boy who takes pleasure in the beauty of the copse and feels a pang when this is shattered. It is a paradox not only of boyhood that two such selves may be conjoined. Wordsworth's experience is recollected with intensity and with integrity; he also sees it in perspective as part of the long process of 'Nature's education' (lines 47-9). Thus, while the destruction saddens and repels, the destroyer is viewed with understanding and even with some amusement. **206**

1-8. *It seems . . . my steps.* The version in Dorothy's letter to Coleridge begins:

> Among the autumnal woods, a figure quaint,
> Equipped with wallet and with crooked stick
> They led me, and I followed in their steps,
> Tricked out, etc.

'They' are the 'guardian spirits' who lead the boy to the copse (see note to lines 13-15). In Wordsworth's longer version 'They' and 'their' become 'Ye' and 'your,' thus identifying the guardian spirits with the 'Powers' whom the speaker has just addressed. (For a summary of this version see note above.)

10. *my frugal dame.* This was Ann Tyson, in whose cottage Wordsworth lodged while at Hawkshead School.

13-15. *Among . . . nook* 1800; *They led me far,/Those guardian spirits, into some dear nook* MSS.

18. *rose* 1800; *towered* MSS.

20-8. *A virgin scene . . . hope.* Much of the feeling of this passage is derived from the sexual metaphor.

47. *being* 1800; *spirit* Dorothy's letter (the MS. of **207** Wordsworth's longer version is cut away after line 32).

48. *feelings* 1800; *being* Dorothy's letter.

53-5. *Then, dearest maiden! . . . woods.* These lines were included in the version sent by Dorothy, but anticipate the 'beginning' Wordsworth was already planning. His longer (and more fictionalised) version opens:

> Ah! what a crash was that! with gentle hand
> Touch these fair hazels—my beloved friend!
> Though 'tis a sight invisible to thee,
> From such rude intercourse the woods all shrink
> As at the blowing of Astolpho's horn.
> Thou, Lucy, art a maiden 'inland bred' . . .

The closing lines would then return the reader to the situation, and to one of the phrases, with which the poem began.

55. *a spirit in the woods.* The spirit or spirits played an important rôle in Wordsworth's longer version of the poem (see general note above). 'When Wordsworth began to write *The Prelude* he still delighted to conceive

207 of Nature not merely as the expression of one divine spirit, but as in its several parts animated by individual spirits who had, like human beings, an independent life and power of action. This was obviously his firm belief in the primitive paganism of his boyhood (see lines 329-50, 405-27); and long after he had given up definite belief in it, he cherished it as more than mere poetic fancy.' (Helen Darbishire, *Prelude*, p. 517; the line references are to Bk. i of the text of 1805.)

207 'THREE YEARS SHE GREW IN SUN AND SHOWER'
(See general note on the 'Lucy' poems, pp. 366-7.) 'Lucy' does not here represent any real person, nor is she a composite figure, but 'an ideal picture of what normal human development might be, in which both the law and the impulse, the kindling and restraining power of nature lead to the perfect development of beauty and grace' (Beatty, p. 213). Her death may have been added to make the poem fit in with the rest of the group. It was 'composed in the Harz forest' (W.W., 1843).

1. *in sun and shower*. In March 1796 Dorothy wrote of Basil Montagu, who was then three years old and had been living with the Wordsworths for six months: 'He is quite metamorphosed from a shivering, half-starved plant to a lusty, blooming, fearless boy. He dreads neither cold nor rain. He has played frequently an hour or two without appearing sensible that the rain was pouring down upon him or the wind blowing about him.' (*E.L.W.*, p. 166.)

7-8. *Myself will . . . impulse* 1800, 1805; *Her teacher I myself will be,/She is my darling* 1802.

208 23. *Grace that shall mould the maiden's form* 1802; *A beauty that shall mould her form* 1800.

209   THE PET LAMB
Written at Town End, Grasmere, in 1800. 'Barbara Lewthwaite' was the name of a beautiful girl then living at Grasmere, though in fact it was not she but another whom Wordsworth saw and overheard (see his note, *P.W.*, i, 364).

WRITTEN IN GERMANY 212

'1798 and 1799. A bitter winter it was when these verses were composed by the side of my sister, in our lodgings at a draper's house in the romantic imperial town of Goslar, on the edge of the Harz forest' (W.W., 1843). The second stanza was omitted from editions after 1815.

THE CHILDLESS FATHER 213

Written at Town-End, Grasmere, in 1800. 'The huntings on foot in which the old man is supposed to join, as here described, were of common, almost habitual occurrence in our vales when I was a boy; and the people took much delight in them' (W.W., 1843). The friend of Timothy's who speaks lines 1-4 presumably then continues the narration ('my ears,' line 19).

One of Wordsworth's favourite subjects is the commonplace action invested with emotional or moral significance: the cutting of a root in *Simon Lee*, the failure to lift a stone in *Michael*. Here the pocketing of a key both recalls (by contrast) times when Ellen was alive and anticipates the empty house to which Timothy will return. That the poem is not, taken as a whole, completely successful is due in part to the bouncy anapæstic metre, suitable for the 'chase' but not for getting a coffin through a door (lines 11-12), for Timothy's 'leisurely motion,' or for the moment of insight into his feelings (line 18).

16. *with a leisurely motion.* The adjective is one of 214 Wordsworth's surprises: *slow* would simply have conveyed the old man's heavy heart, his diminished eagerness for hunting; *leisurely* gives a fuller sense of the situation by emphasising his continuing life, his selfpossession and physical firmness; perhaps also by suggesting the small unwanted compensations of the bereaved who have 'no one to please but themselves.'

THE OLD CUMBERLAND BEGGAR 214

'Observed, and with great benefit to my own heart, when I was a child; written at Racedown and Alfoxden in my twenty-eighth year' (W.W., 1843). 'The class of

214 beggars to which the old man here described belongs
will probably soon be extinct. It consisted of poor and,
mostly, old and infirm persons who confined themselves
to a stated round in their neighbourhood, and had certain fixed days on which at different houses they regularly received alms, sometimes in money but mostly in
provisions.' (Wordsworth's prefatory note.)

The poem has three main phases. Lines 1-21 describe
the beggar seated at his meal, alone amid the 'wild unpeopled hills.' Lines 22-66 show him on his journeys—
'he travels on'—and though he is still referred to as 'a
solitary man,' his encounters with the turnpike-woman,
the post-boy, the village children, etc., present him in
relation to rural society. Lines 67-154 justify the beggar's
way of life in terms of his value to this community,
whose charities he helps to keep alive; and lines 155-89
conclude this final phase with a plea that he should not
be sent to the workhouse.

The opening section is purely descriptive, but has a
peculiarly Wordsworthian intensity: the beggar must
have been one of the earliest of those solitary figures
seen amid wide landscapes which so stirred Wordsworth's
imagination (*cf. Resolution and Independence*, and figures
in *The Prelude* and *The Excursion*). This intensity is lost
as the poem becomes more discursive, and though each
phase has good poetry of its kind the declamatory ending
leaves a sense of disappointment. MSS. show that
Wordsworth began the poem in 1796-7 as 'a description'
and added the defence of the beggar later—partly, perhaps, to make the poem seem more complete and purposeful (*cf.* his treatment of *Animal Tranquillity* and
'*There was a Boy*,' and the opening devised for *Nutting*).
The defence is none the less sincere and strongly felt.

1-21. *I saw . . . his staff*. This passage illustrates Wordsworth's power of vivid and detailed recollection, and of
what he calls 'looking steadily at my subject' (Preface,
p. 26). Conventional treatment would have made the
scene comic, or pathetic, or picturesque: in Wordsworth's hands it is none of these things. The beggar's
age, solitude and serious calm are noted, and so equally

386

are the showers of crumbs and his failure to catch them. **214**
The result is unclassifiable but authentic, like something seen by the fresh and fascinated eye of a child.

24, 44. *He travels on*: cf. *Animal Tranquillity and Decay*, **215**
p. 52, line 3. Lines 1-14 of *Animal Tranquillity* originally belonged to this section of *The Old Cumberland Beggar*.

67. *But deem not this man useless*, etc. The transition **216**
from description to rhetorical moralising is rather abrupt.
Lamb wrote:

> . . . it appears to me a fault in the *Beggar*, that the
> instructions conveyed in it are too direct and like a
> lecture: they don't slide into the mind of the reader,
> while he is imagining no such matter. An intelligent
> reader finds a sort of insult in being told 'I will teach
> you how to think upon this subject.'   (*Lamb*, i, 239.)

After *useless* Wordsworth originally included some lines
beginning:

> Not perhaps
> Less useful than the smooth and portly squire,
> Who with his steady coachman, steady steeds
> All slick and bright with comfortable gloss,
> Doth in his broad glassed chariot drive along . . .
>   (Alfoxden MS., *P.W.*, iv, 236, *app. crit.*)

67-70. *Statesmen! ye . . . nuisances*. 'The political
economists were about that time [1797-8] beginning
their war upon mendicity in all its forms, and by implication, if not directly, almsgiving also. This heartless
process has been carried as far as it can go by the *amended*
Poor Law Bill [of 1834] . . .' (W.W., 1843). In 1797-8
and for many years afterwards poverty and unemployment were acute in country districts. Wordsworth was
well aware of this, but objected to such relief measures
as the setting-up of workhouses and 'soup-shops' on the
grounds that these would weaken the spirit of independence, and also the 'domestic affections,' among the
poor. See his letter to Charles James Fox of January
1801 (*E.L.W.*, pp. 312-5).

73-9. *'Tis Nature's law . . . linked*. For Wordsworth it is
not by accident that the beggar has his uses: he has his

216 part to play in the 'system of benevolence.' See note on Hartley, pp. 274-6; *cf.* also *The Excursion*, Bk. ix, lines 1-20 and *app. crit.* (*P.W.*, v, 286-7).

217 79. After *linked*, the following lines were inserted in 1837:

> Then be assured
> That least of all can aught that ever owned
> That heaven-regarding eye and front sublime
> That man is born to, sink, howe'er depressed,
> So low as to be scorned without a sin;
> Without offence to God cast out of view;
> Like the dry remnant of a garden-flower
> Whose seeds are shed, or as an implement
> Worn-out and worthless.

These later lines imply that the beggar is to be valued, not because he is useful in the general scheme of things, but because he is a human being. *Cf.* Coleridge's discussion in 1809 of 'the sacred principle . . . that a person can never become a thing, nor be treated as such [i.e. purely as a means to an end] without wrong' (*The Friend*, ed. Rooke, 1969, i, 190). Wordsworth may already have felt this in 1800 (see especially the closing section of the poem), but his explicit defence of the beggar is utilitarian.

99-101. The Alfoxden MS. here reads:

> And meditative, in which reason falls
> Like a strong radiance of the setting sun
> On each minutest feeling of the heart,
> Illuminates, and to their view brings forth
> In one harmonious prospect; minds like these, etc.

This seems a description of the poet Wordsworth himself would have wished to be, whereas the published text gives only the general account of a great writer. *Cf.* also the MS. reading at line 103, which carries a stronger suggestion of autobiographical fact.

103. *have perchance received* 1800-20; *did perchance receive* Alfoxden MS.; *haply have received* 1827.

219 167/8. *Waste not on him your busy tenderness* MS.

172. *House . . . of Industry*. A workhouse: 'misnamed' because conditions seldom encouraged industry, and in

many cases no work was provided. Unlicensed begging, **219** however, was illegal, and where workhouses existed (as at Cockermouth) paupers could be made to go there before receiving any assistance from the parish. See Dorothy Marshall, *The English Poor in the Eighteenth Century* (Routledge, 1926), pp. 128, 146-8, 237.

173. *that pent-up din*, etc. Eighteenth-century workhouses varied (see Marshall, *op. cit.*, chapt. iv); but most commonly they were dark (hence 'let the light . . . orbs,' lines 182-3), dirty, ill-ventilated, crowded and comfortless. Wordsworth knew by heart Crabbe's description of a workhouse in *The Village* (1783), Bk. i, lines 238-49 (see *M.M.*, i, 55). Crabbe mentions 'the clamour of the crowd'; the 'din' would be increased where such trades were practised as spinning, weaving, and the beating of hemp and flax.

177-8. 'Here the mind knowingly passes a fiction upon herself, first substituting her own feelings for the beggar's, and, in the same breath detecting the fallacy, will not part with the wish' (*Lamb*, i, 239).

RURAL ARCHITECTURE **220**

Written at Grasmere in 1800. 'These structures . . . are common among our hills, being built by shepherds as conspicuous marks, occasionally by boys in sport' (W.W., 1843). A fourth stanza appears in all edns. but those of 1805 and 1815:

—Some little I've seen of blind boisterous works
By Christian disturbers more savage than Turks,
Spirits busy to do and undo:
At remembrance whereof my blood sometimes will
flag;
Then, light-hearted boys, to the top of the crag;
And I'll build up a giant with you.

4. '*Great How* is a single and conspicuous hill which rises towards the foot of Thirlmere, on the western side of the beautiful dale of Legberthwaite, along the high road between Keswick and Ambleside' (Wordsworth's footnote).

A POET'S EPITAPH

Cf. Theocritus, Epigram XIX: 'Here lies the poet Hipponax! If thou art a sinner draw not near this tomb, but if thou are a true man, and the son of righteous sires, sit boldly down here, yea, and sleep if thou wilt.' (Lang's translation, quoted in *P.W.*, iv, 414, where the Greek text is also given.) Wordsworth had read Theocritus and discusses his Idylls in a letter of February 1799, the year in which this poem was written (*E.L.W.*, p. 255).

A Poet's Epitaph is extraordinarily uneven in quality, passing from conventional satire to devastating scorn and from a sentimental sketch of the poet-recluse to an effective summary of some of Wordsworth's most important conceptions. After lines 1-36 it is difficult to accept, as the poet's *alter ego*, the modest figure who appears in line 37. The poem shows the strength of the anti-rationalist element in Wordsworth (lines 17-36), and shows too how his independence of mind could sometimes pass over into arrogance and absurdity.

1. *statesman* 1800-32; *statist* 1837. (A 'statist' is a statistician.)

2. *business* 1800-32; *conflicts* 1837.

6-8. Softened in 1820 to:

> Go, carry to some fitter place
> The keenness of that practised eye,
> The hardness of that sallow face.

11. *Doctor.* Not a physician (see line 17) but a Doctor of Divinity, or more generally a parson. Lamb objected to 'the vulgar satire upon parsons and lawyers in the beginning' of this poem: see *Lamb*, i, 239. By 'vulgar' Lamb means 'commonplace.'

18. *Philosopher*, i.e. scientist (*cf.* Preface, p. 21, line 36 and note). Confusingly, 'moralist' in line 25 bears a sense which today might best be rendered by the term 'philosopher' (see note to lines 25-36).

21. *sensual fleece.* The implication of this very compressed metaphor seems to be that the scientist deals only in the kind of knowledge that can readily be verified by the

senses: he ignores 'impulses of deeper birth.' This habit **221**
is seen as a mental 'fleece,' protecting him from other
kinds of knowledge as a sheep's wool protects it from the
weather. The metaphor also transfers some of the
sheep's animality and stupidity to the scientist.

24. *Thy pin-point of a soul* 1800-5; *That abject thing, thy
soul*, 1815-32; *Thy ever-dwindling soul* 1837. In 1801
Lamb criticised 'pin-point' as a 'coarse epithet' (*loc.
cit.*).

25-36. *A moralist . . . dust.* A 'moralist' was an exponent
or follower of some ethical system; the term sometimes
implied a secular morality. Scientist and 'moralist' are
both presented as heartless reasoners but of complementary kinds, one confined to the data supplied by his
senses, the other to the abstractions created by his
mind. The scientist is 'all eyes,' the moralist 'has
neither eyes nor ears'; the former is insulated by a
'sensual fleece,' the latter by an 'intellectual crust.' More
than one moral system of the period might be said to
rely too confidently upon abstractions, e.g. those of
Bentham (*Principles of Morals and Legislation*, 1789)
and Godwin (*Political Justice*, 1793). Wordsworth is
attacking a tendency rather than any one 'moralist' or
his doctrines.

45-52. *The outward shows . . . his own heart.* The poet **222**
combines the separate powers of the scientist and the
moralist, in that he can both observe and reflect. Moreover his observations, made in a state of quiet receptive-
ness, are more comprehensive and more fruitful than
the scientist's; just as the 'random truths' evolved from
his experience of nature are more valuable than the
systematic truths of the moralist.

51. *The harvest of a quiet eye.* This line conveys a sense
both of the observing and of the reflecting process
described above. The 'quiet eye' is both the organ
which receives nature's impressions in a 'wise passiveness' (*cf. Expostulation and Reply*, p. 50, lines 17-24),
and the 'eye made quiet by the power/Of harmony, and
the deep power of joy' which may later 'see into the life
of things' (*Tintern Abbey*, p. 139, lines 48-50).

223

A FRAGMENT

Written in Germany in 1799; later called *The Danish Boy*. 'These stanzas were designed to introduce a ballad upon the story of a Danish prince who had fled from battle and, for the sake of the valuables about him, was murdered by the inhabitant of a cottage in which he had taken refuge. The house fell under a curse, and the spirit of the youth, it was believed, haunted the valley where the crime had been committed.' (Wordsworth's note, 1827.)

225

'IT WAS AN APRIL MORNING'

'Grasmere, 1800. This poem was suggested on the banks of the brook that runs through Easedale, which is, in some parts of its course, as wild and beautiful as brook can be. I have composed thousands of verses by the side of it.' (W.W., 1843.) 'The Dell can be identified as by Easedale Beck, a little above Goody Bridge' (E. de Selincourt, *P.W.*, ii, 486).

11. *various*, i.e. progressively changing, as in Latin *varius*. *Cf*. Milton, *Paradise Lost*, Bk. iv, line 669; Dryden, *Absalom and Achitophel*, line 545. By italicising the word Wordsworth acknowledged that in this sense it is no longer part of 'the language really used by men'; in 1845 he reconstructed the passage on more English lines (*P.W.*, ii, 111).

226 39. *My Emma*. 'The poem is unquestionably addressed to Dorothy' (E. de Selincourt, *P.W.*, ii, 486).

226

TO JOANNA

Joanna Hutchinson (1780-1843) was the youngest sister of Mary, whom Wordsworth married in 1802. The poem was written at Grasmere in 1800. As E. de Selincourt points out (*P.W.*, ii, 487) it should not be taken literally: for example, Joanna Hutchinson was not brought up 'amid the smoke of cities.' Also, 'the effect of her laugh is an extravagance; though the effect of the reverberation of voices in some parts of the mountains is very striking' (W.W., 1843).

Wordsworth was pleased with this poem: in 1801

he believed that *To Joanna* and *Nutting* showed 'the **226** greatest genius of any poems in the second volume' (see *M.M.*, i, 506). The following analysis of the poem appears in one of his notebooks:

The poem supposes that at the rock something had taken place in my mind either then, or afterwards in thinking upon what then took place, which if related will cause the vicar to smile. For something like this you are prepared by the phrase 'Now by those dear immunities,' etc. I begin to relate the story, meaning in a certain degree to divert or partly play upon the vicar. I begin—my mind partly forgets its purpose, being softened by the images of beauty in the description of the rock and the delicious morning, and when I come to the two lines 'The rock like something,' etc., I am caught in the trap of my own imagination. I entirely lose sight of my first purpose. I take fire in the lines 'That ancient woman.' I go on in that strain of fancy 'Old Skiddaw' and terminate the description in tumult 'And Kirkstone,' etc., describing what for a moment I believed actually took place at the time or [what,] when I have been reflecting on what did take place, I have had a temporary belief, in some fit of imagination, did really or might have taken place. When the description is closed, or perhaps partly before I waken from the dream and see that the vicar thinks I have been extravagating, as I intended he should, I then tell the story as it happened really; and as the recollection of it exists permanently and regularly in my mind, mingling allusions suffused with humour, partly to the trance in which I have been, and partly to the trick I have been playing on the vicar. The poem then concludes in a strain of deep tenderness.   (MS. 2, quoted in *P.W.*, ii, 487.)

28. *I, like a runic priest* etc. 'In Cumberland and West- **227** morland are several inscriptions upon the native rock which, from the wasting of time and the rudeness of the workmanship, have been mistaken for runic. They

227 are, without doubt, Roman.' (Wordsworth's footnote.)
31. 'The Rotha . . . is the river which, flowing through
the lakes of Grasmere and Rydal, falls into Winandermere' (Wordsworth's footnote).

228 54-65. *The rock, like something . . . misty head.* Coleridge
quotes a parallel from Drayton's *Poly-Olbion*: see *B.L.*,
chapt. xx, p. 233, or *P.W.*, ii, 488.

56-7. *That ancient woman . . . cavern.* 'On Helm Crag,
that impressive single mountain at the head of the Vale
of Grasmere, is a rock which from most points of view
bears a striking resemblance to an old woman cowering.
Close by this rock is one of those fissures or caverns
which in the language of the country are called dungeons.
Most of the mountains here mentioned immediately
surround the Vale of Grasmere; of the others, some
are at a considerable distance, but they belong to the
same cluster.' (Wordsworth's footnote.)

229   'THERE IS AN EMINENCE'

'1800. It is not accurate that the eminence here alluded
to could be seen from our orchard-seat. It rises above
the road by the side of Grasmere lake, towards Keswick,
and its name is Stone-Arthur.' (W.W., 1843.)

5. *cliff* 1800-36; *peak* 1843.

10. *The star of Jove.* Wordsworth's favourite: *cf.*
'Jupiter, my own beloved star,' *Prelude*, p. 120 (Bk. iv,
line 239 in text of 1805).

13. Wordsworth enjoyed solitude and lonely places,
and drew strength from them: see R. D. Havens, *The
Mind of a Poet*, chapt. iv.

14. *She who dwells with me:* Dorothy.

17. so 1800-5; *Hath to this lonely summit given my name*
1815.

229 'A NARROW GIRDLE OF ROUGH STONES AND CRAGS'
Written in October 1800 (see *D.W.J.*, i, 65). 'The character of the eastern shore of Grasmere Lake is quite
changed, since these verses were written, by the public
road being carried along its side. The friends spoken

of were Coleridge and my sister, and the fact occurred **229**
strictly as recorded.' (W.W., 1843.)

16. *wreck*. A form of 'wrack' found chiefly in Scottish **230**
and Northern speech: here probably loose water-plants
and other deposits, but possibly growing weeds.

19-23. *which, seeming lifeless . . . now there* so 1800-5;
> That skimmed the surface of the dead calm lake,
> Suddenly halting now—a lifeless stand!
>
> And starting off again with freak as sudden   (1815.)

35-6. *that tall fern . . . named*. Royal moonwort, or
Osmunda regalis.

38. *Naiad*. In Greek and Roman mythology, the god-
dess of a river, spring, well or fountain, represented as
a young and beautiful virgin.

41. *sweet* 1800-20; *bright* 1827.

53-5. *That way we turned . . . same voice* so 1800-20; **231**
omitted 1827.

56-7. *We all cried out . . . lose a day* so 1800-5 and, substantially, 1815-20; '*Improvident and reckless*,' *we exclaimed*,/'*That man must be, who thus can lose a day* 1827.

83-5. *a memorial name . . . coast*. Wordsworth has in
mind such commemorative names as Deception Island,
Anxious Bay and Cape Catastrophe.

TO M.H. **232**

'To Mary Hutchinson, two years before our marriage.
The pool alluded to is in Rydal Upper Park' (W.W.,
1843). The poem was in fact written in December 1799,
nearly three years before Wordsworth's marriage (see
P.W., ii, 118, 488).

24. *beeches* all edns.; *poplars* MS. *for* 1802-5; *from* 1800,
1815.

LINES WRITTEN WHEN SAILING IN A **233**
BOAT AT EVENING

Begun *c*. 1789. 'The title is scarcely correct. It was
during a solitary walk on the banks of the Cam that I
was first struck with this appearance, and applied it to
my own feelings in the manner here expressed, changing
the scene to the Thames near Windsor [?Richmond].
This and the three stanzas of the following poem,

233 *Remembrance of Collins,* formed one piece: but upon the recommendation of Coleridge the three last stanzas were separated from the other.' (W.W., 1843.) The earliest MS. version of this material shows Wordsworth apparently working towards an Italian sonnet. Early in 1797 he converted it into the five-stanza poem described by his note (see Reed, pp. 22-3, 305-6). This poem was published in *L.B.* (*1798*) under the title *Lines written near Richmond, upon the Thames, at Evening*; it was divided in 1800.

1-2. *How rich the wave . . . hues* so 1798-1805; *How richly glows the water's breast/Before us, tinged with evening hues* 1815.

9-16. *such views . . . tomorrow.* Wordsworth was again thinking of 'mighty poets in their misery dead' in 1800, when the incident commemorated in *Resolution and Independence* took place:

> I thought of Chatterton, the marvellous boy,
> The sleepless soul that perished in his pride;
> Of him who walked in glory and in joy
> Following his plough, along the mountain-side:
> By our own spirits are we deified:
> We poets in our youth begin in gladness;
> But thereof come in the end despondency and
> madness.

233   REMEMBRANCE OF COLLINS

Called in 1800 *Lines written near Richmond upon the Thames* (see notes to preceding poem). Richmond was the home of the poet James Thomson, whose death in 1748 was commemorated by his friend William Collins in the ode mentioned by Wordsworth (see footnote). Like *Lycidas*, Collins's ode enacts a funeral rite, of which 'the scene is supposed to lie on the Thames near Richmond.' Eleven years after writing this ode Collins himself died at the age of thirty-eight, disappointed by the reception of his poems and broken in physical and mental health.

13. *Such as* 1800; *Such heart* 1798.   *the poet*: Collins.

14. *pouring* 1798-1805; *murmuring* 1815. *a later ditty*. In 1798 *later* was italicised, presumably to help the reader through the rapid changes of time (lines 9-12, the

present; 13, Collins's hopeful youth; 14-16, his em- **233**
bittered later life).
18. This line makes the promised allusion to Collins's **234**
Ode on the Death of Thomson: cf.

> Remembrance oft shall haunt the shore
> > When Thames in summer wreaths is dressed,
> And oft *suspend the dashing oar*
> > To bid his gentle spirit rest.   (stanza iv)

20. *that poet's sorrows* 1802; *his freezing sorrows* 1798-1800.

THE TWO THIEVES   234

Written in 1800. 'This is described from the life as I
was in the habit of observing when a boy at Hawkshead
School. Daniel was more than eighty years older than
myself when he was daily thus occupied, under my
notice. No book could have so early taught me to think
of the changes to which human life is subject, and while
looking at him I could not but say to myself: "We may
any of us, I, or the happiest of my playmates, live to
become still more the object of pity than this old man,
this half-doting pilferer." ' (W.W., 1843.)

1-6. *O now . . . the land* so all edns.; MS.—

> Oh! now that the boxwood and graver were mine,
> Of the poet who lives on the banks of the Tyne!
> Who has plied his rude tools with more fortunate
> > toil
> Than Reynolds e'er brought to his canvas and oil.

> Then books, and book-learning, I'd ring out your
> > knell,
> The vicar should scarce know an A from an L.

1. *Bewick.* Thomas Bewick (1753-1828) restored the art
of wood-engraving in England. Philip James writes in
English Book Illustration 1800-1900 (Penguin Books,
1947):

> Through his craft he became 'a silent poet of the
> waysides and hedges,' a poet who combined an
> astonishing accuracy of observation with sincerity,
> humour, occasionally a streak of healthy indelicacy,
> and not a little homely pathos. . . . In [Bewick's vig-

234   nettes and tail-pieces] every feature of the countryside is lovingly recorded; its denizens, its implements, its aspect under rain, wind, sun and snow, and its trees and foliage in all seasons.   (pp. 19-20.)

235   11. *the Prodigal Son*, etc. Pictures illustrating Bible stories were often hung or pasted up in small inns and alehouses; *cf.* the 'pictures placed for ornament and use' (i.e. instruction) at the inn of Goldsmith's *Deserted Village* (1770).

236   40-1. *Every face . . . they roam*. Another instance of that humanity shown to one another by the poor which Wordsworth admired: *cf. The Old Cumberland Beggar*, pp. 218-19, lines 135-54.

236   'A WHIRL-BLAST FROM BEHIND THE HILL'
Written in the holly grove at Alfoxden in the spring of 1798 (see *P.W.*, ii, 489; Reed, p. 227).
    11. *You could not lay a hair between*. This line was omitted from editions after 1815.

237   19-27. An early MS. version ends simply:
> The withered leaves jump up and spring
> As if each were a living thing.
> This long description why indite?
> Because it was a pleasant sight.   (*P.W.*, ii, 128.)

24-7. *Oh! grant me . . . mind*. These lines were omitted after 1805.

237   SONG FOR THE WANDERING JEW
Written in 1800. Mediæval legend tells of a Jew who refused to let Jesus rest on his way to Golgotha, and was therefore doomed to wander on earth until the Second Coming. A ballad on this theme appears in Percy's *Reliques* (ii, 291-6). The Wandering Jew enjoyed a vogue in the literature of the late eighteenth century, and appears in several other works known to Wordsworth, to Coleridge or to both: see Lowes, *The Road to Xanadu*, pp. 242-54. In the closing lines of Wordsworth's tragedy *The Borderers* (written 1796-7), 'Mar-

maduke becomes, in all essentials, the Wanderer him- **237**
self' (Lowes, p. 246). The stanzas of this poem were
subsequently rearranged, and in 1827 two others, dealing with the wanderings of clouds and of 'the fleet
ostrich,' were included.

MICHAEL 238

Written between October 11th and December 9th 1800
(see *P.W.*, ii, 479). On the former date Wordsworth and
Dorothy visited a sheepfold in Greenhead Gill which an
old shepherd had taken seven years to build. Wordsworth also had in mind the story of an aged couple,
former owners of the Wordsworths' cottage and some
land in Grasmere, whose son had 'become dissolute
and run away from his parents' (*P.W.*, ii, 478).

Probably the strongest impulse behind both this
poem and *The Brothers* is Wordsworth's desire to pay
tribute to the shepherds of Cumberland and Westmorland and to put on record something of their way of life,
which he felt to be threatened by new economic
developments. In *The Brothers* this theme is largely confined to lines 118-81, perhaps the most interesting
passage of the poem but structurally a digression from
an already rather straggling narrative. But *Michael* is so
conceived that virtually the whole poem records this
pastoral life in minute and faithful detail, and in terms
which convey the simple grandeur Wordsworth found
in it. Michael himself is a product of this life, and
almost a personification of its virtues: hard work,
frugality, independence, uprightness, strong family
feeling and an unconscious love for the countryside in
which his days are passed. He is also completely convincing as a person.

Five weeks after completing *Michael* Wordsworth
sent Charles James Fox a copy of *L.B.* (*1800*), together
with a long letter drawing particular attention to this
poem and to *The Brothers*:

In the two poems *The Brothers* and *Michael* I have
attempted to draw a picture of the domestic affections

238   as I know they exist amongst a class of men who are now almost confined to the North of England. They are small independent *proprietors* of land, here called statesmen, men of respectable education who daily labour on their own little properties. The domestic affections will always be strong amongst men who live in a country not crowded with population, if these men are placed above poverty. But if they are proprietors of small estates, which have descended to them from their ancestors, the power which these affections will acquire amongst such men is inconceivable by those who have only had an opportunity of observing hired labourers, farmers, and the manufacturing poor. Their little tract of land serves as a kind of permanent rallying-point for their domestic feelings, as a tablet upon which they are written, which makes them objects of memory in a thousand instances when they would otherwise be forgotten. It is a fountain fitted to the nature of social man, from which supplies of affection, as pure as his heart was intended for, are daily drawn. This class of men is rapidly disappearing. . . . The two poems which I have mentioned were written with a view to show that men who do not wear fine clothes can feel deeply.   (*E.L.W.*, pp. 314-15.)

The language of the poem justifies Wordsworth's general thesis, in the Preface, that serious and accurate writing needs no rhetorical heightening to make it impressive. For several substantial passages of verse excluded from the published text see *P.W.*, ii, 479–84.

A Pastoral Poem. See general note to *The Brothers*, p. 363.
2. *Gill* so 1800-5; the spelling *Ghyll* of later editions seems to have been introduced into the language by Wordsworth (see *O.E.D.*).
6. *beside* 1800-20; *around* 1827.

239 40. *forest-side.* 'The eastern side of the lake, between Greenhead Ghyll and Town End' (E. de Selincourt, *P.W.*, ii, 484).

62-4. *And grossly . . . thoughts.* A rejected passage **239**
begins:

> No doubt if you in terms direct had asked
> Whether he loved the mountains, true it is
> That with blunt repetition of your words
> He might have stared at you, and said that they
> Were frightful to behold; but had you then
> Discoursed with him in some particular sort
> Of his own business, and the goings-on
> Of earth and sky, then truly had you seen
> That in his thoughts there were obscurities,
> Wonders and admirations, things that wrought
> Not less than a religion in his heart. (*P.W.*, ii, 482.)

65-79. *Fields, where . . . life itself.* Wordsworth's poems
on 'Nature's education' are chiefly concerned with the
process by which natural sights and sounds encourage
human development or reinforce, by association, a
moral impulse. Here he makes it clear that the process
works both ways: the hills have impressed the incidents
of Michael's life, and their meaning, on his mind, and
it is the incidents which have endeared the hills to
Michael.

73-6. *So grateful . . . blood* so 1800-27; *The certainty of* **240**
honourable gain;/Those fields, those hills 1832.

74/5. *Where all his forefathers had lived and died* MS.

78. *blind*, i.e. involuntary and unconscious (*cf.* line 148).
Both the meaning and the texture of this line, with its
five labials, suggest a baby feeding at its mother's breast:
cf. Wordsworth's explicit use of this analogy to express
his sense of man's 'filial bond' with nature in *The
Prelude*, p. 56 (Bk. ii, lines 237-64 in the text of 1805).

79. *The pleasure . . . life itself.* Wordsworth implies that
if 'just being alive' is a pleasure it is because we are
gratified by countless associations (themselves established by pleasure) of which, like Michael, we are unconscious. *Cf.* 'the grand elementary principle of
pleasure, by which [man] knows, and feels, and lives,
and moves' (Preface, p. 33).

102. *mess of pottage*: helping of stew (made with
vegetables or meat) or soup. The phrase momentarily

240 connects Michael and his household with the shepherds of the Old Testament: 'pottage,' already archaic in 1800, was remembered chiefly from Genesis xxv, and 'mess of pottage' occurs in the heading for that chapter in the Genevan Bible. *Cf.* the Biblical turn of phrase in line 156.

241 122-3. *neither gay . . . hopes.* An example of Wordsworth's accuracy, realism, and refusal to write the expected.

130/1. The following additional passage occurs in a copy of the poem sent by Wordsworth to Thomas Poole on April 9th, 1801:

> Though in these occupations they would pass
> Whole hours with but small interchange of speech,
> Yet there were times in which they did not want
> Discourse both wise and pleasant, shrewd remarks
> Of daily prudence, clothed in images
> Lively and beautiful, in rural forms
> That made their conversation fresh and fair
> As is a landscape. And the shepherd oft
> Would draw out of his heart the obscurities
> And admirations that were there, of God
> And of his works, or, yielding to the bent
> Of his peculiar humour, would let loose
> His tongue and give it the mind's freedom—then,
> Discoursing on remote imaginations, strong
> Conceits, devices, day-dreams, thoughts and
>   schemes,
> The fancies of a solitary man.

(*E.L.W.*, p. 324.)

136. *Dunmal*: later edns. give the more usual form *Dunmail*.

242 141. *the Evening Star.* The name was in fact that of a house in Grasmere, on the same side of the valley as the Wordsworths' (see *P.W.*, ii, 478).

146-9. *Effect which might . . . Or that* so 1800-20; *Less from instinctive tenderness . . . Than that* 1827.

153-5. *From such . . . on earth.* Omitted after 1820.

243 174. *The Clipping Tree.* 'Clipping is the word used in the North of England for shearing' (Wordsworth's footnote).

223-6. *This unlooked-for claim . . . lost.* 'The old man of **244**
eighty makes a new and surprising discovery concerning
himself. Pity is not invited, but neither is it excluded
from our response. It would in fact be inadequate rather
than inappropriate. Michael, though stricken, is not
disabled. He arms himself "with strength to look his
trouble in the face." ' (John Danby, *William Wordsworth: The Prelude and other Poems* (Arnold, 1963),
p. 28.)

227-9. So 1800-32: 1836—
        As soon as he had armed himself with strength
        To look his trouble in the face, it seemed
        The shepherd's sole resource to sell at once
        A portion, etc.

264-76. *There's Richard Bateman,* etc. 'The story **245**
alluded to here is well known in the country. The chapel
is called Ings Chapel, and is on the right-hand side of
the road leading from Kendal to Ambleside' (Wordsworth's note, 1802-5). Bateman's first name was really
Robert, and Ings Chapel was rebuilt at his expense
c. 1743 (see *P.W.*, ii, 484).

265. *a parish-boy*, i.e. a destitute boy brought up at the
expense of the parish. Such children were usually
boarded and lodged among the parishioners until they
could be placed out as apprentices.

330. *a sheep-fold.* 'It may be proper to inform some read- **247**
ers that a sheep-fold in these mountains is an unroofed
building of stone walls, with different divisions. It is
generally placed by the side of a brook, for the con-
venience of washing the sheep; but it is also useful as a
shelter for them, and as a place to drive them into to
enable the shepherds conveniently to single out one or
more for any particular purpose.' (Wordsworth's note,
1802-5.)

412-6. So 1802: 1800—   **249**
        Be thy companions, let this sheep-fold be
        Thy anchor and thy shield; amid all fear
        And all temptation, let it be to thee
        An emblem of the life thy fathers lived, etc.

447-52. *Meantime Luke began . . . seas.* The rapid **250**

250 account of Luke's delinquency is disconcerting. Luke must have made some resistance before succumbing to the pressures of London, yet of this struggle we are given no sense. His failure, however, must be accepted as a datum: Wordsworth's concern is with the effect of the heavy news upon Michael, whose poem this is. Michael's grief is not directly described, as are his earlier love and anxiety; it is suggested in several oblique ways, and the element of shock is conveyed largely by this swift transition from Michael's 'confident and cheerful thoughts' to Luke's ignominy.

251 455. *Would break the heart: old Michael found it so* 1800-15; *Would overset the brain, or break the heart* 1820.

459-60. *His bodily frame . . . strength.* Cf. lines 43-4, and note the effect of the repetition in a changed context.

471. *And never lifted up a single stone.* See Matthew Arnold's comment, quoted on p. 414. (Arnold fails to indicate that the line draws most of its force from what has gone before: to a reader who did not know the poem it would not seem particularly striking.)

473. *with that* 1800-32; *or with* 1836.

NOTES ON WORDSWORTH'S APPENDIX

In the first two paragraphs Wordsworth explains the 252
phenomenon of 'poetic diction' by giving an account
of the rise of figurative language in poetry. Like
Longinus and the English writers who followed him,
Wordsworth assumes that figurative language comes
naturally to impassioned men (*cf.* p. 29, lines 9-10 and
p. 31, line 26 to p. 32, line 6, and notes). Primitive poets,
he explains, wrote under the stimulus of strong feelings
and therefore used figurative language; this language
was afterwards imitated by less impassioned poets and
finally degenerated into a mere convention. Wordsworth's
account of the matter is of course quite unhistorical. It
is true, however, that some eighteenth-century poets who
shared Wordsworth's notions about primitive poetry
had tried to reproduce its effects by using elaborate
rhetoric. René Wellek writes, in *The Rise of English
Literary History* (University of North Carolina Press,
Chapel Hill, 1941):

> We must not forget that even the highly ornate and
> to our mind extremely artificial style of Gray's odes
> was a conscious attempt to recapture that 'oriental,'
> elevated, sublime, metaphorical style which was
> supposed to be nearest to the language of the heart
> and thus to the poetry of original unspoilt natural
> man.   (p. 89.)

Wordsworth perceived that whatever effect this
highly figurative style achieved it was not that of
passion; and his inference, expressed in the quotation
from Quintilian on p. 49, is that genuine feeling is more
important to the poet than a knowledge of tropes. The
rest of the Appendix is interesting chiefly for the examples
Wordsworth gives of the deadening effect of poetic diction, and for his unusually close criticism of the lines by
Cowper.

3. *agitation and confusion of mind were* 1802-32; *emotion* 253
was 1836.

9-10. *and with the spirit of a fraternity they arrogated it* 254
to themselves as their own omitted 1836.

254 30-33. *in impressing a notion . . . with that character.*
Wordsworth is pointing out that poetic diction appeals
to a kind of cultural snobbery in the reader.

255 15. *Pope's Messiah.* 'Messiah: A Sacred Eclogue' first
appeared in 1712 (*Spectator*, no. 378). It is a very free
rendering, in pastoral form and in couplet verse, of
some passages from Isaiah traditionally believed to
foretell the birth of Jesus:

Ye nymphs of Solyma! begin the song:

To heavenly themes sublimer strains belong, etc.

Pope offers the poem as an imitation of Virgil's *Pollio*,
in which similar prophetic passages had been discovered.

15-16. *'Did sweeter sounds adorn my flowing tongue'*: the
first line of *Charity: A Paraphrase upon the Thirteenth
Chapter of the First Epistle to the Corinthians*, first
published in 1704. See *The Literary Works of Matthew
Prior*, ed. H. Bunker Wright and M. K. Spears (O.U.P.,
1959), i, 207-8.

16-17. *'Though I speak with the tongues of men and of
angels'*: the opening of the passage from the Authorised
Version paraphrased by Prior.

20. *Turn on the prudent Ant*, etc. A slightly different
and more authoritative text of *The Ant* appears in *The
Poems of Samuel Johnson*, ed. D. Nichol Smith and E.
Laming McAdam (O.U.P., 1941), pp. 151-2. The
poem was first published in 1766.

256 9/10. *Proverbs, chap. vith./One more quotation.* Between
these two sentences the following cancelled passage
appears among the printer's copy for *L.B.* (*1802*):

In order further to point out some of the ordinary
and less disgusting shapes which Misdiction puts on
at the present day I will transcribe a poem published
a few years ago which, though of great merit, is
crowded with these defects.

Could then the babes from yon *unsheltered* cot
Implore thy *passing charity* in vain?
Too thoughtless youth! what though *thy happier lot*
Insult their life of poverty and pain.
What though their Maker doomed them thus forlorn
To brook the mockery of the *taunting throng*,

Beneath the *oppressor's iron scourge* to mourn,   **256**
To mourn, but not to murmur at his wrong?
Yet when their *last late* evening shall decline,
Their evening cheerful though their day distressed,
A hope perhaps more *heavenly bright* than thine,
A grace by thee unsought, and unpossessed,
A faith more fixed, a rapture more divine,
Shall gild their passage to eternal rest.   (Russell.)
The reader has only to translate this sonnet into such
language as any person of good sense and lively
sensibility—one, I mean, who does not talk out of
books—would use upon such an occasion in real life,
and he will at once perceive in what manner the passages printed in italics are defective. (*P.W.*, ii, 407-8.)
The sonnet here criticised is by Thomas Russell (1762-
88), and is no. x in his *Sonnets and Miscellaneous Poems*
(1789). Despite these objections Wordsworth admired
Russell's work, and thirty years later transferred the
last four lines of this sonnet (between quotation-marks)
to his own sonnet *Iona, upon Landing* (see *P.W.*, iv,
42-3 and note).

13. *Religion! what treasure untold*, etc. These are
stanzas iv-v of Cowper's poem, which begins 'I am
monarch of all I survey' (*Poetical Works* ed. H. S.
Milford (O.U.P., 1934), pp. 311-12). It was first published in 1782.

17-23. *a sentiment . . . the same language.* So 1802-32; **257**
a principle which ought never to be lost sight of, and
which has been my chief guide in all I have said—
namely, that in works of *imagination and sentiment*, for
of these only have I been treating, in proportion as
ideas and feelings are valuable, whether the composition be in prose or in verse they require and
exact one and the same language. Metre is but advent-
itious to composition, and the phraseology for which
that passport is necessary, even where it may be graceful at all, will be little valued by the judicious. 1836.
The printer's copy for *L.B.* (*1802*) includes a cancelled
final paragraph apologising for Wordsworth's apparent
temerity in criticising other poets (see *P.W.*, ii, 409).

COLERIDGE'S ACCOUNT OF THE ORIGINS
OF *LYRICAL BALLADS*
FROM *BIOGRAPHIA LITERARIA* (1817)

During the first year that Mr. Wordsworth and I were neighbours, our conversations turned frequently on the two cardinal points of poetry: the power of exciting the sympathy of the reader by a faithful adherence to the truth of nature, and the power of giving the interest of novelty by the modifying colours of imagination. The sudden charm which accidents of light and shade, which moonlight or sunset, diffused over a known and familiar landscape appeared to represent the practicability of combining both. These are the poetry of nature. The thought suggested itself (to which of us I do not recollect) that a series of poems might be composed, of two sorts. In the one the incidents and agents were to be, in part at least, supernatural; and the excellence aimed at was to consist in the interesting of the affections by the dramatic truth of such emotions as would naturally accompany such situations, supposing them real. And real in *this* sense they have been to every human being who, from whatever source of delusion, has at any time believed himself under supernatural agency. For the second class, subjects were to be chosen from ordinary life: the characters and incidents were to be such as will be found in every village and its vicinity where there is a meditative and feeling mind to seek after them, or to notice them when they present themselves.

In this idea originated the plan of the *Lyrical Ballads*: in which it was agreed that my endeavours should be directed to persons and characters supernatural, or at least romantic; yet so as to transfer from our inward nature a human interest and a semblance of truth sufficient to procure for these shadows of imagination that willing suspension of disbelief, for the moment, which constitutes poetic faith. Mr. Wordsworth, on the other hand, was to propose to himself as his object to give the charm of novelty to things of every day, and to excite a feeling analogous to the supernatural by awakening the mind's attention from the lethargy of custom, and directing it to the loveliness and the wonders of the world before us: an inexhaustible treasure, but for which, in consequence of the film of familiarity and selfish solicitude, we have eyes yet see not, ears that hear not, and hearts that neither feel nor understand.

With this view I wrote *The Ancient Mariner*, and was preparing, among other poems, *The Dark Ladie* and the *Christabel*, in which I should have more nearly realised my ideal than I had done in my first attempt. But Mr. Wordsworth's industry had proved so much more successful and the number of his poems so much greater that my compositions, instead of forming a balance, appeared rather an interpolation of heterogeneous matter. Mr. Wordsworth added two or three poems written in his own character, in the impassioned, lofty and sustained diction which is characteristic of his genius. In this form the *Lyrical Ballads* were published. . . .

From: B.L., chapt. xiv, pp. 168-9.

[Critics have differed as to the historical value of this account, written nearly twenty years after the event. In the above notes (pp. 262-4 and elsewhere) it is suggested that Wordsworth and Coleridge did have such a scheme in view for some six to nine weeks during the spring of 1798, and that *The Thorn*, *Goody Blake* and *The Idiot Boy*, besides other poems excluded from *Lyrical Ballads*, were written within its framework. *The Ancient Mariner*, however, seems to have been written before the scheme was devised.]

Critical Extracts

FRANCIS JEFFREY

The followers of simplicity are . . . at all times in danger of occasional degradation; but the simplicity of this new school seems intended to ensure it. *Their* simplicity does not consist by any means in the rejection of glaring or superfluous ornament—in the substitution of elegance to splendour, or in that refinement of art which seeks concealment in its own perfection. It consists, on the contrary, in a very great degree, in the positive and *bona fide* rejection of art altogether, and in the bold use of those rude and negligent expressions which would be banished by a little discrimination. One of their own authors indeed has very ingenuously set forth (in a kind of manifesto that preceded one of their most flagrant acts of hostility) that it was their capital object 'to adapt to the uses of poetry the ordinary language of conversation among the middling and lower orders of the people.' What advantages are to be gained by the success of this project we confess ourselves unable to conjecture. The language of the higher and more cultivated orders may fairly be presumed to be better than that of their inferiors: at any rate it has all those associations in its favour by means of which a style can ever appear beautiful or exalted, and is adapted to the purposes of poetry by having been long consecrated to its use. The language of the vulgar, on the other hand, has all the opposite associations to contend with; and must seem unfit for poetry (if there were no other reason) merely because it has scarcely ever been employed in it. A great genius may indeed overcome these disadvantages, but we can scarcely conceive that he should court them. We may excuse a certain homeliness of language in the productions of a ploughman or a milkwoman; but we cannot bring ourselves to admire it in an author who has had occasion to indite odes to his college bell and inscribe hymns to the Penates.

410

But the mischief of this new system is not confined to the depravation of language only: it extends to the sentiments and emotions, and leads to the debasement of all those feelings which poetry is designed to communicate. It is absurd to suppose that an author should make use of the language of the vulgar to express the sentiments of the refined. His professed object in employing that language is to bring his compositions nearer to the true standard of nature; and his intention to copy the sentiments of the lower orders is implied in his resolution to make use of their style. Now the different classes of society have each of them a distinct character as well as a separate idiom; and the names of the various passions to which they are subject respectively have a signification that varies essentially according to the condition of the persons to whom they are applied. The love, or grief, or indignation of an enlightened and refined character is not only expressed in a different language but is in itself a different emotion from the love, or grief, or anger of a clown, a tradesman or a market-wench. . . . The question therefore comes simply to be: which of them is the most proper object for poetical imitation? It is needless for us to answer a question which the practice of all the world has long ago decided irrevocably. The poor and vulgar may interest us in poetry by their *situation*, but never, we apprehend, by any sentiments that are peculiar to their condition, and still less by any language that is characteristic of it. The truth is that it is impossible to copy their diction or their sentiments correctly in a serious composition: and this not merely because poverty makes men ridiculous, but because just taste and refined sentiment are rarely to be met with among the uncultivated part of mankind; and a language fitted for their expression can still more rarely form any part of their 'ordinary conversation.' . . .

In making these strictures on the perverted taste for simplicity that seems to distinguish our modern school of poetry we have no particular allusion to Mr. Southey, or to the production now before us. On the contrary, he appears to us to be less addicted to this fault than most of his fraternity; and if we were in want of examples to illustrate the preceding observations we should certainly look for them in the effusions of that poet who commemorates with so much effect the chattering of Harry Gill's teeth, tells the tale of the one-eyed huntsman 'who had a cheek like a cherry,' and beautifully warns his studious friend of the risk he ran of 'growing double.'

From: Edinburgh Review, i (Oct. 1802), 65-8, in a review of Southey's *Thalaba*.

WILLIAM HAZLITT

Every one is by habit and familiarity strongly attached to the place of his birth, or to objects that recall the most pleasing and eventful circumstances of his life. But to the author of the *Lyrical Ballads*, nature is a kind of home; and he may be said to take a personal interest in the universe. There is no image so insignificant that it has not in some mood or other found the way into his heart; no sound that does not awaken the memory of other years.

To him the meanest flower that blows can give
Thoughts that do often lie too deep for tears.

The daisy looks up to him with a sparkling eye as an old acquaintance; the cuckoo haunts him with sounds of early youth not to be expressed; a linnet's nest startles him with boyish delight; an old withered thorn is weighed down with a heap of recollections; a grey cloak, seen on some wild moor, torn by the wind, or drenched in the rain, afterwards becomes an object of imagination to him; even the lichens on the rock have a life and being in his thoughts. He has described all these objects in a way and with an intensity of feeling that no one else had done before him, and has given a new view or aspect of nature. He is in this sense the most original poet now living, and the one whose writings could the least be spared: for they have no substitute elsewhere. The vulgar do not read them, the learned, who see all things through books, do not understand them, the great despise, the fashionable may ridicule them: but the author has created himself an interest in the heart of the retired and lonely student of nature, which can never die. Persons of this class will still continue to feel what he has felt; he has expressed what they might in vain wish to express, except with glistening eye and faltering tongue! There is a lofty philosophic tone, a thoughtful humanity, infused into his pastoral vein. Remote from the passions and events of the great world, he has communicated interest and dignity to the primal movements of the heart of man, and ingrafted his own conscious reflections on the casual thoughts of hinds and shepherds. Nursed amidst the grandeur of mountain scenery, he has stooped to have a nearer view of the daisy under his feet, or plucked a branch of whitethorn from the spray: but in describing it, his mind seems imbued with the majesty and solemnity of the objects around him. The tall rock lifts its head in the erectness of his spirit; the cataract roars in the sound of his verse; and in its dim and mysterious meaning, the mists seem to gather in the hollows of Helvellyn, and the forked Skiddaw hovers in the distance. There is little mention of mountainous scenery in Mr. Wordsworth's poetry; but by internal evidence one might be almost sure that it was written in a mountainous country, from its bareness, its simplicity, its loftiness and its depth!

From: 'Mr. Wordsworth,' in *The Spirit of the Age* (first published 1825).

MATTHEW ARNOLD

Wordsworth's poetry is great because of the extraordinary power with which Wordsworth feels the joy offered to us in nature, the joy offered to us in the simple primary affections and duties; and because of the extraordinary power with which, in case after case, he shows us this joy and renders it so as to make us share it. The source of joy from which he thus draws is the truest and most unfailing source of joy accessible to man. It is also accessible universally. Wordsworth brings us word, therefore—according to his own strong and characteristic line—he brings us word 'of joy in widest commonalty spread.' Here is an immense advantage for a poet. Wordsworth tells us of what all seek, and tells of it at its truest and best source, and yet a source where all may go and draw for it.

413

Nevertheless we are not to suppose that everything is precious which Wordsworth, standing even at this perennial and beautiful source, may give us. Wordsworthians are apt to talk as if it must be. They will speak with the same reverence of *The Sailor's Mother*, for example, as of *Lucy Gray*. They do their master harm by such lack of discrimination. *Lucy Gray* is a beautiful success: *The Sailor's Mother* is a failure. To give aright what he wishes to give, to interpret and render successfully, is not always within Wordsworth's own command. . . . No poet, perhaps, is so evidently filled with a new and sacred energy when the inspiration is upon him: no poet, when it fails him, is so left 'weak as is a breaking wave.' I remember hearing him say that 'Goethe's poetry was not inevitable enough.' The remark is striking and true: no line in Goethe, as Goethe said himself, but its maker knew well how it came there. . . . But Wordsworth's poetry, when he is at his best, is inevitable, as inevitable as Nature herself. It might seem that Nature not only gave him the matter for his poem, but wrote his poem for him. He has no style. He was too conversant with Milton not to catch at times his master's manner, and he has fine Miltonic lines; but he has no assured poetic style of his own like Milton. When he seeks to have a style he falls into ponderosity and pomposity. In *The Excursion* we have his style, as an artistic product of his own creation: and although Jeffrey completely failed to recognise Wordsworth's real greatness, he was yet not wrong in saying of *The Excursion*, as a work of poetic style, 'This will never do.' And yet magical as is that power, which Wordsworth has not, of assured and possessed poetic style, he has something which is an equivalent for it. . . .

The right sort of verse to choose from Wordsworth, if we are to seize his true and most characteristic form of expression, is a line like this from *Michael*:

And never lifted up a single stone.

There is nothing subtle in it, no heightening, no study of poetic style, strictly so called, at all: yet it is expression of the highest and most truly expressive kind. . . . Nature herself seems, I say, to take the pen out of his hand and to write for him with her own bare, sheer, penetrating power.

This arises from two causes: from the profound sincereness with which Wordsworth feels his subject, and also from the profoundly sincere and natural character of his subject itself. He can and will treat such a subject with nothing but the most plain, first-hand, almost austere naturalness. His expression may often be called bald, as for instance in the poem of *Resolution and Independence*; but it is bald as the bare mountain tops are bald, with a baldness which is full of grandeur.

> From: 'Wordsworth' (1879), in *Essays in Criticism:*
> *Second Series.*

DAVID NICHOL SMITH

There was nothing too humble for Wordsworth; he only required that it should be familiar. But the subjects that he nominally chooses may not be the real subjects of his poems. The titles afford as a rule little clue to what the poems contain. Wordsworth does not value anything for itself so much as for what it can tell us of ourselves. There was no need for him to search for material outside the beaten track when everywhere around him things were 'for ever speaking' and he had only to listen. He can 'find a tale in every thing,' and he shows his readers how they too may find it in what they pass by as worthless or insignificant in the hurry of their daily pursuits. He has

> among least things
> An under-sense of greatest; sees the parts
> As parts, but with a feeling of the whole.

His poem called *The Small Celandine* is a poem on the human lot.

> Thanks to the human heart by which we live,
> Thanks to its tenderness, its joys, and fears,
> To me the meanest flower that blows can give
> Thoughts that do often lie too deep for tears.

Wordsworth could not be expected to take any interest in plot for its own sake. More than this, he took little interest in the study of character as it is generally understood—in the traits which distinguish one man from another. He finds his theme in the qualities that are common to all men. The persons of his stories are a leech-gatherer, a schoolmaster, an old shepherd and his son, or an aged beggar. It does not matter what names he gives them. They have no habits of mind that are necessarily connected with their occupations; they are not drawn as clearly marked types; much less are they individuals. They are simply men, old or young, or women, or children, as nature makes them, and as little affected as may be by the conventions of society.

He tried to abandon, as far as he could, the conventions of the language of poetry, using instead 'a selection of the language really spoken by men.' Here, too, he sought the essential and the permanent as much as in the matter of the poems. Unfortunately, in his preface to *Lyrical Ballads*, he approached the difficult question of poetic diction too much in the manner of a challenge, and without fully considering all that was involved. Coleridge, who was a greater adept in theoretical discussion, had no difficulty in showing the weak points in the argument; and unfriendly critics have not failed to take their opportunity. But the diction of Wordsworth's poetry would have raised no questions if he had not himself directed attention to it. He could not keep in every poem to the maxims which he stated somewhat unwarily in this early preface; no poet can always use the language of ordinary speech. He meant to plead for simplicity, and in the ardour of his attack on 'gaudiness and inane phraseology' he had allowed his plea, sound in itself and not untimely, to develop into a provocative manifesto. What has never to be forgotten is that the plea was only a consequence, and a necessary consequence, of the guiding principle of his poetry, and that in some of his greatest passages he does use the language really spoken by men. . . .

Nature was to Wordsworth a living soul that reveals herself alike in the movement of the stars, the yearnings of the heart, the sleep of a great city, or the decay of a flower. . . . His poetry makes no division between man and the world in which he lives. He thinks of all created things, human or inanimate, as parts of one great whole, filling their appointed place, moving in their established order. He is our greatest nature poet because he is the poet of more than external nature; he is, in a higher degree, the poet of man. No other

416

poet is more consistently original and faithful in his pictures of what the eye can see, more luminous in his interpretation of it. But he could never dissociate it from the human heart.

From: Introduction to *Wordsworth: Poetry and Prose* (The Clarendon Press, Oxford, 1921), pp. xiii-xviii.

CHARLES BURNEY

The author's first piece, *The Rime of the Ancyent Marinere*, in imitation of the *style* as well as the spirit of the elder poets, is the strangest story of a cock and a bull that we ever saw on paper: yet, though it seems a rhapsody of unintelligible wildness and incoherence (of which we do not perceive the drift, unless the joke lies in depriving the wedding guest of his share of the feast), there are in it poetical touches of an exquisite kind.

From: Monthly Review, Ser. 2, xxix (June 1799), 204, in a review of *L.B. (1798).*

LESLIE STEPHEN

The germ of all Coleridge's utterances may be found—by a little ingenuity—in *The Ancient Mariner*. For what is the secret of the strange charm of that unique achievement? . . . Part at least of the secret is the ease with which Coleridge moves in a world of which the machinery (as the old critics called it) is supplied by the mystic philosopher. Milton, as Penseroso, implores

> The spirit of Plato to unfold
> What worlds or what vast systems hold
> The spirit of man that hath forsook
> Her mansion in this fleshy nook,
> And of those demons that are found
> In fire, air, flood, and underground,
> Whose powers have a true consent
> With planet and with element.

If such a man fell asleep in his 'high lonely tower' his dreams would present to him in sensuous imagery the very world in which the strange history of *The Ancient Mariner* was transacted. It is a world in which both animated things, and stones, and brooks, and clouds, and plants are moved by spiritual agency; in which, as he would put it, the veil of the senses is nothing but a symbolism everywhere telling of unseen and supernatural forces. What we call the solid and the substantial becomes a dream; and the dream is the true underlying reality. The difference between such poetry and the poetry of Pope, or even of Gray, or Goldsmith, or Cowper—poetry which is the direct utterance of a string of moral, political, or religious reflections—implies a literary revolution. . . . Indeed, the moral, which would apparently be that people who sympathise with a man who shoots an albatross will die in prolonged torture of thirst, is open to obvious objections.

From: Hours in a Library (1892), iii, 358-9.

C. M. BOWRA

The triumph of *The Ancient Mariner* is that it presents a series of incredible events through a method of narration which makes them not only convincing and exciting but in some sense a criticism of life. No other poet of the supernatural has quite done this, at least on such a scale and with such abundance of authentic poetry. In his conquest of the unknown, Coleridge went outside the commonplace thrills of horror. Of course, he evokes these, and his opening verses, in which the Mariner stays the Wedding-Guest, suggest that at first Coleridge followed familiar precedents in appealing to a kind of horrified fear. But as he worked at his poem, he widened its scope and created something much richer and more human. . . . Instead of confining himself to an outworn dread of spectres and phantoms, he moves over a wide range of emotions and touches equally on guilt and remorse, suffering and relief, hate and forgiveness, grief and joy. Nor has his creation the misty dimness commonly associated with the supernatural. What he imagines is indeed weird, but he sees it with so sharp a vision that it lives vividly before our eyes. . . .

What Wordsworth found in a world of vision, Coleridge found in the supernatural. It clarified his ideas for him and enabled him to present in concrete shapes many feelings and apprehensions which were not less haunting because they were undefined. He was both fascinated by the unknown and in some sense afraid of it. This helped him to make *The Ancient Mariner*. It gave him the thrill of excitement which he needed before he could concentrate his mind on a subject, and through it he sharpened his vision and purified his mind of many disturbing and distracting elements. . . .

Both in the main plan of the Mariner's crime and in the spiritual forces who battle over him, Coleridge emphasises the state of man between persecuting horrors and enchanting beauties. Such a state was no doubt his own. He, whose genius in Hazlitt's words 'had angelic wings, and fed on manna,' was destined to know many dark and guilty hours of sloth and regret. *The Ancient Mariner* is his greatest poem because he put most of himself into it and in it spoke most fully from his inner being. The brilliant reality which he gives to this invention of his imagination comes from his prophetic insight into himself. He was to suffer, as few poets have suffered, from the discordant contrast between reality and dream, between blissful confidence and bitter, broken hopes, between the warmth of human ties and the cold solitude of the haunted soul. It was from some foretaste or premonition of these contrasts and struggles that Coleridge made his poem, and they provide its relation to life. He was too modest when he said that all he wished to secure was 'that willing suspension of disbelief for the moment, which constitutes poetic faith.' His poem creates not a negative but a positive condition, a state of faith which is complete and satisfying because it is founded on realities in the living world and in the human heart.

From: 'The Ancient Mariner,' in *The Romantic Imagination* (O.U.P., 1950), pp. 55-6, 74-5.

Bibliography

Principal Editions

Lyrical Ballads was first published, in one volume, in 1798. An enlarged edition in two volumes, with Wordsworth's Preface, appeared in January 1801 (dated 1800). The work was revised and rearranged in 1802, and further revised in 1805 (for fuller details see pp. 265-8). For these editions the abbreviations *L.B.* (*1798*), *L.B.* (*1800*), etc., have been used. Modern reprints include:

Lyrical Ballads (*1798*), ed. Thomas Hutchinson (Duckworth, 1898). The introduction and notes contain a great deal of information, which now inevitably needs to be corrected or supplemented in places. Other writings of *c.* 1798 by Wordsworth and Coleridge are included in an appendix.

Lyrical Ballads (*1798-1805*), ed. George Sampson (Methuen, 1903). Still a useful reprint of *L.B.* (*1805*), with footnotes showing the readings of earlier editions.

Lyrical Ballads (*1798*), ed. H. Littledale (O.U.P., 1924). A page-for-page reprint of the first edition.

Lyrical Ballads, ed. R. L. Brett and A. R. Jones (Methuen, 1963). Reprints *L.B.* (*1798*) and the second volume of *L.B.* (*1800*). Brief notes, but a long and interesting introduction. An appendix gives extracts from some early reviews as reprinted by Elsie Smith in *An Estimate of William Wordsworth* (*q.v.*).

Lyrical Ballads (*1798*), ed. W. J. B. Owen (O.U.P., 1967). An up-to-date reprint of the first edition, with a good introduction and notes.

Lyrical Ballads (*1798*) (Scolar Press, Menston, Yorks., 1971). A photographic facsimile of Southey's copy of the first edition.

See also:
Wordsworth's Preface to 'Lyrical Ballads,' ed. with an introduction and commentary by W. J. B. Owen (*Anglistica*, ix; Copenhagen, 1957).

Other Editions and Principal Sources

The Poetical Works of William Wordsworth (5 vols., O.U.P., 1940-9). Vols. i-ii ed. E. de Selincourt, iii-v ed. E. de Selincourt and Helen Darbishire. [*P.W.*]

WILLIAM WORDSWORTH, *The Prelude, or Growth of a Poet's Mind*, ed. E. de Selincourt (O.U.P., 1926; 2nd edn., revd. Helen Darbishire, 1959). [*Prelude*]

The Prose Works of William Wordsworth, ed. W. J. B. Owen and Jane Worthington Smyser (3 vols., O.U.P., 1974).

The Early Letters of William and Dorothy Wordsworth (1787-1805), ed. E. de Selincourt, revd. C. L. Shaver (O.U.P., 1967). [*E.L.W.*]

Journals of Dorothy Wordsworth, ed. E. de Selincourt (2 vols., Macmillan, 1941). [*D.W.J.*]

MARY MOORMAN, *William Wordsworth, a Biography* (2 vols., O.U.P., 1957-65). [*M.M.*]

An Estimate of William Wordsworth by his Contemporaries, 1793-1822, ed. Elsie Smith (Blackwell, 1932). A collection of extracts, not always accurately transcribed, from reviews and other criticisms. [E. Smith]

MARK L. REED, *Wordsworth: The Chronology of the Early Years, 1770-1799* (Harvard University Press, 1967). A masterly guide to a huge mass of complex material. [Reed]

The Complete Poetical Works of Samuel Taylor Coleridge, ed. Ernest Hartley Coleridge (2 vols., O.U.P., 1912). Vol. i, poems; vol. ii, plays and appendixes. See also *The Poems of Samuel Taylor Coleridge*, ed. Ernest Hartley Coleridge (O.U.P., 1912): this volume in the Oxford Standard Authors

series reprints vol. i of the *Complete Poetical Works*, using the same pagination, and adds some material from vol ii.
[*C.P.W.*]

The Collected Works of Samuel Taylor Coleridge, gen. ed. Kathleen Coburn (Routledge and Princeton Univ. Press, 1969-). Four vols. have appeared and another twelve are in preparation, including *Poetical Works* (ed. G. Whalley) and *Biographia Literaria* (ed. M. Abrams).

SAMUEL TAYLOR COLERIDGE, *Biographia Literaria*, ed. with an introduction by George Watson (Everyman's Library, Dent, 1956; reprinted with additions and corrections, 1965). [*B.L.*]

SAMUEL TAYLOR COLERIDGE, *Biographia Literaria, with his Aesthetical Essays*, ed. J. Shawcross (2 vols., O.U.P., 1907; corr. ed. 1954). Less up-to-date but more fully annotated than Watson's edition.

Collected Letters of Samuel Taylor Coleridge, ed. Earl Leslie Griggs (6 vols., O.U.P., 1956-71). [*C.L.*]

The Notebooks of Samuel Taylor Coleridge, ed. Kathleen Coburn (three vols. so far published, Routledge, 1957-73).
[*C.N.*]

The Letters of Charles Lamb, to which are added those of his sister Mary Lamb, ed. E. V. Lucas (3 vols., Dent and Methuen, 1935). [*Lamb*]

THOMAS PERCY, *Reliques of Ancient English Poetry*, ed. H. B. Wheatley (3 vols., Swan Sonnenschein & Co., 1889). Wheatley gives the text of the 4th edn. (1794). [*Reliques*]

Suggestions for Further Reading

(i) *Recommended for use in both schools and universities*

WALTER JACKSON BATE, *Coleridge* (Macmillan Co., New York, 1968; Weidenfeld, 1969). A short clear account of Coleridge's life and the development of his thought.

F. W. BATESON, 'Poetic Diction and the Sublime,' in *English Critical Essays: Twentieth Century*, Ser. 2 (O.U.P., World's Classics, 1958), pp. 169-80.

BIBLIOGRAPHY

C. M. BOWRA, 'The Ancient Mariner,' in *The Romantic Imagination* (O.U.P., 1950), pp. 51-75.

JOHN DANBY, *The Simple Wordsworth* (Routledge, 1960). Valuable for its close and sensitive readings of *Simon Lee* and other poems. [Danby]

HELEN DARBISHIRE, *The Poet Wordsworth: The Clark Lectures, 1949* (O.U.P., 1950; corrected impression, 1958).

LAWRENCE HANSON, *The Life of Samuel Taylor Coleridge: The Early Years* (1938).

D. W. HARDING, 'The Theme of *The Ancient Mariner*,' *Scrutiny*, ix (1941), 334-42. Deals with the fundamental problem, 'What kind of relation has this poem to real human experience?' A modified version of this essay appears in Harding's *Experience into Words* (Chatto, 1963), pp. 53-71.

HUMPHRY HOUSE, *Coleridge: The Clark Lectures, 1951-52* (Hart-Davis, 1953). An admirable introduction to Coleridge, learned and sensitive. Chapter iv, on *The Ancient Mariner*, gives rather disproportionate prominence to Robert Penn Warren's essay (*q.v.*).

H. M. MARGOLIOUTH, *Wordsworth and Coleridge, 1795-1834* (O.U.P., Home University Library, 1953). A short dual biography: a good account of the two men's relationship.

J. C. SMITH, *A Study of Wordsworth* (Oliver and Boyd, 1944).

(ii) *Recommended more particularly for university students*

F. W. BATESON, *Wordsworth, a Re-interpretation* (Longmans, 1954; revd. edn., 1956). A bold reassessment of Wordsworth's character and poetry; contains some good criticism which is valid whether or not one accepts particular biographical suggestions. [Bateson]

F. R. LEAVIS, 'Wordsworth,' in *Revaluation* (Chatto, 1936), pp. 154-202. A searching essay, best appreciated by those familiar with a fairly wide range of Wordsworth's poetry.

423

BIBLIOGRAPHY

JOHN LIVINGSTON LOWES, *The Road to Xanadu: A Study in the Ways of the Imagination* (Constable, 1927). A long and important study of the part played in *The Ancient Mariner* and *Kubla Khan* by Coleridge's conscious and unconscious memories of his reading.   [Lowes]

ROBERT MAYO, 'The Contemporaneity of the *Lyrical Ballads*,' *P.M.L.A.*, lxix (1954), 486-522. Mayo shows that many of the themes and forms of *Lyrical Ballads* must have been familiar to contemporary readers; also that most of the poems were readily accepted on their first appearance. An excellent corrective to conventional accounts of how they 'burst upon an astonished world.' Mayo also suggests ways in which the poems really were original.

ROGER N. MURRAY, *Wordsworth's Style: Figures and Themes in the Lyrical Ballads of 1800* (Nebraska Univ. Press, 1967).

MARK REED, 'Wordsworth, Coleridge, and the "Plan" of the *Lyrical Ballads*,' *University of Toronto Quarterly*, xxxiv (1965), 238-53.

ROGER SHARROCK, 'Wordsworth's Revolt against Literature,' *Essays in Criticism*, iii (1953), 396-412.

PAUL D. SHEATS, *The Making of Wordsworth's Poetry, 1785-1798* (Harvard Univ. Press and O.U.P., 1973).

E. M. W. TILLYARD, 'The Ancient Mariner,' in *Poetry and its Background* (Chatto, 1955; originally pubd. as *Five Poems*, 1948). Taking a long historical view, Tillyard shows how much the general conception of the poem owes to the period at which it was written.

CHAUNCEY BREWSTER TINKER, *Nature's Simple Plan: A Phase of Radical Thought in the mid-Eighteenth Century* (Princeton University Press and O.U.P., 1922). Presents shortly and simply some aspects of the primitivism which influenced Wordsworth's attitude towards the language and the themes of 'low and rustic life.'

F. M. TODD, *Politics and the Poet: A Study of Wordsworth* (Methuen, 1957). Outlines an important side of Wordsworth's development and connects, for example, the choice of themes in *Lyrical Ballads* with his political outlook.

JONATHAN WORDSWORTH, *The Music of Humanity* (Harper, New York and Evanston, 1969). Texts of 'The Ruined Cottage,' with introductory and critical material highly relevant to *Lyrical Ballads*.

R. O. C. WINKLER, 'Wordsworth's Poetry,' in *The Pelican Guide to English Literature*, v (1957), 152-85. Some good close criticism, notably of *Tintern Abbey* and *Michael*.

(iii) *Recommended for advanced university students*

JOSEPH WARREN BEACH, *The Concept of Nature in Nineteenth-Century English Poetry* (Macmillan Co., New York, 1936), chapts. i-vi. An admirable study: describes very fully Wordsworth's theories about nature and shows how he came to hold them.   [Beach]

ARTHUR BEATTY, *William Wordsworth: His Doctrine and Art in their Historical Relations* (University of Wisconsin Studies, Madison, 2nd edn., 1927). Gives a clear and detailed account of Hartley's philosophical and psychological system; makes the most of Hartley's influence on Wordsworth. Useful for following up ideas covered more rapidly and more imaginatively by Willey (*q.v.*)   [Beatty]

R. N. DANIEL, 'The Publication of the *Lyrical Ballads*,' *Modern Language Review*, xxxiii (1938), 406-10.

ERNEST DE SELINCOURT, *Dorothy Wordsworth, a Biography* (O.U.P., 1933).

WILLIAM EMPSON and DAVID PIRIE, eds. *Coleridge's Verse: A Selection* (Faber, 1972). Includes a long introduction by Empson and a critical reconstruction of *The Ancient Mariner*: 'The reader has a right to the true poem, and . . . even its own author must not be allowed to conceal it any longer' (Pirie, p. 216).

D. F. FOXON, 'The Printing of *Lyrical Ballads*, 1798,' *The Library*, ser. 5, ix (1954), 221-41.

BIBLIOGRAPHY

GEOFFREY H. HARTMAN, *Wordsworth's Poetry, 1787-1814* (Yale Univ. Press, 1964; repr. with a 'Retrospect,' 1971). Not a general study, but an exploration of Wordsworth's 'apocalyptic' imagination.

RAYMOND DEXTER HAVENS, *The Mind of a Poet* (Johns Hopkins Press, Baltimore, 1941). Part I gives an intelligent and comprehensive account of some of Wordsworth's personal characteristics and attitudes, based mainly on a study of *The Prelude*. Part II is a lively detailed commentary on that poem.

W. J. B. OWEN, *Wordsworth as Critic* (Toronto Univ. Press and O.U.P., 1969).

STEPHEN MAXFIELD PARRISH, *The Art of the Lyrical Ballads* (Harvard Univ. Press, 1973). The two most notable of these essays deal with dramatic technique in such poems as 'The Thorn.'

H. W. PIPER, *The Active Universe: Pantheism and the Concept of Imagination* (Univ. of London, Athlone Press, 1962). Particularly interesting on the belief, expressed in some of the *Lyrical Ballads*, that plants and even apparently inorganic objects have some kind of life and intelligence.

ROBERT PENN WARREN, 'A Poem of Pure Imagination,' *Kenyon Review*, viii (1946), 391-427; a shortened form of the essay prefixed to Warren's edition of *The Ancient Mariner* (New York, 1946). Propounds an intricate scheme of unconscious symbolism in the poem. Suggestive and often illuminating, though somewhat too systematic.

GEORGE WATSON, *Coleridge the Poet* (Routledge, 1966). Emphasises presence of traditional literary forms, e.g. the ballad in *The Ancient Mariner*.

BASIL WILLEY, *The Eighteenth-Century Background: Studies on the Idea of Nature in the Thought of the Period* (Chatto, 1940). Chapt. xii relates Wordsworth's view of nature, not only to 'the thought of the period,' but also to political events and to his personal life.

BIBLIOGRAPHY

Bibliographical Works

The following works may be helpful to students who would like to explore the literature of this subject further.

WERNER W. BEYER, *The Enchanted Forest* (Blackwell, Oxford, 1963). Includes a bibliography (pp. 261-6) especially useful for German influences on Coleridge's poetry.

R. L. BRETT, ed. *S. T. Coleridge* ('Writers and their Background,' Bell, 1971). Includes a bibliography by George Whalley (pp. 271-81).

A. E. DYSON, ed. *English Poetry: Select Bibliographical Guides* (O.U.P., 1971). Bibliographies of Wordsworth (by J. C. Maxwell and S. C. Gill, pp. 167-87) and Coleridge (by John Beer, pp. 188-210) are preceded by helpful discussions.

GEOFFREY H. HARTMAN, *Wordsworth's Poetry, 1787-1814* (see above) includes a critical bibliography of writings on *Lyrical Ballads* (pp. 371-7).

RICHARD HAVEN, *Coleridge 1793-1970: An Annotated Bibliography* (projected).

ELTON F. HENLEY and DAVID H. STAM, *Wordsworthian Criticism, 1945-1964: An Annotated Bibliography* (New York Public Library, 1965). This volume and its successor (below) provide a comprehensive register of post-war criticism; especially helpful is the listing of book-reviews.

DAVID H. STAM, *Wordsworthian Criticism, 1964-1973: An Annotated Bibliography* (New York Public Library and Readex Books, 1974).

GEORGE WATSON, ed. *The New Cambridge Bibliography of English Literature*. Vol. iii (1969) includes sections on Wordsworth (by W. J. B. Owen, cols. 182-211) and Coleridge (by George Whalley, cols. 211-54).

New studies are reported annually in the *Annual Bibliography of English Language and Literature*; in the *MLA International Bibliography*; in 'The Romantic Movement: A Selective and Critical Bibliography,' published by *Modern Language Notes*; and in *The Year's Work in English Studies*.

427

'ADVERTISEMENT' TO *LYRICAL BALLADS* (1798)

It is the honourable characteristic of poetry that its materials are to be found in every subject which can interest the human mind. The evidence of this fact is to be sought, not in the writings of critics, but in those of poets themselves.

The majority of the following poems are to be considered as experiments. They were written chiefly with a view to ascertain how far the language of conversation in the middle and lower classes of society is adapted to the purposes of poetic pleasure. Readers accustomed to the gaudiness and inane phraseology of many modern writers, if they persist in reading this book to its conclusion, will perhaps frequently have to struggle with feelings of strangeness and awkwardness: they will look round for poetry, and will be induced to enquire by what species of courtesy these attempts can be permitted to assume that title. It is desirable that such readers, for their own sakes, should not suffer the solitary word *poetry* (a word of very disputed meaning) to stand in the way of their gratification; but that while they are perusing this book they should ask themselves if it contains a natural delineation of human passions, human characters and human incidents; and if the answer be favourable to the author's wishes, that they should consent to be pleased in spite of that most dreadful enemy to our pleasures, our own pre-established codes of decision.

Readers of superior judgment may disapprove of the style in which many of these pieces are executed: it must be expected that many lines and phrases will not exactly suit their taste. It will perhaps appear to them that, wishing to avoid the prevalent fault of the day, the author has sometimes descended too low, and that many of his expressions are too familiar and not of sufficient dignity. It is apprehended that the more conversant the reader is with our elder writers, and with those in modern times who have been the most successful in painting manners and passions, the fewer complaints of this kind will he have to make.

An accurate taste in poetry and in all the other arts, Sir Joshua Reynolds has observed, is an acquired talent, which can only be produced by severe thought and a long-continued intercourse with the best models of composition. This is mentioned, not with so ridiculous a purpose as to prevent the most inexperienced reader from judging for himself, but merely to temper the rashness of decision; and to suggest that if poetry be a subject on which much time has not been bestowed the judgment may be erroneous, and that in many cases it necessarily will be so.

The tale of *Goody Blake and Harry Gill* is founded on a well-authenticated fact which happened in Warwickshire. Of the other poems in the collection it may be proper to say that they are either absolute inventions of the author, or facts which took place within his personal observation or that of his friends. The poem of *The Thorn*, as the reader will soon discover, is not supposed to be spoken in the author's own person; the character of the loquacious narrator will sufficiently show itself in the course of the story. *The Rime of the Ancyent Marinere* was professedly written in imitation of the *style* as well as of the spirit of the elder poets; but with a few exceptions the author believes that the language adopted in it has been equally intelligible for these three last centuries. The lines entitled *Expostulation and Reply*, and those which follow, arose out of conversation with a friend who was somewhat unreasonably attached to modern books of moral philosophy.

LYRICAL BALLADS (1798)

The following is a list of poems in the first edition of *Lyrical Ballads*, in the order in which they originally appeared. Page numbers refer to the present edition. For details of poems omitted after 1798 see p. 268.

Index of First Lines

431